6/20/95

To: Ray Hall

With my Best wishes ~

Best of luck,
Helen L. Shireman
great granddaughter

# MAJOR-GENERAL
# JOHN FREDERICK HARTRANFT
## *CITIZEN SOLDIER AND PENNSYLVANIA STATESMAN*

**Major-General John F. Hartranft**

This is the official photo of the Pennsylvania National Guard, circa 1882. This photo copy by Frank D'Amico.

*Courtesy of Pennsylvania National Guard.*

# MAJOR-GENERAL
# JOHN FREDERICK HARTRANFT

*CITIZEN SOLDIER AND PENNSYLVANIA STATESMAN*

A. M. Gambone

First Edition
Butternut and Blue
1995

ISBN  0-935523-46-4

Printed in the United States of America
on acid-free paper.

Published in 1995
as the eighth volume of
the *Army of the Potomac Series*

by

**Butternut and Blue**
**3411 Northwind Road**
**Baltimore, MD  21234**
**410-256-9220**

# DEDICATION

TO MY WIFE NANCY,
FOR HER LOVE AND UNTIRING PATIENCE.

# TABLE OF CONTENTS

# PREFACE

Perhaps the casual observer of the American Civil War might wonder why we need another biography about another general when the Library of Congress is already host to thousands of volumes on the subject and its personalities. Actually, the reasons are many but might be best understood by the scholars and buffs of the era who can attest to the vast lack of credible knowledge that still exists on many of the war's participants.

Many Civil War biographies pay much attention to principal commanders like Lieutenant-General Ulysses S. Grant, General Robert E. Lee, Lieutenant-General Thomas [Stonewall] J. Jackson and Major-General William T. Sherman, to name a few. In some cases, even their subordinate officers have had one or two biographies published about their lives and contributions. More frequently, however, at those lower levels, meaningful information has a tendency to drop off sharply, sending us searching for information on the vital activities of many forgotten men. Consequently, we are often provided with only a distorted glimpse of the heroic, and sometimes not so heroic, deeds of those who might be important to our knowledge of the war. The study of brigade and division commanders is a matter of utmost importance if we are ever going to really understand that terrible conflagration.

Napoleon once stated, "soldiers generally win battles; generals get credit for them." This lack of individual recognition for soldiers also applies to many subordinate generals, like Major-General John Frederick Hartranft. Too frequently, like Napoleon's soldiers, the Civil War officers of the second and third rank lie silent in their graves and history is impoverished about their exploits and accomplishments. Once we realize that these are the men who actually directed the fighting of the war, we can better understand the importance of their contributions.

As a native of Norristown, Pennsylvania, I attended Washington Elementary School in the east end of town, then Rittenhouse Junior High School, and finally, I graduated from the Eisenhower Senior High School in 1957. During those developing years I was aware that my hometown had the Hartranft and Hancock Elementary Schools, but those school names were just that, and represented individuals who never meant anything to me. To the best of my recollection, those names never meant anything even to the students [and perhaps the teachers] who attended those particular institutions. In fact, during my elementary and secondary education, there was never any local recognition of either of these two generals, though they both came from Norristown and its environs. The reader might appreciate that if Hartranft and Hancock were handled in such an indifferent manner,

i

there was absolutely no mention of other Norristown area Civil War heroes including Generals Matthew R. McClennan, Adam J. Slemmer, and Samuel K. Zook. As for lower ranking officers and enlisted men, there was virtually no hope of recognition.

At the outbreak of the war in 1861, the population of Norristown was about 8,000 people. Perhaps no other American town of that size, North or South, made such an equal military contribution of five generals. Yet, few Norristown area citizens are familiar with this distinction or any of the men and their accomplishments.

In addition to these historical omissions, I was never introduced to other area generals such as Major-Generals George B. McClellan and George G. Meade of Philadelphia, John G. Parke of Coatesville, and John F. Reynolds of Lancaster. I suspect that such a historical information gap is not unique to Norristown but indicative of failings in many schools and towns throughout the country. My intent here is not to criticize the teachers, schools, and leaders of my hometown, but rather to emphasize the need that all of us must be more mindful of the roots of our historically important people. Perhaps we all need to realize that heroes need not come from "some other place."

The Civil War is a tragic tale of military horror of brother against brother and a great human struggle which cries out for its proper place in our history and understanding. It still reverberates and its aftershocks will continue for decades to come. No other national event stands at the crux of our modern existence as does the immortal conflict between the Blue and the Gray. If we fail to understand and teach the war and its participants properly, we are doomed to lose its lesson to ignorance and distortion.

All of the generals from the Norristown area are buried in Montgomery Cemetery, located at the foot of Hartranft Avenue. While technically located in West Norriton Township, the cemetery lies immediately adjacent to the west end of Norristown. With five generals and two hundred other officers and enlisted men who served in the Civil War, Montgomery Cemetery should be a very significant historical landmark for the locale and the state. Instead, it lies in unforgivable ruin and remains virtually unknown to most of the local population and certainly throughout the state.

Plagued by vandalism and only modest grounds maintenance, only Hartranft's and Hancock's gravesites receive any individual care, and that comes mainly from a few private citizens or the Old Baldy Civil War Round Table of Philadelphia. Recent legal difficulties have exacerbated the cemetery's problems and have frustrated efforts to purchase that hallowed ground by the local Historical Society of Montgomery County.

Hartranft's obscurity is not solely related to Norristown. My research on him brought me into contact with numerous libraries and historical societies throughout Pennsylvania. In many cases, staff members had never heard of Hartranft, either as a general or governor of the state. Another good indicator of his fall into the unknown is his beautiful equestrian statue in front of the Capitol in Harrisburg. Its nickname, "The General in the Park", tells how little is remembered of the man and his period. As for most of the other Norristown area veterans interred at Montgomery Cemetery, sadly, one can barely find their graves.

Fortunately, the histories of some locals such as McClellan, Meade and Hancock have survived through their biographies. They have monuments to their memories and their feats are widely told. With Hartranft, as with others, the story is dramatically different. Aside from the occasional references and local distorted biographies, no single volume serves as an information source to a man considered so important during his time. Since Hartranft fell into oblivion after his death, the objective of this volume is to attempt to restore him to his rightful position in American and Pennsylvania history.

Active with hometown and state militia, Hartranft became the colonel of the 4th Pennsylvania Volunteers, whose body walked off the field the morning of the battle of First Bull Run. He then raised the famous 51st Pennsylvania, which served with distinction in both the eastern and western theaters, finally gaining promotion to brigadier-general in 1864. In March of 1865, he was quickly brevetted to major-general by Lieutenant-General Ulysses S. Grant after his dramatic recapture of Fort Stedman. During the Lincoln conspiracy trial, President Andrew Johnson appointed him Special Provost Marshal General of Washington D. C. There he was responsible for all of the defendants and had the unpleasant responsibility to execute David Herold, George Atzerodt, Lewis Paine, and Mrs. Mary E. Surratt.

After the war, he declined the offer of a permanent military career for political office in his beloved Pennsylvania, where he served as Auditor General and two terms as Governor. As the Keystone State's Chief Executive, he was instrumental in forming the modern Pennsylvania National Guard, which he commanded from 1879 until his untimely death in 1889. During his two terms as governor, he also decisively confronted great economic and labor disorders including railroad and coal mining strikes along with the infamous Molly Maguires. Yet Hartranft maintained a strong degree of trust in his many associates, and at times, that trust proved to be sorely misplaced and costly to his career.

My decision to write about Hartranft grew out of my hometown loyalty and my respect for his significant military and political accomplishments. He embodies the concept of a true soldier who has to carry out orders that may be contrary to personal thinking and mores. But, his keen mind and instinctive military nature made him understand that orders must always be interpreted based upon prevailing conditions of the moment and site. Consequently, he promptly and correctly disobeyed orders at Fort Stedman and proceeded with a counterattack which defeated Lee's last offensive move. Had he delayed there, the Confederate attack might have gained strength, or at least, the cost to Lee's army would have been relatively minor instead of the heavy toll it exacted. In either case, the war probably would have extended beyond Lee's surrender date of April 9, 1865.

The product of a German heritage, Hartranft had his roots in the Schwenkfelder sect of Christianity. Although a devout man, he grew apart from any particular church and, like President Lincoln, kept formal religion at arms length. In terms of the war, he felt the preservation of the Union was paramount and though his education did not prepare him for combat, as a citizen soldier he quickly adapted to the art of the military. With a keen mind for engineering and law, he had the mental agility to transfer the principles of those disciplines to strict military demands which allowed him to perfect his soldierly responsibilities as few men did. In a war that frequently rewarded individuals because of their political or military connections, Hartranft found himself void of any such shallow relationships and realized that he was "marked" by the cowardly actions of the 4th. All of this meant he would have to earn any stature by sheer effort and results.

I cannot pretend that this volume is an in depth study of the various Civil War battles or political confrontations that Hartranft encountered during his career. Rather, the conflicts and incidents only serve as highlights and references to his contributions and participation. The author feels that those bloody military and exasperating political clashes are far better documented by others whose expertise is better suited for such matters. However, even though the battles herein have been written about many times, virtually none has been presented from Hartranft's vantage point. Consequently, for the students of the Civil War, it is appropriate to focus upon the efforts of Hartranft in those conflicts to clarify some of the misconceptions of what he, or others, did or did not accomplish. In this way, I hope John Frederick Hartranft's contributions to the nation and his state will be better understood and appreciated.

# ACKNOWLEDGMENTS

It is impossible for me to conceive of any historical work being written without the assistance of many who are frequently, and unfortunately, unnoticed. Perhaps the greatest privilege given to any author is meeting those helpful individuals and specialists. That is certainly the case with this volume and my only fear is that I may miss someone who gave much to me and the cause of this work. Should that failing occur in any manner, please accept my sincere apology. Let me be prompt to add however, that any omissions or errors contained in this volume are my sole responsibility and not those from whom I have drawn so much support. To the following I offer my sincere gratitude.

To Mr. Donald Stepanck, Director of the Parks & Recreation Department in Watertown, Connecticut, who intensified my Civil War studies by providing me the opportunity to begin an extended lecture series on the subject. Because of Don's kind consideration, his prototype lecture series developed into a five year program that presents 225 hours of holistic profile on the conflict. To my very good friend and traveling companion, Frank D'Amico, who is also responsible for many of the photographs contained herein. Mrs. Judith A. Meier of the Historical Society of Montgomery County at Norristown, Pennsylvania, who labored so diligently and efficiently to my endless requests. Without her, I certainly would have missed many details about Hartranft. Mr. Dennis Moyer and Miss Claire Conway of the Schwenkfelder Library in Pennsburg, Pennsylvania, who proved extremely helpful in the research of Hartranft's Schwenkfelder genealogy. Lieutenant-Colonel [Ret.] William O. Hickok of the Pennsylvania National Guard in Harrisburg, who constantly provided assistance and guidance on Hartranft's relationship with the Guard. Dr. Richard Sauers, the past Military Historian of the Pennsylvania Capitol Preservation Committee, for his assistance with parts of my text. All of the flag photographs herein are the result of Dr. Sauers and his staff while active with the Committee. Dr. Charles H. Glatfelter, Professor Emeritus of History, Gettysburg College, for his critical review on portions of Hartranft's political career. Mr. Charles B. Oellig, Curator for the Pennsylvania National Guard Museum, for his critical reviews on significant portions of Hartranft's military career and participation in the creation of the modern Guard. Mrs. Ester Steele who, along with Mrs. Margaret Boyd were willing to pursue early data on Hartranft in the Pennsylvania coal mining region which was essential to my research. The staff at the Recorder of Deeds Office of Montgomery County, Pennsylvania, and in particular, Mr. Sam Fulton and Mrs. Gladys Quartucci who spent many hours

researching Hartranft's many real estate transactions. Mrs. Dorothy
Ferguson, who was willing to supply the insightful private letters and papers
of her grandfather, Brevet Brigadier-General William E. Doster, who was
legal counsel for Paine and Atzerodt during the Lincoln conspiracy trial.
Mr. Joseph Cunningham, who kindly reviewed the entire manuscript and
made numerous editorial suggestions. Mr. John Fournier who gave me
much technical assistance with my writing and Mr. Anthony J. Saraceni who
labored over the tedious task of preparing maps and other drawings so they
might be better understood. To his wife, Joan Saraceni, for her persistent
pursuit of local Norristown banks to find the original currency honoring
General Hartranft, and her other research efforts in the Norristown area.

There are institutions and departments of all types that lent their
assistance including the Libraries at Norristown and Pottstown,
Pennsylvania. Mrs. Ellen Gambini and, in particular, Mrs. Candice Lamb of
the Silas Bronson Library in Waterbury, Connecticut. Mrs. Jill Smith and
her capable staff at the Library of Woodbury, Connecticut, with particular
thanks to Mrs. Linda Petersen. Ms. Mary Yeager of the Scranton Public
Library and Archivist Ms. Ellen Fladger of Union College in Schenectady,
New York. Archivist Ernest Staley at Mercersburg Academy in
Mercersburg, Pennsylvania and Mr. John J. Slonaker and Dr. Richard
Sommers of the U. S. Army Military History Institute at Carlisle,
Pennsylvania. Mrs. Joan Rintleman and her staff at the Watertown,
Connecticut Library. To Mr. David Hedrick of Gettysburg College and
author John Michael Priest for sharing his important papers on the battle of
Antietam. To Mr. William Norwood, Principal of the Heminway Park
School in Watertown, Connecticut, who took so much time to review and
make the many corrections to my grammar. To Ms. Holly Green of
Boyertown, Pennsylvania, who did much research into the life of the
Hartranft family in that area. To Dr. Ian Lawson for his personal guidance
through the deep labyrinth of medical science that attends the physical
problems related to Hartranft. Mr. Michael Kauffman who gave so freely of
his time, thoughts and records relating to the Lincoln Conspiracy Trial and
Mr. John Smarsh, for his assistance in better identifying some of the
Hartranft photographs.

The Pennsylvania State Library and Archives at Harrisburg plus the
National Archives and the Library of Congress. Mr. Shawn Weldon of the
Core States Financial Corp., and my young administrative assistant, Katrina
Salzer for all her many hours at the copy machine. To my private secretary,
Judith Van Stone for her endless patience and diligence to orchestrate much
of the tedious follow up effort connected with such a volume. A very special
note of thanks to Mrs. Helen Shireman, Hartranft's great-granddaughter,
and her husband Ron, who so graciously opened their home and offered the

general's papers which truly represent the centerpiece of this book. Mrs. Shireman and her family spared no inconvenience to further this work and it was a particular privilege to have worked with them.

Lastly, and perhaps most importantly, my wife Nancy for her endless patience during my long hours, days, weeks, and months spent upon this endeavor which was primarily conducted from my household office known as the "hole". She has read and reread the entire volume many times and offered her support and suggestions for style and grammar. Her encouragement made possible the progress when matters seemed lost and confused. Many times before I have read similar statements from authors but now I can appreciate the real value and truth in such notations.

To all of these, and to any I may have forgotten, I extend my sincere apologies, gratitude, and respect.

A. M. Gambone
Woodbury, Connecticut
April 9, 1994

# LIST OF PHOTOGRAPHS

# LIST OF MAPS AND DIAGRAMS

# ABBREVIATIONS

AOH ............................................................ The Ancient Order of Hibernians
AOTP ...................................................................... The Army of the Potomac
*Bolton Diary* ........... *Diary of Captain William J. Bolton of the 51st Pennsylvania*
*Genealogical Record* ....... *The Genealogical Record of the Schwenkfelder Families*
JFH ............................................................................... John F. Hartranft
HMCP ...................................... *History of Montgomery County Pennsylvania*,
    edited by Theodore W. Bean.
HSMC ..................... Historical Society of Montgomery County Pennsylvania
    at Norristown
*O. R.* ........................... *The Official Records of the Union and Confederate Armies*
SEH .............................................. Samuel E. Hartranft, the General's Father
SSH ............................................. Sallie Sebring Hartranft, the General's Wife
*S. H. S. P.* ................................................. *The Southern Historical Society Papers*
Shireman Collection ......... Personal and official records and correspondence
    kept by General Hartranft
USAMHI ................ U. S. Army Military History Institute, Carlisle Barracks,
    Pennsylvania

# CHAPTER ONE

## *"IN THE BEGINNING ..."*

As the early burning summer sun rose higher in the sky, July 7, 1865 promised to be another hot oppressive day. Planted along the riverbanks of the confluence of the Potomac and Anacostia rivers rested the Washington Arsenal, which had recently gained new notoriety as a prison since it now held the defendants charged in the conspiracy to murder President Abraham Lincoln. The seven week trial was over, and the inmates knew the fate that awaited them. In particular, three men and one woman were almost oblivious to the heat of that blistering sun as they wrestled with fear and trepidation about the scheduled major event for that fateful day. For George A. Atzerodt, Lewis Paine, David E. Herold, and a dolorous widow, Mary E. Surratt, this day would be their last on earth unless the newest occupant of the White House, President Andrew Johnson, deemed it prudent to offer them any form of clemency. All had been found guilty of conspiring with John Wilkes Booth to murder President Abraham Lincoln.

Also "confined" within those stark prison walls was the jailer of the accused, who had efficiently carried out his duties during the trial while attempting to balance some sign of human concern. The morning heat was no less oppressive for Brevet Major-General John Frederick Hartranft, as he busied himself with last moment papers and made a meager attempt to consume some breakfast. The entire legal ordeal had exacted its toll upon him too, but he managed to appear indifferent, avoiding any possible impression of favoritism to any one of the condemned.

As the hot morning slowly became early afternoon, the heat became even more unbearable. A crowd, comprised mainly of soldiers, began to swell within the courtyard of the prison as invited visitors looked upon the hastily constructed gallows with mixed emotions that vacillated between morbid fascination and horror. Finally, shortly after one o'clock that afternoon, Hartranft saw the futility of waiting any longer for a reprieve from the President.

Passing the word to begin the gruesome task, he personally walked the corridors of the prison, though history leaves us no precise record of any verbal comment he may have made. No matter, because we can be certain that he found no pleasure in this day's duties irrespective of how many horrors of war he had witnessed over the past four years. With the nod of his head, or the point of his finger, a solemn procession began out of the prison and into the baking courtyard.

1

First in line was Mary Surratt, followed by Paine, then Atzerodt, and finally Herold. All walked with varying difficulties to the scaffold and then up the thirteen traditional, virulent steps. Immediately behind them was Hartranft, in a clean uniform complete with gold braid and brass buttons, representing the awesome power of the U. S. Government. He too mounted those steps and then, drawing a deep breath, he began to read the charges followed by the court's guilty verdict and sentence, which was death by hanging! With some of the defendants being sheltered from the brutal sun with umbrellas, and Mary Surratt half dead from fright, Hartranft stepped back off the platform, and down the steps once more.

Suddenly, there were three loud hand claps and the traps fell. The crowd sighed, and the four fell heavily towards the earth only to be rudely interrupted in their drop by a sharp jerk of the rope now held tightly around each neck. True to his military bearing, Hartranft looked upon the entire event without any outward sign of emotion. However, no one, not even his wife Sallie, would ever know the pain and anguish he had suffered that day.

As the four bodies finally stopped their writhing, Hartranft's personal revulsion perhaps became suspended somewhere between heaven and earth as well. As he took one last look upon the four lifeless forms hanging there, he might have thought that at times, the rigors of military duty are almost greater than the heart can tolerate.

Thus, the military career of the 34-year-old general came to an abrupt end, and he would now return to his native state of Pennsylvania to embark on an entirely new political career. But the modest birth and background of General Hartranft certainly did not portend any reason to anticipate an individual who was destined to become important in so many of America's darkest days.

In the beginning, the small English sailing ship *Saint Andrew* was moored at the foot of Walnut Street in Philadelphia, on September 22, 1734.[1] Aboard were 184 tired, hungry, and frightened passengers who had just completed a long and trying crossing of the Atlantic to their new home in search of religious freedom.[2] Ironically, the captain of that vessel was a John Stedman, who carried a family name that was to mean so much to the future general some one hundred and thirty years hence.[3]

Included in that band of German religious refugees was the Herterranft family headed by Tobias and his wife Barbara [Jäckel].[4] All of those passengers were followers of Caspar Schwenckfeld von Ossig [1489-1561], who had adopted a passive form of Christianity which also took its founder's name.[5]

With Tobias and Barbara were their five children including Maria, sixteen, a set of fifteen-year old twins, Anna and Rosina, and two sons, George and Melchior, thirteen and eight respectively. Later, another son

2

Abraham was born, probably in America, with his death recorded in 1766.[6] Shortly after their arrival, the entire group of immigrants began to disperse in and around the Philadelphia area, including the southeastern counties of Berks, Bucks, Lehigh, and Montgomery.[7]

Tobias moved his family into the area known today as the "Pennsylvania Dutch Country", in Salford [now Marlborough] Township in Montgomery County. That, rich farm land, northwest of Philadelphia, had been originally settled around 1735, and was only a short distance from the growing hamlets of Norristown and Pottstown.[8]

With the passing of time, Tobias' family name of Herterranft would be Anglicized into Hartranft, composed of two names, "Hart", meaning bold and "Ragenfrid", meaning powerful in peace. The original Herterranft went through several changes including Ranft, Ranf, Ranfd, Ranph, Rauft, Ramph, Hartranfft, and finally to Hartranft.[9] While it is not possible to pinpoint the exact time of the name changes, at the time of his death, Tobias was already using the kindred spelling of Hartranfft, indicating a rapid change. Whatever the precise timing, Tobias' eldest son George was the first to use the final form of Hartranft.

Tobias died on October 4, 1758. While his grave has not been positively identified, it is believed to be in the cemetery of St. Paul's Lutheran Church near Red Hill, Pennsylvania. Barbara died on February 15, 1764, and her remains were placed in the local Washington Schwenkfelder Cemetery; the reason for their separation is unknown.[10]

Abraham, the son of Tobias and Barbara would marry Susanna Schubert who gave birth to a son Leonard. Leonard married Christine Moyer and they had fifteen children including a son, Leonard Jr. who married Mary Elizabeth Engle and from that union sprang nine children including a son, Samuel E. Hartranft.[11]

Samuel E., father of the future general, was born on October 6, 1806, in New Hanover Township and he married Lydia Bucher of the same locale in 1829.[12] The couple purchased a private home and on December 16, 1830, John Frederick Hartranft, their only child, was born as the sixth generation of the Hartranft family in America.[13] Even before Hartranft's birth however, at least some of his family had begun to drift from the Schwenkfelder Church as witnessed by the baptism of John Hartramph, a relative, at the Falkner Swamp Reformed Church at Gilbertsville, on January 16, 1785. Even his father Samuel was baptized at St. Paul's Lutheran Church in Red Hill and the general, like his relative, was also baptized at the Falkner Swamp Reformed Church on January 2, 1831.[14]

The home where Hartranft was born is a house of modest proportions with twenty-inch-thick stonewalls that was probably built in 1774, and most likely, upon the foundation of an even earlier house. In

**Hartranft's Home at Birth**

The home where General Hartranft was born.

*Photographer: Frank D'Amico*

1750, Michael Bachman bought the property from Henry Van Bibber and gave the original home and a tract of 103 acres to the Falkner Swamp Reformed Church and School. It was probably used as the church's parsonage for a while, and records clearly indicate that the present home was built with communal spirit which incurred the cost of "rum, boarding and building materials."[15] Tradition says that General "Mad" Anthony Wayne used the house as his headquarters just prior to the Valley Forge encampment, though there is no historical proof of that claim. Today, the house is located at 117 Cross Road in New Hanover Township, just outside the tiny village of Fagleysville. While the home has undergone some modern improvements, the basics of the house and its original construction are readily apparent, and it appears that what is the front today, was undoubtedly the rear of the home in the past.

In 1841, Samuel became an innkeeper and moved his small family to his newly-purchased Swamp Inn, near current Gilbertsville.[16] Later, he moved to nearby Boyertown to another inn which had been built upon the ruins of the older Union House, and still serves as the Boyertown Inn. While living in that area, Samuel also became a captain in the Boyertown Militia.

While young Hartranft may have received some local schooling in the area where he was born, it is more probable that he obtained much of his early education at home from his parents. From his mother he would draw a rich, soft background of tolerant Christian heritage while his father imparted a sense of business and a lifelong love of horses. Eventually, the lack of suitable schooling for their thirteen-year-old son became a major factor in Samuel and Lydia's decision to move to Norristown, which they did in March of 1844. In that thriving town, only 18 miles west of Philadelphia, Samuel and Lydia could find suitable educational facilities for their son, while the area also offered new business opportunities for the senior Hartranft. With a good head for business, Samuel soon purchased the Pennsylvania Farmer Inn for $7,000, which he sold in 1852 for $17,000; quite a nice profit for the time![17] In addition to the inn, Samuel ran a stage line and speculated in real estate, which was an area his son would also pursue.

From the very beginning there developed a lifelong, close relationship between father and son which was marked by great trust in each other's insight and abilities. Samuel and Lydia both encouraged their son to become self-sufficient but even after his marriage, Hartranft always demonstrated great respect for his parents and his father in particular.

With the move to Norristown, Hartranft began his education in earnest and studied under Dr. John F. Evans for about two years.[18] Afterwards, he went to the distinguished Treemount Seminary in Norristown, which educated almost five thousand students during its thirty-nine-year history.[19] That private institution was directed by the industrious

5

Reverend Samuel Aaron and his associate, Philip Cressman. Young Hartranft proved to be only an adequate student. But, his strong parental influence was already beginning to surface as exemplified by Reverend Aaron's remarks in the "Character Book" dated March 22, 1847, wherein he stated, "John Hartranft has always conducted himself in my class like a gentleman and has my sincere respect."[20]

In 1850, following his graduation from Treemount, Hartranft entered Marshall College in Mercersburg, Pennsylvania, though the precise timing of his attendance is subject to debate.[21] He remained there for only a short while before entering Union College in Schenectady, New York in September of 1850.[22] His reasons for changing schools remain unclear and speculation runs from financial considerations to the influence of friends.[23] Nonetheless, at Union, he studied engineering and in 1851, he became a member of the Sigma Phi Fraternity where he received the nickname "Fred", undoubtedly because of his middle name.[24] By that time, Hartranft's appreciation of education had vastly improved and a partial list of his studies included geometry, Greek, trigonometry, chemistry, French, German, mechanics, and engineering mensuration. Out of a total of thirty-three final grades, only eleven were below 100, and none lower then 96. He was so far advanced that while he did not attend his final semester, he was still awarded an A. B. in Civil Engineering in the spring of 1853.[25]

Returning to Norristown at the age of 22, Hartranft pursued a brief engineering career with the Water Gap Railroad in Easton, Pennsylvania.[26] There, he served as a rodman, or surveyor's apprentice, and assisted in running the Mauch Chunk [modern Jim Thorpe] and Wilkes-Barre Railroad.[27] However, the labors in the outer regions did not really suit the young engineer and he soon left that job and returned to the Norristown area to assist his father in his real estate and stage line business. In 1854, Samuel introduced his son to Michael C. Boyer, the Democratic Sheriff of Montgomery County, who offered Hartranft his first political position as a deputy sheriff. Young Hartranft eagerly accepted, and held that position for about four and one-half years.[28] Like his father, the young engineer-turned sheriff was dedicated to the Democratic party, and while his political allegiance would later change, Boyer's offer exposed him to his first experience with political "favors." The position of deputy sheriff also served to whet his appetite for law, and he began studying that discipline under Colonel James Boyd, Esquire, and later, A. B. Longaker, Esquire, in Norristown. On October 24, 1860, upon the motion of Longaker, Hartranft was admitted to the Montgomery County Bar.[29]

Before becoming a lawyer however, many other important events took place in Hartranft's life; not the least of these was his marriage to pretty Sallie Douglas Sebring, of Easton, Pennsylvania. Sallie's father was

**John F. Hartranft**

Hartranft as a student at Union College (circa 1853).
*Source:  Union College.*

Judge William L. Sebring of Easton and her mother was Ann Davis of Plymouth, in Montgomery County.[30] Hartranft and Sallie were married on January 26, 1854, when he was just twenty-three and she was not yet nineteen.[31] From their union, seven children would be born, though two of them would die at a very early age and another on the day of birth.[32]

With the added responsibility of a wife, and charged with the vigor of youth, Hartranft set about on a very active lifestyle for Sallie and himself. He became a member of the Montgomery Hose and Steam Fire Engine Company in Norristown, and was soon elected auditor.[33] In 1858, he was elected president of the Company and his close bonds to it would remain for the rest of his life.

During the seven years between the time of his marriage to Sallie and the outbreak of the Civil War, Hartranft continued pursuing his business, legal, community, and militia interests while beginning a modest real estate investment and still assisting in his father's business activities. Around 1857, though the precise date is unknown, he joined the Norris Rifles, a local militia company, and was elected lieutenant, and later, captain.[34] During this same period, he also became active with the state militia, and in 1859 found himself elected a lieutenant-colonel.[35] He became a Mason in 1858 and was elected to the Borough Council in the same year while still maintaining his position as deputy sheriff and conducting his own business as a stock broker, para-legal and a real estate broker.[36] In addition to all of this, he was active with the Montgomery County Agricultural and Mechanical Society, and the Committee to Improve Roads, Streets and Bridges.[37] Now twenty-eight years old, he and Sallie already had three of their seven children. Their eldest son Samuel had been born on October 30, 1855, while their first daughter Ada was born on March 4, 1857 and their second son Wilson, was born on December 1, 1859.[38] His growing family did not deter Hartranft's ambitions, and in 1860, he and several friends incorporated the Stony Creek Railroad Company, which never advanced much beyond the paper stage.[39]

By early 1861, war clouds had formed over much of the nation. Seven southern states had already seceded and stood hoping for similar decisions from North Carolina, Virginia, and others. President James Buchanan of Pennsylvania sat in the White House, vacillating and attempting to appease the departed southern states, which accomplished little except to frustrate officials of both sides.

Still, despite the growing national tensions, most Americans hoped for, and sincerely anticipated, a peaceful solution to the potential tragedy of war. Those fallen hopes were based upon the national experience over the past eighty five years during which America had always found a way to compromise. But, for some, the election of Abraham Lincoln, considered by many to be unfit for the presidential post, only exacerbated strains over the national unrest. In the South, many saw the president-elect as a threat to their established life style, their coveted state rights and their legal right to own slaves. In the North, when secession occurred, it was simply a matter of preservation of the Union.

There was never any doubt about Hartranft's feelings and loyalties, which were founded upon Lincoln's premise of an undivided Union. If war came, he was committed to do whatever he could, even if that meant going off to fight. Certainly, his experience with the local and state militias did not prepare him for such demanding pressures, since those organizations had become little more than a parade spectacle and a forum for social functions. Yet, his commitment to the Union was absolute.

Youthful and sturdy, standing about five feet ten inches, Hartranft had a large crop of black hair set above piercing blue eyes, which looked out over a full-flowing black mustache.[40] His strong, commanding stature upon a horse lent a regal air to his countenance, and his striking facial features made him a model of a soldier for the mid-nineteenth century. However, he also had a substantial "Pennsylvania Dutch" accent reflecting the parochial nature of his family background.[41] While that never hampered his spirit and resolve, he was never fond of making speeches, even after he entered politics. But, like countless numbers of other immigrants and their offspring, Hartranft had a deep-seated pride in his German ancestry and later, while governor, he found time to write and speak on the significant contributions made by those that shared his heritage.[42]

Following the Confederate attack on Fort Sumter on April 12, 1861, President Lincoln called for 75,000 militia to put down the rebellion. Hartranft gave an immediate response on April 17th by presenting himself before Pennsylvania Governor Andrew Curtin to offer the services of the entire 1st Regiment, Second Brigade, Second Division of the state militia. Curtin, who was eager to please Lincoln and a firm believer in the Union, promptly accepted the offer and authorized him to return home and raise a regiment. The Governor's only proviso was that the new regiment had to report for duty within four days.[43] Without any delay, Hartranft returned to Norristown and began to solicit men for a ninety-day period, and he soon had a regiment of about 600 volunteers.

After forming his ranks, the appropriate speeches were made along with the presentation of flags from the local women, and Lieutenant-Colonel John F. Hartranft and his men departed Norristown on Saturday, April 20, 1861.[44] Leaving his wife Sallie and three children behind, the neophyte militarist and his equally naive command set off to Camp Curtin in Harrisburg, "to see the elephant."[45]

Reaching Camp Curtin later that afternoon, the regiment followed the common practice of electing their officers. Four men, all from Norristown, were to be in command -- Colonel John F. Hartranft, Lieutenant-Colonel Edward Schall, Major Edwin Schall, and Charles Hunsicker as Adjutant. Since Curtin's deadline was met, on April 21 the Pennsylvania governor officially commissioned Hartranft a colonel and the regiment was formally designated as the 4th Pennsylvania.[46]

On the very day of its induction, the 4th was ordered by Major-General Robert Patterson, Commander of the Department of Pennsylvania, to proceed to Perryville, Maryland.[47] They were to hurry and report to Colonel Charles P. Dare of the 23rd Pennsylvania, to assist in the securing of that port town from Confederate sympathizers who might interfere with Union troop movements. As a result, their departure was in such haste that it prevented the men from obtaining proper uniforms and equipment. In fact, they were so poorly provisioned that ammunition had to be carried in their pockets because they had no cap or cartridge boxes.[48]

That entire hasty movement was the result of the civilian attack upon the 6th Massachusetts in Baltimore which occurred on the 19th.[49] That incident, which resulted in about thirty-nine killed and wounded, precipitated much fear in Washington and a flurry of ominous telegrams between officials from the U.S. Capitol to Harrisburg. One of the many related telegrams was General Orders No. 3 from Brevet Lieutenant-General Winfield Scott announcing that General Patterson's scope of responsibility had just been expanded to include Delaware, Maryland, and Washington and that he,

> ... will, as fast as they [troops] are mustered into the service, post the volunteers of Pennsylvania all along the road from Wilmington, Del., to Washington City, in sufficient numbers and in such proximity as may give a reasonable protection to the lines of parallel wires, to the road, its rails, bridges, cars and stations.[50]

Hartranft soon joined Dare, who led the newly-inducted 4th along with one his own companies into Perryville, which was occupied without incident. Shortly afterwards, the 4th was ordered on to Washington. Meanwhile, Hartranft's provision problems continued to simmer as he made every effort to secure proper clothing and equipment for his men. Unfortunately, the army's initial disorganization continued to frustrate his efforts resulting in the 4th being considered among "the worst-clothed troops that Pennsylvania had sent to the field."[51]  Compounding those difficulties was the lack of pay for his men. Newspapers had advertised an attractive pay rate of $20.00 per month for privates. When U.S. government funds were finally dispersed, only $11.00 was given to the privates of the 4th who were told that the balance was to be received from their state government. That balance was not forthcoming and the financial strain placed upon those men and their dependent families was sore indeed.[52]

When the order directing the 4th to move to Washington was received, Dare thought it prudent to send only Hartranft and half the regiment, while maintaining the remainder in Perryville under Major Edwin Schall for added security.[53]

It was during that very period when the telegrams between President Lincoln, Maryland Governor Thomas H. Hicks, and Brigadier-General Benjamin F. Butler became very intense. Hicks was upset with the movement of any Federal troops through Maryland, and he advised the President, "I feel it my duty most respectfully to advise you that no more troops be ordered or allowed to pass through Maryland, and that the troops now off Annapolis be sent elsewhere, ... so that the effusion of blood may be prevented."[54]

Those pleas and threats from Hicks did not alter Lincoln's decision to have troops land at Annapolis and marched to Washington. General Butler twice telegraphed Hicks on the 22nd attempting to appease him while standing by his orders. In his second telegraph Butler's patience was wearing thin and he emphasized to the governor that in regard to his troops, *"They are not Northern troops; they are part of the whole militia of the United States, obeying the call of the President."*[55]  [emphasis is original]

Butler was not acting independently because Secretary of War Simon Cameron made it clear that in view of the threats posed by any such interference, "Governor Hicks has neither right nor authority to stop troops coming to Washington. Send them on prepared to fight their way through if necessary."[56]

Each passing telegram seemed to fan the flames of the moment, and since Hicks was preparing to meet with the state legislature at Annapolis, General Scott told Butler,

> The undersigned, General-in-Chief of the Army, has received from the President the following instructions respecting the legislature of Maryland, now about to assemble at Annapolis, viz: It is "left to the commanding general to watch and await their action, which, if it shall be to arm their people against the United States, he is to

11

adopt the most prompt and efficient means to counteract, even if necessary to the bombardment of their cities, and in the extremest necessity suspension of the writ of habeas corpus."[57]


Hartranft and the first half of the 4th arrived at Annapolis on the 28th and were housed in the buildings of the Naval Academy under the command of General Butler. Within several days, Major Schall arrived with the balance of the 4th, and they too were housed in the same manner.[58] Fortunately, none of those Union troops were called upon to fire upon any Maryland residents and Union troops began to move freely.

On May 8, the entire 4th entered Washington and because neither the state nor federal governments had provided any camp equipment, Hartranft was forced to quarter his men in assembly buildings and a nearby church. Owing to the cramped quarters in those buildings, his ranks were set upon by a new worry, camp illness. To further aggravate matters, the 4th had still not received their much-needed uniforms, which supposedly had been shipped on April 28.[59]

Almost one month later, in early June, proper camp equipment arrived, followed by uniforms, and Hartranft was again ordered to move his regiment into a new camp about two miles outside of Washington, near Bladensburg.[60] When that move was complete, Hartranft renewed his daily and constant drilling. Unfortunately, many in his ranks were too guileless to appreciate the value of that drill routine, and they complained bitterly. Nonetheless, despite his lack of military training and experience, he knew that a well-disciplined unit made for better soldiers under fire, and he worked hard to make the regimen second nature to his ranks. Still, idleness, cramped quarters, petty military duty and, more recently, the camp illness wore thin on those new glory-minded soldiers.

Difficulties aside, on June 17, Hartranft wrote Sallie,


I never had any thing to do in my life that pleased me so well as my present occupation, and I do sincerely regret that I never had a military education. I am growing fat and robust...I cannot think for one moment of returning home from the field until this war is ended - I have my heart and soul in it and <u>will</u> [emphasis is original] keep the 4th Regt. in the field though many stay at home.[61]

On the 24th, the 4th was ordered to move once again, and this time, towards Alexandria where they were told to anticipate a fight. When they got into the area, Hartranft encamped them on Shuter's Hill, and in lieu of a fight, the men were subjected to still more of their commander's drills.[62]

However, the first "fight" for the 4th came on Sunday, June 30, about 2:00 A.M. Some of the men, under the direction of Lieutenant [and later General] Matthew R. McClennan were unsuspectingly approached by a group of fourteen Confederates while on picket duty along the Fairfax Road around Camp Hale in Alexandria. Unable to see clearly in the dark, the men of the 4th offered the challenge and the rebels responded, "Go to hell - we'll kill all of you."[63] With that, both sides began to fire upon each other. The noise from those reports sent Colonels Hartranft and Schall rushing towards the shots, along with other members of the 4th from an adjoining post. Those Pennsylvanians also encountered the Confederates, and they immediately began to fire upon each other, mortally wounding Private Thomas Murray and severely wounding Private Llewelyn Rhumer of the 4th. The Confederates lost one killed and several wounded before retiring.[64] Later that same day, Hartranft wired Sallie that "Thos. Murray, Norristown, W. Lewellen [sic] Rumer, Blue Bell [Pennsylvania] wounded being attacked while on picket. Both of Co. E Capt. [George] Amery. let their friends know our men did well killing two of them and wounding one. ... J. F. Hartranft."[65]

While this clash was relatively insignificant, it brought home the ugly reality of war and the mortality of the men, which was underlined when word was later received of Murray's death. The incident made the 4th the first Pennsylvania regiment to see actual combat, and won them the obligatory praise of many, including Secretary of War Simon Cameron.[66] Cameron, who was also the political boss of Pennsylvania, verbally expressed a strong desire to Hartranft to keep the 4th active, but typical of many politicians, he failed to follow through on any of his promises to help. Cameron's lack of action, coupled with the continuing delays in uniforms, equipment, and pay, further eroded the morale of the Keystone men.[67]

When Brigadier-General Irvin McDowell was placed in charge of all Federal troops south of the Potomac, the 4th was reassigned to the First Brigade, Third Division, which was commanded by Colonel William B. Franklin. As always, with summer coming on, the weather in Washington became hot and humid. Those weather conditions, and a sense of meaningless duty, further inflamed the regiment's already tried patience. Still unaware of the deep dissension brewing within his ranks, Hartranft continued to write home expressing his pleasure with the progress of his raw regiment. On June 21, just one month before the fateful battle of First Bull Run, with supplies vastly improved, he wrote Sallie that, "The boys [The

13

regiment] feel well-plenty to eat and well clothed."[68] Hartranft naively felt his command was content and progressing in good order. Besides, as July started, it was clear to everyone that a major battle would soon be fought, and that would give every man the opportunity to show his valor and justify his joining the inefficient Union army.

ENDNOTES FOR CHAPTER ONE
"IN THE BEGINNING ..."

1. Brecht, Samuel Kriebel, ed. *Genealogical Record of the Schwenkfelder Families*, New York: Rand McNally & Company, 1923, p. 13. Hereafter referred to as *Genealogical Record*.
2. Anders, James Meschter, "Schwenkfelder Accomplishments", *Who Are the Schwenkfelders*, Pennsburg, Pennsylvania: The Board of Publication of the Schwenkfelder Church, 1923, p. 2. Hereafter referred to as "Schwenkfelder Accomplishments."
3. Records of the Schwenkfelder Library.
4. Brecht, *Genealogical Record*, p. 684.
5. Anders, "Schwenkfelder Accomplishments," p. 3.
6. Brecht, *Genealogical Record*, p. 684.
7. Anders, "Schwenkfelder Accomplishments," p. 2.
8. Kriebel, Howard W., "Historical Tours", *150th Anniversary of Montgomery County, Pennsylvania, Historical Society of Montgomery County*, [September 1934]; p. 19.
9. Brecht, *Genealogical Record*, p. 684.
10. Ibid.
11. Ibid., 684-690.
     *Also see* Barrett, Eugene A., "John Frederic Hartranft; Life and Services", *The Bulletin of the Historical Society of Montgomery County*, 7, [April, 1951] p. 299.
12. Brecht, *Genealogical Record*, p. 701.
13. Ibid., pp. 684, 728.
14. Records of the Falkner Swamp Reformed Church of the United Church of Christ, Gilbertsville, Pennsylvania.
     *Also see* Brecht, *Genealogical Record*, p. 701.
15. Hauze, Gary C., *Is This Not the Promised Land?, A History of America's Oldest German Reformed Church*, Gilbertsville, Pennsylvania: Falkner Swamp Reformed Church, 1975, pp. 20-21.
     *Also see Norristown Times Herald*, August 10, 1955.
16. Record of Deeds, Berks County Courthouse, vol. 47, p. 479.
17. Barrett, "John Frederic Hartranft; Life and Services", p. 300.
18. Armor, William C., *Lives of the Governors of Pennsylvania*, New York: Charles Scribner's Sons, 1907; reprint, Dayton, Ohio: Morningside Bookshop, 1977, p. 494.
19. "Historical Sketches", *The Bulletin of the Historical Society of Montgomery County*, 4, [1929], p. 376.
20. Barrett, "John Frederic Hartranft; Life and Services", pp. 302-303.

21. Records of Franklin & Marshall College, in author's possession.
22. Records from Union College, submitted by Ms. Ellen H. Fladger, Archivist, to author, June 19, 1990. Hereafter referred to as Records from Union College.
23. Barrett, "John Frederic Hartranft: Life and Services", p. 304. Unfortunately, a 1927 fire at Marshall College destroyed many of the records of earlier students including Hartranft's. We will probably never know all the reasons for his change of schools.
24. Records from Union College.
    *Also see* letter from James M. Dundas [a classmate] to JFH, December 16, 1852, Shireman Collection. The Shireman Collection contains numerous letters that span the periods of college to Hartranft's terms as governor where he received letters from classmates that were addressed as "Dear Fred".
25. Records from Union College. N.B. -- The degree awarded Hartranft was a Bachelor of Arts since the degree of Bachelor of Science did not exist in 1853. Courtesy of Union College.
26. Barrett, "John Frederic Hartranft: Life and Services", p. 305.
27. Bates, Samuel P., *Martial Deeds of Pennsylvania*, Philadelphia: T. H. Davis & Co., 1875, p. 662.
28. Barrett, "John Frederic Hartranft: Life and Services", p. 305.
    *Also see* Bates, *Martial Deeds of Pennsylvania*, p. 662.
29. Montgomery County, Pennsylvania, Bar Association ledger book-1860.
30. Records of the Easton Library, Marriages and Deaths 1799-1851.
31. Brecht, *Genealogical Record*, p. 728.
32. Ibid., p. 729.
33. Barrett, "John Frederic Hartranft: Life and Services", p. 307.
34. Bean, Theodore E., ed. *HMCP*, Philadelphia: Everts & Peck, 1884, p. 196.
35. Ibid.
36. *The Norristown Register and Montgomery Democrat*. March 23, 1858. Hereafter referred to as *The Norristown Register*.
37. Ibid., April 6, 1858.
38. Brecht, *Genealogical Records*, p. 728.
39. Corporation documents, courtesy of the Schwenkfeld Library.
40. Pennypacker, Samuel Whitaker, *The Autobiography of a Pennsylvanian*, Philadelphia: J. C. Winston Company, 1918, p. 87.
41. Townsend, George Alfred, Scrapbook #133, p. 89.
42. Hartranft, John F., "Memorial Day Address", *The Schwenkfeldian*, [October, 1914], p. 161.
43. Bean, *HMCP*, p. 196.
44. Ibid., p. 196.

45. A common expression during the war meaning those soldiers who had actually experienced combat.
46. Bean, *HMCP*, p. 196.
47. Armor, *Lives of the Governors of Pennsylvania*, p. 494.
48. *The Norristown Herald & Free Press*, July 16, 1861.
49. Armor, *Lives of the Governors of Pennsylvania*, p. 494.
50. *O. R.* I, vol. II, p. 579. In that same telegram, Scott announced that Patterson's responsibilities now included the District of Columbia, Maryland, Delaware, and Pennsylvania.
51. JFH to SSH, July 3, 1861, Shireman Collection.
      *Also see* Armor, *Lives of the Governors of Pennsylvania*, p. 494.
52. *The Norristown Herald & Free Press*, July 16, 1861.
53. There were two Schall brothers in the 4th, and later the 51st. In the 4th, Edward was a lieutenant-colonel while Edwin was a Major.
54. *O. R.* I, vol. II, pp. 588-589.
55. Ibid., p. 590.
56. Ibid., p. 578.
57. Ibid., pp. 601-602.
58. Bean, *HMCP*, p. 196.
59. Ibid., pp. 196-197.
60. Ibid., p. 197.
61. JFH to SSH, June 17, 1861, Shireman Collection.
62. Bean, *HMCP*, p. 197.
63. *The Norristown Herald and Free Press*, July 16, 1861.
64. Ibid., July 2, 1861.
65. JFH to SEH, June 30, 1861, Shireman Collection. Note the discrepancies in the casualty reports which were very common during the war.
66. JFH to SEH, July 3, 1861, Shireman Collection.
67. Bean, *HMCP*, p. 196.
68. JFH to SSH, June 21, 1861, Shireman Collection.

# CHAPTER TWO

## *"IGNOMINIOUS FLIGHT"*

By July of 1861, both the North and the South were bracing for some sort of decisive military confrontation. However, in both camps the thought of battle was mostly romantic and much of that sentimental notion was based upon a mixture of historical data and the popular belief that one Confederate could whip twenty Yankees, and one Yankee a like number of Confederates. Equally important was the earlier American military history which accounted for relatively small numbers of casualties and even fewer fatalities. The entire American Revolution resulted in only 4,435 fatalities while the War of 1812 had only 2,260. The Mexican War, which concluded after two years in 1848, was the greatest American conflict up to that point and it numbered only 13,284 dead.[1] The citizens of 1861 could not fathom that single campaigns would soon account for more than the total 20,000 casualties of those three combined conflicts.

The early days of the Civil War were filled with passionate speeches which avoided any reference to the horrible realities of war. Volunteering for the army was a grand affair promoted by politicians, women, and the strains of stirring martial music. It was an opportunity that gave much color to many otherwise dreary lives.

The call of war also gave rise to a large number of men with diverse backgrounds who suddenly found themselves thrown into sectional and national spotlights. Many individuals of military and non-military backgrounds were forced to decide between the North or the South. Men of the cloth, politicians, businessmen, inventors, teachers, tradesmen, and others felt the need to offer their services to the military. Men like P.G.T. Beauregard, Joseph E. Johnston, James Ewell Brown Stuart, Lenonidas Polk, Braxton Bragg, John A. McClernand, Daniel Edgar Sickles, Joseph Hooker, George Armstrong Custer, Philip Sheridan, Robert E. Lee, and Ulysses S. Grant all felt the call in their own way.

Montgomery County and Norristown in particular had its share of fathers, sons, and brothers who were also swept up in the spirit. Men like Captain William J. Bolton, Sergeant John A. Wills, Privates George H. Kulp, William P. Earle, and James C. Saylor all rushed to offer their services in response to Lincoln's call.[2] They joined the ranks of fellow townsmen which included men like Winfield Scott Hancock, Matthew R. McClennan, Adam J. Slemmer, Samuel K. Zook, and John Frederick Hartranft. They were, for the most part, men in the flower of their youth whose "...hearts were touched by fire."[3]

The quick response that Hartranft offered to the North was repeated many times from men everywhere in the country. It did not really matter that warfare was on the cusp of a modern age, and that strategy, discipline, and technology were as important as passion. These were unconsidered ingredients and the thrill of following the tradition of fathers and grandfathers who had participated in the Revolution was enough.

Even prior to President Lincoln's call for 75,000 troops, the Confederacy had already begun amassing an army of approximately 100,000 men. So great was the response to that initial Southern call that thousands had to be sent home because the new, budding government did not have adequate supplies with which to equip them. In the North, matters were not much better, since Lincoln was not certain how, if at all, the states would respond to his call for troops. Yet, despite their mutual problems and trepidations, both sides were successful of organizing early armies, though the term "armies" was in fact just a term in 1861. In their haste to assemble their war machines, North and South alike neglected the necessity of proper training which really left both sides with only armed mobs.

These were the general conditions facing almost every period officer including the twenty-nine year old Hartranft and the 4th as they entered the Washington area. They brought with them a strong sense of local, state, and national pride. Convinced that the concept of union was correct, those Keystone men worried sorely that they would not get to see battle before the entire matter was settled; a common fear on both sides. Conditions were changing rapidly and it had only taken four days from the time of Lincoln's call until the departure of the 4th from Norristown and that alone was a testimony to the anxiety and commitment frequently seen in the early days of the conflict.

Still, despite the appearance of inept government, both sides finally began to crystallize their war machines. In the South, Brigadier-General Joseph E. Johnston, an 1829 graduate of West Point, along with Brigadier-General Pierre Gustave Toutant Beauregard, an 1838 graduate of West Point, were placed in charge of the Confederate forces in Virginia.[4] Johnston, the senior officer, was in charge of the Army of the Shenandoah while Beauregard took command of the Army of the Potomac. Both had served with distinction in the U.S. Army during the Mexican War. The combined commands of these two generals would later be known as the Army of Northern Virginia, under Robert E. Lee.

For the North, Brigadier-General Irvin McDowell was given command of the Department of Northeastern Virginia.[5] His army would be known as the Division of the Potomac until later, when Major-General George B. McClellan was appointed Supreme Commander and he personally renamed it, "The Army of the Potomac."[6] McDowell too had graduated from West Point in 1838, and was a classmate of Beauregard.[7] As with many of the professional officers during the Civil War, McDowell had acquired his battlefield experience during the Mexican War. Despite his over-fondness for fine food and wine, he was a very capable officer.

In May of 1861, General Johnston was positioned at Harper's Ferry, Virginia, while Beauregard was positioned south of Washington, D. C.[8] At the time, McDowell wasn't exactly anxious to engage the Rebels since he wanted more time to better train his raw recruits. The desire for more training was also shared by the supreme commander, General Winfield Scott. Unfortunately for McDowell and others, political pressures would dictate the first major conflict quicker than desired and when that pressure was applied, McDowell pleaded with Lincoln that his troops were not yet prepared. The new President basically agreed but retorted that, "You are green, it is true; but they are green also. You are all green alike."[9] Consequently, the hapless McDowell was forced to make his battle plans and was soon assigned headquarters at the Lee Mansion in Arlington. Only a short while before, the U. S. Government had seized that home under the pretext of unpaid taxes.[10]

For the 4th, the long days of June and early July went by and petty frustrations continued to mount. Nonetheless, there is little doubt about the sense of excitement and fear that runs through an army before any major battle, and weeks prior to the first major conflict, most everyone spoke about an impending and decisive fight. As July wore on, McDowell sent his army toward Manassas Junction, Virginia, an important railroad junction approximately 25 miles southwest of Washington, located near Bull Run Creek. That junction was considered important to the Confederates as well, and their presence in the area was considered a threat, or at least an affront, to the Union.

The first Battle of Bull Run took place on Sunday, July 21, 1861. For many, it was the long awaited conflict expected to settle the matter of union or secession once and for all. Word had spread throughout Washington that that particular Sunday would provide a wonderful spectacle. Consequently, many in Washington made arrangements to go out early to ensure a suitable position upon which to picnic, enjoy the "festivities", and watch the Rebels being taught a lesson about Union determination.

Meanwhile, Hartranft's continual regimental training resulted in frequent praise from his superior officers for the 4th's exceptional performance on drill. The 4th's brigade commander, Colonel William B. Franklin, also a West Point graduate, tendered his compliments to Hartranft directly by telling his aides that, "Hartranft was the best Colonel in his Brigade."[11]  Irrespective of their impressive maneuvering abilities, everything was not calm in the ranks of those Pennsylvanians.

While becoming somewhat concerned with the rising amount of bickering in his ranks, Hartranft was still buoyed by Franklin's positive comments and appeared to discount any serious discontent. Yet the 4th was becoming more distraught about the lack of proper equipment plus the mundane manual duty they were frequently assigned. Apparently, Hartranft believed the unrest to be nothing more than soldierly "belly aching" and he even wrote Sallie that the regiment was anxious for battle.[12]  He also told Sallie that he was enjoying military life and continued his expression of confidence in the 4th,

> I have not been anxious heretofore to push the regiment forward because the men did not feel like soldiers - but now [with proper provisions] they feel prepared and anxious to try their steel.[13]

For the people in Norristown, encouraging and patriotic newspaper reports kept them informed of virtually all the details of their heroes. One example:

> The railroad leading from Alexandria to Manassas Junction is now in running order, and troops have been transported over it some five miles beyond our camp [Hale].  As the shrill whistle announces the approach of our men the rebels gracefully retire and will doubtless fall back upon Richmond, as the Junction has no natural advantage as a military post, and its only protection is the breastworks thrown up by the Negroes in the service of the rebel army.[14]

Another, more dramatic and overly confident local newspaper report, told of impressive impending success:

> Perhaps Gen. Scott has been awakened by the [New York] Tribune's continued cry 'forward to Richmond', and is moving in that direction. If this be really the case, you may prepare for decisive and rapid movements against the

rebels, for the old Hero never moves until he is ready, and never attacks an enemy until he is ready to overwhelm and crush him at a blow. I am led to believe there will be little fighting this side of Richmond. Fairfax Court House is now almost deserted by the rebel troops, and as we advance upon Manassas Junction, they will doubtless retire to their strongholds at Richmond ... But the same Chieftain who stormed the almost inaccessible heights of Chapultepec [Mexico] directs the forces which are about to attempt the capture of Richmond. When he is prepared, and the order goes forth to 'take Richmond', rest assured it will be done. [Emphasis is original] Our brave volunteers are now well disciplined, and always obey orders.[15]

The "Chieftain" referred to in this article was obviously General Winfield Scott, a native Virginian who was one of the heroes of the War of 1812 and the Mexican War. Scott always remained loyal to the Union but at the outbreak of the war he was seventy-five years old and weighed 325 pounds.[16] Scott would soon be replaced by General George B. McClellan.

During the middle of July, the 4th was assigned to protect Fort Ellsworth, which was deemed an honor since that martyred officer was still an important sentiment in the North. Honors aside, the enlistment term of the 4th was also coming to its end, and the local Norristown newspaper printed an ominous letter excerpt from one of the regimental members, "Our term of enlistment will expire on Sunday, the 21st inst., but the 'mustering out' of a regiment always requires time. We will not reach Norristown for some days after that time."[17]

Certainly, the boys of the 4th knew their calendar and their petty frustrations were beginning to flagrantly boil within their ranks. The visionary glory of battle was diminishing rapidly and as the month of July began to pass, they openly discussed their deep frustrations and options among themselves. Frustrations were made all the worse when they remembered how Hartranft had implored their own Secretary of War, Simon Cameron, for more soldierly duty and he did absolutely nothing.[18]

Still, Hartranft continued to proudly praise the progress of his regiment and on July 14th, just before the 4th set out for Manassas, he wrote to his father, "As it looks like a fight soon it may be that we will not be home at the expiration of our three months."[19] Hartranft was obviously aware of the regiment's expiration of enlistment, but his note clearly indicated his belief that they would remain at least for the coming fight. Nothing in his letters even hinted at any major difficulty and he remained confident about his command's willingness to perform.

Meanwhile, McDowell planned a two-pronged approach which was designed to catch Beauregard by surprise, roll up his left flank, and crush the balance of the Rebel army. The Union army was approximately 35,000 strong, while Beauregard had about 24,000 which would soon be aided by Johnston and another 8,500.[20]

Upon orders, Hartranft moved the 4th closer to Centreville, Virginia, and sometime on July 20, he must have received a small group of men representing the regiment. We can only imagine his shock to hear that his ranks had decided that since their ninety days were complete, they wanted to go home immediately.[21] Dismayed at the thought of such leave on the eve of battle, he tried to rationalize with the men but found himself unable to change their minds. His only success came from Captain Walter H. Cook, who commanded Company K, Sergeant Major C. Jones Iredell and Privates Joseph C. Reed and Thomas Simpson.[22] Ultimately, he had no option but to report the grievous matter to his commanders which led to personal pleas from McDowell and Cameron.[23] Despite even those pleas, the men remained adamant and except for those noted, every other member of the 4th walked off the field early on the morning of the battle. That bleak incident quickly became a point of contention between supporters and detractors of Hartranft and the 4th. However, it is clear from General McDowell's Special Order No. 37, written at Centreville, that the 4th did have the technical right to be discharged. While most today find such military license to be incredible, the reader must be careful to try and understand the attitude that existed in 1861. Still, McDowell vainly tried to change their minds in his Special Order No. 37:

> The general Commanding has learned with regret that the term of service of the Fourth Regiment Pennsylvania Volunteers is about to expire. The services of this regiment have been so important, its good conduct so general, its patience under privations so constant, its state of efficiency so good, that the departure of the regiment at this time can only be considered an important loss to the Army.[24]

Searching for any means to evince a change of heart, McDowell continued and promised,

Fully recognizing the *right* [emphasis added] of the regiment to its discharge and payment at the time agreed upon when it was mustered into service, and determined to carry out literally the agreement of the Government in this respect, the general commanding, nevertheless, request the regiment *to continue in service a few days longer*, [emphasis added] pledging himself that the postponement of the date of muster out of service shall not exceed two weeks. Such members of the regiment as do not accede to this request will be placed under the command of proper officers to be marched to the rear, mustered out of service, and paid as soon as possible after the expiration of their terms of service.

By command of General McDowell:
JAMES B. FRY
Assistant Adjutant-General[25]

That attempt failed to even change one other man's mind in the 4th and their decision to leave could only cast a terrible shadow upon their reputation. No justification, no matter how well founded and qualified, could excuse their refusal to follow the examples set by Colonel Hartranft, Captain Cook, and their other three comrades.

On the same day that McDowell issued his Special Order No. 37, and after it had been rejected, he reassigned Hartranft and told the 4th that,

The Fourth Regiment Pennsylvania Volunteers, having completed the period of its enlistment, is hereby *HONORABLY* [Emphasis added] discharged from the service of the United States. The regiment will, under command of the lieutenant-colonel, take up the march to-morrow for Alexandria, and on its arrival at that place will report to General Runyon to be mustered out of the service.[26]

Captain William J. Bolton, commander of Company A, confided to his diary of the 20th, what appears to be an early attempt at justification of the regiments actions,

...the fact of the matter was, the men had been badly used--they had a right to their discharge. Many had already made provisions to re-enlist in the service after a short stay at home. I myself had a part of a company already for the new call of three year men -- the General seeing that nothing could be done, ... ordered the regiment ... to be mustered out.[27]

The 8th New York Militia exercised the same right and they too were also honorably discharged at the same time.[28] Early in the morning of the 21st, as McDowell's army began moving toward the battlefield of Bull Run, the 4th Pennsylvania, led by Lieutenant-Colonel Schall began its march to Camp Hale, some twenty-four miles to the rear.[29] Again, Bolton's diary:

Laid in Bivouac all day and night near Centreville with nothing to eat--The term of the enlistment of the regiment expired to-day--General McDowell has made an appeal ... Difference of opinion prevailed throughout the whole regiment, but there was no concert of action, many willing to remain, I among the number... [The regiment] reached Camp Hail [sic] late in the afternoon [July 21].[30]

Despondent and embarrassed as he must have been at the thought of his men leaving at such a critical moment, Hartranft reported to his First Brigade Commander, Colonel William B. Franklin, of Colonel Samuel P. Heintzelman's Third Division, as an aide-de-camp.[31]   Under Colonel Franklin's command were the 5th and 11th Massachusetts, the 1st Minnesota, the 1st U. S. Artillery, and, until its departure, the 4th Pennsylvania.[32]   Captain Cook was assigned to the staff of Colonel David Hunter, who commanded the 3rd U.S. Cavalry, Second Division. Sergeant Major Iredell spent his time aiding the wounded as a volunteer, while Privates Reed and Simpson were sent to the rear as reserves and were not employed in active combat that day.[33]

As a member of Franklin's staff, Hartranft witnessed the movement of the First Brigade as it moved away from the Centreville area at about 2:30 A.M. on the morning of the 21st. Franklin's ranks had been issued three days' rations, and the entire Third Division was to be part of the main attacking group to cross Sudley Ford.

Upon reaching Centreville, the First Brigade was delayed to permit other columns to pass in front and after a delay of about two hours, Franklin's men finally pushed forward reaching Bull Run at about 11:00 A.M. That march of about twelve miles required nearly eight and one half hours, indicating the density of Union troops on the road.[34]

Initially positioning his brigade on both sides of Bull Run, near Sudley's Ford, Heintzelman and Franklin encountered sharp resistance which tore into their lead elements. The 5th and 11th Massachusetts were brought across the stream and sent to the center as support for the six 10-pound Parrotts belonging to Captain James B. Ricketts of Company I, 1st U. S. Artillery. Unfortunately for Ricketts, he and his crew came under severe Confederate fire where he was seriously wounded and his guns disabled. Meanwhile, the two supporting Bay State regiments, which were only under slight fire because of their position, panicked, leaving the guns on the field. Because Ricketts' guns were so important, the 5th and 11th were ordered back to support the battery and were soon assisted by the 1st Minnesota. Unfortunately, the hot Rebel fire again drove off the 5th and 11th, and no attempt by Franklin, Hartranft, or other members of his staff could restore order. Only the steady, determined support of the Minnesota boys prevented a major disaster though the heavy Rebel fire finally drove even them from the site and the guns were lost.[35]

At about 2:30 P.M., the arrival of Confederate Colonel Jubal Early with his Sixth Brigade to support Brigadier-General James Longstreet and his Fifth Brigade, triggered the first signs of the great Union rout. Early's reinforcements meant greater Rebel resistance and the Federals in front of Longstreet began to move back.[36] Between 3:30 and 4:00 P.M., both Early and Brigadier-General Edmund Kirby Smith and his Fourth Brigade were placed on Beauregard's left, and when the Rebel offensive began, the Union line began to withdraw. It didn't take long before the orderly retrenchment became wild confusion, panic, and pandemonium which drove large parts of the Union army into a rout.[37]

When the ranks of Colonel Franklin's First Brigade were thrown into disarray, Hartranft moved quickly in an attempt to maintain order. With authority and confidence, he ordered Franklin's lines to hold their position and maintain ranks unless they wished to destroy others in their haste. For a little while, Hartranft's commands minimized damage to Franklin's men and supplies but, as the rout gained momentum, no amount of commands, rationale, or heroics was adequate to control the masses who became bent on saving only themselves. Finally, Franklin's men joined many other Federals making their way across the Warrenton Road, back toward Sudley's Ford and Washington.

While the entire rout became a sore Federal embarrassment, many individual feats of courage were noted and in Hartranft's case, Franklin reported,

> Colonel Hartranft, of the Fourth Pennsylvania Regiment, whose regiment refused to march forward that morning, accompanied me to the field as an aide-de-camp. His services were exceedingly valuable to me, and he distinguished himself in his attempts to rally the regiments which had been thrown into confusion.[38]

Well after the battle of first Bull Run, Franklin, by then a brigadier-general, sent Hartranft a copy of his battle report. Realizing that the actions of the 4th that day might cause Hartranft difficulties, Franklin hoped that his comments might prove helpful when he wrote,

> Dear Colonel, Above you have my report. You are welcome to use it in any way that you may consider most advantageous to yourself. What I have said about you hardly seems strong enough now. I meant to say that I appreciated your services in the highest possible manner, as I certainly felt at the time I wrote.[39]

Hartranft had displayed a strong ability to control both himself and others under extremely trying conditions. His stoic attitude prohibited him from leaving the army when it needed him most, and his calm and deliberate style brought some control to conditions on the brink of disaster.

Nonetheless, the 4th's default would haunt Hartranft for years to come, slowing his rise in the army. More than once, the new Secretary of War, Edwin Stanton, would wryly state, "Why, this is the Colonel of the Fourth Pennsylvania Regiment that refused to go into service at First Bull Run."[40] Certainly, that alone was a bitter pill for Hartranft to swallow, but to further his miseries, the 4th was the only regiment from Pennsylvania which brought no honors to his great Keystone State. Over the next three years, Hartranft would frequently find himself in charge of brigades and even divisions without the privilege of appropriate rank and he rightly

27

reasoned that his lack of promotion lay squarely rooted in the sad events of First Bull Run.

As might be expected, the departure of the 4th created numerous charges and countercharges. Many from the regiment pointed toward McDowell as being incompetent and accused him of distorting their performance to cover his own ineptitude. Not long after the battle, one member of the 4th stated, "we awaited anxiously the appearance of the official [battle] report of Gen. McDowell, hoping that he would do the regiment the simple justice to give a fair, plain, and truthful statement in reference to their departure from Centreville, on the morning previous to the slaughter at Bull's Run. But in this we were mistaken."[41]

But, on August 4, McDowell attempted to write an objective profile of his defeat and his report essentially stated that the Union army was simply untrained and really not prepared for combat. As for his comments about the 4th, he candidly and accurately observed,

> On the eve of the battle the Fourth Pennsylvania Regiment of Volunteers and the battery of Volunteer Artillery of the Eighth New York Militia, whose term of service expired, insisted on their discharge. I wrote to the regiment as pressing a request as I could pen, and the honorable Secretary of War [Simon Cameron], who was at the time on the ground, tried to induce the battery to remain at least five days, but in vain. They insisted on their discharge that night. It was granted; and the next morning, when the Army moved forward into battle, these troops moved to the rear to the sound of the enemy's cannon.[42]

Among apologists for the 4th, Captain [later Major-General of the Pennsylvania National Guard] Bolton offered that McDowell suggested that if the 4th Pennsylvania and the 8th New York had not walked off the field, the Union would have had a victory that fateful day.[43] Bolton's charge here is simply not true. McDowell claimed nothing of the kind. Instead, his total reference to both units was directly as stated in the above report. There were no further statements on the matter from McDowell and not the slightest hint that the departure of either group caused his failure at Bull Run.

Further, McDowell was even-handed with his treatment of the 4th and as late as July 20, he warned army headquarters that the enlistments of several units were ready to expire which signaled potential problems. He then stressed,

I am somewhat embarrassed by the inability of the troops to take care enough of their rations to make them last the time they should, and by the expiration of the term of service of many of them. The Fourth Pennsylvania goes out to-day, and others succeed rapidly. I have made a request to the regiment to remain a few days longer, but do not hope for much success. In a few days *I shall lose many thousands* of the best of this force. [Emphasis added] Will it suit the views of the General and the Government that they shall be replaced by long-service regiments? The numbers may be replaced, but it will not be an equal force.[44]

Other charges leveled against McDowell by men who left the field can only be considered self-serving and unfounded. For example, one soldier complained about McDowell's statement regarding the 4th as they, "moved to the rear to the sound of the enemy's cannon." This individual contends that the 4th left the area early on the morning of the 21st and the actual battle did not begin until about 10:30 A.M. Consequently, the regiment was long out of hearing range of any cannon fire. Another argued that McDowell never indicated, in his Special Order No. 37, that an attack was even imminent![45]

It is impractical to give these two points too much credence, yet they should be addressed. There is ample proof that by evening of the 20th, everyone in the Union camp knew a battle was to occur on the 21st. Heavy Confederate train arrivals at Manassas Junction on the 20th told every listener that troops and supplies were on the move.[46] Hartranft himself wrote his father as early as the 14th, stating, "I now understand the movement for this week - We will go below Fairfax & will march about 27 miles into Virginia, which will have the effect to surround them [the Rebels] at Manassas - Don't show this letter to anyone."[47] The possibility that those Pennsylvanians did not realize a battle was imminent is simply preposterous.

But all the facts demonstrating the threshold of battle did not preclude those inclined to make their outlandish charges. For example, another claim hurled at McDowell, most likely from Private George N. Corson of Company B, charged that, "No mention is here [McDowell's Special Order No. 37] made of any expected attack."[48] Private Corson's statement here only reflects the civilian familiarity mindset of the volunteer soldiers of the day which professional officers hated. Perhaps Private Corson expected a personal memo from the commanding general.

As for the 4th not being within hearing distance of the cannon, Union troop activity began as early as 2:00 A.M. on the morning of the 21st. Confederate small arms fire was reported as early as 6:00 A.M. which resulted in a Union response from a 30-pounder cannon, fired by Lieutenant Peter C. Hains.[49] The only reports on the 4th's departure is from Bolton's diary which states they left the area for Camp Hale "early in the morning."[50] With all the preparations and early morning fire being conducted, it is highly doubtful that they were out of earshot as early as 6:00 A.M. When all things are considered, the matter of their ability to hear or not is almost senseless because there is no doubt that they were witness to the rest of the army, as it headed for battle.

Another anonymous, caustic newspaper report referred to the men of the 4th as cowards since they left the field "while the noise of the cannon was ringing on their ears and the blood of their noble comrades was being spilled in defense of the glorious Stars and Stripes." In heated response to that comment, Corson again replied that, "As far as the above charge retakes [sic] to the 4th Pennsylvania regiment, we will say that it is entirely false. ...The 4th Pennsylvania regiment on Saturday, the 20th of July, knew nothing of the intended battle...."[51] Corson also lashed out to yet another charge with patriotic, popular, self-serving rhetoric,

> But those who were enjoying their peaceful homes when the members of the Fourth Pennsylvania Regiment were rushed on through great danger, much privation and terrible suffering, to the defense of the Nations Capitol and the National honor, now dare to speak of the 'ignominious flight' of these brave men, and to call them cowards! Let the croaking reporters do an hundredth part the service of one member of the Fourth, and he will be rewarded in Heaven beyond all the merit of a whole life spent in writing sensation letters, not to say false communications, for publication.[52]

Harsh criticism of McDowell continued by many returning soldiers of the 4th and, with some understandable pride in their local volunteers, other Norristownians began to attack McDowell's character too as one local historian commented,

General McDowell, when he found himself defeated in the battle which ensued, looking about for some causes to which he could attribute his failure, towards the close of his official report drags in this regiment [the 4th] for a share of blame, to whose service he had no more rightful claim, and whose conduct he could no more justly censure, than that of a regiment a week or a month earlier discharged.[53]

However, all those vicious attacks on McDowell, which continued until the end of the war, become more perplexing when the very Pennsylvanians who claim to revere General William T. Sherman, ignore his evaluation of that commander. Pointedly, Sherman considered McDowell's plan for First Bull Run as excellent, but doomed by events beyond his control.[54] Hardly the terms used to define an incompetent!

On January 18, 1863, McDowell finally, if belatedly, addressed Hartranft's contribution at First Bull Run when he wrote the colonel,

I am glad to see your name has been sent to the Senate for promotion. I have written to the chairman of the Committee on Military Affairs of the Senate in your behalf and asking him to take favorable action on your nomination! I trust he may do so and that the Senate may confirm your nomination where there are so many and more than the law allows there is danger - and therefore I wrote.

I always regretted I did not make an exception in your case in my report of the battle of Bull Run and name you in that report for your good conduct - instead of leaving it with Genl. Franklin. I regret this the more as Genl. Franklin's report was not pointed.

I am much obliged for the kind expressions in your report and hope you may have no occasion to change them-

Very Sincerely,
Truly Yours,
Irvin McDowell, Maj. Genl[55]

31

As for Hartranft's feelings on McDowell, there is no evidence to contradict that he ever felt that McDowell did anything but his very best at Bull Run. In fact, his personal correspondence offers little on the entire matter and he quietly kept his own counsel and simply offered to raise a new regiment. For young Hartranft, he had learned a valuable lesson and the important matter was saving the Union rather than any personal gain or justification.

As for the 4th's performance on July 21, we can only conclude that the bulk of the regiment proved a sad surprise to everyone and Hartranft in particular. All the reasons for leaving the field at such a critical moment may never be known but, the men's fateful decision was inexcusable. That does not discount the hardships endured by the 4th, but it does recognize that other regiments were in a similar position and they chose to stay and fight. This conclusion was also shared by the eyewitness English reporter for the London *Times*, William Howard Russell, who wrote that the battle of Bull Run, "was terminated by the most singularly disgraceful panic and flight on record..." Russell continues that he was appalled at the cowardice of many of the Union troops during the rout and even mentions that he saw the [4th] Pennsylvania regiment, "which deserted the field on the day of battle *because* [their] *time was up*...."[56] [emphasis is original]

The 4th arrived in Norristown on July 28, and, according to Bolton, it took part in a brief parade that ended at the County Courthouse where they were addressed by Judge Daniel M. Smyser.[57]  Upon reaching the public square, Judge Smyser said,

> I have been charged by your fellow citizens of Norristown, with the performance of an agreeable duty-that of bidding you a warm and cordial welcome on your return 'home from the Wars'.
>
> Three months ago, when you marched to the field, I had the honor of presenting to the regiment a stand of colors, the gift of your fair compatriots, the ladies of Norristown.  It was a fitting gift for beauty to bestow and for soldiers to receive; and, in redemption of the pledge then given, you now bring it back, as I say, without a stain upon its honor or your own. The loose allegations and still more idle rumors which at one time reached us, in the midst of the agony of excitement consequent upon the disaster of Manassas, are already discredited, refuted, and

forgotten; and I proclaim and assert that the Fourth Pennsylvania 'has deserved well of the country'.[58]

Suitably, Judge Smyser's presentation was made in the middle of the night at 3:00 A.M. Perhaps, correspondent Russell's observation of the 4th's performance was the most pointed. Thought by many of the period to be pro-Southern, as Russell approached the battlefield area at approximately 9:30 A.M. on the morning of the 21st, he encountered "a body of men...on the road, with their backs toward Centreville [near the battle] and their faces toward Alexandria." Russell noted that the body was in fact a regiment marching away from the guns in the distance.[59]

Russell stopped at a stream and asked an officer, "Where are your men going, sir?"

"Well, we're going home sir, I reckon-to Pennsylvania." Russell then commented that "there is severe work going on behind you, judging from the firing." The response from the soldier was "Well, I reckon, sir,there is. We're going home...because the men's time is up. We had three months of this work." This caused Russell to reflect as he thought about the "feelings of a general who sees half a brigade walk quietly away on the very morning of an action...coolly turning their backs on it when in its utmost peril, because the letter of their engagement bound them no further...." Russell noted "it was the 4th Pennsylvania Regiment...."[60]

Long after the war was over, both Cook and Hartranft received proper recognition for their tenacity and performances at Bull Run. On August 26, 1886, Hartranft received the Congressional Medal of Honor for having, "voluntarily served as an aide and participated in the battle after the expiration of his term of service, distinguishing himself in rallying several regiments which had been thrown into confusion."[61] However, similar to so many matters related to his military career, he even had to pursue the War Department in 1886 to make certain that his decoration did not get lost.[62]

Cook too received the Medal of Honor on May 19, 1887, the award stating that he too had, "voluntarily served as an aide on the staff of Col. David Hunter and participated in the battle, his term of service having expired on the previous day."[63] Finally, after twenty-five years, both were given their just due for honor and valor to their country.

The conflict had just begun, and the initial battle of Bull Run made it clear that the romantic notions of war were dead. The nation was now locked in a deadly contest and the shock, dismay, and anger over Bull Run acted as the herald of change for the armies of both sides and Hartranft too.

ENDNOTES FOR CHAPTER TWO
"IGNOMINIOUS FLIGHT"

1. Frances H. Kennedy, ed. *The Civil War Battlefield Guide*, Boston: Houghton Mifflin Company, 1990, p. 302.
2. After the Civil War, Bolton became a Major-General of the Pennsylvania National Guard.
    *Also see Diary of William J. Bolton of the 51st Pennsylvania*, p. 16 hereafter referred to as *Bolton Diary*.
3. Oliver Wendell Holmes. All five men noted here rose to the rank of Brigadier or Major-General. Author's note.
4. Warner, Ezra J., *Generals in Gray*, Baton Rouge: Louisiana State University Press, 1959, pp. 22, 159.
5. Davis, William C., *Battle at Bull Run*, Garden City, New York: Doubleday & Company, Inc., 1977, p. 12.
6. Sears, Stephens W., *George B. McClellan, The Young Napoleon*, New York: Ticknor & Fields, 1988, pp. 95 & 100.
7. Warner, *Generals in Blue*, p. 298.
8. West Virginia was admitted to the Union as its own State identity on June 20, 1863.
9. Catton, Bruce, *The Civil War*, New York: Bonanza Books, 1960, p. 98.
10. Ibid., p. 148.
    *Also see* Davis, *Battle at Bull Run*, p. 13.
11. JFH to SEH, July 14, 1861, Shireman Collection.
12. JFH to SSH, June 17, 1861, Shireman Collection.
13. Ibid.
14. *The Norristown Herald & Free Press*, July 16, 1861.
15. Ibid.
16. Warner, *Generals in Blue*, p. 430.
17. *The Norristown Herald & Free Press*, July 20, 1861.
18. JFH to SEH, July 14, 1861, Shireman Collection.
19. Ibid.
20. Macdonald, John, *Great Battles of the Civil War*, New York: Macmillan Publishing Company, 1988, p. 23.
21. Such technicalities can hardly be condoned in modern terms but some apologist of the period felt that these were very valid terms. Author's note.
22. *The Norristown Herald & Free Press*, July 30, 1861.
23. *O. R.* I, vol. II, p. 325.
24. Ibid., p. 745.
25. Ibid.
26. Ibid.

27. *Bolton Diary*, p. 12.
28. Ibid.
29. Ibid., p. 15.
30. Ibid., pp. 12 & 15.
31. *O. R.* I. vol. II, p. 745.
32. Ibid., p. 315.
33. *The Norristown Herald & Free Press*, July 30, 1861.
34. *O. R.* I, vol. II, pp. 405-406.
35. Ibid., p. 405.
36. Ibid., p. 462.
37. Ibid., pp. 496-497.
38. Ibid., p. 406.
39. Copy of Franklin's report dated July 28, 1861, sent to JFH, Shireman Collection.
40. Barrett, Eugene A., "The Civil War Services of John F. Hartranft", *Pennsylvania History*, 23, (April, 1965): pp. 166-187
41. *The Norristown Herald & Free Press*, August 13, 1861.
42. *O. R.* I, vol. II, p. 325.
43. *Bolton Diary*, p. 15.
44. *O. R.* I, vol. II, p. 308.
45. *The Norristown Herald & Free Press*, August 13, 1861.
46. Davis, *Battle at Bull Run*, p. 163. Colonels William T. Sherman and Oliver O. Howard both plainly reported that they knew of the coming battle.
47. JFH to SEH, July 14, 1861, Shireman Collection.
48. *The Norristown Herald & Free Press*, August 13, 1861.
49. Davis, *Battle at Bull Run*, p. 163.
50. *Bolton Diary*, p. 15. Some reports place the firing of that large cannon as early as 5:00 A.M. See, Editors of *Civil War Times Illustrated*, *Great Battles of the Civil War*, New York: Gallery Books, 1989, p. 66.
51. *The Norristown Herald & Free Press*, July 30, 1861.
52. Ibid.
53. Bean, *HMCP*, p. 197.
54. Lewis, Lloyd, *Sherman, Fighting Prophet*, New York: Harcourt, Brace and Company, 1932, p. 171.
55. McDowell's letter to JFH, January 28, 1863, Shireman Collection.
56. Sideman, Belle Becker and Lillian Friedman, eds., *Europe Looks at the Civil War*, New York: The Orion Press, 1960, pp. 49-50.
57. *Bolton Diary*, p. 16.
58. *The Norristown Herald & Free Press*, July 28, 1861.
59. Wheeler, Richard, *A Rising Thunder*, New York: Harper Collins Publishers, 1994, p. 351.

60. Ibid.  Note, the officer has not been identified.
61. *The Congressional Medal of Honor, The Names, The Deeds*, Forest Ranch, California: Sharp and Dunnigan, 1984, p. 795.
62. War Department letter to JFH, August 9, 1886, Shireman Collection.
63. *The Congressional Medal of Honor, The Names, The Deeds*, p. 750.

# CHAPTER THREE

## *ROANOKE ISLAND TO FREDERICKSBURG*

Following First Bull Run, Hartranft returned to the Norristown area to raise a new regiment, the 51st Pennsylvania Volunteers. By the end of September, 1861, his new command rendezvoused at Camp Curtin in Harrisburg, which had been named in honor of the Keystone State's governor. Many of the soldiers who had been a part of the ill-fated 4th now rejoined their favorite colonel, "Old Johnny" as he was also known, and five companies came from Montgomery County alone. Most of the others hailed from interior Pennsylvania counties including Centre, Dauphin, Lycoming, Northampton, Snyder, and Union.[1]

While waiting for his regiment to come up to full strength, Hartranft kept busy training his new charge. While only less than 60 miles away from home, his demanding schedule kept him from making frequent family visits while the mail and money matters were his constant, if sometimes exasperating, companions. On September 12, he wrote to Sallie,

> I am progressing finely with my regiment. But find that my attention is required here and that I cannot well come home before Monday next. And as you want some money please get it from Father until I come home - If I find leisure time I will come home sooner.
>
> I am yours most Obediently
> JFH[2]

Though only little more than a month had passed since the 4th had walked off the field at Bull Run, Hartranft had become wiser by that experience. He had learned that constant drilling and strict discipline, combined with a sensitivity toward his men were the principle points for regimental success. With those guidelines, his ranks appeared to be in good spirits and they endured the rigors of camp life well. On September 28, the 51st was officially mustered into the United States Army despite their not being up to full strength which would take until November.[3] As was common, the regiment elected its officers which included: Colonel, John F. Hartranft; Lieutenant-Colonel, Thomas S. Bell; Major, Edwin Schall; Quartermaster, John J. Freedley; Surgeon, John P. Hosack; Assistant

Surgeon, James D. Noble; Adjutant, Daniel P. Bible; and Chaplain, Daniel G. Mallory.[4] In addition to these officers, Hartranft's uncle, Abraham, also signed on as one of the regiment's sutlers.[5]

While they waited for formal assignment, and under orders to the contrary, a group of twelve members of the 51st went out to forage and came upon a rather substantial pig. Knowing how much their mates would appreciate that prize, but equally conscious of their colonel's orders against foraging, they quickly devised an ingenious method to bring the animal back to camp. Quietly, they killed the pig, doing all manner of things to suppress the noise. Successful with that, they stretched the two hundred pound hog in a military blanket and formed around it as if carrying a sick comrade.

As the small group entered the picket lines, they were halted and challenged. One creative member of the team told the guard that the "man" in the blanket was terribly sick and the doctor had ordered that absolutely no air be allowed upon him. With that "practical" explanation, the men were allowed through the lines, only to skillfully manage another, and similar, narrow escape with an officer. When that challenge too was surmounted, the pig was brought back into camp, but only after a long, six-hour ordeal. Nonetheless, the smiles of the rank and file, as they enjoyed the roasted treat, made the entire effort worth-while.[6] No record exists about Hartranft's knowledge of the prank.

On November 5, 1861, Governor Curtin presented the 51st with its state colors and on the morning of the 16th, the regiment embarked upon their initial journey to Maryland. Ultimately, the 51st would fight in both theaters of the war, participate in nineteen major battles and dozens of skirmishes, travel more than ten thousand miles and win themselves a prized reputation for valor.[7]

The regiment's first destination was Annapolis Junction, near the Naval Academy. There, along with many other regiments, the 51st went into winter quarters at Camp Union. As was the custom in many army camps, the 51st adorned its area with a variety of decorations including arches of evergreens, a Keystone to salute the state, a number of pine trees, and a ninety-foot-high flag pole.[8] Obviously, the Pennsylvania boys did not wish to be overlooked!

While pleased with his new and developing command, Hartranft was very uncertain about their combined futures. He feared that the stain of the 4th's departure at Bull Run would be held against them, and when he saw a possibility to join Brigadier-General Ambrose E. Burnside's new expedition, he implored General Franklin to intercede for him. Only too eager to assist, Franklin wrote Burnside and explained that while the 4th did not stay on the field, Hartranft personally rendered valuable service to him that fateful day. Franklin concluded, "I know no Colonel of a regiment whom I would rather have under my command with his regiment than Col. Hartranft, and I hope there will be no difficulty in the way of his accompanying you."[9]

A couple of weeks later and still fearing repercussions, Hartranft also wrote to McDowell to request his recommendation and stressed, "I am also informed that strong efforts are being made at Washington to displace my Regiment...I am fearful that those disposed to make the change [replacement of his Regiment] may attach to me the action of the Fourth Regt. I therefore ask you for a letter of recommendation to General Burnside...."[10] Unfortunately, McDowell's letter would not materialize until well after Burnside's North Carolina expedition though the lack of it certainly didn't interfere with Burnside's decision to accept Hartranft and the 51st.

Despite all of his duties and concerns, Hartranft kept himself informed of local, national, and international news because he was intrigued by the potential political consequences if England and France recognized the Confederacy. It is clear that he strongly doubted any possibility of a military confrontation with the two European giants and on December 19, he told Sallie, "I have no very serious apprehension that we will drift into a war with England and France at this time notwithstanding the press. But if we do we must stand firm and not yield an inch."[11] Many Northerners shared Hartranft's concern about potential war with England and France.

As a regimental commander, Hartranft was also responsible to mete out punishment whenever his soldiers violated military rules. Commensurate with his Teutonic love of discipline, on the day after Christmas 1861, he instituted what became known as the "overcoat" for errant soldiers, a unique device that utilized a barrel without a bottom and enough of the top removed to permit a man's head to pass through. When placed over a soldier's head, it made the offender blush with embarrassment while affording his comrades some amusement.[12] While records fail to note if the devise was used while the soldier was fully dressed or not, it is easy to imagine the opposite and the further embarrassment it would cause. Nonetheless, it became an effective form of punishment and Hartranft utilized it freely.

Around the middle of December, Burnside was officially appointed as commander of the newly-created Department of North Carolina.[13] For weeks, he had been busy planning a massive invasion of the Chesapeake Bay area which was thought to be crucial by both sides. In the process, he had assembled an armada which consisted of almost one hundred ships of every shape, size, and variety along with a substantial army.

Around the same time, Company A of the 51st was assigned to provost and patrol duty which meant it had to arrest drunken soldiers and citizens along with those who did not know the proper code words. When one soldier approached their line he was halted and routinely asked the countersign. Unable to recall the proper response, Private Levi Bolton immediately took the man by the arm and began to lead him to the guard house. Apparently, the thought of arrest sharpened that soldier's memory for he soon was able to provide Bolton with the correct message. While the entire matter was undoubtedly embarrassing to Levi, General Burnside was high in his praise for the soldier's vigilance despite his own temporary inconvenience.[14]

On December 29, Hartranft was pleased to learn that the 51st was ordered to move out as part of General Burnside's special expedition. The regiment was assigned to the Second Brigade which was led by the highly respected Brigadier-General Jesse Lee Reno. After a few minor delays, the regiment boarded the ships *Cossack* and *Scout* which weighed anchor on January 9, 1862.[15] The entire trip would prove a most miserable sea voyage for everyone involved.

While developing his plans, Burnside had worked quietly and held the details and objectives in the strictest confidence. Few knew where they were headed or when they might arrive and on the morning of the 9th, prior to departure, he deliberately passed by all of the ships in his armada to encourage the men and their captains. Responding to the loud huzzas of his men, the general gave a hearty wave and felt confident of success. His constant attention to secrecy led Hartranft to entice Sallie's imagination with, "The government steamer and ships are all painted black and their names do not appear - But each vessel has a small flag with the number of its designation on it - viz the Red flag designating the First Brigade, the Blue the Second, White the third."[16] However, despite all of Burnside's successful clandestine work in the north, as the flotilla departed, Henry T. Clark, Governor of North Carolina, correctly speculated that Burnside was now thought to be enroute to Pamlico Sound.[17]

While Confederates theorized about Burnside's destination, his own men also guessed about their objective as witnessed by Hartranft's letter to Sallie dated January 8,

> As to our destination I have not made up my mind - Our boats which contain our Regt. are sea worthy and would sail To New Orleans in safety - But I do not think that some of the other boats are sea worthy and therefore cannot sail to N. Orleans I have therefore thought that we would not go farther South than North Carolina.[18]

Though unknown at that moment, Hartranft's deductions were correct and he and the entire flotilla would soon make history at Roanoke Island and New Bern [*], North Carolina. On the 15th, he again told Sallie that, "I am entirely in the dark as to our work...."[19]

Even Confederate Cavalryman, Brigadier-General J.E.B. Stuart, dabbled in guessing Burnside's objective, for on January 9, he told his friend and comrade, Brigadier-General Daniel Harvey Hill that, "The Potomac Burnside fleet has not yet developed itself, but we are anxiously expectant."[20]   Obviously, the Northern threat was a grave concern to everyone.

Almost from the very start of its voyage, Burnside's flotilla was plagued by a continuous string of violent storms which tossed his ships and soldiers about in great fright. Time and again, his troop ships were hung up on sand bars or tossed about like corks on the high seas. Seasick men sustained with only thin rations and little fresh water made the normally stifling living conditions a living hell. Hartranft too suffered greatly and poor information about the depths of shoals and the drafts on the ships only made matters worse.[21] Ship owners had lied about the draft of their ships to acquire the rental fees from the government and all of these conditions added to the woes of the Union commander.

Day after day, Burnside's flotilla encountered endless obstacles and harrowing near death experiences. Still, they slowly progressed, and Burnside directed a Mr. Sheldon, a civilian, to take word directly to Washington about his many difficulties and delays. As Sheldon related all of the plaguing problems, President Lincoln grew decidedly dour. Finally, suffering from the pressures laid upon him by Sheldon, the President ventured to say "They had better come back at once." "Oh no", replied Sheldon, who immediately went on to let Lincoln know that despite his many hardships, Burnside was actually making progress. That alone was enough to lift the sagging spirits of the President.[22]

While Burnside was having weather difficulties, his land-based adversary, Confederate Brigadier-General Henry Wise, was having his own problems with Richmond. Wise, who had been Governor of Virginia and won fame when he signed the death warrant for John Brown after his unsuccessful raid at Harper's Ferry, also married the sister of Union Major-General George Gordon Meade. Oddly enough, his hatred of the Yankees was still great and he became committed to Burnside's destruction.

---

[*] The period spelling of the town's name was Newbern. The author has adopted the modern spelling, New Bern, for consistency.

Around the middle of January, Burnside's lead ships were finally beginning to arrive around Roanoke Island and among them was *Cossack* with Hartranft and approximately one-half of his command. On the 15th, Hartranft rightly predicted that, "Roanoke Island will be most contested and may have a severe fight but if we gain that, the other places will fall with light blows - We will in all probability visit Roanoke tomorrow."[23] On page 43 is a map that Hartranft drew and included in his letter so Sallie could better understand his whereabouts.

While the Confederacy showed some ability in divining Burnside's plan, a letter from General Joseph E. Johnston to Brigadier-General William H. C. Whiting clearly shows that not everyone in the southern command felt secure about their ability to meet such a potential attack. Johnston noted, "As to what Burnside may or can do, it depends so much upon the preparations our Government has made ... our people ought to be able to drive them away from the Roanoke if they attempt to enter it."[24]

Burnside made land on January 13 and he immediately sought to obtain credible, detailed information about the area. One young black, Tom, told him about an excellent harbor at a point called Ashby's Landing, "located on the west side of Roanoke, about two miles south of Fort Bartow."[25] After consulting his maps, Burnside decided that was the place for his landing, and began a training program so that all of the soldiers knew how to row a boat to shore and how to alight from it. Those light rowboats were a variety of sizes and models but they would serve the purpose.

In anticipation of such a Yankee landing, Wise had made several requests to Secretary of War Judah P. Benjamin for reinforcements. His failure to receive any troops only increased his fears and pleas to Benjamin. In frustration, Wise left the island to speak personally with Benjamin who promptly sent him back to his post empty-handed. But, instead of returning immediately, Wise made a week-long stop at his home in Norfolk where he raised a loud voice against the Secretary.[26]

President Jefferson Davis didn't help matters when he had Benjamin order Wise to have his 2,500-man garrison on Roanoke Island to hold their position as best they could.[27] What the President didn't know, was that Wise only had a total of 1,900 men with about 1,400 effectives.[28] Certainly, no match for Burnside's nearly 13,000 soldiers.[29]

Hartranft continued to guess at events and was not exactly confident and prophetically noted, "I predict this expedition will fall into entire insignificance having foreshadowed all its glory without ever realizing any of it. I fear that too much is already expected by our people...."[30]

Each day saw more of the Union flotilla arrive as the soldiers on board offered every kind of thankful prayer for their safe arrival upon the land. One officer of the 24th Massachusetts noted of the passage, "...

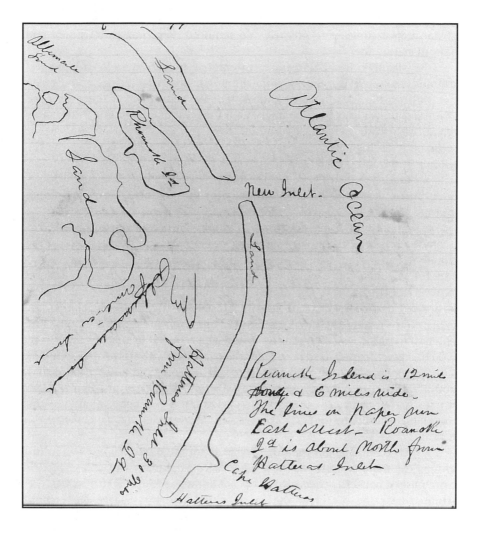

**Hartranft's Drawing of the Roanoke Island Area**

*Courtesy, Shireman Collection*

43

obstacles overcome were greater, and required more persistent pluck and patient endurance."[31]

Through it all, Hartranft attempted to continue his regimental training, though living aboard ships did not sit well with his men and made the drilling of arms almost impossible. To add to their miseries, the Pennsylvania soldiers became angry with their sutlers, including Hartranft's uncle, who were charging exorbitant rates for their goods. With cheese selling for as high as $1.00 per pound and cigars at 10 cents each, the soldiers were outraged. The oblivious sutlers offered a final insult when they sold a brand of bad whiskey for the incredible price of $3.00 per bottle.[32] Such prices were impossible to fathom when the customers were earning a mere $13 a month.

Finally, on Friday morning, February 7, Burnside gave the order to begin the attack of Roanoke Island. Naval gunboats, on the westside of the island near Ashby's Harbor, placed themselves in assigned positions and at 11:23 A.M., opened fire which was immediately returned by the Confederate cannon in Fort Bartow. The exchange of gunfire continued throughout the entire day and only began to fall off late in the afternoon. At about 5:00 P.M., after viewing the day-long bombardment from the deck of the ship, Hartranft boarded the gunboat *Delaware* which was to bring him ashore. By 9:00 that evening, the 51st, along with ten thousand Union troops belonging to the First, Second and Third Brigades, finally landed on Roanoke Island, about 1 1/2 miles below Fort Bartow. During the entire process, a heavy driving rain drenched the men who struggled through a damp dinner and did their best to prepare themselves for the fight that was sure to come in the morning.

By 6:30 A.M. on the 8th, the battle for Roanoke Island was in full swing. The main contest was in a thick pine tree forest, and as the Rebels were pushed back, they headed for a point known as "Suple's Hill" which was situated near the center of the island which held three large Rebel field pieces.[33] The Rebel position was almost totally surrounded by water, swamp, and briars which made any passage most difficult and sometimes impossible. That terrain comforted the Confederates who thought that the swamps were impassable. The commanding Confederate officers were Colonel Henry Shaw of the 8th North Carolina and Lieutenant-Colonel Frank Anderson of the 59th Virginia. One of the men under Anderson's command was the son of General Wise, Captain O. Jennings Wise.

In anticipation of any Union attack, the Confederates had felled many trees along the main approach to their fort, which would further hamper any Union advancement. Consequently, Yankee soldiers found any movement extremely difficult and slow. For the first two hours of the fight, the 51st had to be content being held in reserve. About 8:30 A.M., Hartranft led his men into the waist deep swamp, and began to move forward at a laborious rate as they supported the advancing Union line.

During that initial phase of the Union attack, Reno and Hartranft followed Brigadier-General John G. Foster's First Brigade, which was leading the Federal attack.[34] As the lead regiment of Foster's brigade became bogged down in the impenetrable swamp, other regiments were sent around to attack the Confederate left. But all of the attacking Union regiments were faced with some herculean effort to make any progress owing to the great swamp. The main approach to the fort, a small dirt road, became clogged with Union soldiers causing Reno to become impatient.[35]

Hartranft's initial objective was to attack the Confederate right flank with the help of the 4th Rhode Island. Slowly hacking their way through the swamp, the 51st was noticed by the defenders whose artillery quickly attacked them with a hail of grape and canister.

That fire, combined with the mounting numbers of bogged Yankees made Hartranft decide to withdraw and move toward the Rebel left. That meant his ranks had to cross in front of the enemy line, making his men prime targets. Fortunately, by remaining low to the ground, the 51st was unscathed by the harsh barrage the Rebels sent.[36] But, the 24th, 25th and 27th Massachusetts regiments plus the 9th New Jersey and 51st New York regiments had suffered greatly in their earlier attack along that front which left many of their dead and wounded in Hartranft's path.

The next few but critical moments gave rise to confusion and misunderstanding as the firing from the 10th Connecticut appears to have set the 9th New York Zouaves in a fleeing frenzy. At the same time, Lieutenant-Colonel Bell was leading a detachment of the 51st out of the swamp, and in front of the Confederate guns when he confronted fleeing members of the 9th. Quickly realizing the danger those frightened New York soldiers could create, Bell ordered his men to fix bayonets and stop their retreat while he personally threatened to shoot any man who attempted to pass.[37] Order promptly returned to the colorfully clad New Yorkers and they soon found themselves at the focal point of the Union attack.

While subject to some debate, [Colonel Rush C.] Hawkins' 9th New York Zouaves redeemed themselves when they, along with the 21st Massachusetts and 51st New York, pushed a flank attack which simply overwhelmed Shaw's right.[38] Meanwhile, Hartranft succeeded crossing in front of the Confederates and in the process, cut a path to the Rebel left where he ordered Bell to lead the attack. "Crossing a ravine obstructed by fallen timber and moving rapidly up the opposite bank, Bell rushed upon the redan, routed the enemy, and planted his flag on the ramparts." General Reno was able to report that, "All of this was gallantly executed, and the

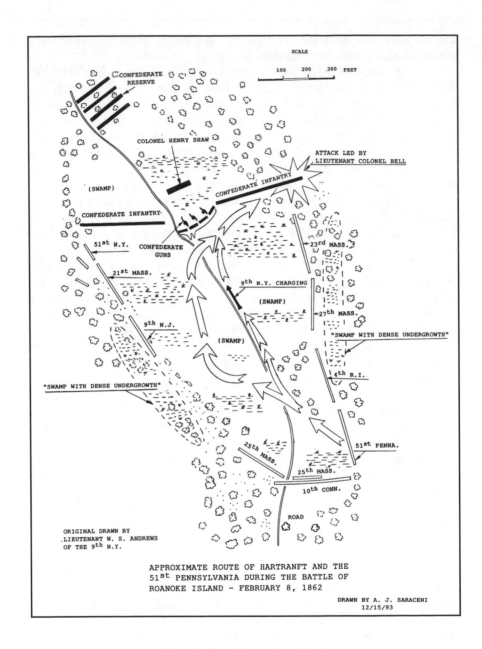

SCALE

100 200 300 FEET

CONFEDERATE RESERVE

COLONEL HENRY SHAW

ATTACK LED BY LIEUTENANT COLONEL BELL

(SWAMP)

CONFEDERATE INFANTRY

CONFEDERATE INFANTRY

51st N.Y.

CONFEDERATE GUNS

21st MASS.

23rd MASS.

9th N.Y. CHARGING

(SWAMP)

27th MASS.

9th N.J.

"SWAMP WITH DENSE UNDERGROWTH"

(SWAMP)

4th R.I.

"SWAMP WITH DENSE UNDERGROWTH"

51st PENNA.

25th MASS.

25th MASS.

10th CONN.

ROAD

ORIGINAL DRAWN BY
LIEUTENANT W. S. ANDREWS
OF THE 9th N.Y.

APPROXIMATE ROUTE OF HARTRANFT AND THE
51st PENNSYLVANIA DURING THE BATTLE OF
ROANOKE ISLAND - FEBRUARY 8, 1862

DRAWN BY A. J. SARACENI
12/15/93

**The Battle of Roanoke Island.**

enemy fled precipitately from all their intrenchments."[39] Shaw then ordered his troops to move back toward the north end of the island since he considered the battle a Confederate loss. Later, about 3:30 P.M., Shaw also decided that further resistance was totally useless and he surrendered his 2,500 men, six forts and 43 pieces of artillery which ended the battle of Roanoke Island.[40]

Shortly after the surrender, a Rebel boat arrived with sorely needed reinforcements for Shaw. Watching them disembark, General Reno sat quietly until the last Southern soldier was ashore. Then, with considerable politeness, and to the great chagrin of the disembarking Confederates, Reno went forward, introduced himself, and informed them they were now Union prisoners.[41]

Word was soon received in Confederate circles that Captain Wise had been killed in the fight. Recklessly, the senior Wise and his family put the blame for the captain's death squarely at the feet of Judah P. Benjamin for not sending the requested supplies and reinforcements. One nephew, Jennings Wise, wrote that, "my grandfather always charged Benjamin with his [the captain's] murder", and a grandson, John Wise, stated that the "fat Jew sitting at his desk" was responsible for the captain's death.[42]

Bitterly, Wise wrote President Davis, "You are aware already, doubtless, of my defeat and disasters. I did my best to prepare for the unequal conflict. Unequal it was. In vain I appealed for re-enforcements; the reply was an order to my post and that 'supplies, hard work, and coolness, not men' were all that was needed. After this there was no election for me but to fight."[43]

Wise never did appreciate that the Confederate government in Richmond knew it had no supplies or men to spare for him or anyone else. Rather than admit that to the world, which would have had invited a wholesale Yankee invasion, Richmond wisely decided to use Roanoke Island as a sacrificial lamb. Benjamin and Davis hoped against hope that the men and materiel already there would suffice or, at least, if the Yankees were successful, would not expand their attacks. For that sad shortage, Benjamin took much blame from the Southern people and press. Not until twenty-five years after the war did the public find out that President Davis knew exactly what was happening and that he and Benjamin both agreed that the secretary would be the "fall guy."[44]

Burnside and his troops were elated over their victory and for the next few days, Hartranft hunted for escaped Rebels, and took some time to sightsee and relax.

# NEW BERN

Having suffered only one combat casualty at Roanoke Island, on Monday, March 3, the 51st was again aboard ship, headed for its next destination, New Bern, North Carolina.[45] Once again, *Cossack* encountered heavy seas as it passed through Cape Hatteras on its way to Ocracoke Inlet. Fortunately, this voyage was not nearly as long, and on Thursday the 13th the regiment landed about 7:00 A.M., at the mouth of Slocum's Creek, thirteen miles south of New Bern.[46] Immediately, they began their march toward the town in a driving rain. As if trudging through the deep mud were not enough, an orderly instructed Lieutenant-Colonel Bell to have some of his men attach ropes to themselves and pull seven* cannon along with them. As Thomas Parker, historian of the 51st, later commented, "If marching with a knapsack, sixty rounds of ammunition, a heavy rifle-musket, three days' rations in haversacks, and other paraphernalia of war, fatigued them; what else, than exhaust them, would carrying all that and dragging a heavy gun and caisson full of shot and shell thirteen miles in the remainder of the day, do?"[47] The men of the 51st struggled under the enormous task of pulling those guns and only slowly made their way toward New Bern. When they finally stopped for the night, about one mile from the Union camps the exhausted soldiers simply fell...upon the ground to sleep at 9:00 P.M.[48] But, they were up again at 2:00 A.M. on the 14th to continue that hard task and pulled the guns even closer to the Rebel lines. Reno himself described the hauling of those guns as "incredible labor."[49] Meanwhile, an unrelenting rain beat unmercifully upon the Yanks and one anonymous marcher remembered it 48 years later,

> ...we had been expecting the ambuscade all day and dreading it. Not that any of the seasoned troops were afraid, but no body likes to be shot at suddenly from behind a blind. Now I couldn't help comparing an open battle with the violence of the wind and rain and the menacing tone of the thunder interspersed with lightning. I decided in favor of battle. You can shoot back at the enemy, but in the hands of the Almighty you are helpless.[50]

* Some reports state eight guns. [Six boat howitzers under Lt. R. S. McCook, USN, and two Wiard cannon from two transports.]

News of the impending attack hit the town of five to six thousand inhabitants and the women and children began to flee New Bern in fear of the Yankee arrival. At 5:00 A.M. on the 14th, Colonel Bell personally woke General Burnside to tell him that the 51st had arrived with the sorely needed artillery. Burnside was ecstatic and, according to Bell, "the General sprang from the bed, carrying some of the clothes with him fast to his spurs, seized him with both hands and said that he would never forget the Fifty-first [Pennsylvania] for that...."[51] Burnside also wrote that "Too much praise cannot be awarded to the officers and men [of the 51st] who performed this very arduous service...",[52] because those guns would constitute the entire Union artillery on the next day.

By 8:30 A.M. Hartranft was placing his weary troops into line of battle immediately behind the 9th New Jersey, when Reno told him to move faster. On the double-quick, Hartranft finished the maneuver and, "halted the regiment and had the men lie down just in time to avoid a fusillade of grape and canister."[53] Placing his troops on a railroad line, Hartranft then ordered a return volley and the battle of New Bern had begun.

The battle was sporadic throughout the morning, but built to a constant roar by 11 A.M. Near-victory shifted back and forth between the Blue and Gray and when Burnside decided to attack off his extreme right, he brought heavy casualties upon the 24th and 27th Massachusetts. Despite those counts, the entire Rebel front was soon under attack from Burnside's forces and Reno ordered Hartranft forward to charge a fort that sat near a brick kiln.[54] At that same moment an incident occurred causing the regimental historian, Parker, to reflect a personal observation about Hartranft's intolerance.

General Burnside had sent one of General Reno's aides, Lieutenant John A. Morris, to reinforce Reno's order for Hartranft to charge. Finding that the regimental commander was momentarily busy elsewhere, the young officer saw a potential moment of glory and took it upon himself to personally lead the charge and called the 51st to the ready. Hartranft had completed his task and now stood silently watching the unsuspecting Morris. When the brash lieutenant ordered the men forward, Hartranft immediately and defiantly called out a loud "halt"!

> As quick as the flash of a gun the line halted, and Hartranft breaking through it, ran up to Morris and passionately asked him 'What in the hell do you mean? I command this regiment and if a charge is to be made I'll make it'. A hasty explanation ensued, ...In a few moments Col. Hartranft saw a slight advantage might be gained in an assault by a few

men on another part of the enemy's works, and he ordered
Lieut. Col. Bell to take the left wing of the 51st P. V. and
make the charge.[55]

Hartranft's attack had the desired effect and, Burnside himself
reported that, "Reno ordered the Fifty-first Pennsylvania, Colonel
Hartranft, to charge the enemies line, which charge was supported by the
remainder of the brigade, causing the enemy to desert his works in great
confusion."[56]

Another commentary noted, "Finally, the 51st [Pennsylvania] was
ordered to lead in a charge on the works. It was planned with judgment and
executed with gallantry. A redan was carried from which the whole rebel line
of works was soon waving with the Stars and Stripes."[57]

In his own report, Hartranft wrote the following about the fight for
New Bern:

> I received the order to proceed to the extreme left and
> support the Ninth New Jersey and resist any attack...The
> Ninth was soon engaged, and under a very heavy fire I
> brought my regiment into line, supporting the Ninth... at
> this point several of my men were wounded, though I
> sheltered them as much as possible by causing them to lie
> down. ...The Ninth moving farther to the front, I moved my
> regiment forward and farther to the left, so as to maintain
> the interval of about 100 feet between my regiment and the
> Ninth.[58]

Reno confirmed Hartranft's skillful handling of his troops when he
noted that the 51st was, "held in reserve at this time, and although exposed
to severe fire, Colonel Hartranft did not allow a single shot to be fired, but
directed the men to lie down, and thus saved them from much loss."[59]

Hartranft continued in his report to state the details of how
Lieutenant-Colonel Bell led the left wing of the 51st to the support of the
sister regiment, the 51st New York. Moving at the double quick Bell
ordered a volley against the Rebel line which made it waver. Hartranft then
ordered Bell to charge and with loud cries the Pennsylvanians moved
forward and soon planted their colors inside the fort.[60]

Despite those valorous movements, Parker's claim that the 51st
Pennsylvania was the first to plant its colors within the Confederate fort, is

impractical to confirm.[61] With the great deal of Union action occurring along the entire Rebel line, it is simply unclear who was first in such a matter.

But, when the lead men of the 51st did enter the fort, Corporal George W. Foote of Company E planted the regiment's national colors on the works. With a sense of great satisfaction it was noted that those colors originally belonged to the 4th Pennsylvania Volunteers.[62]

By 4:00 P.M., Burnside had taken New Bern and in their flight, the Rebels set fire to parts of the city including the Trent River railroad bridge which truly ended the fight. During the entire engagement, the 51st was most fortunate and suffered only 10 men wounded.[63]

It was interesting for the Yankees, most of whom had never met a slave before, to listen to the local Blacks describe their impressions of the boys in blue. When one black woman was asked what she thought of the Yankees, she stated that,

> I find dey looks like our people, an I said so yesterday when I seed you pass our house, for my massa had always tole us dat de Yankees wa'r great big people, tall as dat pine tree dar, wid one eye in de centre ob der for'ed and one in de back of dar heds, and dat if dey got a holt ob a nigger, dey jist munched dem up wid dar grate big teef, and dat would be de last of de coon. Why, my massa said dat your teef was a long as der arms, and wid one crunch would bite a hoss in two, and a heap of oder things, he tole us 'bout you, but I guess he only tole us dat to try to fritin us so dat we wouldn't run away from him and come to you folkses.[64]

For the next few days, the Union Army relaxed with only light duty. Hartranft and the 51st were assigned to perform some bridge burnings near Pollocksville which was located about twenty-three miles from New Bern.[65] Meanwhile, Burnside and his staff also took time to relish their victory and on March 22, the commanding general was informed of his promotion to major-general as his reward.[66] On March 28, the 51st went into camp about one mile outside New Bern and in honor of their colonel, the men named their new temporary home "Camp Hartranft."[67]

Other matters also occupied Hartranft's mind as letters from home beseeched him to return quickly. Sad news about two of his children strained his mind and on March 4, Sallie had written him that "Ada's [photograph] is not so good [since] suffering had changed her so much, Oh;

51

those children, there is so much scarlet fever about."[68] Sallie's pleas were strong, warning Hartranft about Ada's and Wilson's failing health. On March 6, Sallie again wrote that, [It is] "Ada's birthday and she stands a fair chance of getting well we all think and the Dr. thinks she is getting better, but has been very low [ill] since last Saturday with the scarlet fever... I am almost worn out with watching [the sick children]...."[69]

Finally, Hartranft took leave and returned home to Norristown, arriving on March 24. Upon entering his home, he was distraught to find his family in deep mourning for his two buried children. Two-and-a-half-year-old Wilson had died on March 17, while five-year-old Ada followed him six days later on March 22.[70]

Sallie, the quintessential mother, was understandably grief-stricken. Although theirs was an era when parents found it common to lose at least one child, she had just lost two who even had to be buried before their father could arrive home. Hartranft naturally had to console Sallie and the surviving children and that family crisis caused him to miss the fight at Camden, North Carolina on April 19. Still, Camden was costly for his regiment and resulted in another twenty-five casualties.[71]

On April 22, Hartranft finally made his way back to the 51st and we can surmise it was a welcomed relief from the recent trauma at Norristown. Yet, he too must have felt the sharp pain of losing two children but, as a pragmatist, he had to go on with his life and responsibilities. In her letters though, Sallie frequently reminded her husband that she badly wanted the photographs of the two children which had been professionally taken just before their deaths. Unfortunately though, despite her many laments, Hartranft was not responsive and, for some unknown reason, he offered her no succor or money to obtain those coveted photographs.

Because of his well-publicized activities at New Bern and Roanoke Island, Hartranft became something of a local hero in southeastern Pennsylvania. On June 11, 1862, Mr. Enoch A. Banks, a friend of the Hartranft family, sent a very sincere letter to the colonel, pleading with him to consider being the Democratic nominee for Pennsylvania's Surveyor General. Banks, who was a member of the Montgomery County Bar and active in local and state politics, went on to inform the colonel that, "I've also talked with others who are your friends and we are disposed to go for you but are in the dark as to whether you would not prefer remaining in the army...."[72]

In response, Hartranft wrote on the 24th of June, "...thank you and my friends in Blair County for your kind intentions, but I do most positively decline to have my name brought before the public as a candidate for office."[73] Not only was Hartranft declining a potential political office which would capitalize on his current fame, he was also undergoing something of a political change himself which ultimately led him to move to the Republican Party.

During the same period, Sallie sent him a copy of a musical score that was written in his honor, entitled "The Colonel Hartranft Quick Step." Initially, Sallie was not certain of its origin and treated the matter with mixed pride and amusement. As it turned out, the tune was written by Thomas O'Neill who taught music in Norristown at the Oakland Female Institute from which Sallie had graduated.[74] Nonetheless, she continued to long for the photos of her dead children and pathetically wrote to the colonel, "I saw the children's pictures last week they are beautiful. I feel like having them at home...Grandpap[Hartranft's father] went to see them but did not ask the price of them...Grandpap gave me $50 of the money you sent up...."[75] It is interesting to note that throughout the entire war, Hartranft sent his money to his father who, in turn, parceled it out to Sallie. Obviously, Sallie felt the loss of her children very deeply and despite her strong desire, she steadfastly refused to ask her father-in-law for the monies to buy those photos. She was convinced that he would view such an expenditure as foolish and frivolous, a rebuke she had no desire to handle.

Despite all of the pressures that such a double trauma can generate, on July 12 Sallie wrote her husband that they were the proud parents of a new baby boy who had been born on June 28. She told her husband that she liked the name John but confessed that when the doctor asked about the name she said maybe "Burnside." She also told Hartranft that she would make no mention of the name McClellan, another possibility, since the doctor was "so down on him."[76] Finally, Sallie decided on Linn as the child's name.

In early July, in response to Lincoln's directive to reinforce McClellan, Burnside began moving his force back north. On July 9, his fleet anchored at Newport News and on the 10th they went ashore. Since Hartranft's departure for the expedition, Cameron had been replaced by Edwin M. Stanton as Secretary of War and Major-General Henry W. Halleck was appointed General-in-Chief. President Lincoln finally tired of McClellan's endless delays and he reached out for a new battlefield commander.

## SECOND BULL RUN

The battle of Second Bull Run took place on August 29 and 30, 1862, on essentially the same field where almost a year earlier, the 4th Pennsylvania had walked off the field. Major-General John Pope who had recently been brought in from the West, would now lead the Union army. Pope placed Burnside, who had only recently formally established the Ninth

Corps, in charge of his right wing which gave temporary command of the Ninth Corps to Reno. From this point forward, the 51st would always serve in the Ninth Corps and they had just arrived in the area of Manassas after coming out of Culpeper, Virginia.

On August 29, Hartranft found himself protecting Captain George W. Durell's Pennsylvania battery and he held his men at the ready with fixed bayonets, but they were not called upon. Instead, after ordering his men to take cover close to the ground, he personally worked with the men of Durell's battery at their guns. For about six hours, Hartranft assisted with the barrage that Captain Durell dropped upon the troops of Major-General James Longstreet.[77] As the day ended, the Confederates began to pull back from their forward positions which was viewed as a sign of retreat by Pope who ordered a strong attack for the next morning.[78]

On the 30th, men of the 51st probably initiated that day's battle when at daybreak, companies A and I, led by Lieutenant-Colonel Joseph K. Bolton and Captain Edwin Schall, were probing in the woods when Confederate pickets opened fire upon them.[79] But, instead of taking part in a sharp infantry engagement, the 51st again supported Durell's battery.

Then, almost like a bad dream, about 4:00 P.M. the Union army began to disintegrate. The roads once again began to clog with the wounded and those Union soldiers attempting to flee the Rebels, and McDowell ordered Reno's division to cover the retreat. McDowell told Reno that his assignment probably meant that he would be captured, but that he [McDowell] couldn't help that.[80] Reno's orders also meant that he and his regiments would also have to protect Captain William M. Graham's Battery K, of the 1st U. S. Artillery which were critically positioned at the rear. Within minutes Hartranft had his regiment into line facing the advancing Rebels and ordered, "Let them have it now, boys."[81] For the next five hours after four o'clock, the 51st hurled all they could to prevent the Confederates access to the Union rear line.

As darkness began to fall and the firing became sporadic, the two sides made camp. Cautiously, Hartranft anticipated some Rebel activity and demanded extra vigilance in the ranks. During the night, voices thought to be Union soldiers were heard crying out in mournful tones for help from the Pennsylvanians. Some of the Keystone men started to respond, thinking to help their comrades when Hartranft immediately stopped them. Quickly he sent an investigating party to take a closer look at the source of the cries and found Rebels pretending to be wounded Yankees. He then ordered a volley which soon silenced any further cries.[82]

At about nine that evening, with the entire army now safely underway, Reno passed the word that Hartranft and his troops could retire from the field toward Centreville. That was welcomed news since, for the past 18 days, the 51st had been constantly on the march and involved with daily fighting.

On September 3, Hartranft told Sallie,

> I am safe - fought on the old field of Bull Run on Friday and Saturday...Our brigade had been victorious in every part of the engagement under which we participated - we stayed the tide of the enemy at Bull Run, saved many of our batteries & stayed on the field, after driving the enemy back until all our army had retired...Your Jackie.[83]

One member of the regiment was sickened by the poor performance of some of the Union's highest military members at Second Bull Run. Specifically, he singled out Generals McClellan and Fitz-John Porter for doing all they could to make certain that Pope did not meet with success. He felt that if there had only been a modest amount of cooperation, "...the result would have been far different."[84] In retrospect, he was probably right!

## CHANTILLY

After its defeat at Second Bull Run, the Union army began to withdraw toward the safety of Washington D. C. In the process, Pope's West Point education certainly taught him that when an army is in retreat, it requires dependable troops and commanders in the rear to prevent total destruction of the main body. Consequently, he ordered Reno and parts of the Ninth Corps, including the 51st, to protect the Washington-bound retreat. Reno was soon joined by two other promising Brigadier-Generals, Philip Kearny of the First Division, Third Corps, who had been described by Brevet-Lieutenant-General Winfield Scott as, "the bravest man I ever knew and a perfect soldier" and, Isaac I. Stevens, and his First Division of the Ninth Corps.[85]

As the Union army was retreating, a heavy rain began to fall adding to the misery of the men. On their way back to Washington, the Union army had to pass an elegant, old plantation known as Chantilly, located on Ox Hill.[86] There on September 1, 1862, the two plodding armies clashed again in the deep mud and endless water. The 51st was marching toward Fairfax Court House with the 21st Massachusetts in their front. Both regiments were part of Reno's Second Brigade and about 4 P.M. the 21st came upon the Confederates in an unusual manner which is best related by Thomas Parker,

The 21st Massachusetts being on the advance it encountered the enemy first, under very peculiar circumstances. A brigade of rebel [sic] infantry was filing out of a neighboring woods into the Fairfax road, just as [Lieutenant] Col. [William S.] Clark, with his 21st Massachusetts regiment, was passing the point into which the enemy were filing; the two colonels saluted each other, as each officer thought they both were of the one army, and as the men of the 21st Massachusetts wore overcoats a good deal of the color of the rebels the delusion was complete. The two colonels rode along together for a few yards, when the rebel colonel asked Col. Clark, 'What's your regiment, colonel?' Col. Clark replied, 'Tis the 21st Massachusetts.' 'My regiment is the [author's note: there was a pregnant pause] _____ Mississippi, and we are enemies,' replied the Rebel colonel, and with his men made a fierce onslaught on the 21st Massachusetts, capturing Col. Clark and a number of his men.[87]

The battle of Chantilly had begun!

The main body of the fight was centered in a cornfield that was surrounded by woods on three sides. Generals Kearny and Stevens were hotly engaged by units belonging to Stonewall Jackson including Brigadier-Generals Ambrose Powell Hill, Alexander R. Lawton and William E. Starke, who blocked the Union advance.[88] As the fight continued, darkness crept over the area, making matters very difficult. However, the Union generals commanding the rear guard held their ground under continuous Rebel attack which kept Hartranft hard-pressed. The terrible weather and the exhausted condition of the men of both sides simply served to make everyone miserable. Driving rain made firing weapons a near impossibility and only heightened the soldiers aggravation. Yet officers of both sides, including Hartranft, pressed their men to their utmost.

Hartranft was kept under frequent Rebel fire in his rear position with Durell's battery. In return, he kept up an unremitting return fire from his batteries, which ultimately demoralized the persistent Rebels. Unaware of the heavy Rebel pressure Hartranft was facing, Reno sent word for him to withdraw. Feeling certain that Reno did not fully realize the challenge and effectiveness of his work, Hartranft ordered the guns to continue their deadly work while he went off to see Reno himself. After a brief discussion with his subordinate, Reno quickly decided that Hartranft's eyewitness account was correct and directed him to remain at his post.[89] This decision made life particularly uncomfortable for the Rebels, as the Norristown colonel placed his guns in a commanding spot and with incessant fire drove back the approaching enemy.

Just as the Rebels appeared to have been driven back, General Kearny found the 21st Massachusetts at the edge of the field, obviously not too willing to fight at that moment.[90] This enraged Kearny, and he attempted to get the 21st to make an attack. One of the regimental officers produced a couple of Southern prisoners to demonstrate that the field was not clear. Kearny was not at all impressed by such a feeble attempt and cried out, "God damn you and your prisoners." He then spurred his horse forward into the dark cornfield. Unable to see clearly in the dark and rain, he came upon some soldiers who turned out to be Rebels. As he turned his horse, the Rebels began to fire at the fleeing Yankee and one bullet found its mark as it traveled, "from the base of the spine to his chest, killing him instantly."[91] Shortly thereafter, General Stevens too, was killed.

The death of the two Union generals seemed to signal the end of the battle, as matters began to sputter to a close at around nine o'clock that evening. For Hartranft, that was a welcome respite though making camp in the heavy rain that night made matters utterly miserable. The battle of Chantilly was brief but costly though Hartranft's rearguard had accomplished its mission of preventing the South from destroying Pope's army and moving upon Washington. Over the next two weeks, the demoralized Union army would pass through Fairfax, and on the morning of the 13th, they crossed the Monocacy River and camped near Frederick, Maryland. At the same time, the full measure of the conflicts at Second Bull Run and Chantilly became known and their numbers were painful for the North. The total casualty count amounted to 16,054 with 1,724 killed outright, 8,372 wounded and 5,958 missing.[92]

## SOUTH MOUNTAIN

Pope's sound defeat at Second Bull Run led Lincoln to re-appoint McClellan to command of the Army of the Potomac. Meanwhile, Lee decided that an attack upon the North might bring relief to Virginia and perhaps encourage recognition from England and France. Lee sent Stonewall Jackson to capture Harpers Ferry, and on September 9th he issued his Special Order 191 which detailed the splitting of his army.

While McClellan's army was in the area of Frederick, two of his soldiers fortuitously found a copy of Lee's Order 191. When the Union commander finished reading Lee's directive, he responded to a telegram from President Lincoln who asked, "How does it look now?", with the following:

"I have the whole rebel force in front of me, but I am confident, and no time shall be lost. I think Lee has made a gross mistake, and that he will be severely punished for it. I have all the plans of the rebels, and will catch them in their own trap if my men are equal to the emergency. Will send you trophies." Later, McClellan said to an aide, "Here is a paper [Lee's Order 191] with which if I cannot whip Bobbie Lee, I will be willing to go home."[93]

About 10-12 miles west of Frederick, and only several miles east of Sharpsburg, lies South Mountain which actually was witness to two battles which were both modest Union victories. On September 14, the battle of Crampton's Gap took place between Major-General William B. Franklin and his Sixth Corps and Confederate Major-General Lafayette McLaws' Division of the First Corps. By the close of the day on the 14th, Franklin had forced McLaws from the field and had taken possession of the pass as well.[94]

The second battle on the 14th directly involved Hartranft at the fight for South Mountain proper. There had been a clash between the two armies at Middleton and, as the Rebel forces pulled out of that small town, they torched private homes and mills before moving up the east side of the mountain. At about two that afternoon the 51st began pursuit up the mountain and it took Hartranft about an hour to position his men directly in front of Durell's battery as they were to again support his guns.

Soon, an artillery duel broke out between Durell and the Rebels, and Hartranft immediately ordered his men to lie prone upon the ground to avoid injury from the muzzles of those big guns. The duel lasted all afternoon and finally ended only as night began to fall when Durell forced the Rebel guns to move back.[95]

The 51st then moved toward the summit and on their climb forward, they passed neatly stacked piles of Confederate corpses. When they reached the top, the men found a cleared field of about three acres, known as Fox's Gap, and Reno directed Hartranft to take, "his regiment across the road into that field, stack arms, and let the men make some coffee."[96] Reno, along with the other officers, believed that the Rebels had fled the area completely.

As Hartranft was moving his men into the field,

> ... companies A, F, D, and I, and part of the color company,
> Co. C, had passed into the field on the right of the road,
> when a most murderous fire of musketry was poured into

58

them from the enemy, who was concealed in a thicket that skirted the field, only about twenty or thirty yards distant from the Fifty-first.[97]

That surprise fusilade caused the 51st to waver for a moment but it quickly regained its composure as Hartranft offered encouragement and prepared his men to return the fire. Soon, the Pennsylvanians responded with a volley of their own which brought a Rebel response. As the 51st took cover, the responding Confederate rounds were too high and passed over Hartranft and fell into the ranks of the newly included 35th Massachusetts, in the rear.[98]

Those uninitiated New Englanders realized they were under Rebel attack and began to return the fire upon the "enemy", not realizing that their shots were leveled directly upon the 51st. This caused a dilemma for Hartranft as he was temporarily pinned down from two sides. Fortunately, the 51st New York was also caught between the two Union regiments and the seasoned New Yorkers quickly threatened to fire upon the 35th if they didn't immediately cease their fire.[99]

Hartranft ordered his regiment out onto the road and placed them behind a low stone wall. He directed Bolton to take Company A and complete the clearing of the immediate area which took Bolton until midnight to accomplish. Despite Bolton's ongoing "mop up" work, the balance of the 51st was constantly harassed throughout the evening by enemy fire, which cost another thirty casualties.[100]

Later, Hartranft learned that General Reno had been wounded during that initial Rebel ambush and was already dying from the shots he had taken in his thigh and groin. As his doctors tended to him, Reno's good friend Brigadier-General Samuel D. Sturgis, of Shippensburg, Pennsylvania, came to see him and asked, "Is it anything serious, Jesse?" Reno's replied, "Sam, it's all up with me."[101] Shortly thereafter, Reno died at age 39.

The battles for South Mountain were over, and the Union had been victorious. However, almost as if it were Standard Operating Procedure, McClellan failed to take advantage of those victories which could have destroyed Lee's Army of Northern Virginia. In the process, he might have brought the war to a close and saved tens of thousands of lives. Unfortunately, that was not McClellan's plan or method, and his inaction led to the bloodiest day in our national history.

# ANTIETAM

The two armies met again on September 17, 1862, on some of the sweetest farmland in America. Situated just above the southern boundary of Maryland, in an area settled by passive Germans known as Dunkers, and just outside the small village of Sharpsburg was to be the site of the next great bloody contest. The town is surrounded by a soft, gently rolling countryside and just east of the village runs Antietam Creek.

The battle actually developed as a segmented engagement, with at least three primary parts. The most famous of all the segments were the cornfield, which was the site of the first real fight of the day; the "Bloody Lane" area, which was witness to the death of so many Americans; and the fight for the Lower or Rohrbach's Bridge which is now known as Burnside's Bridge. That beautiful stone bridge, with its three graceful arches, is just as comely today as it was on that fateful day of September 17. For Hartranft and the 51st, the bridge was the focal point of their efforts that day.

The battle began around 6:00 A.M., when Major-General Joseph Hooker ordered the 10 brigades of his First Corps infantry out of the North Woods toward the little white Dunker church. Directly in front of their path lay the cornfield whose stalks still stood high and straight. As the men of the First Corps made their way through the rows of cornstalks, they formed an eerie group as they filled the paths between the rows with their bayonets which protruded beyond the tops of the stalks. It didn't take long before the Union met fierce resistance from portions of Jackson's Second Corps including Brigadier-Generals Alexander R. Lawton, David R. Jones and John B. Hood. The fight was on! For the next hour and a half, control of the cornfield passed back and forth and words don't even begin to describe the incredible horror in that field. Captain Cook of the 12th Massachusetts wrote, "Rifles are shot to pieces in the hands of the soldiers, canteens, haversacks are riddled with bullets, the dead and wounded go down in scores." By 7:00 A.M., the 12th Massachusetts lost 224 of its 334 men while in fifteen minutes, the Louisiana Tigers, or more properly the Louisiana 8th, lost 325 of their 500 men.[102] Death was everywhere.

By 7:30 A.M., casualties to Hooker's First Corps, already had climbed to 2,600 dead and wounded, while Confederate General Hood responded to the question, "where is your division?", with the sad retort, "dead on the field." By 9:00 A.M., more than 8,000 Americans lay dead or wounded on that field, and the fight had only just begun.[103]

The next area was the sunken road which was held by a group of Confederate soldiers led by Colonel John Brown Gordon, commander of the 6th Alabama, who positioned his men along the roadway and told Lee that he would stay there until "Victory or Sundown" had arrived. For

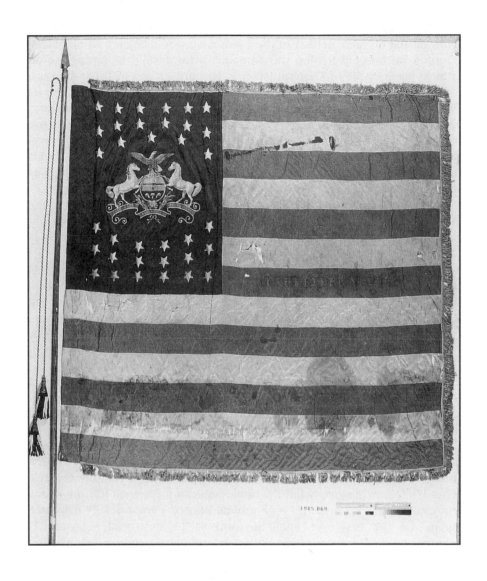

**Flag of the 51st Pennsylvania Volunteers**

*Photographer: Capitol Preservation Committee.*
*Source: Capitol Preservation Committee.*

Gordon and his men, neither of these two goals would be met. Nonetheless, Gordon, an intrepid fighter, was wounded twice during the strong Union attacks made by Major-General Israel B. Richardson and his First Division of the Second Corps plus the coordinated efforts led by Brigadier-General William H. French and his Third Division. While the Confederates successfully repulsed those attacks, on one occasion a minie ball tore through Gordon's cap, leaving only a hole. Shortly thereafter, Gordon was hit in the head by another ball, causing him to fall forward, his face in his hat. Thanks only to the earlier minie ball hole, his profuse bleeding was permitted to exit, thereby saving Gordon from drowning in his own blood.

Soon after Gordon's wounding, Colonel Francis C. Barlow led the 61st and 64th New York regiments down upon the Rebels in the sunken road and broke their hold as his men laid in an enfilading fire which was described as "shooting them like sheep in a pen."[104]

Meanwhile, Burnside and his Ninth Corps were situated on the north side of the Antietam Creek and McClellan had been urging him to move across the creek to bring relief to the Federal left. A few attempts had been made but all were thwarted, because 125 men of the 2nd Georgia were settled on the high ground just beyond the opposite side of the creek. The boys from the Peach Tree State were led by Lieutenant-Colonel William R. Holmes who was part of Brigadier-General Robert Toombs' Brigade.

The 11th Ohio made the first attempt to cross Rohrbach's Bridge around 9:00 that morning and was easily repulsed. Then, one hour later, the 11th Connecticut made another attempt and took heavy losses before the survivors withdrew. Next came Brigadier-General James Nagle with his First Brigade, Second Division of the Ninth Corps, which made a third attempt. As the 2nd Maryland and 6th New Hampshire regiments formed below the bridge, they found themselves also under continuous fire from the Georgia boys.[105] When they moved at the double-quick up the road leading to the bridge, the Rebels on the far high ground poured a most deadly fire upon them. Of the first one hundred Yankees to spearhead that attack, approximately 90 were either killed or wounded, ending yet another attempt.[106]

Burnside now became frustrated, and called upon his Second Division commander, General Sturgis who in turn, called upon his Second Brigade commander, Brigadier-General Edward Ferrero, to take the bridge.[107] Ferrero had been a dance instructor at West Point and was not respected by many of his command including Hartranft. Nonetheless, the order falling upon Ferrero was to take the bridge and at that moment, the two 51st regiments of Pennsylvania and New York were close to each other, with the New Yorkers being led by Colonel Robert B. Potter.[108]

Eager to make a good impression, Ferrero went to the area of the "twin" regiments and reining in his horse, he stood before the troops and called for the 51st to move "forward." In a silent and embarrassing moment, he soon realized that nothing was happening and in the process lost his calm and shouted "Why in hell don't you [move] forward?" In a quiet, cutting voice, Hartranft responded, "Who do you want to [move] forward?" Suddenly, Ferrero realized that he had two 51sts on his hands and then declared, "The Fifty-first Pennsylvania." With that a defiant Hartranft coolly answered, "Why don't you say what you mean when you want *me* to move?"[109] [Emphasis added]

As Ferrero attempted to restore some modicum of control, he let out a yell, "Attention, Second Brigade. It is General Burnside's special request that the two 51sts take the bridge. Will you do it?" Now the Keystone State boys were forbidden any whiskey rations owing to some infraction over the past several days. Consequently, after a quick and reflective moment to Ferrero's question, Corporal Lewis Patterson of Company I of the 51st Pennsylvania called out, "Will you give us our whiskey, Colonel [sic], if we take it?"[110]

Ferrero responded, "Yes, by God! ...You shall have as much as you want, if you take the bridge. I don't mean the whole brigade, but you two regiments shall have just as much as you want, if it is in the commissary or I have to send to New York to get it, and pay for it out of my own purse; that is if I live to see you through it. Will you take it?"[111]

With that, a resounding yell of yes filled the air as the soldiers gave Ferrero exactly what he was searching for. Like so many things in the war, Patterson's request was rather unique, since he was a teetotaler and did not imbibe.[112]

As the men of the two regiments formed a line of attack, the Georgians on the other side could see that their recent good fortune was fast coming to an end. Their commander, Colonel Henry L. Benning, noticed that a part of his right flank had simply vanished. In addition, the balance of his men were rapidly running out of ammunition, so he ordered them to, "pull back."[113] Meanwhile, the 51st Pennsylvania began to move forward and Hartranft was warned not to "go up the road" leading to the bridge. That advice came from Lieutenant-Colonel J. Eugene Duryea who had made an earlier attempt with the 2nd Maryland. Heeding Duryea's comment, Hartranft related,

> Turning my attention to some other way I found a depression back of a rising ground opposite and overlooking the approaches to the bridge. I moved the regiment by the right flank under cover of this and formed

63

it in close column of division just behind the crest. When the formation was complete I ordered the movement upon the bridge....[114]

As he was leading the ranks toward the bridge, Hartranft encountered a fence that was connected to its upper wall. He described that fence as a "serious obstacle" but his ranks simply climbed over it and then took the lower wall. As portions of the 51st began to come upon the center of the bridge they realized that they had to run to the far end to avoid the heavy Georgia fire. Hartranft continued,

> While the men replied to the fire of the enemy I was at the end of the upper wing wall and had the two panels of fence nearest the bridge torn down. In the meantime Colonel Potter came up with his regiment, the Fifty-first N.Y., and formed along the fence to the left of the bridge. The fence afforded little or no protection and the Fifty-first N.Y. was losing heavily. This also impelled me to arouse my regiment to another effort...Passing through the opening in the fence with the colors and a few officers and men we got on to the bridge, and the others passed on. I turned and called on the rest of the regiment to follow. While thus engaged Colonel Potter came up, likewise calling to his regiment. Both regiments responded promptly and passed rapidly over the bridge. The Fifty-first Pennsylvania was leading, filed to the right on the roadway, and the Fifty-first N. Y. to the left. This was about noon.[115]

As Hartranft was leading and encouraging his regiment to move, Captain William Allebaugh, who commanded Company C, responded first and led his men forward. Heavy fire from the Georgians soon struck down Lieutenant Davis Hunsicker causing Allebaugh to make some quick changes in his approach to the bridge. While Hartranft was yelling encouragement at the top of his voice, Allebaugh, along with "three colorbearers, one color-guard and his first sergeant, William F. Thomas", was the first to cross the bridge through a hail of shot. The rest of the men of both regiments were close behind as Hartranft yelled "Come on, boys, for I can't hallo any more."[116]   As the men in blue began to pour across the bridge, the Confederates quickly realized that matters had shifted in favor of the Union

### Antietam Bridge

A modern view of Antietam bridge. Hartranft moved his troops from left to right, over the bridge.

*Photographer: Frank D'Amico.*

65

**Antietam Bridge**

This would be the general view of what Hartranft and his men saw as they crossed the bridge on September 17, 1862. The Georgia troops were located slightly to the left of the bridge behind the trees.

*Photographer: Frank D'Amico.*

and the Rebel snipers in the trees on the far side of the bridge began to leave their positions. Others decided to surrender and used pieces of paper attached to their ramrods as white flags.[117] The entire charge took about twelve minutes, but the cost was high, with 21 killed outright and 99 wounded.[118]

It was shortly after the crossing, while Hartranft was waiting for further instructions from Ferrero, that he sent Lieutenant-Colonel Bell to find the brigade commander. Bell crossed back across the bridge, found Ferrero and was on his way back to tell Hartranft that Ferrero wanted him to move to the top of the hill when Bell was fatally struck in the left temple.[119] The complete list of casualties for the 51st Pennsylvania upon the bridge can be found in Appendix C.

With the 51st across the Antietam, Hartranft settled his men along the dirt path on the far side. Shortly thereafter, he could hear someone calling out for the commander of the Pennsylvania regiment, and he was approached by Lieutenant John Williams Hudson of the 35th Massachusetts, whom Ferrero has sent to ask why Hartranft had not advanced his regiment to support the 35th? Hartranft answered abruptly, "I've no ammunition."[120] With that Hudson returned to Ferrero and gave him Hartranft's reply.

In his battle report, Ferrero noted that, "The Fifty-first Pennsylvania Volunteers, commanded by Col. J. F. Hartranft, led the charge, [over the bridge] followed by the Fifty-first New York Volunteers, Lieut. Col. R. B. Potter;" Ferrero continued that those same officers and regiments were "worthy of particular praise."[121]

General Toombs noted that during the fight to take the bridge, Lieutenant-Colonel William R. Holmes had been killed during the attack. He further stated that with the heavy losses incurred by the defending Georgians, "I deemed it my duty, ... to withdraw my command..." from their position across from the bridge. However, Toombs also noted that after the bridge had been taken, that, "Though the bridge and upper ford were thus left open to the enemy, he moved with such extreme caution and slowness that he[Burnside] lost nearly two hours in crossing and getting into action on our side of the river ...."[122]

Impressed by Hartranft's actions at the bridge, on September 25th, Burnside wrote to McClellan requesting promotion for Hartranft.[123] While Burnside's request was not granted, it had been noticed by other high ranking officers, Brigadier-General Samuel P. Heintzelman for example, who wrote Hartranft,

Colonel - I have read General Burnside's letter recommending Colonel [William S.] Clark and yourself for Brigadier-Generals. I well recollect your gallant service on General Franklin's staff at the first Bull Run battle, and have followed with interest your career in North Carolina. It will afford me much pleasure to hear that your services have been rewarded in this manner.[124]

Unfortunately, Hartranft was destined to remain a colonel for many more months.

## FREDERICKSBURG

Following the battle of Antietam, President Abraham Lincoln strongly urged McClellan to pursue Lee and his army, which he failed to do. McClellan's reluctance exasperated the president and Lincoln finally relieved McClellan on November 7, replacing him with General Burnside. The pride within the ranks of his Ninth Corps can be imagined.

The next major military event in Hartranft's career was the battle of Fredericksburg, on December 13, 1862. While the change in command did not disturb Hartranft greatly, he did confess to Sallie on the 11th of December, that he "respected" McClellan.[125]

The 51st was still part of General Ferrero's Second Brigade, Sturgis's Second Division, and with Burnside's promotion, Brigadier-General Orlando B. Willcox had taken temporary command of the Ninth Corps. At Fredericksburg, the Second and Ninth Corps both reported to Major-General Edwin V. Sumner, the oldest general in the Union Army.

The 51st crossed the Rappahannock on the morning of the 12th and for the rest of that day bivouacked in Fredericksburg, taking care to keep out of sight of the Confederate guns. Shortly after noon on the 13th, Hartranft led the regiment "to the lower end of the city...and up a street that terminated abruptly by a large brick-kiln."[126]  Quickly coming under heavy Rebel artillery fire, Hartranft ordered his men to the ground knowing that the kiln would offer some protection. He quickly found a better position in the railroad cut to his front and he ordered the entire regiment to its safety.[127]

Pausing only a few moments to let his men gain their breath, Hartranft found that General Ferrero was also in that cut. Attempting to inspire the 51st, Ferrero yelled at the top of his lungs, "go in and give it to them."[128]  With that charge, plus some added hot Rebel fire upon them, the regiment lost no time in vacating the cut. Its next objective, Marye's

Heights, meant the line had to cross a clear field which extended for about one third of a mile. Since other Union units had preceded the 51st, it was now obvious that they could expect heavy Confederate artillery fire plus the incredible volleys emanating from behind the stone wall just in front of a sunken road. Nonetheless, Hartranft ordered the regiment forward and like a giant blue serpent, his troops began to follow him at a full run. Parker here comments,

> Before the regiment has reached its position its way was somewhat impeded by a series of high board fences that inclosed [sic] some of the land, and instead of the regiment being able to advance in an unbroken line of battle, it had to divide into several squads to pass through the apertures of the fence. The boards being nailed on perpendicularly, with stout nails and plenty of them, it was only here and there that a board had been wrenched off, and the passages through the fences were blocked up with heaps of dead, dying and wounded, who had to be trampled upon in order to get through. The groans of the dying and wounded soldiers when trodden on were heartrending in the extreme, but it was no time or place to stop to evince sympathy for the brave fellows who lay weltering in their gore. All felt it, but as each one knew not how soon he was to fall and share the same fate, he passed on heedless of all cries for aid. The men of the 51st were falling at every step, some killed outright, some with a leg or arm torn off, some with their bowels or brains oozing out, and some falling as if they had been hit, but in fact had only fallen to impress their officers that they had been wounded, and thus escape proceeding any further.[129]

When Hartranft reached his final position, perhaps 75-100 yards from the wall in front of the sunken road, the 51st opened fire. Some of his men carried as many as one hundred rounds, and from about noon to four o'clock the regiment fired constantly. After the Pennsylvania boys had shared and consumed all of their own ammunition, they begged for more from other units and even emptied the cartridge boxes of their dead comrades.[130]

With the regiment out of ammunition, and their exposed position still accented by the remaining daylight, they could not pull back and allow replacements to afford them a break. Instead, Hartranft, along with many others, was forced to remain at his position with the incessant Confederate fire until 8:00 P.M., with the aid of darkness, he could safely lead his men off the field.

The cost to the Union was monumental. Burnside began this battle with about 120,000 men and records show a total casualty list of 12,653, or almost eleven per cent.[131] Burnside realized that the battle had been a dismal failure and wanted to renew the fight in the morning, personally leading his old Ninth Corps. His top advisors opposed such a plan, and convinced him of its futility.

Instead, the Army of the Potomac began to retreat across the Rappahannock during the night of the 15th. Again, the 51st acted as rearguard and Hartranft returned to the same position he vacated on the 13th near the stonewall, just below Marye's Heights. Because of a shortage of tools, and the severe cold weather, the 51st could barely create a breastwork for their own protection. Yet for the next twenty-six hours the men were forced to remain in this position without food, water or relief.[132] Finally, Hartranft was able to find another regiment to replace his strained men and led his regiment back to camp.

On the 17th, those detailed for burial duty, including men from the 51st, brought back horror stories of bodies stripped of all clothing and left naked on the field. They also told of Rebel offers to pay as much as $25 in greenbacks for a blanket or an overcoat.[133] Since most Yankees realized that the greenbacks had belonged to their dead comrades, most of those offers were refused.

The 51st had again demonstrated its valor, and despite Hartranft's personal animosity, Ferrero was again lavish in his praise of the Norristown commander. In his report, Ferrero stated that, "The highest praise is due Colonel Hartranft, the senior colonel of the brigade, for his gallant conduct and valuable service...."[134] In little over one year, Hartranft and the 51st had fought at Roanoke Island, New Bern, Camden, Second Bull Run, South Mountain, Antietam, and now Fredericksburg. Before the last battle, he could only count 270 able-bodied men in his regiment. When the fight for Fredericksburg was over that number had dropped to a mere 180 effectives which meant a loss of another 90 men.[135]

Hartranft's patience was sorely tested by the failure at Fredericksburg and he vented some of his frustrations upon Sallie when he wrote,

> We have again passed through one of the severest fighting
> battles of the campaign [Fredericksburg]... What the army

**Flag of the 51st Pennsylvania Volunteers**

Flag remnants of the 51st Pennsylvania. The main body of the flag has been torn away by heavy enemy fire.

*Photographer: Capitol Preservation Committee.*
*Source: Capitol Preservation Committee.*

may do now is rather doubtful, I think the winter campaign is pretty well settled. Our loss in killed is 1500, wounded 6500 without gaining a point and the moral affect [sic] of a defeat to overcome. Not that I consider a defeat was actually sustained by us because we held every inch of ground we took, and our brigade with 900 men held theirs all day on Monday, But our army could not advance upon the Batteries beyond the line we occupied without losing almost all, and our Generals decided to withdraw for the present... We may then go into winter quarters, as I think that to take Richmond now by this route is doubtful....[136]

Burnside's army prepared for winter quarters, while its commander prepared another attack against Lee. On January 20, 1863, Burnside set out again, but, unfortunately, heavy rains turned the roads into a veritable quagmire and the entire campaign became famous as "Burnside's Mud March" which had to be cancelled. Major-General Joseph Hooker soon replaced Burnside as commander of the Army of the Potomac.

When Burnside left his post as commanding general on January 26, 1863, the Ninth Corps was briefly led by Major-General John Sedgwick of Connecticut. Shortly afterward, when Burnside was ordered to the west, he requested his old Ninth Corps and the War Department agreed. In the early Spring of 1863, the 51st struck its tents and began to head West while Hartranft went home for a much-deserved leave.[137]

# ENDNOTES TO CHAPTER THREE
## ROANOKE ISLAND TO FREDERICKSBURG

1. Parker, Thomas H., *History of the 51st Regiment of P.V. and V.V.*, Philadelphia: King & Baird, Printers, 1869, p. 11. Hereafter referred to as *History of the 51st*.
2. JFH to SSH, September 12, 1861, Shireman Collection.
3. Parker, *History of the 51st*, p. 25.
4. Ibid., p. 14.
5. Ibid., p. 35.
6. Ibid., pp 20-22.
7. Ibid., pp. 690-691.
8. Ibid., pp. 30-31.
9. W. B. Franklin to Ambrose Burnside, November 12, 1861, Shireman Collection.
10. JFH to Irvin McDowell, December 10, 1861, Shireman Collection.
11. JFH to SSH, December 19, 1861, Shireman Collection.
12. Parker, *History of the 51st*, p. 38.
13. Marvel, William, *Burnside*, Chapel Hill, North Carolina: University of North Carolina Press, 1991, p. 42.
14. Parker, *History of the 51st*, pp. 36-37.
15. Ibid., pp. 43-45.
16. JFH to SSH, January 8, 1862, Shireman collection.
17. Marvel, *Burnside*, p. 42.
18. JFH to SSH, January 8, 1862, Shireman Collection.
19. JFH to SSH, January 13, 1862, Shireman Collection.
20. *O. R.* I, vol. V, p. 1025.
21. JFH to SSH, January 15, 1862, Shireman Collection.
    *Also see* Marvel, *Burnside*, p. 45.
22. Marvel, *Burnside*, p. 48.
23. JFH to SSH, January 15, 1862, Shireman Collection.
24. *O. R.* Series I, vol. V, p. 1069.
25. Sauers, Richard A., "General Ambrose E. Burnside's 1862 North Carolina Campaign", (Ph. D. diss., Pennsylvania State University Graduate School, 1987) p. 150. Hereafter known as "General Burnside's Expedition".
26. Marvel, *Burnside*, p. 51-52.
27. Sauers, "General Burnside's Expedition", pp. 166-167.
28. Evans, Eli N., *Judah P. Benjamin, The Jewish Confederate*, New York: The Free Press, 1988, p. 146.
29. Sauers, "General Burnside's Expedition", p. 157.
30. JFH to SSH, January 17, 1862, Shireman Collection.

31. Sauers, "General Burnside's Expedition", p. 144.
32. Parker, *History of the 51st*, p. 69.
33. Ibid., p. 75.
34. Sauers, "General Burnside's Expedition", p. 196.
      *Also see* Parker, *History of the 51st*, p. 75.
35. Sauers, "General Burnside's Expedition", p. 202.
36. Parker, *History of the 51st*, p. 76-77.
37. Sauers, "General Burnside's Expedition", p. 211.
38. Parker, *History of the 51st*, p. 77.
      Also see, *O. R.* Series I, vol. IX, p. 98.
39. *O. R.* Series I, vol. IX, pp. 221-222.
40. Armor, *Lives of the Governors of Pennsylvania*, pp. 496-497.
41. Parker, *History of the 51st*, p. 79.
42. Evans, Judah P. Benjamin, The Jewish Confederate, p. 147.
43. *O. R.* Series I., vol. IX, pp. 111-112.
44. Evans, *Judah P. Benjamin, The Jewish Confederate*, p. 147.
45. Parker, *History of the 51st*, p. 78.
46. Ibid., p. 98.
47. Ibid., p. 100.
48. *O. R.* Series I, vol. IX, p. 233.
49. Sauers, "General Burnside's Expedition", p. 298.
      *Also see O. R.* Series I. vol. IX, p. 223.
50. *Philadelphia Daily Evening Telegraph*, March 14, 1910.
51. Sauers, "General Burnside's Expedition", pp. 242, 298.
52. *O. R.* Series I, vol. IX, p. 202.
53. Sauers, "General Burnside's Expedition", p. 344.
54. *O. R.* Series I. vol. IX, p. 203.
55. Parker, *History of the 51st*, pp. 105-106.
56. *O. R.* Series I., vol. IX, p. 204.
57. Bates, Samuel P., *Martial Deeds of Pennsylvania*, Philadelphia: T. H.
      Davis & Co., 1875, p. 664.
58. *O. R.* Series I. vol. IX, p. 231.
59. Ibid., p. 221.
60. Ibid., pp. 231-232.
61. Parker, *History of the 51st*, p. 115.
62. *Bolton Diary*, p. 33.
63. Parker, *History of the 51st*, pp. 107-108.
64. Ibid., p. 109-110.
65. Ibid., p. 115.
66. *O. R.* Series I, vol. IX, p. 207.
67. *Bolton Diary*, p. 40.
68. SSH to JFH, March 4, 1852, Shireman Collection.

69. SSH to JFH, March 6, 1862, Shireman Collection.
70. Brecht, *Genealogical Records*, pp. 728-729.
71. *Bolton Diary*, p. 46.
72. E. A. Banks to JFH, June 11, 1862, Shireman Collection.
      *Also see* Beane, ed., *HMCP*, p. 547.
73. JFH to E. A. Banks, June 24, 1862, Shireman Collection.
74. SSH to JFH, June 16, 1862, Shireman Collection.
75. SSH to JFH, August 1, 1862, Shireman Collection.
76. SSH to JFH, July 12, 1862, Shireman Collection.
77. Parker, *History of the 51st*, p. 211.
78. Boatner, Mark M., III, *The Civil War Dictionary*, New York: David
      McKay Company, Inc., 1959, p. 105.
79. *Bolton Diary*, p. 71.
80. Parker, *History of the 51st*, p. 214.
81. Ibid.
82. Ibid., p. 216.
83. JFH to SSH, September 3, 1862, Shireman Collection.
84. *Bolton Diary*, p. 73.
85. Warner, *Generals in Blue*, p. 395.
86. Boatner, *The Civil War Dictionary*, p. 105.
87. Parker, *History of the 51st*, pp. 219-220.
88. Chambers, Lenoir, *Stonewall Jackson*, 2 vols., New York: William
      Morrow & Co., 1959, p. 173.
89. Bates, *Martial Deeds of Pennsylvania*, p. 665.
90. Parker, *History of the 51st*, p. 220.
91. Constable, George et al, eds., *Lee takes Command*, Alexandria, Virginia:
      Time-Life Books, 1984, p. 166.
92. Livermore, Thomas L., *Numbers and Losses in the Civil War*,
      Bloomington, Indiana: Indiana University Press, 1957, p. 88.
93. Bailey, Ronald H., ed. *The Bloodiest Day-The Battle of Antietam*,
      Alexandria, Virginia: Time-Life Books, 1984, pp. 28, 38.
94. Boatner, *The Civil War Dictionary*, p. 20.
95. Parker, *History of the 51st*, p. 224.
96. Ibid., pp. 224-225.
97. Ibid., p. 225.
98. Ibid.
99. Ibid., p. 226.
100. Bates, *Martial Deeds of Pennsylvania*, p. 665.
      Also see Parker, *History of the 51st*, pp. 226-227.
101. Parker, *History of the 51st*, p. 227.
102. Bailey, *The Bloodiest Day-The Battle of Antietam*, p. 73.
103. Ibid., p. 79.

104. Ibid., p. 102.
105. Priest, John M., *Antietam: The Soldiers Battle*, Shippensburg,
 Pennsylvania: White Mane Publishing Company, Inc., 1989, p. 219.
106. Luvaas, Jay and Harold W. Nelson, eds., *The U. S. Army War College
 Guide to the Battle of Antietam*, New York: HarperCollins
 Publishers, 1987, pp. 224-225.
107. *O. R.* SeriesI, vol. XIX, part I, p. 419.
108. Priest, *Antietam: The Soldiers Battle*, p. 230.
109. Ibid.
110. Parker, *History of the 51st*, p. 232.
111. Ibid.
112. Ibid.
113. Priest, *Antietam: The Soldiers Battle*, p. 239.
114. Hartranft, John F., Oration. *Report of the Sixth Annual Meeting of the
 Association of the 51st Regiment P. V., Dedication of Monument at
 Antietam Bridge*, October 8, 1887. Shireman Collection.
115. Ibid.
116. Parker, *History of the 51st*, pp. 234-235.
117. Frassanito, William A., *The Photographic Legacy of America's Bloodiest
 Day*, New York: Charles Scribner's Sons, 1978, p. 237.
118. Parker, *History of the 51st*, p. 235.
119. Ibid. p. 237.
120. Letter from Lieutenent John William Hudson, of the 35th
 Massachusetts, written in early October, 1862. Courtesy of John M.
 Priest. Original located in the Maryland Room, Washington County
 Free Library.
121. *O. R.* Series I, vol. XIX, part I, p. 448.
122. Ibid., pp. 890-891.
123. Armor, *Lives of the Governors of Pennsylvania*, p. 502.
124. Ibid., pp. 502-503.
125. JFH to SSH, December 11, 1862, Shireman Collection.
126. Parker, *History of the 51st*, p. 269.
127. Ibid., p. 270.
128. Ibid.
129. Ibid., pp. 270-271.
130. Ibid., p. 273.
131. Livermore, *Numbers and Losses in the Civil War*, p. 96.
132. Parker, *History of the 51st*, p. 275.
133. Ibid., p. 277.
134. *O. R.* Series I, vol. XXI, p. 326.
135. Parker, *History of the 51st*, p. 277.
136. JFH to SSH, December 16, 1862, Shireman Collection.

137. Parker, *History of the 51st*, p. 289.

# CHAPTER FOUR

*VICKSBURG TO KNOXVILLE*
*"ALMOST A GENERAL"*


With the coming spring of 1863, Hartranft and the men of the 51st were ordered to the West. They struck their tents at Newport News on March 26, and embarked upon a trip that would take them more than two-and-one-half months to complete.[1] Hartranft took advantage of that travel time and went home on furlough. For the rest of the 51st, on Monday the 30th, they arrived in Columbus, Ohio, and from there, they moved to Cincinnati, then to Paris, Kentucky, and finally, Mt. Sterling, Kentucky, where on the 7th of April, Hartranft rejoined the regiment.[2]

On the 14th, Hartranft and the 51st lost one of their most loyal comrades when Captain Edward Schall of Company D, resigned his commission to return to Norristown.[3] Schall's brother, Edwin, was the regimental lieutenant-colonel and also owned a popular newspaper, the *National Defender*.[4] With such good eyewitness reporters, the *National Defender* was able to keep the families in Norristown well updated on the efforts of the 51st.

The trip West proved to be trying and matters were compounded since the men of the 51st were not always certain where they were headed. On June 3rd, while the 51st was in Stanford, Kentucky, Hartranft received an urgent telegram from General Burnside directing him to move as rapidly as possible towards Vicksburg.[5] Since Burnside was to remain in Tennessee, command of the Ninth Corps fell to Major-General John G. Parke. Hartranft force-marched the 51st for thirty-four miles to Nicholasville where they boarded a train for the "Queen City of the Bluff."[6] Yet typical military confusion existed and even Hartranft was not exactly certain which way the train was headed until it pulled out of the station. He wrote to Sallie that, "We are again on the move, but instead of moving toward the front, we are moving towards Lexington and from there I do not know."[7]

The detachment of the Ninth Corps, including the 51st, finally arrived at Vicksburg on June 17th and was placed in the rear of Grant's army with the left flank near Snyder's Bluff and the right at Jones Templeton's Plantation.[8] Captain Parker, who constantly sent a string of letters back to the *National Defender*, quickly deduced that, "We are here... for the purpose of checking [CSA General] Joe Johnston from getting in the rear of Grant, while the siege continues."[9]

There were many signs that the siege of Vicksburg was already creating hard times for the inhabitants of the city, as many horses and mules had been sighted floating down the Mississippi. This was a clear indication that those animals had died of starvation while others that had been set free to fend for themselves, were captured by the Union troops.[10]

Grant's siege grip of the city certainly predated the arrival of the 51st, and when the Pennsylvanians went into camp, life actually became routine and boring as Hartranft ordered drill, drill, and more drill. Grant was not going to take any chances and he, more than anyone, realized that if General Johnston attacked his rear, there could be serious trouble so he prepared to avoid a two-front battle if possible.[11] Consequently, the Ninth and Hartranft, who was placed in temporary charge of Edward Fererro's Second Brigade, were again relegated to that all-important but potentially boring rear position along with Major-General William T. Sherman.[12]

Constant rumors about General Johnston's alleged attack kept most of the Union troops on edge. It was "common knowledge" that Richmond didn't want to see Vicksburg fall. It was equally certain that Johnston would soon attack and bring relief to the Confederate commander from Philadelphia, Lieutenant-General John C. Pemberton, and his 30,000 troops locked inside the city.[13]

Unknown to the Union men, however, Johnston had given up all hope of saving Vicksburg. He had only 31,000 troops, and knew they were not adequate to successfully attack Grant.[14] Johnston had pleaded with Richmond, and Secretary of War James A. Seddon in particular, for reinforcements, but did not get very far since Richmond simply did not have the resources available. It was now a war of nerves and propaganda for Johnston and his army.

The day following the arrival of the 51st, the *Daily Citizen* in Richmond optimistically told the public that, "we have nothing to record of his [Johnston's] movements, except that we may look forward at any time to his approach. We may repose the utmost confidence in his appearance within a very few days."[15] Apparently, no one, absolutely no one, in Richmond really understood how desperate and hopeless conditions were for salvaging Vicksburg.

Finally, on the 15th of June, Johnston wired Secretary Seddon and told him that if he did not get additional troops, "I consider saving Vicksburg hopeless."[16] Seddon fired back that "Vicksburg must not be lost without a desperate struggle. The interest and the honor of the Confederacy forbid it."[17] Johnston, who saw the utter hopelessness of the situation, very diplomatically answered, "I will do all I can."[18] Unfortunately for Johnston, Pemberton and the Confederacy, that was not nearly enough.

Ultimately, Johnston's attack never came, and Grant's grip made Pemberton realize that he could not continue to hold out inside the city without risking the lives of the civilians and soldiers. Consequently,

Pemberton began negotiations and, feeling he would get much better terms for a surrender on Independence Day, Pemberton agreed to capitulate accordingly. The day after Lee's defeat at Gettysburg, Grant took command of the city along with 30,000 Rebel prisoners.

For Hartranft, the 51st, and the entire Union army, the nightmare of Vicksburg came to an end and the Pennsylvanians felt fortunate since they did not have to face combat again. According to Reverend D. G. Mallory, chaplain of the 51st, "Early in the morning [July 4th] I listened with all my ears for the opening fight, but heard only the national salute to the Day...A happy day, because bloodless, victory."[19]

Hartranft and the boys of the 51st were thrilled at the thought of Grant's victory but they were allowed no time for celebration and were ordered to prepare to move out immediately. According to Parker, "The beleaguered city of Vicksburg having surrendered to Gen. Grant at 10 o'clock on the morning of the 4th inst., we immediately packed up our 'knapsacks' and started off on a march that same afternoon...."[20] The destination of the 51st was the capital city of Jackson, Mississippi where Hartranft and his Pennsylvanians arrived on July 17th.[21]

The 51st and the members of the Ninth Corps, under General Parke, were now going to be part of General Sherman's offensive move against General Joseph E. Johnston. In this campaign, Sherman would lay siege to Jackson in an effort to dislodge Johnston.[22] At that time, Hartranft was again in temporary command of the Second Brigade of the Second Division which included the 35th Massachusetts, 11th New Hampshire, and the "twin" 51st regiments from New York and Pennsylvania.

On July 10th, as the Union Army moved to within six miles of Jackson, Hartranft issued an order calling upon all regimental commanders to "hold their commands in readiness to move upon the enemy at a moment's notice."[23] At that time, Hartranft had come down with a severe case of dysentery and was confined to bed. Not one to be kept down, he relegated himself to an ambulance, and handled the brigade from a wagon. According to Parker "he [Hartranft] being unable, from sickness, to sit up, but reclining on the cushions of the seats, he dispatched orders and manoeuvred his command as skillfully as if able to sit on his horse and attend to the details in person."[24] While the colonel attempted to fight off the pestilence of the "dreaded disease", it took its toll upon him, and he would later return to Norristown on a sixty-day leave to restore his health.[25]

Immediately after receipt of orders, Hartranft directed his brigade toward Jackson and after moving about two miles, they encamped for the night.[26] The next morning, Saturday the 11th, while the brigade was moving slowly towards the city, the Rebels opened fire and sent a hail of shot and shell over their heads.[27] In response, Hartranft quickly placed his command in line of battle but the Rebels scattered and the only further pelting the brigade received that day was from a cooling rain. On Sunday the 12th, the Union men got the news of Lee's defeat at Gettysburg which lifted their morale immeasurably.

Each day, Hartranft and his brigade came closer to Jackson but in an agonizingly slow pace. Early in the morning of Thursday the 16th, men of the 51st were sent forward as skirmishers just outside of the city.[28] Throughout the prior evening, the Pennsylvanians on picket duty could hear the rumble of wagons and the marching of troops. With the advent of dawn, the skirmishers of the 51st moved closer to town only to find that the Confederates had gone.[29]

Hartranft and his Second Brigade were first into the city by a full hour before any other troops, and his men planted their colors upon the dome of the capitol.[30] When the balance of the Union army made its way into Jackson, men of the Ninth Corps and the Second Brigade in particular taunted the Westerners by calling out "Boys, you are too late, the whiskey is all gone, the Ninth Army Corps got all of it an hour ago."[31] The siege of Jackson was over and it was another bloodless coup for the Union.

But the "sacking" of Jackson was about to begin, and many men of the 51st participated in the poor sport. Those Union troops looked first for tobacco and then whiskey which they found both in abundance. Groceries were taken and men started to ransack the shelves of clothing stores and acted like giddy children.[32] Despite his burning fever, Hartranft ordered his men to Milldale and the sacking came to an abrupt end. On July 31st, while camped at Milldale, the Pennsylvanians and all the men of the Ninth Corps received the praise of General Grant who told them that,

> The endurance, valor and general good conduct of the Ninth Corps are admired by all, and its valuable co-operation, is gratefully acknowledged by the Army of the Tennessee.
>
> Maj. Gen. Parke will cause the different regiments and batteries of his command to inscribe upon their banners and guidons, "Vicksburg and Jackson."
>
> By order of...Maj. Gen. U. S. Grant.[33]

After the fall of Jackson, Colonels Zenas R. Bliss of the 27th Rhode Island, Simon G. Griffin, First Brigade, First Division of the Ninth Corps, and Hartranft were all strongly recommended for promotion to Major-

General Grant. In turn, Grant heartily endorsed those recommendations with the notation that the Ninth Corps was also short of generals and these three, who had commanded brigades, had "done well."[34] Word was passed to each of the three candidates which, understandably, caused much excitement with them.

Colonel Orville E. Babcock of Grant's staff prematurely told Colonel Bliss that "This [promotion] is no joke, we have got them now, and I congratulate you on your promotion which will come immediately and no one can stop it."[35] Of course, these comments made their way back to Griffin and Hartranft as well.

Several days later as Bliss passed Griffin and Hartranft, he noticed that both men had donned their new general's coats. Bliss remarked to Hartranft that "he [Hartranft] got his coat very promptly." In response, Hartranft asked his comrade if he had ordered his own new coat as yet. When Bliss asked why he should do so, Hartranft said, "Why didn't you see the recommendations [for promotion]?"[36] Unfortunately for all three, none of the promotions ever materialized despite the combined pleas of Generals Grant and Parke. Consequently, Hartranft and his two comrades would have to remain content with the rank of colonel and the bitter pride of being "almost a general."

On the 6th of August, the 51st was off again, this time headed for Kentucky. When the regiment arrived in Cincinnati, it stopped by the Burnet House, where General Burnside made his headquarters. Burnside, who had not been able to follow his Ninth Corps to Vicksburg, made a brief speech to the men and afterwards, a soldier from Hartranft's regiment yelled out to Burnside, "We want you along with us, General." Smiling for a moment, Burnside quickly reflected and told the men that "I'll be with you in heart, if not in person."[37] For Hartranft, his bout with the "remittent fever" had taken its toll and he took advantage of the lull and made his way home to restore his health.

Meanwhile, the 51st entered Kentucky and encamped just outside of Covington and then moved to Nicholasville and finally to Crab Orchard.[38] Around the middle of September, orders directed the 51st to join General Burnside at Knoxville, in eastern Tennessee.[39] However, this order was quickly rescinded and the Pennsylvania boys garrisoned Crab Orchard instead.[40]

On September 29th, Lieutenant-Colonel Schall, who was in command during Hartranft's absence, received orders to move his men toward Knoxville and the 51st began a march of 157 miles which was completed in under twenty days.[41] After a few days of rest, the 51st moved toward Loudon, and finally, on Monday, November the 16th, it participated in the battle of Campbell's Station, which was to be one of Hartranft's proudest victories.

There, at this small crossroads, CSA Lieutenant-General James Longstreet, Lee's "Old War Horse", wanted to take possession of the area which would then give him easy access to Knoxville.[42] The critical nature of Campbell's Station becomes more evident when we note that some authors have deemed it the "decisive battle of the Campaign."[43] At Campbell's Station there were roads that went in six different directions; the major highway being the Kingston Road.[44]

Longstreet had arrived in the area on the 14th with about 20,000 troops and on the 15th, he and members of Burnside's army clashed at Hough's Ferry, which drove the Rebels back about two miles.[45] Burnside decided that on the morrow he would lead another attack, but that evening he received a directive from General Grant ordering him to move back to Knoxville with his 6,000 men.[46] Grant went on to say,

> I do not know how to impress on you the necessity of holding on to East Tennessee in strong enough terms. ...it would seem that you should, if pressed to do it, hold on to Knoxville and that portion of the valley you will necessarily possess holding to that point. Should Longstreet move his whole force across the Little Tennessee, an effort should be made to cut his pontoons on that stream *even if it sacrificed half the cavalry of the Ohio army*. [Emphasis added]

That same day, Burnside also received a message from Henry Halleck telling him to hold his position for a few more days and, "If you retreat now it will be disastrous to the campaign."[47] Consequently, if there had been any doubt in Burnside's mind beforehand, he certainly now knew just how important his position was.

Very early in the morning of the 16th, Longstreet had a lucky break when a local told him how he could take a shortcut and beat the Yanks to the crossroads at Campbell's Station.[48] Elated at the thought of success, Longstreet ordered Major-General Lafayette McLaws' Division forward, and in the process they brushed with Burnside's right flank. Quickly grasping the situation, Burnside ordered Hartranft to take temporary command of the Second Division and move to Campbell's Station with all haste.[49] The colonel's new command consisted of the First Brigade, led by Colonel Joshua F. Sigfried with the 2nd Maryland, 21st Massachusetts, and 48th Pennsylvania regiments. The Second Brigade, led by Lieutenant-

Colonel Moses N. Collins, included the 35th Massachusetts, 11th New Hampshire, and the 51st Pennsylvania regiments.[50] Just before daylight, Hartranft led out the Second Division with Colonel William Humphrey's Third Brigade, First Division following.[51] The march was extremely difficult because of the driving rain and mud. Hartranft himself wrote that "the mud was so terrible that the two batteries I was to take with me had to be helped along. One of them, Benjamin's 20lb. battery stuck frequently and only the agonizing labor of men with long ropes could pull them out. From early evening until 2 o'clock A.M., I had not moved two miles."[52]

Hartranft had been made aware of McLaws' movement toward the crossroads, and despite the muddy roadbed, he urged his men to move as quickly as possible.[53] But pressing forward was no easy matter and the men struggled to drag along the seven fieldpieces, which included four heavy 20-pound Parrotts.[54] A private in the 79th New York Highlanders wrote that "the mud was deep and the road full of wagons and artillery, which we were frequently obliged to help out of the mud holes." A correspondent also wrote that, "Wagons sank to their boxes in the liquid mud, ...while driver, teamsters and artillerymen became so covered with the spattering mud that it was difficult to tell them from the surrounding soil."[55] Even Burnside's First Division commander, Brigadier-General Edward Ferrero, noted that it took as many as sixteen to twenty horses or mules to pull one gun.[56] Nonetheless, Hartranft continued to drive his men forward, and they arrived at the Kingston Road a full fifteen minutes before McLaws.[57] That gave "Old Johnny" precious time to deploy his men "in a beautiful position."

Just as soon as Hartranft's men were put into place, the head of McLaws' line could be seen coming toward them. The fight for Campbell's Station had begun! Hartranft immediately ordered his modest cavalry escort to attack the Rebel front line, which temporarily drove the Confederates back.[58] According to Hartranft, because of that cavalry attack, "the enemy did not immediately annoy me in front but tried to work around my right and, I had considerable trouble to hold the cavalry on that flank. They [the Rebels] attempted to come back but I forced them out."[59] As the fight at Campbell's Station held the Confederates, Burnside moved the bulk of his army to Knoxville as Grant had ordered. Meanwhile, McLaws kept up constant pressure in front of Hartranft while Colonel Humphrey was being hotly engaged by Brigadier-General Micah Jenkins, who led the division belonging to Major-General John Bell Hood [who was still recuperating from his severe Chickamauga wounds]. Despite the pressure, "Hartranft steadfastly held his ground until the remainder of the army and all the trains passed the threatened point."[60] Fighting became so intense on Hartranft's front that when he finally received the word to pull back to a nearby hill, one of his regiments was completely out of ammunition.[61]

84

Just before three o'clock that afternoon, Burnside ordered his lines to move back toward a range of small hills believing that Longstreet was planning another attack. Bracing, Burnside formed his lines into the shape of a rectangle with Hartranft holding the left, where he expected Longstreet's attack to impact. Almost on cue, with a tremendous screaming yell, the Rebels charged directly for Hartranft's line.[62]

Moving constantly along his front, Hartranft told his men to remain steady and fire low. The Johnnies appeared to be oblivious to that hard fire and continued to move forward, until the Union batteries opened with a rain of grape and canister which promptly drove them back. In his report, General Ferrero wrote, "Never did troops [Hartranft's] manoeuvre so beautifully and with such precision."[63] With Longstreet's attack repulsed, Burnside led his remaining troops into Knoxville, which offered natural fortification, and, to await the certain siege that Longstreet was to begin.[64]

As the Union men began pouring into the city, they noticed that the streets were crowded with local citizens who had come in from the countryside to avoid being caught in the middle of the battle. Conversely, the main road out of Knoxville was also clogged with residents who wanted to flee the city for the same reason. Amidst all of the civilian confusion, the Confederate troops kept up a sharp taunt upon the men in blue making every attempt to dishearten them.[65]

Still, the Union men could be justifiably proud of their action that day, though they noted that their ranks had been thinned by 318 casualties.[66] Hartranft too could take pride in holding "the enemy in check until the entire [Union] army at Lenoir was up."[67] That same night, Private David Benfer, a member of the 51st Pennsylvania wrote home and told his family "to day we had a fight at Camels [sic] station, we had three men wounded in our regt. tow [sic] sergeant[s] out of my Co., we fell back during the night to knoxville [sic] and the rebels on our heels."[68]

Safely inside Knoxville, Burnside began to fortify his position and from November 17th through December 5th, General Longstreet effectively held Knoxville in a stage of siege. During that time, the Union army enjoyed relative safety because of the natural protection afforded the men and Burnside's main concern was how long the supplies would hold.

Inside the city, the 51st was positioned on the Union right, with its line crossing the principal road leading from Cumberland Gap.[69] Immediately on Hartranft's right stood a mill which was fed by a small stream and shortly after entering the city, he issued an order to impress all the "idle Negroes about the city, and put them at work on the fortification."[70] The following day, Hartranft directed his men, along with the local blacks, to begin building a dam across the stream. His intent was to flood the area, which would offer great protection to his line. When the dam was complete, it spread the water for several miles on the front and right of his line with a depth ranging from four to twelve feet.[71] So effective was this ploy that the Rebels were unable to make any sort of attack against the Pennsylvanians. Hartranft was pleased with his fortifications and mused that "forty thousand men cannot take this place."[72]

Meanwhile, Longstreet continued to probe for a soft point in the Yankee line, and as the days passed, Federal supplies began to dwindle. Nonetheless, Burnside became ever more vigilant and in the early gray morning hours of the 29th, the men of the Ninth Corps braced themselves as three brigades of Longstreet's men approached their line at Fort Sanders.

> They struck and stumbled over the wires amidst the deadly fire of our men. This obstruction was soon passed. A number fell amidst the entanglement, but the weight of the column carried it through. They came steadily on, with a courage which exhorted the admiration of their antagonist. They cut away the abattis, never faltering beneath the withering musketry fire, and the destructive projectiles of the artillery. They filled the ditch. Their way was marked by carnage and death. Would nothing stop those devoted [Southern] men? A few mounted the parapet. But they could go no further.[73]

No matter the brave dedication of the Rebel troops, the Union men inside Fort Sanders had been lifted to a greater resolve and steadfastly beat back the attacking enemy. At times, Yanks stuffed triple canister into their guns and simply blasted away the faces of the foe as they continued their superhuman but hopeless effort.[74]

One newspaper correspondent who watched the Union valor and Rebel destruction wrote, "The earth, was sated in blood-men waded in blood, and struggled up the scarp, and slipping in blood fell back to join their mangled predecessors in the gory mud below. The shouts of the foiled and infuriated Rebels, the groans of the dying and shrieks of the wounded arose above the din of the cannon."[75] Captain Henry Burrage of the 36th Massachusetts could only say that "it was Fredericksburg reversed."[76]

Finally, after severe carnage, the attack faltered and Longstreet called his men back but not before he counted losses numbering fourteen hundred including the near total annihilation of the 17th Mississippi.[77]

Burnside held Knoxville just as Grant ordered him to do. The fight for Fort Sanders was the last major event in the entire campaign, and

86

**Flag of the 51st Pennsylvania Volunteers**

Flag remnants of the 51st Pennsylvania. Note the many important battles from both theaters in the war.

*Photographer: Capitol Preservation Committee.*
*Source: Capitol Preservation Committee.*

Hartranft could be pleased with his own performance. Both he and the men of the 51st had distinguished themselves, and once again, he had proven his ability with a larger command by directing the efforts of a division. Yet, despite those laurels, he was still months away from receiving any real recognition.

In late December of 1863, Hartranft received a most gracious and unsolicited compliment upon his military career. In a letter sent to U. S. Senator Henry Wilson, Mr. Calvin Cutter, who was the surgeon for the 21st Massachusetts, strongly urged Hartranft's promotion to brigadier-general. Cutter explained to the senator that Hartranft has demonstrated himself to be cool, never agitated and blessed with good common sense and "never drunk." He continued,

> To be more particular at Antietam, Md., Col. Hartranft was the hero of the 9th A.C. leading the successful charge by which the Antietam bridge was carried.
>
> Here in Tenn., at the battle of Campbell's Station, when we were twice outflanked by the enemy, Col. Hartranft was the man who, by changing the position of his Division, relieved our peril. This was done cooly [sic], promptly, quietly and in perfect order. Thus saving the Army from confusion and disaster.
>
> At Knoxville, his management, and actions seemed to me equal, if not superior to that of any other officer. This is saying much when all did so well. I regard Col. Hartranft as equal to, if not superior, to any other man in the Army Corps - [and capable] to command a Brigade, a Division, or even The Corps.[78]

Regardless of the flattering nature of this plea, Hartranft would still not be promoted. Instead, he and the 51st would soon be headed home for a well deserved furlough. The colonel, having previously written to Sallie about his coming home, received a letter from her dated January 17th. Her joy at learning that her husband would soon be home was nearly electric, "I am so happy you are coming home. I could not sleep last night. I was so glad, you will think that I am a baby... I should think that the Norris[town] people would have a grand time when the 51st arrives in town...They have allways [sic] said that the 51st should have a grand reception... Your Sallie."[79]

ENDNOTES FOR CHAPTER FOUR
VICKSBURG TO KNOXVILLE
"ALMOST A GENERAL"

1. Parker, *History of the 51st*, p. 289.
2. Ibid., pp. 291-297.
3. Ibid., p. 298.
4. Ibid., p. 303.
5. Bearss, Edwin Cole, *The Vicksburg Campaign*, 3 vols., Dayton, Ohio: Morningside House, Inc., 1985, vol. 3, p. 1074.
6. Ibid., p. 1075.
7. JFH to SSH, June 3, 1863, Shireman Collection.
8. Bearss, *The Vicksburg Campaign*, vol. 3, p. 1079.
9. Parker, *History of the 51st*, p. 320.
10. Ibid.
11. Carter, Samuel III, *The Final Fortress: The Campaign for Vicksburg, 1862-1863*, New York: St. Martin's Press, 1980, p. 266.
12. Ibid.
13. Warner, *Generals in Gray*, p. 232.
14. Carter, *The Final Fortress: The Campaign for Vicksburg 1862-1863*, p. 265.
15. Ibid.
16. Ibid.
17. Ibid.
18. Ibid., p. 266.
19. Parker, *History of the 51st*, p. 327.
20. Ibid., p. 333.
21. Ibid.
22. Boatner, *The Civil War Dictionary*, p. 429.
23. Parker, *History of the 51st*, p. 349.
24. Ibid., p. 356.
25. JFH to J. M. Bishop, January 29, 1887, Shireman Collection.
26. Parker, *History of the 51st*, p. 349.
27. Ibid., p. 350.
28. Ibid., p. 351.
29. Ibid.
30. Ibid.
31. Ibid., p. 352.
32. Ibid., pp. 365-366.
33. Woodbury, Augustus, *Major-General Ambrose E. Burnside and the Ninth Army Corps*, Providence, Rhode Island: Sidney S. Rider & Brother, 1867, pp. 344-345.
34. *Papers of Zenas R. Bliss*, Vol. IV, Chapter I, pp. 83-84. Courtesy,

USAMHI.
35. Ibid.
36. Ibid.
37. Parker, *History of the 51st*, p. 386.
38. Ibid.
39. Ibid., p. 388.
40. Ibid., p. 390.
41. Ibid., pp. 395 & 401.
42. Woodbury, *Major-General Ambrose E. Burnside and the Ninth Army Corps*, p. 334.
43. Ibid.
44. Ibid.
45. Ibid., pp. 332-333.
46. Ibid., pp. 344-345.
47. *O. R.* I., vol. XXXI, Part III , p. 560.
48. Korn, Jerry, et al., eds., *The Fight for Chattanooga, Chickamauga to Missionary Ridge*, Alexandria, Virginia: Time Life Books, 1985, pp. 107-108. Hereafter referred to as The Fight for Chattanooga.
49. *O. R.*, I, vol XXXI, Part III, p. 560.
50. Woodbury, *Major-General Ambrose E. Burnside and the Ninth Army Corps*, p. 335.
51. JFH to J. M. Bishop, January 29, 1887, Shireman Collection.
52. *Battles & Leaders*, vol. 3, p. 733.
53. Marvel, William, *Burnside*, p. 312.
54. Korn, *The Fight for Chattanooga*, p. 108.
55. Longstreet, James, *From Manassas to Appomattox*, reprint; The Blue and Grey Press, Secaucus, New Jersey: 1984, p. 492.
56. Woodbury, *Major-General Ambrose E. Burnside and the Ninth Army Corps*, p. 335. Also note that estimates here vary from 15 minutes to about an hour before McLaws' arrival. Author's note.
57. Ibid.
58. JFH to J. M. Bishop, January 29, 1887, Shireman Collection.
59. Ibid.
60. Woodbury, *Major-General Ambrose E. Burnside and the Ninth Army Corps*, p. 335.
61. Marvel, *Burnside*, p. 314.
62. Woodbury, *Major-General Ambrose E. Burnside and the Ninth Army Corps*, pp. 336 & 337.
63. Ibid., p. 337.
64. *Battles & Leaders*, vol. 3, p. 734.
65. *The Norristown Herald & Free Press*, December 15, 1863.
66. Boatner, *The Civil War Dictionary*, p. 116.

67. Parker, *History of the 51st*, p. 435.
68. Letter from David Benfer, Courtesy, USAMHI.
69. Bean, *HMCP*, p. 209.
70. Parker, *History of the 51st*, p. 449.
71. Ibid.
72. Parker, *History of the 51st*, p. 448.
73. Woodbury, *Major-General Ambrose E. Burnside and the Ninth Army Corps*, p. 348.
74. Ibid.
75. Korn, *The Fight for Chattanooga*, p. 114.
76. Ibid., p. 115.
77. Woodbury, *Major-General Ambrose E. Burnside and the Ninth Army Corps*, p. 349.
78. Letter from Mr. Calvin Cutter to U. S. Senator Henry Wilson dated December 1863, Shireman Collection.
79. SSH to JFH January 17, 1864, Shireman Collection.

# CHAPTER FIVE

## *THE WILDERNESS TO PETERSBURG*
## *"A SPECIAL TRUST AND CONFIDENCE"*

With the arrival of New Year's Eve 1863, Hartranft and the 51st were preparing to return to the East. As colonel, Hartranft had a number of administrative duties to attend to, and one important detail was the rapidly closing deadline of the three-year tour for many of his men. Therefore, eager to have his soldiers reenlist, on that last day of the year, the government prudently made certain that the men were paid. Shortly afterwards, Hartranft appeared before the entire regiment, making a heart-felt plea to the men to reenlist. When he finished with his impassioned call, the troops were dismissed and they made their way back to their quarters in a silent, reflective mood.[1]

Also typical of the time, Hartranft tried to make some minor concessions to his men in order to further induce reenlistments. Unfortunately, those concessions, which frequently took the form of promotions, were often disrupted by Governor Curtin, who wanted his office to share in those tributes. On the 4th, an overly expectant Hartranft wrote to his father and told him that "the regiment has reenlisted almost to a man of those that were present."[2] Yet, despite the political handicaps, Hartranft was able to induce one hundred and eighty men to reenlist by January 5, 1864.[3] He also told his father that he wanted to bring his men home for a furlough and added that "the men are very anxious to march into Norristown as a Regt - they expect a 'big time'."[4]

On January 13th, news was received that the men of the 51st could go home for a thirty-day leave. What joy spread through the camp that night! Everyone had their own particular visions as their minds raced to the warm firesides of home, wives, mothers and sweethearts.

But even such good news had to be tempered by the practical responsibilities of leading a regiment. Hartranft, who wanted to go home as badly as anyone, had to first make certain that his men had ample adequate clothing.[5] The journey back to Norristown was not to be swift or simple, as the men would meet many travel delays, detours, and weather problems which would undoubtedly lead to frustrations. A full year had passed since most of the 51st had been home with their families, and, despite the many traveling difficulties they would encounter, nothing was going to stand in their way. As the men drew ever nearer to home, a number of telegrams were sent to Norristown to keep the families informed of their progress and estimated arrival time. In response, Norristown planned a grand welcome for her brave young men, and a variety of flowery statements began to appear in the hometown newspapers that were meant as welcoming messages.[6]

The Norristown area members of the 51st arrived home on February 9th, around 1:00 P.M. Crowds came out to welcome their heroes, and the young ladies waved and blushed at the sight of each and every soldier. Joy was everywhere in that small town as the beloved fathers, sons, and sweethearts began to disembark from the train. Many were the friends and family members who stood on the train platform, eagerly awaiting the emergence of their "special" soldier.

But "war is hell" and that phrase was frequently used whenever communications failed. Joyful anticipations were frequently dashed and hopes could be destroyed at a moment's notice when yesterday's news did not arrive. And so it was as the men of the 51st dis-embarked, and Parker again took notice and recorded the following situation which undoubtedly took place thousands of times across this nation.

An aged man whose silvery hair betokened threescore years and ten, had come in his carriage with a daughter, and an empty seat to take the loved one home where they could have him all to themselves. The mother remained at home to have prepared something nice to tempt a dainty appetite, but alas! seeing the 1st sergeant of his dear "Dick's" company he elbows his way through the crowd and reaches the sergeant with the inquiry, "Has Dick got out of the cars yet?", the sergeant used to seeing death around, answered in an indifferent tone. "Why Dick's dead and buried long ago, didn't you know it?" The old man's heart was crushed, his chin dropped on his bosom, and he returned to his daughter who was sitting in the carriage awaiting the father and brother's appearance, but there came no brother - he lay sleeping his last sleep afar off at Camp Nelson, Ky.[7]

Somehow, soldiers do become indifferent to such tragic moments and realize they must make the most of any given opportunity to relax lest they should be the next "Dick". The men of the 51st were home and they meant to enjoy every moment of their leave.

The townspeople gave the men a hero's welcome and were lavish in their praise to Hartranft in particular. Mr. Benjamin E. Chain, a noted

Norristown banker and county district attorney, delivered the welcoming speech and told the people gathered that "It is to you, Colonel, that the regiment owes the character it bears. Your discipline in the camp, your foresight on the march, your coolness, bravery and judgment on the battlefield, have won the confidence and love of your men, and made them heroes in the fight. They knew that you never ordered where you did not lead."[8]

Hartranft then briefly addressed the crowd whose constant chatter made it impractical to discern his every word. But the colonel made it clear that he appreciated the reception offered by the town and thanked them for their support. He then addressed the growing issue of those who wanted to make a settlement with the Confederacy [Copperheads] stating, "I would rather see the flag burned, and its ashes scattered to the winds, that it should be disgraced by a dishonorable peace."[9]

Hartranft's comments here now put a different hue on his feelings for General McClellan, who was thought to favor such a peace. After his brief speech, the colonel entered the Market House for a celebration, and afterwards hurried home to drink in the love of Sallie and their children.

On the 9th of March, after a full thirty-day leave, the 51st began to make its way back to active duty by forming at Camp Curtin in Harrisburg and then, moving to Annapolis. From the naval center, a Norristown newspaper printed a letter from an unknown member of the 51st that told the tale of attrition in such a regiment. "Of the nine hundred men then [two years prior] here, there are about three hundred and fifty left. Many have gone to their long homes, others have been discharged on account of disability. It is a sad thought, that the many who to-day are in full bloom of health, will in a short time be cut down, never to rise in life again."[10]

While at Annapolis, Hartranft was charged with discriminating against blacks. A colonel of a colored regiment complained to the New York Union League that Hartranft refused to issue tents to black soldiers because he needed them for white soldiers.[11] Little is really known of the complaint and we can only assume that it did not become a major issue.

On April 14th, exactly one year prior to the assassination of President Lincoln, the men of the 51st had a brief visit from the new Supreme Commander of the U. S. Army, Lieutenant-General Ulysses S. Grant, who was accompanied by General Burnside. Both men received a resounding welcome from the entire body at Annapolis, while almost everyone was making some effort at trying to guess their next objective. All of that was soon cleared up, for on the 21st of April, the Pennsylvanians prepared to move and by the 29th, they had marched to Warrenton Junction.[12] On the 30th, Hartranft told Sallie in a letter that, "A great many troops have been ordered to the front & it really looks as if something would be done soon - But what, time alone will tell."[13]

No one in the 51st, or the rest of the Union army, really knew or understood the changes that were taking place at the top levels of the Army of the Potomac. General George Gordon Meade, who had been put in charge just before Gettysburg, still retained that office and Grant, had decided to take to the field with the Eastern Army rather than remain in a Washington office. The quiet man from Galena was on the verge of changing the entire complexion of the war with his dedication to "fight", as Lincoln desired. Shortly after he was appointed to his new position, Grant stated that he was going to "hammer continuously against the armed forces of the enemy and his resources until by mere attrition, if by nothing else, there should be nothing left for him but an equal submission with the loyal section of our common country to the Constitution and the laws."[14] That was Grant's plainly articulated objective.

It was just too early to appreciate that fighting would now be, whenever possible, the ongoing directive so Lee's army and the entire concept of a Confederate nation would be destroyed.

On May 1, General Burnside wrote to Secretary of War Edwin Stanton to follow up on an earlier request to have Hartranft promoted to brigadier-general. He informed the Secretary that "I would like to have it carried through to-morrow."[15] At the same time, Hartranft was given command of the First Brigade of the Third Division, commanded by Brigadier-General Orlando B. Willcox, Ninth Corps which included the 2nd, 8th, 17th, and 27th [including the 1rst and 2nd Companies of Michigan Sharpshooters attached] Michigan regiments plus the 109th New York and, of course, the 51st Pennsylvania.[16]

## THE WILDERNESS

On the 5th, the men of the 51st were rudely aroused from a sound sleep at 4:00 A.M. and told to eat a hasty breakfast and by 11:00 that morning, they had arrived at Germanna Ford on the Rapidan River where they would spend the day on picket duty.[17] The battle of the Wilderness had already begun between Grant and his 118,000 men and Lee with 61,000 men.[18] There, in that maze of thick underbrush and twisted growth which made cannon virtually useless, the determined Grant was to meet the redoubtable Lee. On the morning of the 6th, the First Brigade was shifted to the front and by 8:00 A.M. the battle was at full pitch. The initial clash fell heaviest upon Willcox's troops, including Hartranft's brigade and until 7:00 P.M. Hartranft and his men fought in that dense thicket among the screams of the wounded and dying.[19] The men of the First Brigade also had to contend with the shrieks coming from those wounded men who couldn't move and were burned to death as the thick underbrush caught fire from the heavy fighting.

About noon, Parker reported that the Rebel fire upon their position slowed, which made it possible for Hartranft to order an advance by his men. Leading the entire First Brigade, Hartranft ordered the 2nd Michigan to be held in reserve while the 17th Michigan was to protect his flank. Then "Old Johnny" led the balance of the blue line forward, "Carrying the enemy's works and held them, but only for a few moments. A panic seized the left, which brought the whole line back in confusion."[20] The entire day was spent in this see-saw type action, while both sides attempted to destroy each other with walls of lead. When Hartranft was again ordered against the Rebel line he quickly saw the futility and certain waste of life that would result, and immediately sent word to Burnside that, "this advance is against my judgment."[21] Trusting to Hartranft's on the spot analysis, Burnside promptly countermanded his order.

At the end of the day, the 51st counted its ranks and found that at least 25 had been killed while another 50 were wounded and 15 were missing.[22] The entire Union army had almost 18,000 casualties with over 2,200 killed while the Confederates suffered about 8,000 casualties.[23] Among those who were severely wounded was CSA General James Longstreet, who took a bullet through his throat when he was accidentally shot by his own men.[24] It was Longstreet and his First Corps that Hartranft and the First Brigade confronted during that day which proved costly as "Old Johnnies" total casualty count was 407.[25]

On the 7th, Hartranft and his First Brigade were again placed on the front line and they could clearly hear the Confederate fire which was being directed at Major-General John Sedgwick's Sixth Corps. Spared the horrors of another battle that day, the brigade was ordered out at 1:30 A.M. on the 8th and headed for Chancellorsville. Arriving there about 4:00 P.M. Hartranft and his men joined General Burnside, and early in the morning of the 9th, he and his men were directed toward the Fredericksburg Plank Road where they engaged the Rebels for "several hours." Despite Meade's declaration that the 9th should be a day of rest, Confederate sharpshooters constantly harassed the Union men.[26]

At one point along the line, General John General Sedgwick was positioning cannon when snipers kept annoying his men, and kept his Union soldiers scurrying. "Uncle John", as he was affectionately known, laughed at his men and yelled to them, "I am ashamed of you! They couldn't hit an elephant at that distance." Moments later, the beloved Connecticut general lay dead with a sniper's bullet in his head.[27]

For the next few days, the First Brigade, along with many other units, were kept constantly engaged on skirmishes with the Rebels. The entire Union army now realized that Grant had no intention of returning across the river to regroup and rest as was normal in the past. Instead, he intended to fight Robert E. Lee at every given moment. Even though Grant's new policy resulted in heavy casualties, the men in blue literally cheered as they pushed southward, instead of north. On the 11th, General Grant sent a wire to General Halleck in Washington wherein he proposed "to fight it out on this line if it takes all summer."

## SPOTSYLVANIA

On May 12th, the regiment was awakened at 2:00 A.M. and moved out an hour later.[28] By 4:30 it could hear the guns being fired between CSA General Richard S. Ewell's Corps and those from the Second Corps of General Winfield Scott Hancock. At that hour, Hancock had amassed about 20,000 troops in front of the "Mule Shoe", and began an attack upon the Confederates. The fighting on Hancock's front became extremely hot and about 2:00 P.M., the entire Third Division was ordered to Hancock's assistance. Hartranft's First, along with Colonel Humphrey's Second Brigade led the way toward the Mule Shoe.[29]

As the two brigades moved forward, they had to first pass through a small woods in their front. As they were doing so, Brigadier-General James H. Lane and his North Carolina brigade were also moving out of the woods to Hartranft's left and across a small clearing that lay between two stands of trees. As Lane's men continued their march they entered the same woods containing Hartranft and Humphrey when suddenly, Lane's men clashed with Hartranft's left.[30] The sudden appearance of Lane's men startled the Union right, and the Rebels quickly advanced and overran the men of the 17th Michigan and took many prisoners and one flag. The North Carolina boys continued their pursuit and next encountered the 51st Pennsylvania. After a bloody fight with Hartranft's old regiment, Lane took two battle flags from the 51st and captured Captain Allebaugh, the first man over the Antietam bridge. Lane and his brigade then encountered the 50th Pennsylvania which they began to capture through tough hand-to-hand combat.[31]

During the fight, Hartranft struggled to keep his brigade under control though Lane's attack was both frightening and confusing to his ranks. One Union soldier even reported being captured twice before getting out of the woods, while a Confederate reported that "everyone was trying to fight his way back to our works."[32] Finally, Lane saw more Yankees headed his way, and decided to pull his forces back, which marked the end of the fighting that day for Hartranft. But, the cost to the First Brigade was 687 casualties though Hartranft initially thought it was much higher.[33]

For Hartranft's command, the next few days were spent in tedious suspense as they lay upon their weapons in a driving rain waiting for the next Rebel attack. On the 15th, while digging traverses in their rifle pits and feeling dejected over the high cost to their ranks and the loss of their colors, the men were heartened to learn that Hartranft was finally going to be recognized for his skill and bravery by his promotion to brigadier-general. The entire brigade, and the 51st in particular, cheered for "Black John", another sobriquet owing to the color of his hair and mustache, whom they loved and respected. When such an appointment was made, the individual was notified and required to indicate his acceptance in writing. The following is Hartranft's youthful response to his notification:


General:

I have the honor to accept the appointment of Brigadier-General of Volunteers in the service of the United States to rank as such from the twelfth day of May 1864.

My full name is John Frederick Hartranft: age 33 years: Residence-Norristown, Montgomery County, Pennsylvania. Accompanying this you will please find my oath of office.

I am General<br>
Your most Obd't Servt<br>
J. F. Hartranft<br>
Brig. Genl Vols.[34]

Coming when it did, his new star did not bring expanded responsibilities since he was already in practical command of the First Brigade. As a new brigadier, his command remained part of the Third Division, which was led by Brigadier-General Orlando B. Willcox. On June 10, his brigade was expanded to include the 38th Wisconsin as well.[35]

In the May 14th citation announcing Hartranft's promotion, it is stated that, "reposing special trust and confidence in the patriotism, valor, fidelity and abilities of J. F. Hartranft, I have nominated, and...do appoint him Brigadier-General of Volunteers." Signed, Edwin M. Stanton, Secretary of War and, Abraham Lincoln.[36]

Some who have written brief biographies on Hartranft tend to exaggerate his activities at Spotsylvania. While we must be careful not to minimize his valor at that fight, he himself was not fully satisfied with his performance. Certainly, he was grateful for the brigadier's star, but objectively he felt his actions at Antietam or Campbell's Station were far more deserving of a star than Spotsylvania.[37] This author agrees.

Nonetheless, on May 30th, the First took up camp in a small, quiet area known as Cold Harbor; only eight miles from Richmond. There, Lee's army of about 59,000 men was to be tested again by Grant's army of 108,000 men. However, Lee had the fortified ground and rightly felt he could defend his position well. Grant had planned a frontal attack which was initially scheduled for June 2nd, but pouring rain and troop movements postponed the assault by one fateful day.[38]

Very early on the morning of the 3rd, Hartranft received orders to move his brigade to the left of its front; Lieutenant-Colonel Schall leading the 51st was first in line.[39] At 5:00 A.M. orders were given that the entire Third Division would make an attack, and the soldiers were ordered to "fix bayonets." Immediately following that order, three lines of blue began to move forward which broke into the double-quick. Meanwhile, the Rebels waited patiently until the Yanks were in sure distance, and with deliberate aim they let loose a devastating wall of lead that made the entire Yankee line waver. Taken completely by surprise, the men in blue were dazed by that Confederate volley which instantly killed Colonel Schall who was soon followed by Lieutenant Isaac Fizone of Company E.[40] According to Major William J. Bolton, who was next to Colonel Schall when he was hit, and afterwards, took command of the regiment, "the two first lines soon gave way, but not so with the third."[41]

The Third Division continued to move forward and got within two hundred yards of the Confederate main line. Meanwhile, the Yanks had virtually no cover and had to make do despite the constant enfilading fire from the Rebel infantry. The men of the Third Division fell to the ground and quickly made modest earthen works in their front "by using their bayonets, tin cups, plates etc."[42] Later in the day another Union attack was considered but at the last moment it was canceled. The First remained in position until well after dark when it was safely relieved.[43]

The cost at Cold Harbor was devastating for the entire Yankee army, and while estimates vary, approximately 8,000 Union soldiers became casualties in about twenty minutes. In his memoirs, Grant wrote that, "I have always regretted that the last assault at Cold Harbor was ever made...no advantage whatever was gained to compensate for the heavy loss we sustained."[44] Perhaps one of the more disturbing points related to this battle was Grant's delay in requesting a truce to gather the dead and wounded when the fight closed that fateful day. Instead of an immediate appeal, the Union commander waited for three days before making such a request for a truce and by that time, many of the wounded had died needlessly.[45] The cost to the Third Brigade was 259 casualties while the 51st alone lost 59 men and officers.[46]

Hartranft wrote home and informed Sallie that, "We have to mourn the loss of Lt. Col. Schall. He was struck while the brigade was advancing & I think bled to death immediately."[47] In the same letter, Hartranft vented some of his own frustrations as he told Sallie,

> Let the North prepare for a desperate conflict. Lee is concentrating every available man, and if the people at home wish Grant to be successful they must continue to reinforce him. Now is the time to drive the rebel army southward, while we have the men in the north to help us, and now is the time for them to come, *the next year may be too late.*[48] [Emphasis added]

### BATTLE OF PETERSBURG

The Union army lost a major opportunity to take Petersburg when it failed to press an early attack against Confederate General P. G. T. Beauregard, who only had about 14,000 men.[49] Still, on June 17th, Hancock and his Second Corps mounted an afternoon assault against Beauregard which was assisted by Burnside and his Ninth Corps. At 2:00 P.M. Burnside gave the command to begin, and General Hartranft was to lead the attack with his First Brigade. However, because of poor communications and observations within the Union army, Hartranft and his entire brigade were sorely repulsed, which resulted in about 800 casualties.[50] According to one historian, "In an error all too typical of the Federal high command that day, Hartranft's men were sent forward at a right angle to the Confederate works, which made them desperately vulnerable." Hartranft's division commander, Brigadier-General Orlando Willcox, reported later that the brigade "melted out of sight" beneath the horrendous fire.[51] During this attack, Hartranft received his only minor wound of the war, when a minie ball slightly grazed his wrist. Shortly thereafter, he had another close call when a ball ripped through his clothing and passed along his chest though no harm came to him.[52] Later that same afternoon, the Third Division was again ordered to attack, and this time had better luck as it took a stand of colors from the 35th North Carolina plus 100 prisoners.[53]

While Hartranft was leading his first attack, which led to the high casualty count, Brigadier-General James H. Ledlie, who had just recently joined the Army of the Potomac, also led his First Division, Ninth Corps, against the Rebels and met the same fate as Hartranft. Captain Charles J. Mills of Ledlie's staff commented that, "...the deep sense of mismanagement and waste of life were almost enough to drive us to despair." Sadly, Ledlie was drunk![54] In another month, Ledlie would again show his capacity for alcohol at the explosion of the Crater when he again failed to direct his troops properly owing to his drinking.

On the 18th, Hartranft and his First Brigade were again on the line of battle from daybreak until darkness when one of his command noted that,

> We were again drawn up in line of battle at daylight ...we charged at a point on the Suffolk and Petersburg Railroad driving the enemy before us. ...Major Morton ...was shot through the heart and fell dead. We charged in good order and took the railroad cut... was about fifteen to twenty feet deep and the sides almost perpendicular. Steps and holes had to be made in the same so as to enable the troops to climb up on the bank, which was commanded by the enemy...Many, however, were killed and wounded here. Between 5 and 6 P.M., the whole division was out of the cut and in the ravine in advance. The troops were again moved forward to attack...our line became exposed to the full view of the enemy, whose fire was too severe to attempt any further advance. Our position, however, held and entrenched during the night...our entrenching tools were tin cups, plates and spoons.
>
> The 2d brigade of our division lost its commander three times on the field all having been shot down at their post.[55]

Since joining Grant's new campaign and crossing the Rapidan River on May 5, the 51st Pennsylvania had a total casualty list of 375 men. That high rate was the result of General Willcox's confidence and frequent calling upon the new brigadier knowing that he could accomplish matters where others would fail.[56] In turn, Hartranft was always eager to call upon the 51st, and later the entire First Brigade, and neither ever let him down.

In the early part of July, Lee sent Lieutenant-General Jubal Early on a raid to the North, which brought him to the very gates of Washington

101

and resulted in the burning of Chambersburg, Pennsylvania. Part of Lee's hope here was that Grant would deplete his ranks by sending a large force after Early to avoid panic in the Yankee Capitol. With that ill-placed belief, the Confederates launched an all-out attack on July 8th against the Union lines, which resulted in heavy losses. During the beginning of that attack, Hartranft was in his tent preparing a report. It had only been the last day or two when he actually received his new stars and as he sat writing, a minie ball entered his tent and promptly, but gently, removed one of those stars from a shoulder. Parker wrote that, "The General thought that [was] an informal way of reducing his rank, and kept on writing as if nothing had happened, or there was no further danger."[57] Later, despite his close encounter, Hartranft wrote to Sallie and told her that he still had, "...full faith in the final success of the Union army under Grant...."[58]

By mid-July, the Union army settled into a siege which would wind up lasting almost ten months. The spade became the mistress for the men as they dug long trenches and began to construct bomb-proofs. Since Grant began this campaign back in May, his army had suffered somewhere between 60-70,000 casualties, and Lincoln's political enemies were profiting from that.[59] In addition, the beleaguered president had sharp difficulties at home too since Mrs. Lincoln thought General Grant a "butcher" for such high casualties. Steadfastly though, Lincoln never wavered upon his dedication to Grant.

The new lifestyle of trench warfare for the soldiers was not easy. One writer noted,

> In this vast maze of trenches, forts, redoubts and tunnels the soldiers of both sides lived, suffered, and died. Constant skirmishing and sharpshooting took its toll, constant shelling back and forth was just another of the nerve-wracking hardships the men had to endure, along with scorching heat and choking dust, then mud and constant wetness, followed by freezing cold and utter loneliness. But in the mud and general filth of the trenches, disease was the greatest killer of all, and one of the most depressing things that had to be endured was complete boredom.[60]

## THE BATTLE OF THE CRATER

The battle of the Crater is one point in Hartranft's history that has received little attention. Clearly, Hartranft was one of the few commanding officers who had the courage to attack soon after the explosion and to live in the center of the entire attack. Fighting for his own life along with those in his charge, Hartranft could also see that the Union army was, for the most part, simply observing the carnage and horror to which he and his men were exposed. While other mini-biographers tend to place heavier emphasis on actions such as the Wilderness and Spotsylvania for Hartranft, this author feels confident that the Crater, despite its being a dismal failure for the North, represents one of Hartranft's most audacious military moments.

Out of boredom came the idea that a mine could be built under a Rebel fort located on Elliot's Salient, which lay directly in front of Hartranft's First Brigade.[61] The men of the 48th Pennsylvania proposed their plan to their commander, Lieutenant-Colonel Henry Pleasants, after he had been overheard as saying, "That God-damned fort is the only thing between us and Petersburg, and I have an idea that we can blow it up."[62]

Work on the mine started on June 25 and the men of the First Brigade did their part by keeping the Rebels from learning of its presence and keeping matters quiet in their own lines. Day after day the men of the 48th, which was comprised of many miners, worked diligently and under duress, as they received little encouragement or assistance from Generals Grant and Meade.

When the mine was complete, it measured 585 feet in length, and the men stacked the end chambers with eight thousand pounds of black powder. General Burnside drew up his plans so that when the explosion took place, he would be able to take full advantage of the confusion that was certain to result. A forceful, quick attack would be the key to destroying the Confederate line.

Just before the explosion, Hartranft's wife had personally viewed the growing erosion of Union war support at home. Sallie had witnessed men who refused to fight which bothered her greatly since she felt that if her husband could do his part, they [especially the many who were not married] could do theirs. She wrote and emptied her frustration upon her husband, who responded, "I see you are very much annoyed by the lack of Patriotism at home - It will do you no good to trouble yourself about it - I think it will all be right yet-wether [sic] Norristown send another man or not."[63]  In reality, by this time, eroding war support was plaguing both armies.

Meanwhile, part of Burnside's initial plan was to have the black regiments of the Fourth Division, led by Brigadier-General Edward Ferrero, make the initial attack after the explosion.[64]  When Burnside made that known to General Meade, the army commander rejected that idea because he feared that if something went wrong, it would prove to be both a political and social disaster. Burnside argued that his black troops were eager to fight and had been practicing for the attack. He further added that he feared the experienced white soldiers were more apt to "dig in" and lose the forward momentum.[65] Of course, Meade won out with Grant's support, who had little real enthusiasm for this type of project after his bad experience with a similar plan during the siege of Vicksburg.

Burnside revised his plan accordingly and Grant sent General Hancock and the Second Corps on a diversionary move, and promised that 100 guns and 54 mortars would support the attacking infantry. In addition, General Meade reminded all corps commanders that, "promptitude, rapidity of execution, and cordial cooperation, are essential to success."[66] The man selected to lead the charge was General Ledlie of the First Division who, like Hartranft, had also been educated at Union College as an engineer.[67] However, that's where their similarities ended.

During the very early morning hours of July 30th, the Union troops began to take their positions. At 3:15 A.M., Lieutenant-Colonel Pleasants lit the fuse and everyone simply held their breath waiting for the spectacular show that was certain to follow. Nothing! At 4:15 A.M., Pleasants allowed two volunteers, Sergeant Henry Rees and Lieutenant Jacob Douty, to enter the shaft and repair the obviously faulty fuse.[68] The two men executed their work with precision and came back to safety. Then, breaking the still, early morning air with a tremendous thunder, at 4:45 A.M. the mine exploded, "...carrying with it men, guns, carriages, and limbers, and spread out like an immense cloud as it reached its altitude...the mass appeared as if it would descend immediately upon the troops [Union] waiting to make the charge...and about ten minutes were consumed in re-forming for the attack."[69] Another eyewitness noted that, "Headless trunks, arms, legs and all parts of the human frame were then mingled with the pieces of broken gun-carriages, guns, blankets, etc.."[70] The explosion created a "crater" approximately 30 feet deep, 80 feet wide, and about 170 feet long and killed or wounded about 270 Rebels.[71] In those early moments following the blast, confusion understandably reigned in the Southern ranks while for the North, the troops of Colonel Elisha G. Marshall's,

> ... heavy artillerymen led the assault with a cheer that a V Corps captain claimed he could hear over the barrage from two miles away. They spilled out of the works in queues, sprinting individually for the demolished fort without stopping to deploy in columns. What infantry obstacles lay in the way disintegrated in a twinkling, and the rapidly deteriorating organization of the second brigade were in the Crater before Five o'clock. In the van was the 14th New York Heavy Artillery; these men repeatedly faltered when

they saw the carnage in the Crater, and the regiment nearly dissolved into a score of rescue parties, digging out their trapped enemies. Lieutenant-Colonel Benjamin Barney's 2nd Pennsylvania Provisional Heavy Artillery swept past the New Yorkers and over the far lip of the Crater, which stretched 125 feet up and down the old Confederate works. The Pennsylvanians clammered up the soft sides of the chasm - it was about 25 feet deep - and took position behind the ruins of the fort. There they remained, digging in just as Burnside had feared, while the crowd in the Crater behind them swelled to unmanageable proportions. William Bartlett's brigade followed Marshall's into the pit, the peglegged General Bartlett stumbling along beside the middle of the column.[72]

Following the blast, Hartranft and most of the First Brigade were formed in the rear of Ledlie's division which faltered when it moved forward. At approximately 5:00 A.M., Hartranft led his men directly toward the Crater though confusion in and out of the Crater was very obvious. Willcox initially wanted Hartranft to take the ground in his front known as Cemetery Hill. Calling upon his men, Hartranft made an attempt but the fire delivered by the rapidly regrouping Confederates made matters impossible.

As the Rebel fire began to intensify, Hartranft was able to bring up one field gun and began to play havoc upon the enemy's line. However, his rifle ammunition was running low and fortunately, the moment was saved when reserve men of the 51st made brave runs of almost two hundred yards to bring "Black John" his precious rounds.[73]

Hartranft then led most of his troops to the left of the crater while others went inside, which was fast becoming clogged with Yankees. Those of his ranks were positioned to the far left inside the crater and when Hartranft personally entered the Crater he saw that two Rebel field pieces were partially buried by the explosion. Immediately, he had them dug out and made ready for some gruesome work. Soon, those two pieces were working havoc upon the Rebel lines, thanks to the heroic efforts of Sergeant Wesley Stanley of the 14th New York Heavy Artillery. Hartranft kept watching the well-oiled motion of the Stanley who had to give a crash course on how to fire the guns, to some of "Old Johnnies" men.[74] Finally, unable to contain his enthusiasm for Stanley any longer, Hartranft called out for three cheers for the Empire State men.[75]

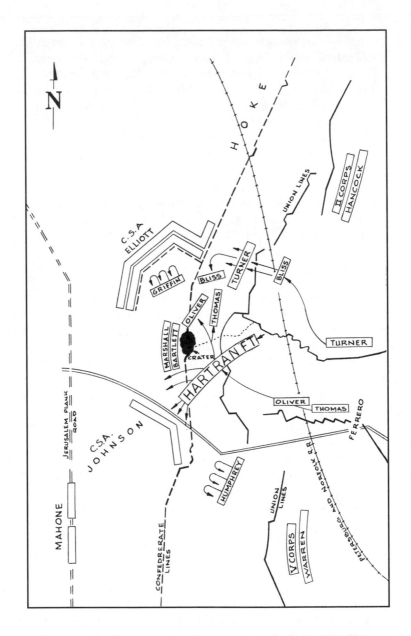

**Hartranft's Attack at the Crater Shortly After the Explosion**

This drawing shows the approach taken by Hartranft and his troops following the explosion at the Crater. The drawing is based upon that which appeared in the book *The Crater* by Richard Slotkin, and has been redrawn by A. J. Saraceni for specific clarity.

It didn't take long before black troops from the Fourth Division entered the Crater where they quickly found themselves under fierce fire as well. About 9:15 A.M., the first Rebel counterattack was ordered by Brigadier-General William Mahone. As the morning wore on, Mahone was able to bring more troops into the area of the Crater and eventually, he would attack on three sides of the pit. His ranks brought up two coehorn mortars which they fired into the pit. He also posted sharpshooters to keep up a deadly fire into the pit. As if to amuse themselves, some of the Rebel infantry picked up discarded rifles with bayonets and sent them javelin-like into the hole creating greater terror.[76] The great Union surprise for the Rebels had turned into their own veritable hell-hole.

Finally, around 12:30 P.M., word was received that the Union men should pull back. As Hartranft waited for a propitious moment to begin the rearward movement, he and his men were again attacked by Rebels and oddly enough, that fight gave some of his men the opportunity to retire while others were sorely treated in the melee.[77]

In the collection of papers that Hartranft left, there exists a portion of an undated, anonymous letter which speaks of the difficulties and horrors in the Crater. The letter makes it clear that the writer was a captain, and it appears as if he is writing the letter to Hartranft's son, perhaps Linn. Certainly, the note is written well after the close of the war, because the writer refers to the "late General Meade", who died on November 6, 1872.[78] The soldier states that, "...my last service with your father [General Hartranft] was July 30th, 1864 on which day I was wounded in the crater before Petersburg, perhaps 4 feet [close?] of the [general?], by the explosion of a 14 inch mortar shell." The author then includes a small crude drawing of the crater as well. He related the death of a Colonel Sarget, who might have been part of the 20th Michigan Volunteers, and who was also physically very close to General Hartranft at the time.

Our unknown author stated that, "Colonel Sargent ...I believe who was killed by the same piece of shell by which I was wounded. The flesh and blood spattered all over General Hartranft. I have been told that he [Sargent] was a brother-in-law of the late General Meade. His heart, and limbs and arms were severed and his body was torn into fragments. The last words of General Hartranft to me were 'Don't try to go to the rear for you will never reach our lines'."[79]

The author of that letter tried and did make it to safety. However, he attributed that safe passage to a bundle of letters and papers about one inch thick which were stuck in his shirt and apparently stopped a minie ball which would have meant certain death otherwise.

This anonymous letter agrees with Hartranft's own written comments on the turmoil that existed inside the Crater. Burnside had ordered his men to pull back since he and other officers of the Ninth Corps in the rear were absolutely stunned by the growing disaster and the inability of his men to retire. Realizing that precious little could be done militarily to assist Hartranft and the others, and perhaps out of sheer frustration, he ordered that a trench be dug for their escape. The specifications for that trench were 8 feet deep and 4 feet wide and approximately 400 feet long which would have taken days to complete.[80]

Hartranft had found himself virtually "stuck" inside the confines of the Crater, and while he was attempting to direct his brigade, two of his orderlies were killed right next to him. Later that morning, Colonel Bolton was hit by a minie ball in the cheek which traveled beneath his shoulder blade, where it remained for many years, undetected. Oddly enough, long after the war, Bolton was beset by a strong coughing spell and in the process, up came the bullet. With Bolton down, command of the 51st fell to Major Lane S. Hart. That day also saw the death of Lieutenant Allen H. Filman of the 51st, who had just received his new commission.[81]

Among the screams, curses, and groans of the wounded and dying, Hartranft initially saw little chance to extricate his men much before darkness. After he and General Simon G. Griffin quickly spoke about their predicament, he felt that one remote possibility was to have Union artillery rain down upon the Rebels and create a diversion for the trapped men. As a result, around 12:45 P.M., Hartranft hastily sent the following note to the rear, with the concurrence of Generals Griffin and Bartlett,

I think the best way to withdraw is by making [an] attack from our pits & batteries bearing on our right & left - the men here are a rabble - and then let them withdraw immediately whenever you approve the plan. They are suffering very much for water, & the troops cannot well be organized.

J. F. Hartranft[82]

General Burnside noted of Hartranft's message, "In testimony to the brutal work of the mortars the Confederates trained upon the Crater, one face of the order is flecked with a black glob that appears to be dried blood."[83] About 2:30 P.M., with the aid of the artillery, Hartranft was able to lead the men out of that "horrid pit".

Unfortunately for Bartlett, who had a cork leg, he was taken prisoner and sent to Libby Prison though others were not so fortunate.[84]

The cost to the Union Army was high, with an estimated 3,798 killed, wounded or missing. Of that total, 3,475, or 91% came from the Ninth Corps, a testimony to the inactivity of the rest of the Union Army. While the losses to Lee's army are difficult to know with certainty, they are estimated to be only about 1,400.[85]

Almost immediately following the Crater fiasco, the finger pointing began, and between Meade and Burnside in particular, matters were not agreeable. Ledlie was severely criticized by Meade, while others accused him of being drunk in his tent.[86]

The battle of the Crater was over. Grant's lack of enthusiasm proved to be well founded, and a potentially great Union victory had been sorely lost through ineptitude. However, the ineptitude rested with the senior officers and not with the "middle management" like Griffin, Bartlett, and Hartranft. Surely, if the man from Norristown had not won his brigadier's star for his efforts at Spotsylvania, he should have certainly received it for his monumental efforts at the Crater. Almost typical of Hartranft's career, while "stuck" inside the Crater he was not officially in charge, and yet he took it upon himself to make decisions for the welfare of all around him.

In his official report dated August 5, 1864, Hartranft recounted the terrible ordeal he and his men had endured. He paid particular tribute to Sergeant Stanley and his work with the fieldpieces, and stated that, "Stanley almost annihilated the [Rebel] attacking column." Later in that report, he had to sadly inform the high command that, "It is with deep regret that I announce the death of Sergt Stanley ... who volunteered to work the captured guns, and did his duty to the last." Finally, he reported that his "loss in Regimental commanders was severe" and closed by offering his special gratitude to a number of officers, including Colonel Bolton of the 51st Pennsylvania.[87]

Typical of military matters, whenever something goes wrong an investigation is ordered, and that is exactly what took place about the Crater. General Meade, amidst some controversy, appointed a court of inquiry which included Major-General Winfield Scott Hancock, Nelson Miles, Romeyn B. Ayres, and Colonel Edward Schriver of his own staff as judge-advocate.[88] In the process of the investigation, many were called including General Hartranft who, when asked if he regarded the attack as a failure, replied, "I did." The Judge-Advocate continued:

Q. "What, in your opinion, were some of the causes of that failure?"
A. "The massing of the troops in the crater where they could not be used with any effect. I think the troops, instead of being sent to the crater, should have been sent to the right and left, so as to have moved in line of

battle, then they could have advanced in some kind of shape; but after they came into the crater in the confusion they were, other troops being brought up only increased the confusion, and by that time the enfilading fire of the enemy's artillery and infantry had become very annoying, which also made it very difficult to rally and form the troops."

Q. "Do you know any reasons why the troops did not go to the right and left of the crater? Were there any physical obstacles to prevent them?"

A. "No; I think troops could have been sent there..."

Q. "If the troops that first went into the crater had not delayed there, could they not, considering the consternation that the explosion of the mine made in an enemy's camp, have got forward to the crest of Cemetery Hill?"

A. "I think they could have moved up to the crest ... I think they would have had to reinforce them speedily in order to hold that hill."

Q. "The re-inforcements were there, were they not?"

A. "Yes, sir."

Q. "And there was nothing to prevent that result?"

A. "No, sir."

Q. "Did you remain [in the Crater] till the troops retired?"

A. "Yes, sir."

Q. "Did they retire in confusion?"

A. "Yes, sir."

Q. "Driven out?"

A. "They were driven out at the same time that I had passed the word to retire. ...General Griffin and myself were together at that time. The order to retire we had endorsed to the effect that we thought we could not withdraw the troops that were there on account of the enfilading fire over the ground ...While we were waiting for the approval of that endorsement and the opening of the fire this assaulting column of the enemy came up, and we concluded - General Griffin and myself - that there was no use in holding it any longer, so we retired."

Q. "What was the fault owing to - owing to the orders that were given, or to the execution of those orders? Was it that the plan was bad, or that the troops or their commanders behaved badly?"

A. "Not being familiar with all the orders and arrangements I could not say. So far as my own command was concerned we did all we could do..."

Q. "How did those color troops behave?"

A. "They passed to the front just as well as any troops, but they were certainly not in very good condition to resist an attack, because in passing through the crater they got confused; their regimental and company organization was completely gone."

110

Q. What general officers where in or about the crater on the enemy's line during all this time?"

A. General Griffin, General Bartlett, and myself, of the Ninth Corps; and general commanding the division of the Tenth Corps that was there [Brigadier-General John W. Turner]. I did not see any others, although there might have been others there."[89]

During the seventeen days of hearings, the tribunal heard much damaging information about the failings of Generals Ledlie and Ferrero. Allegations of intoxication, coupled with their being in a bomb-proof during the attack, would prove to be damaging, but not fatal to their careers.[90] More importantly, the findings proved most destructive to General Burnside, who was found guilty of failing, "to obey the orders of the commanding general."[91]

The court was also unhappy with General Willcox, and felt that he did not do enough to, "cause his troops to go forward to that point [Cemetery Hill]." The court conveniently went on to state that they felt that, "explicit orders should have been given assigning one officer to the command of all the troops intended to engage in the assault when the commanding general was not present in person to witness the operations."[92] Perhaps the greater reality is that the court sought a scape goat for the disaster, and in the end behaved more like a political body rather than a military tribunal. The court really never gave Willcox the proper credit for directing Hartranft's initial efforts towards Cemetery Hill or that the harsh fire from the Confederates was simply too hot to tolerate, and he was simply forced back or risk annihilation.

The tribunal signaled the end of Burnside's military career, while never addressing the deep tensions between he and General Meade. As for General Ledlie, "he was sent on a 20-day sick leave which was extended for four months. Returning on December 8, he was sent home the next day to await orders which never came."[93] As for Ferrero, despite a harsh view from the court, he retained his commission and was even brevetted to major-general in December of 1864. When the war was over, he returned to his teaching of dancing.[94]

On August 1, 1864, Major-General John Grubb Parke was placed in charge of the Ninth Corps to replace General Burnside, who decided to take a leave after the trial but prior to their ultimate findings. Fully expecting to return to his command when his leave was completed, Burnside wired Grant accordingly and asked where he should await orders. Grant responded that he, "ought not return to his Corps just then."[95]

Hartranft found himself sickened by the entire proceeding and felt that the disaster at the Crater was caused by pettiness of the Union hierarchy rather than the military prowess of the Rebels. On August 1st he wrote home to Sallie:

> We lost the best opportunity of a Grand Victory on the 30th I have ever seen ... The Army of the Potomac stood on the hills and cooly [sic] looked upon the struggle, but not a man would they send to reinforce or secure a victory. I was in the crater when the color [sic] troops were repulsed by the enemy. All the ground then gained was lost besides many prisoners of white troops as well as blacks - my troops were then in part of the fort not blown up, where I used two brass guns against the enemy as they continued to advance, with the guns and infantry we killed and wounded nearly their entire force coming against us [about 500] we soon afterwards received the order to retire from this part of the rebel line to our original line - But before we were ready to do so they again attacked us and I gave the order to retire - But I know that we could have repulsed them again, if we had not been ordered to retire - I had two of my orderlies killed by my side in the crater - a morter [sic] shell exploded within six feet of me but not a scratch did I receive - I did not expose myself unnecessarily but I think I did my duty to the best of my understanding ...I am thankful to HIM who orders our destinies that I am safe....[96]

On a lighter note, on August 18th, Hartranft wrote Sallie and told her that he would send his father a clay pipe made from the soil taken out of the Crater and to her, he would send the bullet which had removed one of his new brigadier stars while he was writing reports.[97]

## WELDON STATION - GLOBE TAVERN

Following the Crater fiasco, Hartranft and his First Brigade had at least a week to regroup and rest. That relaxed posture came to an end on August 8th, when they were ordered to Yellow Tavern on the Weldon Railroad, which was absolutely vital for Lee since it represented the last source of supplies from the South. Its capture would represent a grand prize for the Union, while for the South it was to be held at "all hazards."

On the 19th, near Yellow Tavern, as Hartranft's brigade was drawing three days of rations, they were suddenly attacked by a Confederate force. The Union men dropped everything they were doing and promptly put up a stiff resistance. Hartranft threw himself into the conflict and while directing his men, a ball passed behind his knee, through his horse, and again behind his other knee. Moments later his horse lay dead but, miraculously, the General was not injured.[98]

Losing no time, Hartranft ordered his men into position in an open field just to the right of Yellow Tavern. Earlier, the woods around the field were filled with Rebels and heavy guns but they had been forced back. Even so, the boys in butternut could still command the area with their big guns, and during one blast of grape, Major Hart, latest commander of the 51st, was seriously wounded. To replace Hart, Hartranft immediately appointed Captain Joseph Bolton, brother of Colonel William J. Bolton.[99]

As the day drew to an end, Hartranft was ordered to the assistance of General Ayres, who was allegedly, still under attack. But Hartranft was puzzled by the order because he had just left Ayres and had not seen any evidence of trouble. Instead, he paused and listened carefully for the most intense fire and, despite his orders, cried out, "I will move in the direction of the fire." Going with his best judgment, Hartranft led his men instead to the aid of Brigadier-General Samuel Crawford, who was taking a stiff pounding from the Rebel General, "Little Billy" Mahone. Fortunately for Crawford, the arrival of Hartranft and his First Brigade stabilized his eroding situation.[100]

After the fight on the 19th, Hartranft wrote Sallie and told her that, "...the enemy attacked the 5th Corps - our division was in reserve - the attack was made at 4'O clock ... I moved forward at once in [the] direction of the attack & met the enemy in less than 20 minutes & checked them again,..."

"This morning at 9:15 the enemy attacked us again - made 4 separate & determined attacks & was repulsed with heavy slaughter. ...on the 19th I had my horse killed with a musket ball ... I have the bullet." ...Your Jackie.[101]

When the fighting for the Weldon Railroad ended, Hartranft and his brigade were forced to stay in the area for a while. On September 8th, he again wrote to Sallie and the notation at the top of his letter, "On Weldon RR before Petersburg":

I never have been as busy as I am at present since I am in the army.

I am at present holding 1 1/4 miles in front of Petersburg with 2/3 of my command ...the other 1/3 is

113

facing to the rear & all building and strengthening our lines.

I did command the 1rst Div. but that has been broken up & at present which is temporary I command the 3rd. Div. but may command it for a month to come.

I have a colored boy, his name is Henry Harden, He will be I think a real nice boy....[102]

My love to all...Your Jackie[103]


In the end, despite the heroic efforts of many, the Union failed to take command of the railroad, but they did maintain control of the ever important Jerusalem Plank Road, a vital access way for the South. The battle for the Weldon Railroad also represented the last major fighting in the east for the balance of 1864 and the two lumbering armies began to slip into winter quarters.

Grant continued to keep his diligent course, which made many at home in the north angry. Growing numbers of his casualties continued to appear in northern newspapers which made Lincoln doubt that he had any chance to be elected for a second term.

Months had now passed since Hartranft and the 51st had joined Grant on his campaign. He and the 51st and now all the members of the First Brigade adapted quickly to Grant's technique of fighting. Winter would come and they would all be confined to the many miles of trenches and little did Hartranft realize, that when the Spring campaign of '65 opened, it would open directly upon him.

As the armies began to prepare for the winter, on November 27th Hartranft had the distinction of capturing CSA General Roger A. Pryor who was serving as a special courier during an informal truce. Pryor was later released at the request of President Lincoln and Hartranft always held this Southern "diplomat" in high esteem.[104]

Around the first of December, Hartranft was assigned six raw new Pennsylvania regiments for his command. With winter now upon the armies, there was little in the way of training that would be accomplished until the spring. Nonetheless, those raw recruits constituted Hartranft's new command when he was placed in charge of the new Third Division of the Ninth Corps.[105] At the time, no one could guess that those contested novices would bring to themselves and their general, their most important plaudits of the entire war.

ENDNOTES FOR CHAPTER FIVE
THE WILDERNESS TO PETERSBURG
"A SPECIAL TRUST AND CONFIDENCE"

1. Parker, *History of the 51st*, pp. 508-509.
2. JFH to SEH, January 4, 1864, Shireman Collection.
3. Parker, *History of the 51st*, p. 511.
4. JFH to SEH, January 4, 1865, Shireman Collection.
5. Parker, *History of the 51st*, pp. 510-511.
6. Ibid., pp. 515, 524.
7. Ibid., pp. 529-30.
8. *The Norristown Herald and Free Press and Republican*, February 16, 1864.
9. Ibid.
10. Ibid., March 15, 1864.
11. Marvel, *Burnside*, p. 342.
12. Bean, *HMCP*, p. 209.
13. JFH to SSH, April 30, 1864, Shireman Collection.
14. Macdonald, *Great Battles of the Civil War*, p. 132.
15. *O. R.* Series I, vol. XXXVI Part II, p. 322.
16. *O. R.* Series I, vol. XXXVI Part I, p. 132.
17. Parker, *History of the 51st*, p. 544.
18. Macdonald, *Great Battles of the Civil War*, p. 143.
19. Bean, *HMCP*, p. 210.
20. Ibid.
21. Armor, *Lives of the Governors of Pennsylvania*, p. 506.
22. Parker, *History of the 51st*, p. 544.
23. Macdonald, *Great Battles of the Civil War*, p. 143.
24. Snow, William P., *Lee and his Generals*, New York: Fairfax Press, 1982, p. 336.
25. *O. R.* Series I, vol. XXXVI, Part I, p. 132.
26. Winslow, Richard Elliot III, *General John Sedgwick*, Novato, California: Presidio, 1982, p. 173.
27. Ibid.
28. Parker, *History of the 51st*, p. 547.
29. Matter, William D., *If It Takes All Summer: The Battle of Spotsylvania*, Chapel Hill, North Carolina: University of North Carolina Press, 1988, p. 240.
30. Ibid.
31. Ibid.
32. Ibid., pp. 241 and 242.
33. *O. R.* Series I, vol. XXXVI, Part I, p. 149. Also, on May 16th, Hartranft

wrote to Sallie and informed her that he thought that he had lost about 1,000 killed and wounded plus another 4-500 taken as prisoners. JFH to SSH dated May 16, 1864, Shireman Collection.

34. JFH to General Ambrose E. Burnside dated July 2, 1864, Shireman Collection.
35. *O. R.* Series I, vol. XXXVI, Part I, p. 176.
36. Courtesy of Pennsylvania State Archives.
37. Armor, *Lives of the Governors of Pennsylvania*, p. 508.
38. Boatner, *The Civil War Dictionary*, p. 163.
39. Parker, *History of the 51st*, p. 560.
40. *Bolton Diary*, p. 259.
41. Ibid.
42. *O. R.* Series I, Vol, XXXVI, Part I, p. 952. This is Hartranft's official report on the battle dated Oct. 25, 1864.
43. *Bolton Diary*, p. 259.
44. Grant, U. S., *Personal Memoirs*, 2 vols. New York: Charles L. Webster & Company, 1886, vol. 2, p. 276.
45. Boatner, *The Civil War Dictionary*, p. 165.
46. *O. R.* Series I, vol. XXXVI, Part I, p. 176.
47. JFH to SSH, June 7, 1864, Shireman Collection.
48. Ibid.
49. Davis, William C., et al., eds. *Death in the Trenches, Grant at Petersburg*, Alexandria, Virginia: Time-Life Books, 1986, p. 44. Hereafter referred to as *Death in the Trenches*.
50. *Bolton Diary*, p. 267.
51. Davis, *Death in the Trenches*, p. 46.
52. Barrett, "John Frederic Hartranft; Life and Services", p. 180.
53. Bolton Diary, p. 267.
54. Davis, *Death in the Trenches*, p. 46.
55. *Bolton Diary*, p. 268.
56. Parker, *History of the 51st*, pp. 568-569.
57. Ibid., p. 572.
58. JFH to SSH, July 12, 1864, Shireman Collection.
59. Cullen, Joseph P., "The Siege of Petersburg", *Civil War Times Illustrated* IX:5, (1970), reprint; Eastern Acorn Press, (1981) p. 15. Hereafter referred to as The Siege of Petersburg.
60. Ibid., p. 17.
61. Ibid. Also see, Parker, *History of the 51st Regiment*, p. 572.
62. Cullen, "The Siege of Petersburg", p. 17.
63. SSH to JFH, July 21, 1864, Shireman Collection.
64. Marvel, *Burnside*, p. 393.
65. Ibid.

66. Cullen, "The Siege of Petersburg", p. 21.
67. Warner, **Generals in Blue**, p. 277.
68. Cullen, "The Siege of Petersburg", p. 21.
69. Ibid.
70. Parker, *History of the 51st*, p. 574.
71. Cullen, "The Siege of Petersburg", p. 22.
72. Cavanaugh, Michael A., and William Marvel, *The Petersburg Campaign, The Battle of the Crater*, Lynchburg, Virginia: H. E. Howard, Inc., 1989, p. 42. Hereafter, referred to as The Battle of the Crater. The author has utilized the entire quotation from the above and considers this volume to be one of the best and most detailed on the subject.
73. Ibid., p. 94.
74. *O. R.* Series I, vol. XXXX, Part I, p. 579.
75. *Battles & Leaders*, vol. 4, p. 562.
76. Cavanaugh and Marvel, *The Battle of the Crater*, p. 94.
77. *O. R.* Series I, vol. XXXX, Part I, p. 579.
78. Anonymous letter, Shireman Collection
79. Ibid.
80. Cavanaugh and Marvel, *The Battle of the Crater*, p. 97.
81. Parker, *History of the 51st Regiment*, p. 576-577.
82. Marvel, *Burnside*, p. 478.
83. Warner, *Generals in Blue*, p. 25.
84. *Battles & Leaders*, vol. 4, p. 560.
85. Cavanaugh and Marvel, *The Battle of the Crater*, pp. 115-116.
86. Message from JFH to General Burnside, Shireman Collection.
87. *O. R.* Series I, vol. XXXX, Part I, p. 579.
88. Ibid., p. 43.
89. Ibid., pp. 101-102.
90. Cavanaugh and Marvel, *The Battle of the Crater*, p. 110.
91. *O. R.* Series I, vol. XXXX, Part I, pp. 128.
92. Ibid., p. 129.
93. Sifakis, Stewart, *Who Was Who in the Civil War*, New York: Facts on File Publications, 1988, p. 378.
94. Ibid., pp. 215-216.
95. Marvel, *Burnside*, p. 413.
96. Barrett, "John Frederic Hartranft; Life and Services", p. 337.
97. JFH to SSH, August 18, 1864, Shireman Collection.
98. Barrett, "John Frederic Hartranft; Life and Services", p. 339.
99. Parker, *History of the 51st Regiment*, p. 580.
100. Bates, *Martial Deeds of Pennsylvania*, p. 670.
101. JFH to SSH, August 21, 1864, Shireman Collection. The bullet

remains as part of the Shireman Collection.

102. It was very common for officers to have black valets. [Author's note]
103. JFH to SSH, September 8, 1864, Shireman Collection.
104. *The Norristown Herald and Free Press and Republican*, May 23, 1876.
105. Bates, Samuel, *Martial Deeds of Pennsylvania*, Philadelphia: T. H. Davis & Co., 1875, p. 670.

# CHAPTER SIX

## *THE BATTLE OF FORT STEDMAN*

With the approach of Spring of 1865, Robert E. Lee found his exhausted Army of Northern Virginia wanting for shoes, food rations, clothing, and materiel. Grant's successive moves around Petersburg had rendered the city a veritable island, incapable of receiving or sending much in the way of supplies. Heated political dissension plagued the government in Richmond and General Sherman was pressing his way into North Carolina. Sherman had an army of 81,000 which was confronted by CSA General Joseph E. Johnston and his 30,000 men. Johnston said of his challenge to Sherman, "I can do no more than annoy him."[1]

Adding to those woes were the poor head counts in Lee's army, which indicated only 35,000 men fit to fight against Grant's estimated 150,000. In addition to his primary Union army invested around Petersburg, Grant had access to another 30,000 troops headed his way from Tennessee under the command of "The Rock of Chickamauga", Major-General George H. Thomas, and another 20,000 operating in the Shenandoah Valley.[2] All of this gave the Union commander a total troop strength approaching 200,000 soldiers that were, by Confederate standards, well fed, clothed, and supplied and ready to combat the determined but beleaguered Rebels.[3]

Because of mounting Southern weariness with the war and various political fractions within the Confederate government, a Southern peace initiative had been attempted with President Lincoln on February 3rd, at Hampton Roads. Representing the South at that meeting was the diminutive Vice President, Alexander H. Stephens, CSA Senator Robert Hunter and Judge John A. Campbell, a former Justice of the United States Supreme Court.[4] Unfortunately for those Southerners, the determined Union President steadfastly refused to negotiate with the South while it was still under arms and continuing in its demand to maintain slavery.[5]

Lincoln's resistance maintained pressure upon the Confederacy, and General Lee suffered constantly for the welfare of his troops. Despite these problems though, Lee knew that he and his army could not simply sit and wait for another major Union attack, especially with the oncoming new battle season. With his odds diminishing, decisive action was necessary, and Lee meant to address the issue promptly and as effectively as possible.

During the first week of March, General Lee called for his Second Corps Commander, Major-General John Brown Gordon. That young Georgian, who was not yet 33, had won Lee's respect owing to his daring and fearless record. Gordon was no scholar of military science, had attended the University of Georgia, and adopted law as his profession prior to the war. Entering the conflict as a captain, Gordon had a record so distinguished that he rapidly rose to the rank of major-general by May 14, 1864. He had been wounded six times during the past three years, and seriously at Antietam.[6]

When Gordon reached Lee's headquarters, he found his commander disturbed by the pressing and eroding conditions. When Lee asked Gordon to review some documents and reports that were scattered on a nearby table, the Georgian promptly set about the task. Those reports, from various Confederate commanders around Petersburg, told Lee of their shrinking ranks and poor supplies.[7] They made Gordon share the sense of frustration, if not despair, that must have settled upon Lee at that particular moment.[8] That data, coupled with his own first-hand knowledge of conditions, only served to reinforce Gordon's own growing concerns.

Finally, Lee asked Gordon for his evaluation of things, and Gordon replied:

"General, there are but three courses, it seems to me.
First, make terms with the enemy,
Second, retreat, abandon Richmond and Petersburg, unite with Johnston in North Carolina and strike Sherman before Grant can join him.
Lastly, fight, and without delay."[9]

After pondering for a while, Lee responded that he agreed with Gordon's analysis and confided that he intended to go to Richmond to confer with President Davis regarding the decaying situation of his army and its limited options.[10] Obviously, Gordon's summary of matters at that time was in agreement with that of Lee.

En route to see the President, Lee stopped to talk to Senator Robert M. T. Hunter, who had been one of the Southern Peace Commissioners at Hampton Roads. Hunter too was sincerely concerned about the deteriorating Southern military conditions and listened eagerly as Lee reported on the worsening conditions of his army. Hunter was struck by the total negative scope of Lee's presentation; later he wrote that Lee had made, "matters clear on the desperate needs of his army."[11] Hunter also noted that, "These and other circumstances betraying the utmost destitution he [Lee] repeated with a melancholy air and tone which I never shall forget."[12] All of this intensified Hunter's concern for Lee and his army but the sympathetic senator had no real means to provide any materiel that was so desperately needed.

Shortly afterwards, Lee met with Davis to review the eroding military conditions and Davis recorded the following,

In the early part of March, ... General Lee held with me a long and free conference. He stated that the circumstances had forced on him the conclusion that the evacuation of Petersburg was but a question of time... To my inquiry whether it would not be better to anticipate the necessity by withdrawing at once, he said that his artillery and draught horses were too weak for the roads in their then condition, and he would have to wait until they [the roads] became firmer.

... General Lee was instinctively averse to retiring from his enemy. He had so often beaten superior numbers, that his thoughts were no doubt directed to every possible expedient which might enable him to avoid retreat. It thus fell out that, in a week or two after the conference above noticed, he presented to me the idea of a sortie against the enemy near to the right of the line. The sortie, if entirely successful, so as to capture and hold the work's on Grant's right, as well as three forts on the commanding ridge in his [Grant's] rear, would threaten his line of communication with his base, City Point, and compel him to move his forces around ours to protect it; if only so far successful as to cause the transfer of his troops from his left to his right, it would relieve our right, and delay the impending disaster for the more convenient season for retreat.[13]

By the time Lee concluded his meeting with President Davis, his sullen attitude had improved markedly, and he hurried back to his headquarters where he again summoned General Gordon, and told him, "There is but one thing to do-Fight. To stand still means death."[14] He then ordered Gordon to study the situation and determine a point for an attack that would break Grant's lock and permit the army to move out and meet with General Joseph E. Johnston.[15] Lee further instructed Gordon that as an extra measure, he wanted to use experienced troops, and the break was to be on the northern end of his line. He then ordered Gordon to "move your troops into the works around the City [Petersburg] as I withdraw one of the other Commands."[16] In this manner, Gordon was to position himself for the clandestine attack which was destined to become the last offensive attack for Lee and his Army of Northern Virginia. Yet, while no one admitted to a last ditch effort, a sense of despair must have been very evident.

Gordon set about his task promptly and moved his own headquarters into Petersburg and immediately started to collect his information. It was very obvious to him that the task was not a light one, and as he began to move his troops as ordered, he wrote that,

> The very narrow space between Lee and Grant's lines, the vigilance of the pickets who stood within speaking range of each other, and the heavily loaded guns which commanded every foot of entrenchments, made the removal of one body of troops and the installation of another impractical by daylight and quite hazardous even at night. We moved however, cautiously through the city to the breastworks, and, as the other corps were secretly withdrawn, my command glided into the vacated trenches as softly and noiselessly as the smooth flow of a river.[17]

During that period of troop transition, Gordon also employed the able assistance of his staff members including "Majors [Edward L.] Moore, [R. W.] Hunter, [V.] Dabney and [James M.] Pace, and Captains [Frank] Markoe, [J.] Wilmer, and [William J.] Jones" to assist in the gathering of the critical information.[18]   While also searching the local terrain, Gordon personally interrogated newly captured Union prisoners and even recent Yank deserters who confused him. Understandably, Gordon couldn't quite understand why any Union troops would want to move into Confederate ranks at this late hour.[19]

Nonetheless, Gordon soon called upon Brigadier-General James A. Walker from Virginia, who led the old Stonewall Brigade which was directly in front of Fort Stedman, at a position known as Colquitt's Salient. Walker too was a competent officer who had been severely wounded at Spotsylvania and had won the solid trust of his former commander, Stonewall Jackson.[20] Gordon asked Walker if he thought his men could hold their position against a Union attack. Walker's quick response was "No!" He felt that the Union lines were too strong and too close but, he added, "I can take their front any morning before breakfast."[21]   Walker obviously felt that moment to be the weakest in terms of the Yankee vigilance. Smiling, Gordon responded, "Don't you forget what you have said; I may call on you to make your words good."[22]

**Colquitt's Salient**

From this exact spot, on March 25, 1865, Gordon began his attack upon Fort Stedman, which is located behind the small trees in the forefront. The land from this point to that in front of Fort Stedman was littered with skirmishers.

*Photographer: Frank D'Amico.*
*Source: Petersburg National Battle Field.*

After a full week of reconnoitering and interrogations, Gordon made his decision and concluded that Fort Stedman, an earthen fort immediately in front of Colquitt's Salient, about two miles from downtown Petersburg, would be the best point for the attack.

Fort Stedman was about three-quarters of an acre in area with a grove of shade trees in its center, and a sally-port or entryway in its rear.[23] The fort was garrisoned by the 14th New York Heavy Artillery, under the command of Major George M. Randall, whose men spilled into nearby Fort Haskell immediately to the south. The immediate area was also supported by the 1st Connecticut Heavy Artillery with a bank of mortars.[24] The fort had received its name in honor of Brevet Brigadier-General Griffen A. Stedman, Jr., of Hartford who was mortally wounded on August 5, 1864, while leading the 11th Connecticut following the debacle of the Mine explosion.[25]

For most, Fort Stedman was a poorly constructed fort, rather unprotected and subject to surprise attack. There was virtually no protection in its rear, while on its right, the line of vision was sorely obstructed by the bomb-proofs erected by the garrison of Battery Number 10 which was immediately adjacent. However, those earthen huts were a testimony to the frequent Rebel shelling of the area.[26]

It is easy to see why Gordon focused upon Fort Stedman. The ground between it and Colquitt's Salient was open and firm and he could move his troops across that area with relative ease. Unlike the woods, marsh and streams in front of nearby Fort Haskell, which would interfere with any movement, the area in front of Stedman would even hold cavalry if required. Just behind Stedman ran the Prince George Court House Road which led directly to Meade Station. That solid road would support Gordon's anticipated rush towards the Union rear.[27]

Gordon had studied the area so well that he knew to the moment the time required to cross from one trench to another. He knew virtually every obstacle in his way and his plan was to be sprinkled with theatrics as he intended that some of his men would pose as Union officers as a result of his recent interrogations.[28]

The troops of both sides between Fort Stedman and Colquitt's Salient, which was known locally as Spring Hill, were approximately seventy-five yards* away from each other; outer pickets even closer. According to CSA Major-General Bryan Grimes, who was selected to lead the Confederate attack, the lines "are so close that you can almost see the whites in the Yankee eyes."[29]

* Estimates vary, author's note.

124

Gordon finally sent word to Lee that he was prepared to present his plan, and he soon found himself before the fifty-eight-year-old commander. Thirty-eight years after the war, Gordon wrote,

The plan of attack on Fort Stedman was fully developed in my own mind; and whether it was good or bad, the responsibility for it was upon me, not because there was any indisposition on General Lee's part to make a plan of his own and order its execution, but because he had called me from the extreme right to his center at Petersburg for this purpose. With him was the final decision-approval or rejection.[30]

Lee finally asked, "What can you do?' Gordon responded, "I can take Fort Stedman, sir."

"How and from what point?" Lee queried.

"By a night assault from Colquitt's Salient, and a sudden, quick rush over ditches, where the enemy's pickets are on watch, running over the pickets and capturing them, or, if they resist, using the bayonet", Gordon responded.[31]

Lee continued his line of questions and comments and challenged Gordon when he said,

"But, the *Chevaux-de-Frise* protecting your front is, I believe, fastened together at Colquitt's Salient with chains and spikes. This obstruction will have to be removed before your column of attack can pass out of our works. Do you think you can move these obstructions without attracting the attention of the Union pickets which are only a few rods* away? You are aware that they are especially vigilant at night, and that any unusual noise on your lines would cause them to give the alarm, arousing the men in their fort, who would quickly turn loose upon you their heavy guns loaded with grape and canister."[32]

* One rod equals 16.5 feet or 5.029 meters.

Obviously, Lee was concerned for the welfare of Gordon and his men and wanted to make certain proper care was being taken with such a dangerous mission. But, Gordon proved to be well prepared by his week-long investigation, and consequently he responded to his chief that, "This [*Chevaux-de-Frise*] is a serious difficulty; but I feel confident it can be

125

overcome. I propose to entrust the delicate task of getting our obstruction removed to a few select men, who will begin the work after dark, and, with the least possible noise, make a passageway for my troops by 4 A.M., at which hour the sally is to be made."[33]

Lee continued his probing posture but the young major-general always responded confidently which demonstrated the thoroughness of his evaluation and planning. After Lee had once again asked him to review the entire program, Gordon emphasized to his commander that,

> During the week of investigation, I have learned the name of every [Union] officer of rank in my front. I propose to select three officers from my corps, who are to command each a body of 100 men. These officers are to assume the names of three Union officers who are in and near Fort Stedman. When I have carried Fort Stedman, each of these selected officers is to rush in the darkness to the rear with his 100 men, shouting: "The Rebels have carried Fort Stedman and our front lines." They are to maintain no regular order, but each body of 100 is to keep close to its leader.[34]

In total, Gordon would have between 10-12,000 men composed of one corps and two divisions. That total accounted for one-third of Lee's thinning army and speaks to the importance of the assault.[35]

Finally, Gordon told Lee that his plan would only work if he had suitable guides who knew the rear area and could lead his men in proper order. Lee, as confident as he could be, told Gordon to proceed with his plan and, "I will endeavor to find ... three men ... to act as guides to your three officers."[36] Since Gordon was not personally familiar with the local terrain, the issue of the guides was crucial to success. Further, the guides were needed because Gordon intended to move quickly beyond Fort Stedman to capture three unidentified additional forts. Celerity was the key ingredient to his plan and not wishing to risk any leaks, Gordon kept matters very secret.

The business of Gordon's clandestine nature was to bring him much criticism later. Yet, it is obvious that he could not tell from one day to the next who might choose to defect from the Confederate lines and destroy his plan. To support his fear, the diary of George Kilmer, a member of the 14th New York Heavy Artillery, noted that, "on the night of February 24th nine deserters came in on our brigade front, and on the next night fourteen, including a commissioned officer, many of them fully armed and equipped."[37] Gordon's concerns are further supported by U. S. military reports that claim approximately 3,000 Rebel deserters to the Union lines between February 15th and March 18th.[38] In fact, Confederate desertion was so rampant that Lee himself admitted that, "These desertions have a very bad effect upon the troops who remain and give rise to painful apprehension."[39] In light of all of this, it is difficult to fault Gordon's style.

Nonetheless, Lee kept his word and found three guides who claimed to be familiar with the local surroundings. Gordon continued his planning efforts and selected 50 strong axmen who were to cut down the *Chevaux-de-Frise* defenses.[40] As Gordon prepared orders that his men wear a white cloth on their arm so they could be identified in the anticipated hand-to-hand night fight, his wife Fanny labored in Petersburg preparing bandages that were sure to be needed once the attack began.

Four o'clock on the morning of Saturday, March 25th, was the time and target date. Gordon promised a thirty-day furlough and a silver medal to all of the selected three hundred men if they were successful.[41] For Gordon personally, with the pride of authorship by his side, the thought of a successful attack must have been intoxicating. He had certainly proven himself to be an able and intrepid soldier, ready to carry out any orders. With the element of surprise, he felt that his chances for success were decent.

For Lee, the eternal pragmatist, the hope of victory must have been a forced but distant dream. No one knew better than he that a disaster was certain to signal total despair for the entire South. Yet, no other practical options existed.

On the 24th, at 4:30 P.M., Lee sent the following wire to Gordon in his own hand writing,

> Genl: I have received yours of 2:20 P.M. and telegraphed Pickett's Division, [General George Pickett of Gettysburg fame] but I do not think it [Pickett's Division] will reach here in time. Still we will try. If you need more troops one or both of Heth's brigades can be called to Colquitt's Salient and [Cadmus M.] Wilcox's to the Baxter road. Dispose of your troops as needed. I pray that a merciful God may grant us success and deliver us from our enemies.
>
> Yours truly,
> R. E. Lee.
> Genl.[42]

Lee's mention of Pickett's Division potentially not being able to reach Gordon in time was either disregarded by Gordon or, he simply felt that fate would make it possible. Later, Gordon would blame the railroad and Pickett's failure to arrive as key elements in his failure.[43]

Fort Stedman is directly to the east of Petersburg and just under one mile south of the Appomattox River. Due east of the fort, by approximately one mile, was Meade's Station, a supply center named for the Union commander. Below Fort Stedman was a string of Union forts including Haskell, Morton, Meikle, and, Sedgwick plus Batteries No. 11 and 12. Immediately north rested Fort McGilvery plus Battery No. 10. [See Map on Page 129] Battery 10 was manned by the 1st Pennsylvania and a portion of the 1st Connecticut Artillery. Batteries 11 and 12 were manned by the 4th Maine and the balance of the 1st Connecticut.[44] In addition, all of the forts had the support of various infantry units and the Union position could set up a galling fire upon any attackers venturing between the lines. Serving as the first line of defense was a single, double or even third line of spiked wooden deterrent known as *Chevaux-de-Frise*, the forerunner of barbed wire.

In general the area looked like a World War I battlefield with its vast network of trenches, bomb-proofs and earthen corridors. Slightly northwest of Fort Stedman was Colquitt's Salient which had been named for General Alfred Holt Colquitt to honor his valor at Olustee, Florida, in 1864. Colquitt lived long after the Civil War and died serving the South in the U. S. Senate in 1894.[45]

The entire area of Fort Stedman was located on a site known locally as Hare's Hill, which bore the name of its owner, Mr. Otway P. Hare. Hare was widely known in the area because of his fine horses and racetrack and he founded a drug store in Petersburg to supplement his income. Until recently, that drug store continued operations though no longer under the Hare family.[46]

Because of numerical disparity between the two ranks at the time, the Union troops in the first or outer line of defense were relieved every several hours. Owing to their dwindling numbers, the Rebels had no such luxury and those young men were frequently forced to remain in their positions all day. Since the same soldiers were frequently assigned such duty, a form of comradery naturally developed between the two lines of pickets.

While Lee and Gordon had been developing their plans, General Grant and his staff were not exactly idle. The Union commander knew that something must happen on his front. Despite the grueling ten months of siege thus far, the Confederacy had demonstrated amazing resilience and, while the two armies were deadlocked, they could not remain forever so. Consequently, in February, Grant sent a precautionary order to Major-

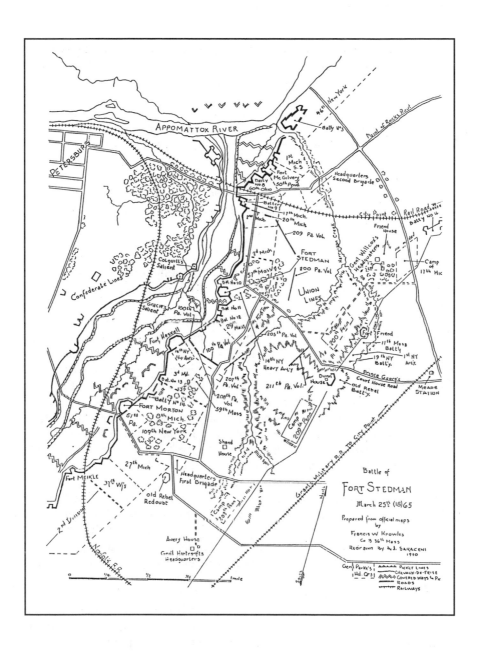

The area just East of Petersburg in 1865 showing the position of Fort Stedman and the area. Redrawn by A. J. Saraceni.

129

General John G. Parke, who was then temporary commander of the Army of the Potomac since General Meade was on leave. Grant's order stated that,

> As there is a possibility of an attack from the enemy at any time, and especially an attempt to break your center, extra vigilance should be kept up both by the pickets and the troops on the line. Let Commanders understand that no time is to be lost awaiting orders, if an attack is made, in bringing all their resources to the point of danger. With proper alacrity in this respect, I would have no objection to seeing the enemy get through.[47]

Grant's choice of words here does not imply praise for a successful Rebel attack but rather in such an event, proper vigilance would certainly destroy such prospects.

On March 20th, Grant invited President Lincoln to visit him at City Point, and the weary President promptly accepted and made his way aboard the boat *River Queen*, arriving on the 24th. That evening, Grant met with Lincoln for a short while and left the tired chief executive at an early hour. With the arrival of the President, General Meade too had arrived back in the area and was staying with his wife Margaret.[48]

General Hartranft was now in command of the Third Division of the Ninth Corps and in December of 1864, he had been assigned six raw Pennsylvania regiments including the 200th, 208th, and 209th, which made up the First Brigade while the 205th, 207th, and 211th made up his Second Brigade. According to Hartranft, each of the new regiments were "all full, numbering one thousand men each."[49] His First Brigade was led by Colonel Charles W. Diven of the 200th while Lieutenant-Colonel William H. H. McCall led that regiment and Colonel A. B. McCalmont led the 208th while Lieutenant-Colonel George W. Frederick led the 209th. Colonel Joseph A. Matthews, of the 205th led the Second Brigade while Lieutenant-Colonel William F. Walter led the regiment and Colonel Robert C. Cox led the 207th and Colonel James H. Trimble the 211th.[50]

Hartranft's Ninth Corps commander was now General Parke, a native of Coatesville, Pennsylvania, near Norristown and a West Point graduate. Parke had been assigned the Ninth Corps to replace General Burnside after the 1864 mine explosion debacle.[51]

Hartranft's position generally ran in a northerly manner for a stretch of about four miles and his command shared the field with the First and Second Divisions of the Ninth Corps which were led by Brigadier-

Generals Orlando Bolivar Willcox and Robert Brown Potter respectively. According to Hartranft,

> The Third Division under my command, was in reserve to these two divisions. ... the [Third] division covered four miles, with [his] headquarters at the Avery House, in the center, the right resting at the Friend House, a mile in the rear of the works, north-east of Fort Stedman and left behind Fort Prescott. ... About 100 yards behind Fort Stedman ... there was a slight rise in the slope, upon which was encamped the 57th Massachusetts, and to the left of this, some old works which the enemy had abandoned as our forces entered the city. Between this camp and these works ran an old country road [Prince George Court House Road], somewhat sunken, from the rear of Stedman to Meade's Station. All the undergrowth and fences had long disappeared, and the ground was generally open.[52]

Hartranft continued that he had placed the 209th Pennsylvania behind Fort Haskell while the 200th was just behind Fort Stedman.

Gordon's plan was now complete and the main attack was to be led by General Walker's Division directly against Stedman while two simultaneous attacks would be made upon the lunettes immediately adjacent to Stedman. Each storming party would consist of fifty picked axmen to clear away the *Chevaux-de-Frise*, followed by one hundred infantrymen. The storming parties were then to be followed by the main assault body.[53]

Just before the attack began, Gordon recalled an incident which demonstrated the type of relations that developed between forward pickets at times.

> The Rev. J. William Jones, D. D., now chaplain-general of the United Confederate Veterans, when standing near this same point [Colquitt's Salient] had his hat carried away by a gust of wind, and it fell near the Union lines. The loss of a hat meant the loss to the chaplain of nearly a month's pay. He turned away sorrowfully, not knowing how he could get another. A heroic young private, George Haner of Virginia, said to him, "Chaplain, I will get your hat." Taking

a pole in his hand, he crawled along the ditch which led to our picket-line, and began to drag the hat in with his pole. At this moment a Yankee bullet went through the sleeve of his jacket. He at once shouted to the Union picket: "Hello, Yank; quit your foolishness. I am doing no harm. I am just trying to get the chaplain's hat." Immediately the reply came: "All right, Johnny; I'll not shoot at you any more. But you better hurry up and get it before the next relief comes."[54]

At 4:00 A.M. on the 25th, about one hour before dawn, the morning was cool, starry and quiet.[55] Between the two lines there were remnants of a cornfield where the Confederates occasionally supplemented their meager diets. Owing to the close proximity of the two forward picket lines, conversation between the two was not unusual. As a result, the small chatter between the two lines that morning gave no hint of what was about to happen.

While some Union reports indicate Rebel activity as early as 3:00 A.M., that was undoubtedly Gordon's own men removing their *Chevaux-de-Frise*; the attack began right on time. As the first Rebel men moved forward onto that cornfield, the noise was quickly picked up by a Federal picket who hollered, "I say, Johnny, what are you doing in that corn?" Calmly and coolly the Confederate response was, "All right, Yank, I am just gathering me a little corn to parch." Totally unaware of the attack, the Union picket replied, "All right, Johnny, I won't shoot." A few moments later, the Yank queried his Southern counterpart again, "I say, Johnny, isn't it almost daylight? I think it is time they were relieving us." In a nonchalant voice, the Rebel response was, "Keep cool, Yank, you'll be relieved in a few minutes."[56]

At that moment, Captain James M. Anderson of the 49th Virginia and Lieutenant Hugh P. Powell of Company A, 13th Virginia, were quietly putting their men into position. Then, General Gordon himself fired three pistol shots in rapid succession to signal the command to attack. At that precise moment, Captain Anderson ordered his men, "Forward-Double-quick."[57] General Walker followed immediately.

As the Confederate line moved forward, the Union picket, only fifty yards away, could clearly hear the approaching troops. Realizing that an attack was unfolding, that singular, hapless soldier went running back toward Fort Stedman yelling, "The Rebels are coming!"[58]

The Rebels were indeed right behind him and they had been wisely instructed not to capture or shoot the Union picket but rather, follow him directly since he would naturally run for the opening in their *Chevaux-de-*

*Frise.* This would make the surprise all the more effective and place the forward Rebel troops in a better position to create confusion among the Union troops.[59]

The first wave of butternuts hit Battery No. 10. Inside, Captain J. P. Cleary, Lieutenant Frank M. Thomson, along with Sergeant J. P. Delack of the 14th New York Heavy Artillery, promptly pulled one of their guns to the sally-port and let loose with a harsh fire upon the attackers.[60] Still, the Rebels continued to come forward with a determined fire from their rifles. Soon, they overpowered the Yanks and in the process, killed Lieutenant E. B. Nye, of the 14th New York while he was attempting to operate his gun.[61] During that brief struggle, the confusion and darkness was so great that some claimed that the men could not distinguish friend from foe and at one time, Yanks were firing a part of the gun while Rebels handled the other.

With Battery No. 10 now in their hands, the Rebels trained their new-found artillery directly on Fort Stedman. At almost the same time, Captain Anderson and Lieutenant Powell were approaching the breastworks of Fort Stedman when an alert thin line of Yankees rose up and let loose with a galling fire and this momentarily stunned the Rebels.

Most of the Federal inhabitants of Fort Stedman were still asleep in a variety of small wooden huts and bomb-proofs, and simply unaware of the attack. However, that first Union volley killed Lieutenant Powell and left Captain Anderson mortally wounded, leaving the storming party without any commissioned officers.[62] But the attackers knew their objective well, and quickly pushed over the breastworks and into the fort. Once inside Fort Stedman's earthen walls, the Rebels let out an incredible yell that was the signal to the rear troops that the fort had been taken and they should move forward.[63] At the same time, those initial Rebels inside the fort set up a rapid and indiscriminate fire upon the Yanks who scattered; many were taken prisoner. Many other officers and men were caught in their beds and that loud Rebel yell quickly brought the main Confederate body forward which precluded any real Union resistance inside the fort.

Yet, Union Major George M. Randall, who had served under Hartranft in the old 4th, commander of Fort Stedman, did everything in his power to rally his men against the sweeping Johnnies. It didn't take long before hand-to-hand fighting broke out but the Rebels were wide awake and delivered crushing blows with their rifle butts to the half-sleeping Yankees. Finally, Randall saw that the cause was lost and he took the colors and made his way to Fort Haskell.

The Yanks had been caught between a surprise closely akin to a nightmare and the confusion that is common when being aroused from the deepest of sleep. In a matter of moments, the first major Southern thrust

**Fort Stedman**

Interior of Fort Stedman shortly after the battle.  Note the "bombproof".

*Source:  Library of Congress.*

**Fort Stedman**

Interior of Fort Stedman shortly after the battle.  Note the "bombproof".

*Source:  Library of Congress.*

had proven successful and Fort Stedman had fallen. Rebel emotions were understandably high as ultimate success for the day appeared to be at hand.

According to General Walker, the Union men inside Stedman did their best to resist and he later wrote that,

> The Officers and men in the fort acted gallantly and tried to form and make resistance, but to form men in the dark just out of sleep, cooped up in a small fort, with a hundred muskets in the hands of an organized body of trained and daring men, pouring forth their deadly contents on every side and making a mark of every head that showed itself, is next to an impossibility.[64]

During those early morning hours General Hartranft was at his headquarters at the Avery House and owing to atmospheric conditions, he did not hear any of the noise related to the initial attack. As might be expected, a number of claims quickly arose about the swift Rebel action. Some Yanks insisted that the surprise was the result of General Grant's offer of payment to any Confederate who deserted to the Union lines with his arms.[65] Some thought this offer precipitated a large number of Southern deserters. In turn, that created a laxness among the Union ranks causing those inside Fort Stedman to believe the actual attack was only more Rebel deserters. None of this appears to be very credible and we are left to applaud the swiftness of the Confederate attack and its initial success.

With Battery No. 10 and Fort Stedman in their possession, the Rebels turned their attention to Battery No. 11 which was just south of Stedman, and garrisoned by the 29th Massachusetts. As Gordon's men made their way toward Battery No. 11, the Bay State boys were initially told to hold their fire, officers believing that Union pickets were returning. At the same time, the Rebels struck with full fury from the rear and their attack resulted in 15-20 minutes of hand-to-hand fighting. Finally, the Rebels again prevailed and the men of the 29th were either driven out or taken prisoner.

Now the important challenge to Gordon was to proceed swiftly to the next Union line, take the three unidentified Union forts which action was certain to cause Grant to shift his troops. However, while he must have felt good about his initial progress, Gordon knew that the first rays of early morning dawn did not bode well for him and his troops and if his good luck was to continue, he must maintain his rapid pace before the entire Union army discovered his action.

For a brief period, the Confederates were in total control of Fort Stedman and the immediate Batteries 10 and 11. All that remained for complete success was to push eastward toward Fort Friend, while continuing the attack on the other forts and lunettes immediately adjacent to Stedman.

The Confederate attack was so swift and surprising that considerable panic and confusion existed within the Union ranks around the immediate area. Men and officers were scurrying into position and yelling orders, while others had to be shaken from their deep slumber. The young drummer boy from the 209th Pennsylvania, I. J. Jamison, instinctively grabbed his drum and ran into the company street and began to beat the alarm. He later wrote, "Everybody seemed panic stricken. Our lieutenants came running along the company quarters, beating the tents with their swords, crying out: Men fall in, or we will all be prisoners ... Fall in!"[66]

The initial Union resistance began when Brigadier-General Napoleon Bonaparte McLaughlen, commanding the Third Brigade of the First Division, Ninth Corps, became alerted and sent scouts to various points along the line. McLaughlen promptly led a counterattack which resulted in the recapture of Battery No. 11. Believing he had turned the tide of events, McLaughlen then pushed directly into Fort Stedman. Totally unaware of the fort's new occupants, he was promptly captured and sent off to Libby Prison in Richmond.[67]

Gordon, who also went to Fort Stedman, reported that he captured one thousand prisoners, nine heavy cannons, eleven mortars, and General McLaughlen. He also reported that the Confederate casualties amounted to fewer than six men,[68] which seems to be most optimistic. Still, his initial wave had proven very effective. He also encountered some unforeseen help from nature, since atmospheric conditions had kept the sounds of the attack from traveling any real distance.

While Gordon could be buoyed by these conditions, he also knew that matters were apt to change rapidly. The sun was beginning to rise and, with the dawn, the Confederates would lose the cover that darkness had afforded them. In part, that cover also inhibited Union artillery fire because of the possibility of killing their own men. By the time Gordon's initial thrust was complete, portions of the Union army had been alerted and would certainly mass for a counterattack.

Although Gordon's initial phase of the attack had gone very well, complete success depended upon positive results of the second phase. His intent was to move forward and capture the three additional forts immediately behind Stedman, which would permit him to open fire on Grant's rear and break the Union line. Here, as with many other details of the war, matters become a little confused and conflicting. Gordon himself does not specify the forts in question but, in the opinion of Mr. O. F.

137

Northington, Jr., Superintendent of the Petersburg National Military Park in 1944,

> Gordon attempted to reach [1] Union Battery 4, which was refaced Confederate Battery 5 of the old, so called, "Dimmock line", [2] Fort Friend, which was known also as the Dunn House Battery and had been Confederate Battery 8 on the same line, and [3] a position on the Dimmock line that covered Meade's Station. This third position may have been for field guns before the fight at Fort Stedman was over.[69]

A close study of the maps extant at the time indicate Mr. Northington's evaluation is most logical and probable.

As Gordon's second phase got underway, a number of factors rapidly developed which would pose some great difficulties. First was his expectation of reinforcements from General George Pickett despite the fact that Lee had warned him that Pickett's timely arrival was not very probable.[70] Secondly, with his stress on secrecy, Gordon did not share much of his plan with his fellow officers and the artillery in particular. Consequently, he left himself uncovered, and while he had ample and capable officers in the rear, they could not be very effective owing to their lack of suitable information.

When Gordon began the second phase, he promptly sent word to General Lee of his initial success, and told his commander that he had sent forward three spearheads to duplicate the initial attack. Shortly thereafter, Gordon's fortunes began to change when he received word from Brigadier-General William G. Lewis, one of the forward commanders, that he had successfully penetrated the Union line under the guise of a Federal officer. Unfortunately, Lewis was unable to find the fort objective since he had lost his guide during the attack upon Fort Stedman. Immediately following Lewis' message, Gordon received similar reports from the other two leading parties, and he immediately notified Robert E. Lee of the confusion.[71] With the coming light, Gordon also diverted men covering the breastworks north and south of Stedman, and sent them forth as a line of skirmishers in his front. This Confederate line was able to advance quickly, but they soon encountered stiff Union resistance.

As the sun began to climb higher, General Lee could plainly see the field from his position on a hill in Gordon's rear. It was obvious that the second phase was already faltering, and Lee knew that Gordon would soon be confronted by heavy Union counterattacks. As a result, he ordered

Gordon to retreat.[72] Some feel that Gordon waited too long to follow that retreat order because of his own vanity. While there may be some truth to that thought, it must also be understood that Gordon realized that retreat was not going to be a simple matter. He and his men would have to cross the open field between Fort Stedman and Colquitt's Salient, and that would provide the Union gunners with a mass of easy targets.

Union Generals Parke, Willcox, and Hartranft had first learned of Gordon's attack about 4:30 A.M.,[73] and Parke immediately ordered general movements to combat the Confederate attack. Willcox was ordered to reoccupy the works that had been taken, while his Chief of Artillery, Colonel John C. Tidball, was ordered to take command of all available ground with reserve artillery while Hartranft was to concentrate his division and reinforce Willcox.[74]

Parke then sent three successive messages to General Meade at headquarters to inform the commander of the attack and to request orders, but all went unanswered. He then sent a fourth urgent message only to find that Meade was at City Point, conferring with Grant, and he found himself in charge of the whole Army of the Potomac. Since the Confederates had cut the telegraph wire to City Point, Parke dispatched a courier to General Grant's headquarters and then set about his work.[75] Events would begin to move quickly now as the full knowledge of the attack became known with the realization that Grant's February warning had materialized.

In the dim gray light of early morning, Generals Willcox and Hartranft were meeting in front of the Friend House when Hartranft reported that, "our attention was called to the puffs of smoke issuing from the wood in the rear, and to the right of Fort Stedman. It was not light enough to see the enemy, nor could any sound be heard, owing to the direction of the wind, but the white puffs indicated musketry firing."[76]

Upon noting these conditions, Hartranft requested of Willcox that Brevet Major L. Curtiss Brackett of the 57th Massachusetts Volunteers lead the 209th Pennsylvania and the 57th toward Stedman, while he would personally lead the 200th Pennsylvania.[77] The 57th and 209th would move in concert upon the rear of Stedman, while Hartranft and the 200th would advance up the Court House Road that ran between Meade's Station and Fort Stedman.

At this point, the Confederates were advancing with a heavy line from the rear of Fort Stedman and covered a good portion of the same road which was to be taken by Hartranft and the 200th. "Old Black John" led his regiment forward in a line of battle which broke through the Rebel skirmishers. He and the 200th soon found themselves confronted with a stubbornly entrenched Confederate force which sent a stiff volley upon the Yanks. In addition, the captured Union guns inside Stedman were now turned upon their rightful owners and they too began to fire upon the 200th and its intrepid leader causing them to momentarily fall back.[78]

Hartranft rallied his beleaguered troops and was relieved to see the approach of the 209th, which had no easy time of responding to his order to "move up." He placed the 209th on his immediate right and his whole line now formed a large, wide "V". Then his right became further extended when the right of the 209th became connected to the 2nd Michigan which was in turn attached to the 17th Michigan, which was anchored to Battery No. 9, just north of Stedman. All of this gave Hartranft great fire power, which would be complemented by the cannon from Battery No. 9 and Fort Haskell which had become trained upon the Rebel line. After quickly inspecting his new line, Hartranft noted,

> Fortunately, upon the line taken, the enemy could not easily deploy for the further advance to Meade's Station and the railroad, the enfilading fires of Battery Nine and Fort Haskell forcing their troops into the bomb-proofs of the captured lines to the right and left to Fort Stedman, which were thus the only openings for their columns to enter and deploy to the rear. Great credit is justly due to the garrisons of these two points for their steadiness in holding them in the confusion and nervousness of a night attack. If they had been lost, the enemy would have had sufficient safe ground on which to recover and form their ranks, and the Third Division would have been overwhelmed and beaten in detail by a greatly superior force. ...The tenacity with which these points were held, therefore, saved the Union army great loss of men, material, and time and enabled the Third Division to signalize itself by a brilliant feat of arms.[79]

Almost simultaneously other Union movements were coming together in rapid fashion. The 20th Michigan had come up and taken a position immediately to the right of Battery No. 9 while to the south, the 208th Pennsylvania, led by Captain Prosper Dalien, was connected from Fort Haskell to the left and toward the rear of Fort Stedman. By this time, the 208th was joined by components of a number of different regiments including men from the 100th Pennsylvania and the 3rd Michigan, and they connected to the left of the 207th Pennsylvania. Meanwhile, Captain J. D. Bertolette of Hartranft's staff, was also taking the 205th and the 207th

Pennsylvania regiments to the right of a ravine on the road leading to Meade's Station.[80]

Tidball's artillery took up position to the rear of Stedman and between it and the artillery at Fort Haskell and Battery No. 9, they were in good position to sweep the Confederates with canister and grape.[81] Meanwhile. the 211th Pennsylvania moved up from their encampment three miles to the rear to the small hills around Fort Meade, and were meant for reserves and to protect the Union right.[82]

In all, Hartranft had approximately four thousand men in a semi-circle around and behind Fort Stedman. His troops stretched for a mile and a half between the most northern and southern lines, and all of the Union men were eager to punish the "Johnnies" for their early morning success.[83]

At about 7:30 A.M., Hartranft received orders from General Parke to retake the line. He immediately sent word to all his regiments that the assault would begin in fifteen minutes, and the signal would be the advance of the 211th Pennsylvania which had moved up and now in full view of the Rebels. The 211th was to be the initial target.[84]

Stedman was now a crowded corral of Confederate troops undoubtedly realizing that a major counterassault was imminent. From various points outside the fort, it was plain to see that the Confederates had positioned themselves in the trenches, parapets, and bombproofs inside the fort. At 7:45 A.M., Hartranft gave the signal for the 211th to begin the attack.[85] Rising from their position, about six hundred men from the Keystone State began rushing across the field which quickly drew Confederate fire. Not to be deterred, the 211th pushed forward which signaled the entire Union line to rise up and follow.[86]

At that critical moment, Hartranft received new orders instructing him to halt any assault until reinforcements from the Sixth Corps could be brought up to assist him. The order troubled Hartranft only for a moment but with a quick look at the positive, forward movement of his first line, he decided it was prudent to disobey the command. He was confident of success, and after the battle he would write, "Just as the 211th moved I received orders to delay the assault until the arrival of a division of the Sixth Army Corps, on its way to support me. As the moment was begun, it was doubtful whether the countermand would reach the regiments on the extreme right and left in time. Beside, I had no doubt of the results, and therefore determined to take the responsibility."[87]

With the 211th leading the attack, the main Federal line began its push against Fort Stedman. With a wild yell, the Yanks came pouring toward the walls of Stedman and in Hartranft's own words, "the 208th stormed batteries XI and XII and the lines to the fort. The 207th carried the west angle of Fort Stedman the 205th and 211th the rear, the 200th the East

141

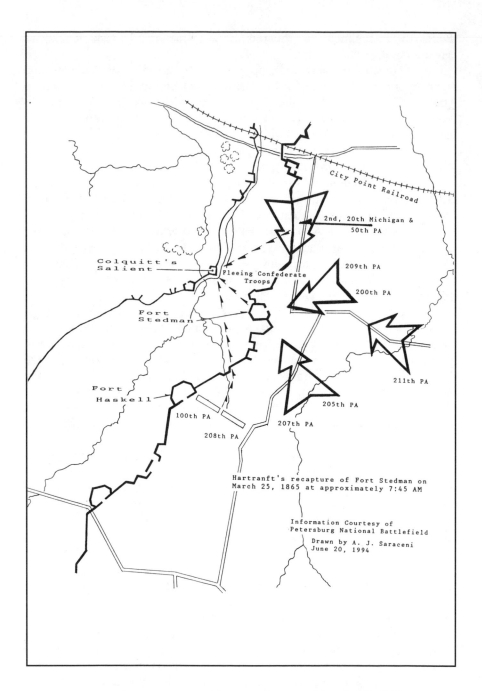

**Hartranft's recapture of Fort Stedman on March 25, 1865.**

142

angle, and the 209th Battery X and the remaining line to the right."[88] Like a thundering blue wave, those raw recruits of Hartranft's First Brigade fell upon Stedman and its immediate environs with such force and rapidity that even he wasn't certain which regimental flag was planted upon the works first.[89]

As the fierce blue line ran forward, a tremendous clash of human bodies crushed into each other and bloody hand-to-hand fighting broke out. Amidst the yelling, screaming and cursing, Americans all were clubbing, and stabbing each other with their bayonets and rifle butts. Cries of agony were mixed with screams of anguish, frustration and joy as the Yanks perceived their victory. Within fifteen minutes, Fort Stedman was retaken. With great enthusiasm, the Yanks ripped the Stars and Bars from the wooden flag pole and promptly raised "Old Glory".

Finally, General Gordon had to give the order to retreat, and in the words of General Walker,

> ... it was a thousand times more hazardous than the advance because it was now in full blaze of daylight and the seventy five yards that lay between Fort Stedman and our shelter was swept by the direct and crossfire of many pieces of artillery posted in both the first and second lines of the enemies works. ...When I reached our works and clambered up to the top, I was so exhausted that I rolled down among the men, and one of them expressed surprise at seeing me by remarking: Here is General Walker, I thought he was killed.[90]

As the Johnnies attempted to make their way back towards Colquitt's Salient, they found themselves raked with canister and rifle fire and much of that from the very guns they held just a short time ago. Many saw the futility in such an attempt and were captured and sent to the rear where the wounded of both sides were given attention.

The Yanks began to take a large number of prisoners, captured firearms and flags. According to Hartranft, "at least fifteen hundred of the prisoners and all the battle flags captured were taken by, and or passed to the rear through the lines of my Division, but were afterwards collected by other troops, while but one battle flag was credited to my command." This situation would later give rise to some Union arguments, but in his report, Hartranft stated that his command was more concerned about retaking and holding the Union position rather than the spoils of war.[91]

As the thrust of the Federal offensive declined and men of both sides could see the horrible physical devastation within the fort and the area, Confederate Major Henry Kyd Douglas of General Gordon's staff appeared with a white flag to request permission to gather the Confederate dead. Hartranft, who was now somewhat physically drained, wasted no words with Douglas and approved the request in a perfunctory manner. The two men spoke briefly, and the general soon found that the major and he had attended the same school, Marshall College, which broke the ice. Douglas asked Hartranft to mail a letter for him and offered a receipt for the Confederate men taken from the field. From that moment forward, a lifelong, warm relationship developed between the two.[92]

The last offensive attack for the Army of Northern Virginia was over, and Lee immediately knew that holding onto Petersburg and Richmond was an impossibility. Struck by his first-hand view of his army's defeat, Lee promptly sent a somber message to President Davis, "it will be impossible to prevent a junction between Grant and Sherman, nor do I deem it prudent that this army should maintain its position until the latter shall approach too near."[93] His spirit all but destroyed, the Gray Fox must have reflected upon the recent words he sent home to his wife in a letter when he said, "I shall... endeavor to do my duty and fight to the last."[94] Within nine days, Lee and his army, having fought "to the last", began their fateful march towards Appomattox. During the evening of the 25th, Lieutenant-Colonel Albert A. Pope, of the 35th Massachusetts, made the following entry into his diary, regarding the day's fighting, "As the day broke one could see the third [sic] division of our corps hurrying to the scene of action. They were soon engaged in charging on the works the rebels had captured in the first onset. The rebels lost heavily a large number of prisoners, stated at as low a number as fifteen hundred, and as high as four thousand."[95]

The cost in casualties was, as is normal for the Civil War, difficult to determine precisely. Hartranft himself estimated the Confederate loss was "probably over three thousand. Two thousand of these were prisoners, the rest killed and wounded."[96]

General Grant estimated the total Rebel casualty cost at six thousand killed, wounded, captured or missing, which appears to be too high.[97] Major William Hodgkins of the 36th Massachusetts reported the Union loss to be 75 killed, 419 wounded, 523 missing for a total of 1017.[98] Unfortunately, General Gordon left no record of his accounting of Confederates casualties and the greater reality is that no one knows for certain the exact count on either side. For members of the Third Division Hartranft reported a total casualty list of 258, with 122 of that from the 200th Pennsylvania alone.[99]

No sooner had the din of battle settled than the standard arguments and finger pointing began on both sides. Questions regarding Gordon's total judgment and understanding of the terrain in the Union lines became fashionable along with blame for his secretive manner. For the North, most of the glory was directed at Hartranft and the 200th Pennsylvania, but they too would come under attack by fellow Keystone State soldiers. None, however, challenged Hartranft's decisiveness and boldness nor questioned his wisdom in disobeying orders. Needless to say, had his judgment rendered a defeat, glory would have turned to scorn. Such are the fortunes of war.

Early Northern newspaper reports carried some confusing information about the fight for Fort Stedman. Instead of identifying Hartranft as the Union leader, Major-General George L. Hartsuff was erroneously given the credit for Stedman's recapture.[100] Hartsuff had won much wider acclaim than Hartranft and had risen to command the Twenty-third Corps.[101] Nonetheless, the matter was soon corrected, and Hartranft was quickly given proper recognition.

Union Generals, Parke, Willcox, and Hartranft in particular were all cited for their brave and decisive actions during that early spring morning. Both Parke and Willcox were lavish in their praise of Hartranft, and various stories began to spring up almost immediately that General Grant and President Lincoln watched the retaking of Fort Stedman from a nearby field. It has been frequently stated that this special audience led to Hartranft's prompt promotion to brevet major-general. Unfortunately, there is very little possibility, and no evidence to support such a claim.

However, early in the afternoon of the 25th, General Parke sent the first official report of the battle to General Meade, wherein he stated that,

> The 1st Brigade of Hartranft's division held in reserve, was brought up and a check given to any further advance [by the Confederates]. One or two attempts to take the hill were made and were only temporarily successful, until the arrival of the 2nd Brigade when a charge was made by that Brigade, aided by the troops of the 1st Div. on either flank, and the enemy were driven out of the fort, with a loss of a number of prisoners, estimated at about 1600. Two battle flags have also been brought in. The enemy also lost heavily in killed outside of our lines. The whole line was quickly reoccupied, and the guns retaken uninjured. I regret to add that Genl. McLaughlen was captured in Fort Stedman. Our loss was otherwise not heavy. Great praise is due to Hartranft for the skill displayed in handling his division,

145

**Painting Depicting Hartranft's Recapture of Fort Stedman**

Hartranft leading the final assault against Fort Stedman on March 25, 1865.
Takn from a painting at Fort Stedman.

*Source: Petersburg National Battle Field.*

which behaved with great gallantry in this its first engagement.[102]

To the officers and men of his command, Hartranft sent the following congratulatory order, later in the day of the 25th. Note his reference to the command's raw status:

HEAD QUARTERS
3rd DIVISION
9th ARMY CORPS,
MARCH 25, 1865
GENERAL ORDERS No. 12.

With feelings of pride and satisfaction the Brigadier-General Commanding tenders his congratulations to the officers and men of his command for their gallant and heroic conduct in the brilliant and triumphant achievement of today, which resulted in the recapture of Fort Stedman and the entire line, together with battle flags, a large number of prisoners and small arms.

You have won a name and reputation of which veterans might feel proud, and have proved yourselves worthy of being the associates of the brave soldiers of the old Ninth Army Corps; and the General Commanding hopes that this, your first engagement and signal victory, will nerve and stimulate you for the performances of future deeds of gallantry.

To the wounded and to the families of those who have so nobly fallen in defense of their country, the General Commanding tenders his most heartfelt sympathies.

By Command of
Brig. Genl. J. F. Hartranft
Jno. D. Bertolette
Asst. Adjt. Genl.[103]

For his quick and decisive action at Fort Stedman, Hartranft was promptly promoted to the rank of brevet major-general. On March 27th, he

**Fort Stedman**

A northerly view of the earthen fort. The marker to the left also indicates the position of the rear sally port.

*Photographer: Frank D'Amico.*
*Source: Petersburg National Battle Field.*

**Fort Stedman**

An exterior view of Fort Stedman. The small path between the trees leads to the sally port referred to at the time of the battle.

*Photographer: Frank D'Amico.*
*Source: Petersburg National Battle Field.*

received written confirmation that President Lincoln had indeed confirmed his appointment accordingly.[104]

On the 28th of March, General Parke sent his congratulations to Hartranft on his promotion as announced by General George Gordon Meade.[105] At the same time, Parke issued a special congratulatory order that said in part,

> This "break" [Stedman] was intended by the enemy to have been a big thing; they intended to strike for City Point and would have made their intentions good, had it not been for the rapidity with which General Hartranft gathered up his scattered forces who were encamped at various places over several miles of territory, and wholly relying on the good discipline that he had inculcated in his command; he saved millions of dollars worth of stores that would have been destroyed by the enemy, had they reached the point. The heart of every soldier on this front swells with gratitude towards him, for his heroic and successful efforts in saving our line. 'SOON AGAIN'.[106]

Even General Meade praised Hartranft and his command for their quick action against the Rebel attack and he went on to point out to all of his commanders that, "no fortified line, however strong, will protect an army from an intrepid and audacious enemy...." With an eye towards the work of the Third, Meade continued to exhort his staff by pointing out that, "no disaster or misfortune is irreparable, when energy and bravery are displayed in the determination to recover what is lost, and to promptly assume the offensive."[107]

Yet, while Hartranft was a humble man he was not devoid of confidence and he knew well the value of his troops. Even his personal diplomacy could not restrain him from softly, but firmly, protecting the image of his men who had acted so well on the 25th. Some of the men of the 100th Pennsylvania, which was part of the Third Brigade, First Division, claimed that after they had taken Fort Haskell, they then moved forward to retake Fort Stedman.[108] These claims essentially state that the men of the 100th entered Stedman and were taking prisoners before Hartranft and his First Brigade ever began their attack.

During combat, understandably, some confusion is always possible, and the mixture of men and units may not always be precise. However, the Stedman claims of the 100th are based upon reports mainly made within the regiment and without concurrence of higher officers within the corps and beyond. The issues that divide the reports between the 100th and General Hartranft are simply too great to disregard.

In the book *The 100th Regiment Pennsylvania Volunteers - The Roundhead Regiment*, there appears a report from Captain Joseph T. Carter, who was part of the 100th. Therein, the Captain wrote, "The 100th took prisoners of all that remained and captured several stands of colours. This ended the Fort Stedman affair with the Roundheads in possession, and although they did not have a Cromwell to lead them, they had an 'Oliver' [color bearer for the 100th] carrying their flag to victory." Captain Carter went on to claim that all of this took place one half hour before Hartranft and the First Brigade began to move. He further stated that Hartranft was not competent to judge which regiment first entered the fort, "because he was not there at that time."[109]

Another report made by Lieutenant John H. Stevenson of the 100th stated that the prisoners taken by Hartranft and his troops had already been captured by Stevenson and sent toward the rear where they encountered Hartranft. Stevenson further claimed that, "These are the men captured by the troops of Hartranft's Division and for which he was brevetted Major General." Stevenson went on to say, "I do not mention this to detract from the services of the gallant Division for it was a gallant one and was led by a gallant and competent Commander, but to vindicate the 3rd Brigade, First Division of the IX Army Corps."[110]

Probably the first public dispute over Fort Stedman appeared in the *Century Magazine* in September 1887, which claimed the Stedman victory for the 100th Pennsylvania. As a result, General Hartranft spoke with both General John B. Gordon and Gordon's assistant adjutant during the conflict, Major Henry Kyd Douglas. From that direct conversation regarding their memory of events that day, Hartranft reported that, "Gordon ...and ...Douglas ...who assure me that for the moment, whatever desultory attacks may have been made on Fort Haskell, they were paying no attention to that work, but were endeavoring to deploy their troops in the rear of the captured line [Fort Stedman] and hurry over supports. They ascribe their failure to the delay of the latter to come up, to the promptness with which the Third Division was assembled, and to the sudden attack of the 200th Pennsylvania." Then, ever gently but resolute in his manner, Hartranft continued his thought on the subject, "In making this criticism and correction I do not wish to be understood as detracting from the merits of the garrison at Fort Haskell, to whose nerve in holding on, under trying circumstances, I had done full justice in the above article long before September, 1887."[111]

Obviously, Hartranft did not concur with the position held by the men of the 100th as it relates to Stedman. He certainly valued their contribution and courage with the activities surrounding Fort Haskell, which were extremely important to the overall success of the Union operation. However, and typically, he could not find it within himself to stoop to name calling and snide remarks, such as were beginning to surface from the 100th.

Certainly the men of the 100th Pennsylvania had a proud career during the Civil War. They are entitled to their rightful position in its history for their own gallant performance on March 25, 1865. Charges and countercharges are always easy to level but difficult to sustain. Some of the disparity between claims of the 100th and Hartranft are perhaps better addressed by the general himself when he wrote about his troops sending prisoner and battle flags to the rear and noted that, "The substantial trophies of the victory were some 1600 prisoners and a large number of small-arms. The prisoners were mostly passed through the lines to the rear, to be picked up and claimed by other commands, and all but one of the captured flags were claimed and taken from the soldiers by unknown officers."[112] Hartranft did not stand alone in his position here, for on March 27, 1865, Lieutenant-Colonel M. T. Heintzelman of the 208th Pennsylvania, reported that, "we captured 250 prisoners making in all 350 prisoners captured by my Regiment, in the meantime the color bearer of the 100th Regt. P.V. entered the fort and took possession of several stands of [Rebel] colors which justly belonged to my Regiment."[113] In the report of Captain James A. Rogers of the 207th Pennsylvania, he noted that, "while I was hurrying my prisoners to the rear, an officer of our Army, wearing the badge of the First Division of the 9th Corps, snatched the [captured Rebel] flag and ran with it to the rear. This officer's name or rank, I did not learn."[114]

Debates aside, matters were now drawing to a rapid close for the Confederacy, and the last real fighting took place on April 2nd.

That day Hartranft's division again saw combat, but not the bloody encounter seen at Stedman. Captain Joseph G. Holmes of the 205th Pennsylvania reported that, "The order was given to charge the enemies works at daylight, which was gradually accomplished - This Regt. captured battery No. 30 with a number of prisoners, also one battle 'Flag' fell into our hands being captured by private John Lilley ... This 'Flag' was forwarded to Brevet Major-General Hartranft."[115]

Another report from the 51st Pennsylvania told how they too made a fight against the Rebel lines and related that as they passed the home of a Confederate Colonel Hobbs, located near the Wilson Station, the men were given something of a treat. As the Pennsylvanians approached the Hobbs home, Colonel Bolton noticed the Stars and Stripes were floating from the

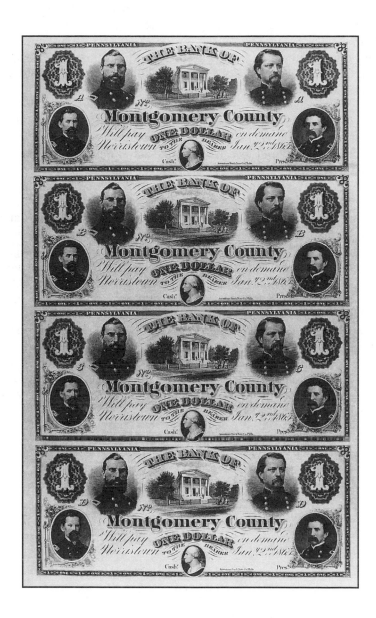

## Bank Notes Honoring Hartranft and Others

Paper currency printed by a Norristown Bank to honor some of her sons. The bills were printed in denominations of $1, $5 and $10. Most, including these originals were not placed in circulation. On the upper left is Brigadier-General Adam Jacoby Slemmer; upper right, Major-general Winfield Scott Hancock; lower right, Brevet-Major-General John F. Hartranft; lower left, Colonel Edwin Schall.

*Source: Core State Financial.*

153

top of the Hobbs home. This caused Bolton to ask Mrs. Hobbs how that flag was put there. After thinking for a moment, the woman told him that, "a Yankee General by the name of Hartranft had given it to them yesterday as he went by with his army, and waited until he saw that we put it up, and told us not to take it down."[116]

Later, on April 21, the men of the 51st Pennsylvania honored Hartranft and presented him with a gold watch as a token of their esteem. "Black John" made a brief speech and spoke about the horror of the Lincoln assassination. Shortly thereafter, Hartranft and the Third Division moved into the area of Washington City, where on May 23rd, he proudly led his division down Pennsylvania Avenue as part of the Grand Review.

Hartranft had already become a local hero back home and one measure of his status was the One, Five, and Ten Dollar bills printed by the Montgomery County Bank in Norristown. Those bills bore his image along with other Norristown men, including General Adam Jacoby Slemmer in the upper left-hand corner, General Winfield Scott Hancock on the upper right, Colonel Edwin Schall on the lower left, and Hartranft on the lower right.[117] No one at that time knew or would have believed, that all of those men, with the relative exception of General Hancock, were destined to fall into total obscurity.

Meanwhile, Sallie, like most wives, was most anxious to have Hartranft back home to share time with her and their family. For the moment, neither she nor the General knew that he was soon to encounter one small, but historic delay.

154

## ENDNOTES TO CHAPTER SIX
## THE BATTLE OF FORT STEDMAN

1. Catton, Bruce, *The American Heritage Picture History of The Civil War*, New York: American Heritage Publishing Company, 1960, p. 563. Hereafter referred to as *The Civil War*.
2. Warner, *Generals in Blue*, p. 501.
3. Davis, Burke, *Gray Fox*, New York: Rinehart, 1956, p. 360.
4. Catton, *The Civil War*, p. 564.
5. Ibid.
6. Warner, *Generals in Gray*, p. 111.
7. Gordon, John Brown, *Reminiscences of the Civil War*, New York: Charles Scribner's Sons, 1903; reprint, Alexandria, Virginia: Time-Life Books, 1981, p. 387.
8. Ibid.
9. Davis, *Gray Fox*, p. 360.
10. Ibid., p. 361.
11. Ibid.
12. Ibid., p. 362.
13. Davis, Jefferson, *The Rise and Fall of the Confederate Government*, 2 vols., New York: Appleton, 1881; reprint, New York: DaCapo Press, 1990, vol. 2, pp. 550-551.
14. Gordon, *Reminiscences of the Civil War*, p. 394.
15. Ibid., p. 396.
16. Davis, *Gray Fox*, p. 363.
17. Gordon, *Reminiscences of the Civil War*, p. 394.
18. Ibid., p. 398.
19. Ibid., pp. 398-399, 402.
20. Warner, *Generals in Gray*, p. 319.
21. Brock, R. A. ed., *Southern Historical Society Papers*, Richmond, Virginia, By The Society, 1903, Vol. 31, p. 23. Hereafter referred to as *SHSP*.
22. Ibid.
23. Hodgkins, William H., *The Battle of Fort Stedman*, Boston: Privately Printed, 1889, p. 10.
24. Ibid., p. 15.
25. Croffut, W.A. & John M. Morris, *The Military and Civil History of Connecticut During the War 1861-5*, New York: Ledyard Bill, 1868, p. 764.
26. *Bolton Diary*, p. 346.
27. *Battles and Leaders*, vol. 4., p. 580.
28. Gordon, *Reminiscences of the Civil War*, p. 404.
29. Hodgkins, *The Battle of Fort Stedman*, p. 15.

30. Gordon, *Reminiscences of the Civil War*, p. 400.

31. Ibid., p. 401.

32. Ibid.

33. Ibid.

34. Ibid., p. 404. Note, the author has found no identification of the three Union officers that Gordon selected. However, on pp. 404 and 411 of his book, *Reminiscences of the Civil War*, Gordon indicates that the name of at least one Union officer came from the 100th Pennsylvania.

35. Estimates vary here from one-third to one-half of Lee's army, even from eyewitness accounts. Author's note.

36. Gordon, *Reminiscences of the Civil War*, p. 405.

37. *Battles and Leaders*, vol. 4., p. 580.

38. Trudeau, Noah, *The Last Citadel*, Boston: Little Brown and Company, 1989, p. 294.

39. Ibid.

40. Gordon, *Reminiscences of the Civil War*, p. 406.

41. Ibid.

42. Ibid., p. 407.

43. Ibid., p. 411.

44. Sommers, Richard J., *Richmond Redeemed*, New York: Doubleday & Company, Inc., 1981, p. 226.

45. Ibid., p. 400.

46. This information, courtesy of Petersburg National Battlefield.

47. Porter, Horace, *Campaigning with Grant*, New York: The Century Company, 1897, p. 403.

48. Ibid., pp. 402-403.

49. Hartranft, John F., "Formation of the Division", written after the Battle of Fort Stedman but, it is not dated. Shireman Collection.

50. *Battles and Leaders*, vol. 4, p. 591.

51. Warner, *Generals in Blue*, pp. 359-360.

52. Hartranft, John F., "The Recapture of Fort Stedman", *The Philadelphia Weekly Press*, March 17, 1886.

53. Gordon, *Reminiscences of the War*, p. 406.

54. Ibid., pp. 408-409.

55. Brock, *SHSP*, vol. 31, p. 24.

56. Ibid., p. 24. There are several variants on this particular moment, but they all tell essentially the same tale. Author's note.

57. Ibid., pp. 24-25.

58. Ibid.

59. Ibid.

60. *Battles and Leaders*, vol. 4, p. 580.

61. Ibid.
62. Brock, *SHSP*, vol. 31, p. 26.
63. Ibid.
64. Ibid.
65. Ibid., p. 580.
66. Trudeau, *The Last Citadel*, p. 343.
67. Wilkinson, Warren, *Mother, May You Never See the Sights I Have Seen*, New York: Harper & Row, 1990, p. 329.
68. Gordon, *Reminiscences of the Civil War*, p. 410.
69. This information, courtesy of Petersburg National Battlefield.
70. Freeman, *R. E. Lee*, 4 vols., New York: Charles Scribner's Sons, 1934, vol. 4, p. 18.
71. Gordon, *Reminiscences of the Civil War*, p. 411.
72. Ibid.
73. Hartranft, "The Recapture of Fort Stedman", *The Philadelphia Weekly Press*, March 17, 1886.
74. Hodgkins, *The Battle of Fort Stedman*, p. 29.
75. Ibid.
76. Ibid.
77. Ibid.
78. Hartranft, "The Recapture of Fort Stedman", *The Philadelphia Weekly Press*, March 17, 1886.
79. Ibid.
80. *Battles and Leaders*, vol. 4, pp. 587-588.
81. Ibid.
82. Hartranft, "The Recapture of Fort Stedman", *The Philadelphia Weekly Press*, March 17, 1886.
83. Ibid.
84. Hodgkins, *The Battle of Fort Stedman*, p. 43.
85. Ibid.
86. Wilkinson, *Mother, May You Never See The Sights I Have Seen*, p. 332.
87. Hartranft, "The Recapture of Fort Stedman", *The Philadelphia Weekly Press*, March 17, 1886.
88. Ibid.
89. *Battles and Leaders*, vol. 4, p. 589.
90. Brock, *SHSP*, vol. 31, p. 29.
91. Hartranft, "The Recapture of Fort Stedman", *The Philadelphia Weekly Press*, March 17, 1886.
92. Douglas, Henry Kyd, *I Rode With Stonewall*, Chapel Hill, North Carolina: The University of North Carolina Press, 1940; reprint, St. Simons Island, Georgia: Mockingbird Books, Inc., 1989, p. 314.
93. Freeman, *R. E. Lee*, vol. 4, p. 20.

94. Ibid., p. 21.
95. Undated copy given to Hartranft after the war, Shireman Collection
96. *Battles and Leaders*, vol. 4., p. 589.
97. Illustrated Life, *Campaigns and Public Service of General Grant*,
    Philadelphia: T. B. Peterson & Brothers, 1865, p. 222.
98. Hodgkins, *The Battle of Fort Stedman*, p. 46.
99. JFH Report on the Battle of Fort Stedman, April 14, 1865., Shireman
    Collection.
100. *Norristown Herald & Free Press and Republican*, April 13, 1865.
101. Warner, *Generals in Blue*, p. 213.
102. Copy of General Parke's original report is part of the Shireman
    Collection.
103. Ibid.
104. Stanton's written confirmation to JFH, Shireman Collection.
105. *Norristown Herald & Free Press and Republican*, April 5, 1865.
106. Ibid.
107. Schmucker, Samuel M., *The History of The Civil War of The United
    States*, Philadelphia: Jones Brothers & Co., 1865, p. 947.
108. Gavin, William, *The 100th Regiment Pennsylvania Volunteers, The
    Roundhead Regiment*, Dayton, Ohio: Morningside House, Inc., 1989,
    pp. 614-630, and, Battles and Leaders, vol. 4., p. 589.
109. Gavin, *The 100th Regiment Pennsylvania Volunteers, The Roundhead
    Regiment*, p. 621.
110. Ibid., p. 620.
111. *Battles and Leaders*, vol. 4, p. 589.
112. Hartranft, "The Recapture of Fort Stedman", *The Philadelphia Weekly
    Press*, March 17, 1886.
113. Report of Lieutenant-Colonel M. T. Heintzelman [of the 207th
    Pennsylvania], March 27, 1865, Shireman Collection.
114. Report of Captain James A. Rogers [of the 207th Pennsylvania],
    March 27, 1865, Shireman Collection.
115. Report of Captain Joseph G. Holmes of the 205th Pennsylvania,
    March 27, 1865, Shireman Collection.
116. Parker, *History of the 51st*, p. 616.
117. Courtesy of Core States Financial Corp.

# CHAPTER SEVEN

## *THE LINCOLN CONSPIRACY TRIAL*

One of the greatest tragedies to come out of the American Civil War was the assassination of President Lincoln at Ford's Theater on April 14, 1865. At the very threshold of being able to rest from the rigors of the past four years, the 56-year-old President was cut down by an assassin's bullet. What followed was to become one of America's most bizarre legal cases and to this very day, endless arguments about improprieties, myths, charges and countercharges surrounding the trial and its participants still continue.

The murder of the sixteenth president resulted in one of the greatest manhunts in American history. Secretary of War Edwin M. Stanton posted a $100,000 reward for the capture of John Wilkes Booth and his accomplices. Booth's reward alone was $50,000 while $25,000 was offered for Daniel C. Harrold, or more precisely, David E. Herold, and another $25,000 for the capture of John H. Surratt, son of Mary Surratt, who herself would soon become one of the key defendants in the trial.[1]

After the President was shot, the U.S. cavalry combed the areas around Washington for any conspirators. During the early morning hours of April 26th, a contingent of the 16th New York Cavalry located Booth and Herold hiding in a tobacco shed on the farm of Richard Garrett, located south of Fredericksburg, Virginia. While the men of the 16th would normally have been under the command of Lieutenant Edward P. Dougherty, the real authority in this pursuit rested with Colonel Lafayette C. Baker, head of the War Department's Secret Police. Baker was aided by his cousin Luther B. Baker and Colonel Everton J. Congers.[2] When the cavalry surrounded Garrett's shed, they called for Booth and Herold to give themselves up which brought out Herold but Booth steadfastly refused to move. With Booth's failure to heed the calls for surrender, Colonel Conger set fire to the barn, which quickly filled the shelter with thick smoke.

Booth still refused to give up and, despite the mounting smoke, he held his ground inside the shed. Ever mindful of Secretary Stanton's wish that Booth be caught alive to stand trial before the public, Colonel Conger, a war veteran and federal detective, emphasized to the twenty-six men of the 16th that all precautions be taken not to kill Booth.

Despite these warnings, as the fire and smoke grew in and around the shed, a single shot unexpectedly rang out and Booth fell. Colonels Baker and Congers immediately ran inside and pulled Booth to the porch of the main house and attempted to make the allegeded assassin more comfortable. But he had been mortally shot through the neck, was paralyzed, and would die within four hours. Immediately Baker and Congers began to question the troops in an attempt to determine who shot Booth. It didn't take long before they learned that Sergeant Boston Corbett claimed to have fired the shot because he felt Booth was "about to shoot one of the officers."[3]

However, even among the eyewitnesses there are confusing reports about the ordeal at Garrett's barn. According to one on site report, written by an aide to Colonel Baker, the shooting of Booth was described as follows:

> Behind the blaze, with his eye to a crack, Conger saw Wilkes Booth standing upright upon a crutch...At the gleam of the fire, Wilkes dropped his crutch and carbine, and on both hands crept to the spot to espy the incendiary and shoot him dead...Booth turned at a man's stride and pushed for the door, carbine poised...
>
> A shock, a shout, a gathering up of his splendid figure, as if to overtip the stature God gave him, and John Wilkes Booth fell headlong to the floor, lying there in a heap, a little life remaining.[4]

"'He shot himself...' cried Colonel Baker, unaware of the source of the report."[5] That source was allegedly made by Sergeant Corbett who was credited with killing Booth. This credit does nothing to clarify the facts surrounding Booth's death, especially when we take a brief look at Corbett.

Thomas H. Corbett was born in England and came to America in search of his fortune. He married here but became a widower when his wife died during childbirth. As a result of that tragedy, he became mentally unsound, a severe alcoholic and a general outcast from society. After a zealous, religious rebirth, Corbett adopted the name Boston, after the city where he lived, as his Christian name, and later, approached by two prostitutes, he castrated himself to prevent his being tempted by the pleasures of the flesh.[6] This was the man that the federal government would offer to the public as the avenger of the president's death.

When Stanton learned that Booth had been shot and killed, the secretary was not as disturbed as was initially feared. Rather, he elevated Corbett to the temporary status of national hero, even though some strongly felt that Booth died from a self-inflicted gunshot. Shortly after the whole assassination affair quieted, Corbett was thought to have gone to Kansas to live upon a government pension, but there is no record of his exact movements and speculation still abounds.[7]

All of these conditions would set the stage for one of the most sensational legal cases in American history. Justice and jurisprudence were about to take on new attitudes as men would discard the proprieties set forth by the Constitution and pursue justice through might. Unfortunately, all of this was done in the name of avenging the death of one of the greatest defenders of the Constitution who ever lived.

Few today would disagree that the assassination of President Lincoln was a tragedy for the man, his family, and the country. The overall handling of the resulting legal proceedings was dreadful and the alleged physical mismanagement of those accused gave rise to accusations of foul play and abuse. Further difficulties arose as the trial unfolded and substantial differences were noted in the testimony of some eyewitnesses and participants. All of this was worsened by the federal government's insistence to try the accused by a military tribunal rather than by a civilian court and its use of illicit methods. In some quarters, this action only served to exacerbate feelings of mistrust and suspicion.

Because the trial has received wide attention from more capable historians on the subject, this author has chosen to draw particular attention to Mary E. Surratt because of her special status as a woman, which brought her to the attention of General Hartranft. That attention is not meant to pass judgment on her guilt or innocence, but rather to demonstrate Hartranft's difficult position and his adroit handling of a sensitive responsibility. Through this approach, it is hoped that the reader will be drawn closer to the personal aspects of the trial and that some of the long-held misconceptions will be dispelled.

With many people still reeling from Lincoln's murder, President Johnson appointed Major-General Winfield Scott Hancock as Military Governor of Washington D. C. The newly elevated President felt certain that Hancock's presence would have a calming effect on the potentially turbulent situation. At the same time, Johnson also appointed General Hartranft as special Provost Marshal General of Washington to "serve the military commission and carry out their decisions."[8] This appointment meant that Hartranft was the military sheriff of the Capital and had full responsibility for the defendants held in the Old Capitol Prison.

By the latter part of April, all the accomplices had been captured, and the men were held in the holds of two sister ironclads, *Montauk* and *Saugus*.[9] Mary Surratt had initially been placed in the Carroll Annex of the Old Capitol Prison, and on April 27, the accussed men were transferred to the prison as well which was still referred to by some as, "Old Penelope". On April 30th, Mary Surratt was also transferred within the same confines, and on May 1st, General Hartranft sent General Hancock a report wherein he stated that, "I took charge of eight prisoners in the cells of this prison...."[10]

The eight prisoners referred to by Hartranft included Lewis Paine [or Powell], David E. Herold, Edward Spangler, George A. Atzerodt, Michael O'Laughlin, Samuel Arnold, Dr. Samuel Mudd and Mrs. Surratt. Eventually, a total of sixteen prisoners would be held at the penitentiary upon some form of conspiracy charges while scores of others, including Union soldiers who dared to express disdain for the murdered Lincoln, were imprisoned elsewhere.

One of Hartranft's first duties was to notify the accused of the charges preferred against them which were, "maliciously, unlawfully, and traitorously conspiring ... to kill Abraham Lincoln." Samuel Arnold left his own recollection of that notice when he wrote,

> I had been but a few days incarcerated at this place, when I was arroused [sic] at midnight in my cell by Major General Hartrauth[sic], holding in his hand a lantren [sic] and some papers, which was seen after the removal of the hood from my head. He asked me if I could read, to which I replied in the affirmative. He then placed in my hands a paper containing the charge and specifications against me and others, which I perused in that silent midnight hour by the dim glimer [sic] of a lantren [sic], after which, the hood being replaced upon my head, he retired, leaving me to ponder the charge, alone in my solitude.[11]

Judging from other eyewitness accounts, all eight accused conspirators were notified of their charges in a very similar manner.

Meanwhile, Booth's body had been buried within the penitentiary walls and despite the fact that the whereabouts of his remains were supposed to be a secret, the *Washington Star* reported their exact location on May 10th.[12] Yet, with Booth dead and a strong handful of suspects to prosecute, Stanton could now direct all of his energies towards the trial of these alleged conspirators.

Stanton was a very capable lawyer with a very strong personality. He accepted his cabinet position as Secretary of War in spite of his disdain for President Lincoln. He had encountered Lincoln some years earlier while in

**George A. Atzerodt**

Atzerodt was hanged on July 7, 1865.

*Photographer: Alexander Gardner.*
*Source: Library of Congress.*

**Samuel Arnold**

Arnold was sentenced to life imprisonment.

*Photographer: Alexander Gardner.*
*Source: Library of Congress.*

**Lewis Paine**

Paine was hanged on July 7, 1865.

*Photographer: Alexander Gardner.*
*Source: Library of Congress.*

**Edmund Spangler**

Spangler got six years of hard labor.

*Photographer: Alexander Gardner.*
*Source: Library of Congress.*

**David E. Herold**

Herold was hanged on July 7, 1865.

*Photographer: Alexander Gardner.*
*Source: Library of Congress.*

**Michael O'Laughlin**

O'Laughlin got life imprisonment.

*Photographer: Alexander Gardner.*
*Source: Library of Congress.*

**Mary E. Surratt**

Mrs. Surratt was hanged on July 7, 1865.

*Source: Library of Congress.*

**Dr. Samuel Mudd**

Mudd got life imprisonment.

*Photographer: Alexander Gardner.*
*Source: Library of Congress.*

the west and engaged in a lawsuit in which Lincoln was also involved. At that time, Stanton chose to ignore and even insult the ungainly Lincoln, thinking the young lawyer to be uncouth. However, as time passed, Stanton grew to realize that Lincoln's mental capacity was far greater than he first suspected and his disdain turned to honest admiration.[13]

Stanton wanted swift justice, and he saw a number of tactical and legal problems that might impair the government's case if the trial were to be conducted in a civil court. First, he felt that President Johnson was not strong enough to satisfy the Northern public and consequently felt the need to "assume" command. Secondly, he knew that if the case were tried in a civil court, matters would become bogged down in legal detail and the desire to move rapidly would falter. Thirdly, and correctly, he felt that if the trial could be held by a military tribunal he could avoid any such civil difficulties and remain somewhat above the law, which afforded the government a distinct advantage. As a result, he moved forcibly and quickly for a military tribunal.

One final difficulty remained in Stanton's plan, and that was the constitutional doctrine that military tribunals could only try civilians where and when the civilian courts were not operable. Certainly, that was not the case in Washington D.C. in May of 1865, and Stanton promptly made his suggestions about a military trial to President Johnson. After convincing the new President that his was the best route, Johnson felt it prudent to submit the matter to Attorney General James Speed. For whatever reasons, Speed decided in favor of Stanton's idea and stated that if the assassins had acted as public enemies they "ought to be tried before a military tribunal."[14]

With Speed's decision, Stanton had his license and began to act quickly. Not everyone supported Speed's decision, and some jurists were repulsed, including Lincoln's first Attorney General, Edward Bates, who stated that Speed, "has been wheedled out of an opinion to the effect that the trial is lawful. If he be, in the lowest degree, qualified for his office, he must know better."[15] The trial was not even underway, and already the controversy had begun and it continues to this very day.

Nonetheless, Stanton was fortified and began to move forward. On May 1st, he selected an old friend and like-minded man, Brigadier-General Joseph Holt, to act as Judge Advocate.[16] Holt was not universally acclaimed as a jurist, and at least one source recorded his description of the new Judge Advocate as,"neither a distinguished legal mind nor a distinguished advocate...He never hesitated in doing his duty, and with his administration of the apparatus for repressing internal subversion he was unsparing and inexorable in using military tribunals to detain and punish those suspected of Confederate sympathies dangerous to the war effort."[17] To assist Holt, Stanton selected two added additional conservatives, Congressman John A.

171

Bingham and Colonel Henry L. Burnett.[18] The trial would run from May 12, through June 30 when the Court went into seclusion to make its final decisions.

From this point forward, the die was essentially cast. Every aspect of the trial would have a military bearing, which ranged from surprise witnesses permitted to be called against the defendants to the ultimate fate of the four destined to hang. The defense counselors immediately saw the pitfalls of a military tribunal and made every attempt to move the proceedings to a civilian court. After being denied such a move by Washington, U. S. Senator Reverdy Johnson of Maryland, a noted lawyer who had accepted the defense of Mrs. Surratt, responded to Attorney General Speed's decision by saying,

> But until this rebellion a military commission like the present, organized in a loyal State or Territory where the proceeding unobstructed...is not to be found sanctioned, or the most remotely recognized, or even military law in England or the United States, or in any legislation of either country. It has its origin in the rebellion, and like the dangerous heresy of secession, out of which that sprung, nothing is more certain in my opinion than that, however pure the motives of its origin, it will be considered, as it is, an almost equally dangerous heresy to constitutional liberty, and the rebellion ended, perish with the other, then and forever.[19]

With all the various points that can be argued about the trial's questionable proceedings, it must be acknowledged that the defendants were allowed to have some of the very best legal counselors of that day. Paine and Atzerodt had William E. Doster, who had received an excellent legal education at Yale and in Europe and had risen to the rank of brevet-brigadier-general in the U.S. Army.[20] In 1862, Doster had served as Provost Marshal for Washington D. C., and at the time of the conspiracy trial, he was out of the army and practicing law in Washington. Mrs. Surratt's counsel was headed by Senator Johnson, who was also one of the nation's finest speakers despite his limited 600 word vocabulary. Most of Johnson's work was handled by two competent, young assistants, Frederick Aiken and John Clampitt. Johnson had some early difficulties with the court, and his personal participation was not as great as some historians would like it to have been.[21] Nonetheless, Mrs. Surratt certainly never wanted for sound legal counsel.

Thomas Ewing, Jr., brother-in-law to General William T. Sherman, and Frederick Stone appeared for Dr. Mudd. Stone also represented Herold, while Ewing also represented Arnold. Walter S. Cox appeared for O'Laughlin.[22]

The counselors were all experienced and well respected in their profession, and when their attempts to move the trial to a civilian court were thwarted, some indicated their own version of what was to come. Doster, who was first employed by Atzerodt and soon "requested" to handle the case for Paine by Assistant Judge Advocate General Burnett, wrote that, "he [Paine] had about as much of a chance to get off, as the other, that is - none at all...considering the excited state of public feeling, and that, in fact, this was a contest in which a few lawyers were on one side, and the whole United States on the other - a case in which, of course, the verdict was known beforehand." Doster went on to succinctly state in his book, *Lincoln and Episodes of the Civil War*, "more than all, it was the period proper for punishment of the rebellion, and somebody must be hanged for example's sake."[23] Doster's words here are very prophetic, though we must bear in mind that they were written long after the trial.

Doster's book also offers us an eyewitness and legal glimpse of the tribunal when he noted,

There were minor circumstances against the defense. The prosecution had had a month assisted by the whole war power of the Government, its railroad, telegraphs, detectives, and military bureau to get its evidence into shape. The prisoners did not receive their charges until the day the trial opened and then they could only communicate sitting in chairs, with a soldier on each side, a great crowd surrounding them, and whisper through the bars of the dock to their counsel. Had counsel been closeted with the prisoners for weeks, with the charges in their hands and the war power of the Government at their disposal, the odds might have been more even.[24]

During the opening moments of the trial, Thomas Ewing also stated,

Conviction may be easier and more certain in this Military Commission, than in our constitutional courts. Inexperienced as most of you are in judicial investigation, you can admit evidence which the courts would reject, and reject what they would admit, and you may convict and sentence on evidence which those courts would hold to be wholly insufficient. Means, too, may be resorted to by the detectives, acting under promise or hope of reward, and operating on the fears or the cupidity of witnesses, to obtain and introduce evidence, which cannot be detected and exposed in this military trial, but could readily in the free, but guarded, course of investigation before our regular judicial tribunal. The Judge-Advocate, with whom chiefly rests the fate of these citizens, is learned in the law, but from his position he cannot be an impartial judge, unless he be more than a man. He is the prosecutor in the most extended sense of the word. As in duty bound, before this court was called, he received the reports of detectives, preexamined [sic] the witnesses, prepared and officially signed the charges, and, as principal counsel for the Government, controlled on the trial the presentation, admission and rejection of evidence.[25]

Ewing then warned his clients, Arnold and Dr. Mudd that, "you have a damned hard court to try you, and as for Judge Holt, he is a god-damned murderer."[26] With such expressions, both before and during the trial, we can be left with little doubt of its outcome.

Nonetheless, as Provost Marshal, Hartranft made daily written reports to Hancock and kept copies of those records for himself. These data were collected in the form of two large notebooks which are now held at the Musselman Library at Gettysburg College. These "daybooks", as they have come to be known, rested dormant for many years in the Hartranft family's collection and in 1965, the general's grandson, Hartranft Stockham, lent the volumes to the college where they have received only a modest amount of attention.[27]

The data in Hartranft's daybooks will not alter the history relating to the Lincoln Conspiracy Trial, since much of that information is redundant detail relating to the physical status, diet, and exercise habits of the prisoners. Nonetheless, what it does provide is some documented insight from a very sober minded individual relating to the manner in which the defendants were treated.

However, in fairness, those records also clearly demonstrate the care he personally afforded those defendants which is counter to popular belief. For example, Hartranft reported that all defendants were inspected twice a day, once by a medical officer and at least once by himself, to make certain that they and their cells were properly kept. Those daily reports were also a vehicle for Hartranft to solicit creature-comfort improvements for some of the prisoners, even if they might be considered modest by present-day standards.

These records clearly show that even Hartranft had to seek the approval of higher authorities for virtually every matter no matter how minor. For those defendants ordered to have ball and chains attached to their feet, even the matter of clean underwear eventually became the focal point of official correspondence since Hartranft had to appeal to Hancock for guidance on such trivial matters. The cell assignment for relatively obscure defendants had to be designated by the higher authorities as well as the need to provide simple boxes for the defendants to sit.[28] Hartranft even had to seek approval for modest amounts of reading materials to occupy the time of the prisoners. *Nothing was to be assumed acceptable,* no matter how insignificant! It is very obvious that Stanton was in charge here and that he was not going to tolerate any possibility that the prisoners might escape or take on the appearance of having soft treatment. While the degree of harsh treatment can be argued, we can acknowledge that the plight of the defendants was anything but pleasant.

With all the pressure applied by Stanton for vigilance, Hartranft then "ordered an infantry brigade, a battery of field guns, and a cavalry battalion to proceed to Greenleaf Point and set up camp outside the grounds. From this formidable force, a regiment of infantry was selected each day to guard the prison. As a precaution, no regiment stood guard more than once, and no soldier held the same position twice."[29]

For many, the most controversial figure involved with the trial was Mrs. Mary Surratt. Secretary Stanton believed, to his dying day, that she was definitely guilty, while others, like General Doster, felt she was not, or at least, not worthy of death.[30] While there are similar debates over most of the other major seven defendants, the arguments over Mrs. Surratt are special due to the softer attitude afforded women at the time. Many have written convincingly about one position or another, but conclusive evidence has yet to be found. This is well demonstrated by the fact that the Surratt Society itself offers no position on her guilt or innocence. We may have to accept the reality that we may never really know the depth of her involvement.

Putting aside the many differences that do exist about Mary Surratt, a brief review of her background may help us to better understand this historically intriguing woman who was the first female in America to suffer capital punishment at the hands of the federal government.

Mrs. Surratt and her husband John had built a house a few miles south of Washington, in a small town in Maryland which had become known as Surrattsville. The house was a modest inn, and had a small saloon which was given ample use by the owner, John Surratt. In addition, it also served as a post office, thereby providing the name Surrattsville. Today, the area is known as Clinton, Maryland, and is located near Andrews Air Force Base.

With the outbreak of the Civil War, Mary and her husband allowed their home to be utilized by Confederates as a resting place and they had one son, Isaac, who served in the Rebel army while another, John, Jr., worked as a Confederate courier.[31] When Lincoln was murdered, John was sought as a conspirator, but he had fled to Canada and then Europe. Later, John Surratt would be extradited to America and tried in a civil court, where the charges against him were dropped owing to legal technicalities.[32]

Mr. Surratt died in 1862, and with the debt he left behind, Mary had to rent out the Surrattsville Inn to a former Washington policeman, John M. Lloyd, and move herself into Washington, D.C.[33] There, on "H" Street she had another home, where she began to take in boarders to augment Lloyd's rental income of $500 per year.[34] At the time, Mary could hardly know that Lloyd and her new Washington boarder, Louis Weichmann, would play such an important part in her fate during the trial. Today, the Surratt boarding house in Washington still stands, where it serves as "Go-Lo's" Oriental Restaurant. The original Inn stands in Clinton, Maryland, headquarters for the Surratt Society.

As a young girl, Mary Elizabeth Jenkins[Surratt] had been raised as an Episcopalian, but about the age of 15 or 16, she converted to Catholicism. Educated at a Catholic school in Alexandria, Mary became quite enamored and involved with the Church and encouraged other members of her family to convert as well.[35] Although not wealthy, Mary was known to be a woman of some refinement, who spoke well and observed the social graces of the period.

As the trial progressed, the two key witnesses against Mary were called. First upon the stand was her boarder, Louis J. Weichmann, who delivered a devastating testimony. For the prosecution, Judge Holt himself examined the witness. A portion of Weichmann's testimony follows:

Q. When did you begin to board at the house of his [John Surratt] mother, Mrs. Surratt, a prisoner here?
A. The 1st of November, 1864.
Q. After this interview at the National Hotel, will you state whether Booth called frequently at Mrs. Surratt's?

**Surratt House and Tavern**

       This is the home/tavern and post office that Mary Surratt and her husband operated. In 1865, the home was located in Surrattsville which is Clinton, Maryland today.

*Source: Surratt Society.*

A. He generally called for Mr. Surratt, - John H. Surratt; and, in the absence of John H. Surratt, he would call for Mrs. Surratt.

Q. Were their interviews always apart from other persons, or in the presence of other persons?

A. They were always apart. I have been in the company of Booth in the parlor; but Booth has taken Surratt out of the room and taken him up-stairs, and engaged in private conversation in rooms up-stairs. Booth would sometimes, when there, engage in a general sort of conversation, and would then say, "John, can you go up-stairs, and spare me a word?" They would go up-stairs and engage in private conversation, which would sometimes last two or three hours.

Q. Did the same thing ever occur with Mrs. Surratt?

A. Yes, sir.

Q. Have you ever seen the prisoner, Atzerodt?

A. I have.

Q. Do you recognize him here?

A. Yes, sir.

Q. Have you seen him at Mrs. Surratt's?

A. He came to Mrs. Surratt's house, as near as I can remember, about three weeks after I formed the acquaintance of Booth.

Q. Were those horses that were kept there [Howard's stable] Surratt's or Booth's?

A. I would state, that, on the Tuesday previous to the Friday of the assassination, I was also sent by Mrs. Surratt to the National Hotel to see Booth for the purpose of getting his buggy. She wished me to drive her into the country on that day; and Booth said that he had sold the buggy, but that he would give me ten dollars instead, and I should hire a buggy. He spoke about the horses that he kept at Brooks' stable; and I remarked to him, "Why, I thought they were Surratt's [John] horses!" Said he, "no: they are mine."

Q. I understand you to say that Booth did give you the ten dollars?

A. Yes, sir, he gave me the ten dollars.

Q. Did you drive Mrs. Surratt out on that day?

A. I did.

Q. To what point in the country?

A. We left the city about nine o'clock, and reached Surrattsville at about half-past twelve o'clock on Tuesday, the 11th of April.

Q. Did you return that day?

A. Yes, sir. We remained at Surrattsville about half an hour- probably not that long; and Mrs. Surratt stated that she went there for the purpose of seeing Mr. [John] Nothey, who owed her some money.

Q. Will you state whether, on the following Friday, that is, the day of the assassination, you drove Mrs. Surratt to the country?

A. Yes, sir. We left about half-past two o'clock in the afternoon. She herself gave me the money on that occasion,- a ten dollar note; and I paid six dollars for the buggy.

Q. Where did you drive her to?

A. To Surrattsville; arriving there about half-past four.

Q. Did you stop at the house of Mr. Lloyd, who keeps tavern there?

A. Yes, sir. Mrs. Surratt went into the parlor, and I remained outside a portion of the time; and a portion of the time I went into the bar-room until Mrs. Surratt sent for me.

Q. Will you state whether you remember, some time in the month of March, of a man calling at Mrs. Surratt's, where you were boarding, and giving himself the name of Wood, and inquiring for John H. Surratt?

A. Yes, sir. I myself went to open the door; and he inquired for Mr. Surratt. I told him Mr. Surratt was not at home; but I could introduce him to the family if he desired it. He thereupon expressed a desire to see Mrs. Surratt; and I accordingly introduced him, having first asked his name. He gave the name of Wood.

Q. Do you recognize him among these prisoners?

A. That is the man [pointing to Lewis Paine, one of the accused].

If this were not enough to implicate Mrs. Surratt, Weichmann added the following damaging information:

Q. Will you state whether, on the afternoon of the 14th of April, the day of the assassination, Mr. Booth did not call and have a private interview with Mrs. Surratt at her house.

A. I will state, that about half-past two o'clock, when I was going to the door, I saw Mr. Booth. He was in the parlor, and Mrs. Surratt was speaking with him.

Q. ...And was it immediately after that you and Mrs. Surratt set out for the country? [The question being related to Mrs. Surratt's visit to her Surrattsville home to deliver a wrapped package to Lloyd]

A. Yes, sir.[36]

Weichmann's testimony when combined with Lloyd's was extremely damaging for Mary Surratt. When called to the stand, Lloyd told the court that five or six weeks before the assassination, he was visited by Mary's son John, Herold and Atzerodt. They asked Lloyd to store two carbines, some rope, ammunition and a wrench. When Lloyd pleaded he had no place suitable for such things, John Surratt showed him a very suitable spot above the storeroom where they could be placed underneath the joist of the second floor.[37]

Then, according to Lloyd's testimony presented in the official U. S. Government compilation, the Innkeeper told the following,

> On the 14th of April I went to Marlboro to attend a trial there; and in the evening, when I got home, which I should judge was about 5 o'clock, I found Mrs. Surratt there. ...She told me to have those shooting-irons ready that night, there would be some parties who would call for them. She gave me something wrapped in a piece of paper, which I took up stairs, and found to be a field-glass. She told me to get two bottles of whiskey ready, and that these things were to be called for that night.
>
> Just about midnight on Friday, Herold came into the house and said "Lloyd, for God's sake, make haste and get those things." I... went straight and got the carbines, supposing they were the parties Mrs. Surratt had referred to, though she didn't mention any names. From the way he spoke he must have been apprised that I already knew what I was to give him. ...I did not give them the rope and monkeywrench. Booth didn't come in. I did not know him, he was a stranger to me. He remained on his horse. Herold came into the house and got a bottle of whiskey , and took it out to him, and he drank while sitting on his horse.
>
> I do not think they remained over five minutes. They only took one of the carbines. Booth said he could not take his, because his leg was broken.[38]
>
> Just as they were about leaving, the man [Booth] who was with Herold said, I will tell you some news, if you want to hear it, or something to that effect. I said "I am not particular; use your own pleasure about telling it." "Well" said he, "I am pretty certain that we have assassinated the President and Secretary Seward."
> ...I was much excited and unnerved at the time.[39]

These two damaging testimonies then would lead the forty-two-year-old Mrs. Surratt to the gallows.[40] When we consider the comments made by Doster about the tribunal's preconceived notions and add these testimonies, it is not too difficult to understand how she would receive a death sentence. And yet Mary Surratt had not lost all of her strength and stature, as was shown during the testimony of W. M. Wannerskerch, who was part of her arresting party. When asked to identify Mrs. Surratt, Wannerskerch said he could not see her face. With that, the court record shows that "slowly, coolly, Mrs. Surratt lifted her veil, looked steadily at him and slowly, coolly lowered the veil again."[41] Wannerskerch made a positive identification.

Sharp controversy exists over the basic treatment afforded all of the eight principal prisoners. Their cells were void of any creature comforts and the prisoners had an empty cell between them, making it impossible for them to speak to each other. The men wore rigid wrist irons while their feet were chained and anchored to a seventy-five pound iron ball.[42]

The most controversial punishment was the use of the head bags that Stanton ordered. These were made from heavy canvas and had about one inch of cotton padding inside. The hoods had only a small opening for eating while no openings existed for the eyes and ears. In fact, there were extra wads of cotton that put constant pressure upon the eyes.[43] The hoods were tied around the neck and they were only removed when the prisoners went into the court room.

The matter of the hoods was initially developed as a means to maintain verbal security among the prisoners.[44] Because of her sex, and Stanton's reluctance to sustain a loud public outcry, Mary Surratt was neither hooded nor chained.[45] The hoods were destined to be removed in the early part of June for all but Paine. In his June 6th report to Hancock, Hartranft wrote that, "The prisoners are suffering very much from the padded hoods, and I would respectfully request that they be removed from all the prisoners except 195[Paine]. This prisoner does not suffer as much as the others, and there may be some necessity for his wearing it, but I do not think there is any for the others."[46]

For General Hartranft, his entire responsibility raised some difficult personal problems. While he had developed into a model soldier who knew the value of obeying orders, this particular duty with civilians and its attendant hardships made him uncomfortable. Such harsh treatment for a woman during that period was unheard of, and the men were being handled in a manner that already found them guilty. His dilemma was to obey orders while bringing some modicum of civility to the prisoners without appearing imprudent and thereby losing favor with his superiors, particularly Stanton. Please remember that Hartranft was also a competent lawyer.

Each day Hartranft personally oversaw the movement of the prisoners to and from the court room, and then he would take up his own position which was at a table near the entrance of the room.[47] At times of court recess, he saw that they were either returned to their cells or brought out into the courtyard for exercise. The twice daily inspection of the prisoners continued as well, and he made certain that the medical officer also made his daily visits. Through the medical officer's reports, Hartranft was able to obtain small but important concessions for the prisoners without appearing as a "soft touch". Yet while it was rare for anyone to move without prior approval, on June 2nd Hartranft took it upon himself to remove the seventy five pound balls attached to the feet of Paine and Atzerodt, since they were both found placing the balls against their heads. Obviously he was concerned about their potential to commit suicide, and everyone, from Secretary Stanton on down, agreed with his decision.[48]

Visitors to the accused were screened carefully to protect their privacy, and right up to the last moments, Hartranft patently refused to permit any of them to become a media sensation.[49] Any visitors, including their counselors, had to have written permission, which was usually granted by individuals like Stanton, Holt, Hancock, or Hartranft himself. At the same time, Hartranft remained fastidious about the cleanliness of the prisoners and their cells. When personal hygiene became impaired because of the ball and chains attached to the feet of the men, he made pleas to Hancock for permission to alter matters so clean underwear could be utilized.[50] However, some reports tend to exaggerate matters of hygiene by reporting that, "No baths or washing of any kind were allowed."[51] This type of information is definitely contrary to the data contained in Hartranft's daybooks, and only tends to add to the confusion surrounding the trial.

Hartranft remained guarded about any type of relationship developing between himself and any of the prisoners. This was particularly true of the male prisoners, and in his report of May 4th, to General Hancock, he provides us with a glimpse of his stoic posture. "The prisoner in [cell] 195 [Paine], after he had finished washing himself, as I was about leaving the cell, and about to lock the door, said, 'General I would like to talk to you if you would condescend to do so - I do not mean now, but when you have time'. I answered 'I have no time'."[52] With that sharp retort, Hartranft left the cell. However, Paine was to have his chat with Hartranft, but that moment was still more than two months away.

But for Mrs. Surratt, matters were slightly different, and her Teutonic jailer simply could not bring himself to treat her exactly like the men. In addition to other privileges afforded the landlady, Hartranft also ordered Brigadier-General Levi A. Dodd to take personal care of her. According to one newspaper report, Dodd, "attended that unfortunate and misguided woman all through the trial, and when she was executed he was by her side."[53] During the war, Dodd had been a regimental commander in Hartranft's division.

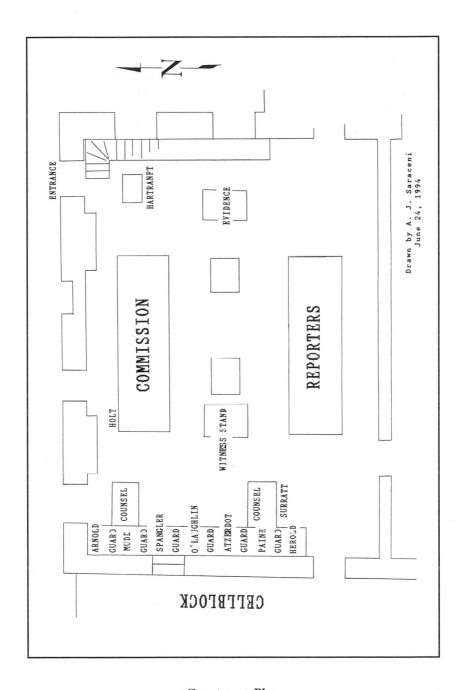

**Courtroom Plan**

Redrawn from the original compiled by Benn Pitman, by A. J. Saraceni and modified to show Hartranft's position, courtesy of Michael Kauffman.

183

Each day Hartranft sent off his daily report to Hancock, wherein he told of the prisoners' conditions along with any request he might have. Those daily reports were the means whereby he might seek out any modest comforts for the prisoners.[54] A good example of his approach, to utilize the medical officer and his comments as a vehicle for improvement is evident in his report of June 18. Therein, Hartranft tells Hancock that Spangler's mind was starting to wander and the doctors decided that he should be placed in the open air for a while. Hartranft followed up on that medical recommendation, but also reminded Hancock that the surgeon recommended open air time for **all** the prisoners, and noted that they should also be provided with some reading materials.[55]

On the 19th of June, Hartranft again reminded Hancock of the doctor's recommendations and also requested a box for each male prisoner to utilize as a seat and an arm chair for Mary Surratt.[56] The men would be given boxes to use as chairs and a rocking chair would be taken from Mrs. Surratt's home to add to her comfort.[57] Mrs. Surratt apparently was undergoing her change of life and consequently was frequently ill which resulted in Hartranft securing approval to have her daughter Annie stay with her.[58] His requests were granted.

Another major controversy surrounds the lack of privacy available to the prisoners, their legal counselors and visitors. It has been often stated that there were no private interviews permitted between the defendants and their counselors. It is true that most frequently, instructions were provided to permit entry of visitors under the "usual restrictions", which meant that any conversations had to be held within hearing distance of a soldier. However, this was not the case at all times, and Hartranft's and other records show a number of directives where soldiers were not present and specifically required not to be present.[59] On May 2, Hartranft wrote to Hancock "I then locked the door, moved the sentinel away from the door, and permitted no one to be so near the cell as to hear the conversation."[60] In that same report, Hartranft again wrote that with another prisoner, that same day, "At 8:50 P.M. I opened cell 195, removed the hood from the prisoner, and Major Eckert entered the cell. I closed the door [not locking it] and removed the sentinel and allowed no one in hearing distance of the conversation in the cell." On May 10th, Judge Holt requested entry for "Mr. Stone, counsel for Dr. Mudd...the interview to take place in the presence of the officer *but not* [emphasis added] requiring the conversation to be in his hearing." Again, on May 21, Hancock sent a note to Hartranft to permit "Mr. Doster to see prisoners Payne and Atzerodt as counsel"; with this request, there were no restrictions.[61] Despite these conditions, which only demonstrate how information becomes distorted, it must still be acnkowledged that the defendants did not enjoy the same privacy or privileges they would have had in a civilian court.

One important observer to report upon Hartranft during the trial was CSA General Henry Kyd Douglas. Douglas had been part of Stonewall Jackson's group and shortly after the war, he was arrested for breaking his parole by wearing his Confederate uniform.[62] Douglas had first met Hartranft, earlier in the year, on the no man's land between Fort Stedman and Colquitt's salient on March 25. Douglas had been instructed by General Gordon to move forward under a flag of truce to gather up the Confederate dead and wounded. Following instructions, Douglas moved forward only to be confronted by a short-tempered General Hartranft.

After listening to Douglas' request, Hartranft addressed him with a quick eye and told him "take your dead and wounded and give us ours, that is all the cartel we need on an occasion like this."[63] However, before parting, enough conversation passed between the two officers to reveal that they had both attended the same school, Marshall College. This brief encounter stayed with Douglas and he became impressed with the Pennsylvanian's courage and humane attitude.

When Douglas was arrested for parole violation, he was sent to Washington D.C. and asked where he would like to stay. The Rebel chieftain quickly replied "I want to be sent to the penitentiary." When the guard asked Douglas why he would want to go there specifically, Douglas responded, "because, General Hartranft is in command, and I will always trust myself in the hands of a soldier with whom I have fought." Douglas later reported that Hartranft had indeed treated him with kindness. Placed in a cell next to Mrs. Surratt, Douglas wrote that "Mrs. Surratt was supposed to be fed on prisoner ration like the others but in fact, Hartranft sent her daily from his table not only the substantials but the delicacies with which it was so abundantly supplied."[64]

As if to emphasize the bizzare nature of the proceedings, Douglas was called to the stand to testify about the suspected efforts of his old unit, the Stonewall Brigade, and Lincoln's murder.[65] After destroying that wild thought, he noted a particular poignant moment that gives us added insight into Hartranft.

On the same day Miss Annie E. Surratt was put upon the stand as witness for her mother. It was a pitiable scene. She was tall, slender, fair, handsome; for her to stand the stare of the cruel, stony eyes riveted upon her was a trying ordeal. She must have known that her testimony made no impression on that tribunal, and toward the close of it she

185

began to show signs of a collapse. The veins and muscles of her neck seemed swollen and she gave evidence of great suffering. General Hartranft was about to go to her, but knowing her horror of him as her mother's jailer, he, with delicate consideration asked me to bring her from the stand.  I brought her out, passing just in front of her mother, and as she reached my room she fell forward and fainted. The door was shut quickly, a doctor called, and at his instance General Hartranft and I carried her below, to his room.[66]


Later, at the end of June, Hartranft himself received a rebuking letter from his wife Sallie, who pleaded with him not to permit himself to be made a hangman. In the end, neither the plea from Sallie or anyone else would keep him from his appointed task.

While in the midst of all of this historical creation, Hartranft also had a personal side of his life that he had to lead. He kept up a lively correspondence with his wife, who was always eager to hear about his challenges, but she also wanted his equal attention in return. On the 28th of June, Sallie wrote her now celebrated husband and told him that she could not now come to visit him. Then, she went on to remonstrate with the major-general with the comment "you say the ladies do not believe that you are married. If I was there they would think [so]." Then, Sallie's ire got the better of her as her handwriting becomes grossly distorted and she ends with the statement that "you should have been [home] some time ago...."[67] Perhaps on the same day he received the above letter, Hartranft received yet another note from Sallie which may have made him blush when she told him, "I am still expecting you home [at the] 4th [of July], if you do not come I will take a big cry - I want to see you so bad and have been thinking all the time how many hundred little things I will do to add to your pleasure and comfort. I am asked all the time to think that you must be penned up in that hateful jail - the idea of making a hangman of you after your 4 years labor, I cannot think of it in any other light."[68]

One other incident during the proceedings carried a strange twist that unfolded years after the trial was complete. One suspect at the penitentiary was a Mr. Harrison who was ultimately acquitted of all charges. As with all prisoners, Harrison too was looked upon each day by the General, which made the officer a very common sight. Years later, when Harrison was a lawyer for the Union Telegraph Company, he was sent to Harrisburg on business. According to Harrison's wife, when the lawyer arrived in the capitol city, he was surprised to learn that the state official he was ordered to deal with was none other than his past jailer. When Harrison came downstairs in the morning at the Lochiel Hotel and saw Hartranft waiting for him in the hall, he threw up his hands, exclaiming, "My God, general, you are not after me again."[69] Both men shook hands, had a good laugh and went off to conduct their business.

When the tribunal finally made its decision on June 29, it would take another seven days before Hartranft was advised.[70] The court's decision was death by hanging for Paine, Herold, Atzerodt, and Mary Surratt and prison terms for the other four men.

Before anyone could be advised, the members of the Commission had to announce their findings to President Johnson first, who had been ill at the time of their decision. Finally, on July 5, Judge Holt went to see the President with the sentences. Attached to Mary Surratt's sentence was a special plea to the President for clemency because of her age and sex.[71]

Unfortunately for Mary Surratt and history, only the President and Holt were in the room together, and when Holt left the President, the Judge Advocate had the Chief Executive's approval on every sentence recommended, including death for Mary Surratt. Later, President Johnson absolutely insisted that Holt never informed or showed him the Court's request for clemency, and that if he had, Mary Surratt's life would have been spared. For his part, Holt spent the rest of his life trying to convince everyone that Johnson indeed read the clemency request. The reality is that no one knows for certain exactly what transpired between the two that day, and will probably never know.

Nonetheless, the tribunal then advised General Hancock of its decision, and he immediately informed Hartranft on the morning of the 6th that, "In accordance with the directions of the President of the United States, the foregoing sentences, in the cases of David E. Herold, G. A. Atzerodt, Lewis Payne and Mary E. Surratt will be duly executed at the Military Prison near the Washington Arsenal between the hours of 10 O'Clock A.M. and Two O'Clock P.M. July 7, 1865. Brevet Major General John F. Hartranft Commandant of the Military Prison is charged with the execution of this order."[72]

Later, during the afternoon of the 6th, both Hancock and Hartranft went to the cells of the four to tell them of the court's decision, which was "*to be hung by the neck.*"[73] With that, Mary Surratt simply burst into tears in an uncontrollable manner and muttered, "I had no hand in the murder of the President."[74]

For both generals, the execution of Mrs. Surratt would be used against them in later years in their political pursuits. Both men would be described as heartless beasts who could do no more than put a helpless woman to death. Those who spoke in this manner had no knowledge of the true feelings of these men. It is a credit to both generals that they simply sustained such ugly remarks and, despite those volleys, forged ahead and won the confidence of the people in their respective political careers.

Hartranft continued to offer a little more insight into the reaction and desires of the four when told of their fate. In a report to General Hancock dated July 8, Hartranft stated that, "in obedience to your orders, I did on July 6th, 1865 between the hours of 11 A.M. & 12 P.M., read the findings & sentences of Lewis Payne, G. A Atzerodt, David Herold and Mary E. Surratt to each of them and also delivered a copy of the same to each. All this in your presence."[75] Hartranft then asked each prisoner if they wished him to send for anyone. In response, Payne said his family was too far away [Florida], but he asked to see Reverend A. P. Stryker of Baltimore and Major Thomas T. Eckert from the Secretary of War's office. Atzerodt asked to see his brother John, his brother-in-law, John Smith, his friend, Marshall McPhail, his lover Rose Wheeler and her daughter, plus an unidentified Southern minister. Apparently, the minister either could not be reached or properly identified because Hartranft himself went to see Reverend Dr. John G. Butler in Washington, who came to attend to the young German.[76] Herold simply asked that his family be notified and that they in turn would send a minister. Mary Surratt wanted to see her daughter Annie, plus Fathers J. Ambrose Walter and Bernardin F. Wigget, and Mr. John P. Brophy, a close family friend.[77] To all of these requests, Hartranft responded immediately and sent for all those named.

Hartranft also summoned Captain Christian Rath of the 17th Michigan Volunteers, who had been assigned to his staff on May 9th.[78] Rath was given the task of building the scaffold and making ready all of the hanging details. While he had never before built a hanging scaffold, Rath began to design one that he felt certain would work. That evening before the hangings, Rath made up the nooses, saving Mrs. Surratt's until last. By the time he got to making her noose, Rath was tired and felt that it wouldn't be needed anyway, since everyone expected her to receive a pardon. As a result, instead of the traditional seven turns, Mrs. Surratt's noose had only five. Many years later, Rath would wryly remark that "a five-turn knot will perform as successful a job as a seven-turn knot." He also had the graves dug just beyond the scaffold, but, owing to some superstitious laborers at the arsenal, the graves were only three feet deep.[79]

Early in the morning of the 7th, Lewis Paine requested permission to speak to Hartranft, who went to the prisoner's cell. There, Paine made a confession of sorts and expressed his feeling that Mrs. Surratt was completely innocent. When the interview was completed, Hartranft returned to his office and wrote a quick note which was immediately sent to the White House, wherein he stated, "The prisoner Payne has just told me that Mrs. Surratt is entirely innocent of the assassination of President Lincoln, or of any knowledge thereof. He also states that she had no knowledge whatever of the abduction plot, that nothing was ever said to her about it, and that her name was never mentioned by the parties connected therewith." Hartranft then fatefully added, "I believe that Payne has told the truth in this matter."[80] Several days later, this note and its contents would come to the attention of General Hancock, who asked Hartranft to explain his thoughts on the note. Hartranft did so on July 15.

Before the hangings, Hartranft had refused to permit newspaper reporters to interview any of the defendants. He was firm in protecting their dignity and refused to let them become objects of the media. During the morning of the hangings, he was pressed with questions and asked to make comments by a variety of people. Steadfastly, he refused to permit the ordeal to take on a circus atmosphere. Yet, no matter how much decorum Hartranft demanded inside the penitentiary, he had no control of that which occurred outside the prison walls. There, on the day of the execution, which was exceptionally hot, vendors were doing a brisk business in pies and lemonade, as if a celebration were being conducted.[81] Shortly before noon, General Hancock arrived at the penitentiary.

About 11:00 A.M., photographer Alexander Gardner showed up with his equipment and his assistant, Timothy O'Sullivan. Gardner would be the only photographer in the yard that day and, after taking some initial shots, O'Sullivan encountered Hartranft and his staff. Realizing the historical importance of the group, O'Sullivan pleaded with the General to permit him to take a photo of him and his staff. Hartranft agreed, and soon he was seated in the center of his staff while O'Sullivan took his photo. Hartranft is in the center while seated, Captain Richard Watt, is on his far right next to Lieutenant-Colonel William H. McCall. On the general's immediate left is Colonel Levi A. Dodd who sits next to the executioner, Captain Christian Rath. The chairs utilized by Hartranft's staff would soon be used by the condemned.[82]

Earlier that morning, Hancock had been ordered to appear before Judge Andrew Wylie with a writ of habeas corpus, demanding his appearance along with that of Mrs. Surratt.[83] Wylie was making a last-ditch effort to save Mrs. Surratt, after he was shaken out of his bed at 2:00 A.M., by Mrs. Surratt's lawyers pleading for his help.[84] At about 11:30 A.M. on the 7th, General Hancock appeared before Wylie with Attorney General James Speed, armed with a presidential order suspending the writ of habeas corpus.[85] According to one Hancock biographer, the general stated, "that the body of Mary E. Surratt is in my possession, under and by virtue of an order of [President] Andrew Johnson... for the purpose in said order expressed."[86] Hancock then declined "to produce said body by reason of the

**General John F. Hartranft and His Staff**

Hartranft and his staff moments before the hanging of the four condemned conspirators. Hartranft is seated in the center of the first row and to his far right is Captain Richard Watt; while next to Watt is Lieutenant-Colonel William H. McCall. To Hartranft's immediate left is Colonel Levi A. Dodd, whom Hartranft assigned to take care of Mrs. Surratt. Captain Christian Rath is seated at the far left. Standing to Hartranft's right is Lieutenant-Colonel G. W. Frederick while immediately behind the General is Lieutenant G. W. Geissinger. Standing to Hartranft's left is Surgeon G. L. Porter.

*Photograhper: Alexander Gardner.*
*Source: Michael Kauffman/Library of Congress.*

order of the President of the United States endorsed upon said writ." [Johnson simply had done away with the writ of habeas corpus like his predecessor, President Lincoln] Hearing all of this, Wylie simply dismissed Hancock, stating that "This court finds itself powerless to take any further action in the premises."[87] Wylie had warned Annie Surratt and the counselors that he had no means to enforce his writ, it being only a piece of paper, while General Hancock had 5,000 rifles to enforce the government's decision. Obviously, he did not expect the President to yield, and he was not mistaken! For his part, Hancock returned to his gruesome duties, feeling confident, however, that Mrs. Surratt would be pardoned at the last moment.

Annie Surratt had also gone to the White House to plead with President Johnson for mercy upon her mother. Johnson's aides did not permit the young woman access to the President and simply left her a crying, heaving heap upon the floor.[88]

According to General Lafayette Baker, who was there, the following took place at the penitentiary, "He [Hancock] enters the room hurriedly, takes General Hartranft aside, and a few words pass between them in a low tone, to which Hartranft nods acquiescence; then, in a louder voice, Hancock says: 'Get ready, General; I want to have everything put in readiness as soon as possible'."[89] This was the signal for the visits of the clergy, relatives, and friends of the prisoners to cease, and for the doomed to prepare for execution.

Perhaps growing weary with the whole trying ordeal, around 1:15 P.M., Hartranft blandly announced to the press that they too should get ready.[90] Even at this late moment however, Hancock still hoped for a last moment reprieve and he stationed riders between the White House and the penitentiary to carry any such message. When all hope was gone, Hancock finally gave the signal to Hartranft to begin.

As the four were led from the prison's interior to the courtyard, Mary Surratt was the first in line, followed by Paine, then Atzerodt, and Herold.[91] Just before she began to move, Mrs. Surratt stated to her confessor, Father Walter, "I wish to say something." The priest, who had attended to Mrs. Surratt for a while, looked warmly at his charge and asked "Well, what is it, my child?" Mary attempted to muster her strength, and in a broken voice she uttered, "I am innocent."[92] Father Walters is not without his detractors because he later wrote a paper on the matter which was read before the United States Catholic Historical Society of New York on May 25, 1891.[93] Some feel that between this final statement and Mary's last confession, wherein she pleaded innocence, he could have been a greater help to her.

With difficulty, especially for Mrs. Surratt, the prisoners made their way up the thirteen steps to the platform. Only Paine appeared to be calm. They were all seated and umbrellas offered them some small relief from the blazing sun. Standing in front of everyone, Hartranft read aloud the charges, verdicts and sentences. Once he was finished, Paine's minister, Dr. A. D. Gillette, stepped forward to offer Hartranft and those on his staff, Paine's personal expression of gratitude for the kindness they had offered him. Similar statements were offered the general from the ministers attending Atzerodt and Herold as well.[94] The priest attending Mrs. Surratt said nothing on her behalf.

With all the legalities completed, Rath began his work of covering the head of each prisoner with makeshift hoods he had fabricated out of a white shelter tent.[95] When the hoods were applied, Rath than affixed the rope around the neck of each prisoner. As he began to place the rope around Mrs. Surratt's neck, her daughter Annie peered out of a window on the second floor of the prison. Next to her was General Doster, who wrote, "To me the most harrowing part of her [Mrs. Surratt] execution was to see her bonnet removed by the two soldiers and the rope put around her neck. It was the meeting of the extremes of what is esteemed sacred and what is deemed infamous. During her execution Anna was present... She stood by one of the windows until the rope was fixed. Then she fell down in a swoon."[96]

While Rath was preparing Mrs. Surratt, an unidentified man in the group below the scaffold called out, "Gentlemen, I tell you this is murder; can you stand and see it done?"[97] Unable to raise any support, he simply stared on in silence.

When Rath got to Paine, the strapping young man assisted the hangman by lifting his head to facilitate the grisly work. Rath said to Paine, "I want you to die quick." Paine replied, "You know best."[98]

With all the last minute details completed, the scaffold was cleared of all but the condemned. Standing there in the 100 plus degree heat, all that was required was the last signal for the four to drop. That "last signal" actually consisted of two last signals, with the first coming from either General Hancock or Hartranft. The final signal came from Rath. It was about 1:25 P.M.[99]

Some reports tell of either Hancock or Hartranft offering three claps of the hand as their final signal while other reports indicate only two claps. While it remains unclear about who or how many claps were heard, that signal caused Rath to give the "final" signal, causing the traps to fall.[100] With that, the four condemned prisoners were promptly suspended between heaven and earth. Again, eyewitness accounts vary somewhat, but it appears that none of the conspirators suffered very long, and Mrs. Surratt the very least. After hanging for almost thirty minutes, the four were cut down and placed in wooden coffins which contained a bottle with their names inside to insure proper identification. Temporarily, they would be buried just behind the scaffolding.

When the signal was given to cut the bodies down, one soldier made a mad dash to secure a souvenir and quickly cut the rope holding Atzerodt which caused the body to fall rudely upond the ground.[101] While that soldier was sharply reprimanded, all of the ropes and the gallows were promptly cut up into lengths of approximately twelve inches and given away as mementos.[102] Those given to General Hartranft can be seen in the photo on page 197.

Now that the four had been executed, it only remained for CSA Captain Henry Wirz, Commandant of Andersonville Prison, to also be hanged on November 10, 1865.[103] With the execution of Wirz, the only real Confederate "official" to be put to death, it appears as if the nation's appetite for blood was at last satisfied.

With the entire trial proceedings complete, Hartranft was relieved of his formal duties by Secretary of War Stanton and in a letter dated July 17, 1865, Stanton wrote,


> Brevet Major General Hartranft,
> General
>
> In relieving you from your recent command at the Washington Arsenal it is due you to express the satisfaction of this Department with the diligent faithful and appropriate manner in which the important duties of your command have been fulfilled. To you and your command the thanks of the Department are herein.
>
>                    Yours very truly
>                    Edwin M. Stanton
>                    Secretary of War[104]


This warm letter to the General was a far cry from the derisive attitude the Secretary had utilized against Hartranft almost four years earlier, when the same citizen soldier was unable to convince his 4th Pennsylvania regiment to remain on the field at First Bull Run. From that fateful day on July 21, 1861, to the present, Hartranft, in his own quiet way,

**Condemned Listen to Death Order**

Condemned Lincoln conspiracy prisoners listen to General Hartranft, under the umbrella holding the white paper, reading the death order.

*Photographer: Alexander Gardner.*
*Source: Library of Congress.*

**Hoods are Placed on Condemned**

The condemned have their hoods applied and nooses adjusted. From left to right, Mary Surratt, seated; Paine with hood applied; Herold and Atzerodt who are both bare-headed.

*Photographer: Alexander Gardner.*
*Source: Library of Congress.*

**Condemned are Hanged**

Condemned Lincoln conspiracy prisoners after the traps had been sprung. Mrs. Surratt is on the far left.

*Photographer: Alexander Gardner.*
*Source: Library of Congress.*

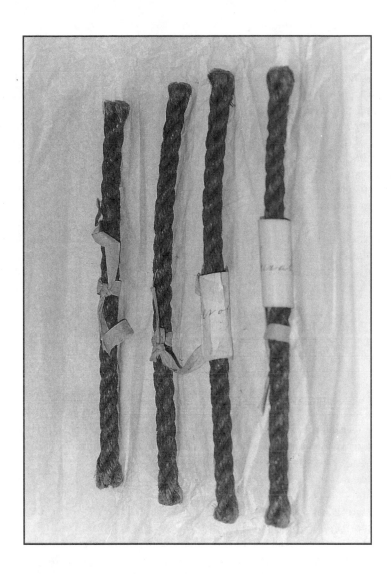

**Pieces of the Ropes That Hanged the Four Condemned Lincoln
Conspirators**

These pieces of rope are contained in Hartranft's collection of papers.
Obviously from the hanging of the four conspirators, two are identified as "Surratt"
and "Herold". However, since the cards bearing these names can be easily removed
from the rope, it is not exactly certain that the identifications are precise.

*Photographer: Frank D'Amico.*
*Source: Shireman Collection.*

had repeatedly proven his ability and won the respect of many, including the secretary.

After the trial proceedings were completed, a number of distortions developed about some of the people and emotions involved in the entire event. One popular notion pomoted that General Hartranft believed Mrs. Surratt to be completely innocent of the charges against her. This thought grew out of the note written by the general and sent to the White House on the morning of July 7, just after his interview with Paine. As noted earlier, this note came to the attention of General Hancock, who asked the Provost Marshal to clarify his thoughts. Even before Hancock's inquiry, Hartranft received a very warm and kind note from Annie Surratt dated July 9th, wherein she too asked him about his statement concerning her mother's innocence. Obviously it didn't take very long for Hartranft's statement to get around, which indicates White House "leaks" even then. While there is no record of a reply from the general to Annie, her letter and Hartranft's response to Hancock's request are fully reproduced here.

Washington D. C.
July 9th, 1865
Genl. Hartranft

Genl. Hancock told Mr. Holohan [a family friend] that you had some things that belonged to my poor Ma, which, with my consent you would deliver to him. Don't forget to send the pillow upon which her head rested, and her prayer beads [rosaries] if you can find them - these things are dear to me.

Someone told me that you wrote the President stating the prisoner Payne had confessed to you the morning of the execution that Ma was entirely innocent of the President's assassination, and had no knowledge of the abduction plot, and that you believe that Payne had confessed the truth. I would like to know if you did it because I wish to remember and thank those who did Ma the least act of kindness. I was spurned and treated with the utmost contempt by everyone at the White House. Remember me to the officers who had charge of Ma, and I shall always think kindly of you.

Yours respectfully,
Anna Surratt[105]

198

The following is Hartranft's response to General Hancock regarding his alleged view of Mrs. Surratt's innocence.

U. S. Arsenal Mil. Prison
Washington D. C.
July 15, 1865

Maj. Genl. W. S. Hancock
Comdg. M. M. Div.
Wash. D. C.

About 10 O'Clock in the forenoon of the day of the execution July 7th, 85, Mr. Brophy came to my quarters, saying that Judge Holt desired Father Walter to put in writing, the statement which Payne had made to him relative to the innocence of Mrs. Surratt. I immediately called Father Walter, who was then in the cell of Mrs. S--- [Surratt], into my room and he proceeded to write the statement. Believing that Judge Holt desired the the best possible evidence as to Payne's sayings, I remarked to Father Walter, that perhaps it would be better for me to add what Payne had said to one to which he assented. I then made the endorsement, which I presume is in the possession of Judge Holt, as nearly in the words of Payne as I could remember and added that I believed Payne had told the truth in this matter. *In this, I did not by any means intend to express my own opinion of the guilt or innocence of Mrs. Surratt but simply that I believed **Payne** had told the truth according to the **best** of his knowledge and belief.* [Emphasis added]

I am Genl.
Your most Obt. Svt.
John F. Hartranft
Bvt. Maj. Genl.
Comdg. Prison[106]

Since Hartranft was in charge of the prisoners within the penitentiary, he had many opportunities to hear comments made by them and their visitors. It is certain that there were at least two requests to speak to him from Paine, and there may have been others as well. Under such close confinement, it is entirely feasible that he heard or was told of Atzerodt's "confession" to Doster wherein that prisoner stated, "That old lady [Mrs. Surratt] is as deep in as any of us."[107]

As for Arnold, O'Laughlin, Spangler and Dr. Mudd, they were brought before General Hartranft on July 17th and he announced that they had been found guilty and would soon be on their way to Fort Jefferson in the Dry Tortugas.[108] That sentencing was conducted in the open courtyard of the penitentiary, and Arnold wrote of his sentencing that, "Genl. Hartrauth [sic], the Military custodian, who was seated at the far end of the yard and the sentence of each were [sic] made known...."[109]

And so the confusion, charges and countercharges still remain. It is important to realize that all of the mystique surrounding the trial was not caused solely by the federal government. The public too contributed its share of distortion and confusion. Shortly after the assassination and the hangings, a number of people sent letters to officials in Washington wishing to offer their thoughts of assistance and vengeance. The following notes are but a small sampling of those received:

* * * * * * * * * *

To Hon. E. M. Stanton

Believing in the efficacy of prayer, and earnestly desiring that the assassin of our beloved President be brought to justice, I clearly dreamed that the assassin was in a man's house by the name of Cromwell, at Reading, Pennsylvania. I am no believer in Spiritualism or fanaticism of any kind, I am a matter-of-fact woman, but for the intelligence I prayed fervently; take it for what it is worth, but I desire that it never be made public. I feel it to be a duty to give my name, but a delicacy prevents me from so doing.

Yours truly,

St. Clairsville, Belmont Co., Ohio[110]

* * * * * * * * * *

PHILADELPHIA, APRIL 20, 1865
To Hon. W. H. Seward:

You may survive the fatal blow which I aimed at your throat but know, thou most cruel, cunning, and remorseless man, that sooner or later you will fall by the very hand which assaulted you last Friday night, and now pens these calm, solemn words.[111]

\* \* \* \* \* \* \* \* \* \*

TANNER, CANADA, APRIL 20, 1865
To Andrew Johnson, President of the
United States or other authority:

With certainty I state to you that John A. Payne and thirteen others are sworn to murder Andrew Johnson, E. M. Stanton, and L. S. Fisher, within thirty days from 23d April, 1865. The arrangements are all made and in progress of execution. I do not know where John A. Payne is now; he was at Montreal and Tanner, Canada when this plot was projected. Seven of the plotters are at Washington, four at Bedford, Bedford Co., Penn. and the thirteenth is with Payne. These are plain facts. Do not reveal this, but arrest John A. Payne and his brother.

Yours very truly,
John P. H. Hall,
Of Tanner, Canada[112]

\* \* \* \* \* \* \* \* \* \*

BOSTON, APRIL 18, 1865

Dear Sir:

As I am willing to do all in my power to aid in the arrest of the assassin Booth, perhaps the following may be of service to you, as I have considerable confidence in my information, which I will let you know about at some future time. Go through Mass. Avenue to 8th Street near the market, to house No. 61, in the rear. Mrs. Caroline or Angeline Wright lives or stays there, and Booth is secreted there. He goes out in the disguise of a negro [sic], and also did before the assassination. He hides upstairs in a concealed closet, which would be difficult to find, unless carefully looked after, as there is a slide or pane. He jumped off his horse after the crime was committed, another man taking his place, to avoid suspicion. The house may be No. 84, and may possibly be some other avenue, but on 8th street, or near the corner. I am just and honest about this matter, but dare not give my name for fear I may be arrested; but should this give any information to you, I shall probably know it.

Yours --------[113]

\* \* \* \* \* \* \* \* \* \*

And, ponder the following:

Oh! What a joke.
Secesh & Co. have treated your honorable body with one of their latest Lincoln jokes. Wilkes Booth & Co. are under a thousand dollar obligation for the pass you have, in your hour of great gratification, granted an intimate friend of his. Your military as well as detective force is not worth powder and lead to kill them. We thank you, honorable Sirs, with sincerity, for your official stupidity, and shall, through a different channel, enable you to patronize the vendors of crape in a wholesome way. Know then, all the rewards you may hereafter offer is of no avail, and further, that we will have the gratification to publish our friends safely at your expense. Oh! what an immense joke. How are you, base, foul Yankee trash. Signed for over ten thousand sworn and tried friends in the District of Columbia. Think of that, base tyrants, and tremble

A Washingtonian[114]

Fifty years after the trial, General Doster reflected upon the trial and attempted to identify how things might have been if it had been a civilian court. While Doster's thoughts here will change nothing and, in a sense, only add to the numbers of theories surrounding the trial, they are important because of his privileged position and erudite manner. Doster concluded that Payne would have been acquitted on the ground of insanity, or, if convicted, would have been sentenced to a long term in a penitentiary. Atzerodt would probably have been convicted, but would have received a light sentence. Herold would have been convicted and sent to the penitentiary for a long term. Arnold, Spangler and Mudd would have been acquitted. Mrs. Surratt would have been confronted again with the testimony of her tenant Lloyd and her boarder Weichmann, who turned

State's evidence to "save their necks" and the court would have been obliged to charge that they could believe these witnesses only as accomplices if they were corroborated. With the previous good character of the defendant, the jury would probably have regarded Mrs. Surratt's declarations as those of an embittered Southern woman, and nothing more, and acquitted her.[115] For Mrs. Surratt in particular, the accusations surrounding her treatment during the trial became particularly vicious. In the September 2, 1873 issue of the *New York Tribune*, there appeared a report made by John T. Ford, the owner of the theater, who stated Mrs. Surratt had been tortured and manacled while in prison. This article caused quite a stir and drew responses from a number of individuals who had been part of the trial. One such response came from Judge Holt, who offered the following letter of rebuttal from Hartranft who was then governor of Pennsylvania,

Executive Chamber,
Harrisburg, Penn., Sept 4, 1873

Dear Sir:

My attention having been directed to a letter dated Washington, Aug. 29, 1873, and signed "Truth," that appeared in the *New York Tribune* a few days since, I think it proper, in justice to you, to declare publicly that its statements, so far as they relate to occurrences within my own observation, are absolute falsehoods.

As Marshal of the Court before whom the conspirators were tried, I had charge of Mrs. Surratt before, during and after the time of her trial, in all a period of about two months; during which she never had a manacle or manacles on either hands or feet; and the thought of manacling her was not, to my knowledge, ever entertained by any one of authority.

During the pendency of the trial I made application to the Secretary of War for permission to remove her from the cell to a comfortably furnished room adjoining the court-room, and for her daughter Anna to occupy the room with her, that she might attend to her wants. This request was granted. She was so removed; her daughter occupied the room with her, and Mrs. Surratt was fully provided for according to her needs and tastes.

A few weeks after her death, Miss Anna Surratt, by letter, thanked me for the kind treatment her mother and herself had received from myself and officers.

You will perhaps remember the name of the young priest who visited Mrs. Surratt so frequently, and which has escaped me. He will certify to her proper treatment and to the falsity of the statements of "Truth".

I have the honor to be your obedient servant,
J. F. Hartranft[116]


Today, the Lincoln conspiracy trial is almost one hundred and thirty years behind us. Yet, those proceedings and personalities still intrigue us as a nation, and the debate continues to swirl about the behavior of many of those involved. On the afternoon of the 7th, after the hangings, *The Washington Chronicle* retorted to those who complained that the four condemned were not given much time to prepare for their death, that President Lincoln was not given *any* time.[117] There is a lot to be said about such a response and for many, it embodies the emotions that this nation felt, and perhaps still feels.

Americans thrive on debate, and many somehow feel "cheated" by Lincoln's murder, which might be the reason that the entire subject is one of our favorite national historical topics. Unfortunately, there are no simple, convincing statements or reports that offer a total solution to the entire event. Perhaps the only solution is to acknowledge that we may have to learn to live with less than complete answers relative to Lincoln's death, the conspiracy trial, and its participants. Since we are a nation bent upon "instant gratification", we may not like that particular prospect, but nothing on the immediate, historical horizon indicates anything different.

With the trial over, Hartranft was faced with an important decision when General Hancock encouraged him to remain in the military and accept a position as a full Colonel; quite an honor for a citizen soldier. In fact, President Johnson and Secretary Stanton had already issued the official notice of his appointment as Colonel of the 34th Regiment of Infantry on August 29, 1865.[118] But his wife Sallie had been waiting patiently for four years, had raised their children and even buried two. Now, she felt very strongly that it was time for "Black John" to come home. Consequently, in October of 1865, he officially declined the appointment.[119] In deference to his wife he decided to go home. But, going home was destined to mean Harrisburg and not Norristown.

1. This is the way that Herold's name was spelled on the reward notice authorized by Stanton.
2. Clark, Champ, et al., eds. *The Assassination, Death of the President*. Alexandria, Virginia: Time-Life Books, 1987, p. 114, 132. Hereafter referred to as *The Assassination*.
3. Ibid., p. 134-135.
4. Baker, L. C., *History of the United States Secret Service*, 2 vols., Philadelphia: By the Author, 1867; reprint; Bowie, Maryland: Heritage Books, Inc., 1992, Vol. 2, pp. 502-3.
5. Ibid.
6. Clark, *The Assassination*, p. 133.
7. Herndon, William H., *Herndon's Life of Lincoln*, Cleveland, Ohio, World Publishing Company, 1942, p. 464.
8. Confidential Letter from the War Department to JFH dated May 8, 1865. Shireman Collection.
9. Chamlee, Roy, Z., *Lincoln's Assassins*, Jefferson, North Carolina, McFarland & Company, 1990, p. 214.
10. Hartranft, *Daybook*, p. 2. Courtesy of Gettysburg College. This is a ledger book kept by Hartranft during the trial. It was lent to the college by the general's grandson, Hartranft Stockham, in 1965.
11. Arnold, Samuel Bland, *Defence and Prison Experience of a Lincoln Conspirator*, Hattiesburg, Mississippi, The Book Farm, 1943, p. 59.
12. Kauffman, Michael, "Fort Lesley McNair and the Lincoln Conspirators", Lincoln Herald Magazine, Vol. 80, No. 4, [Winter 1978]: p. 180. Hereafter known as "Fort Lesley McNair".
13. Thomas, Benjamin P., & Hyman, *Harold M., Stanton, The Life & Times of Lincoln's Secretary of War*, New York, Alfred A. Knopf, 1962, pp. 64-65, 382.
14. Clark, *The Assassination*, p. 140.
15. Ibid.
16. Ibid.
17. Pittman, Benn, *The Assassination of President Lincoln & the Trial of the Conspirators*, New York: Wilstach & Baldwin, 1865; reprint, Birmingham, Alabama: The Legal Classics Library, Gryphon Editions, Ltd., 1982, p. 9. Hereafter referred to as *The Assassination of President Lincoln*.
18. Clark, *The Assassination*, p. 141.
19. Steiner, Bernard C., *Life of Reverdy Johnson*, n. p.: The Norman Remington Co., 1914, pp. 14-15.

20. Doster, William E., *Lincoln and Episodes of the Civil War*, New York: G. P. Putnam's Sons, 1915, p. 257.
21. Kunhardt, Dorothy & Philip, *Twenty Days*, North Hollywood, California: Newcastle Publishing Co., Inc., 1985, p. 194.
22. Ibid.
23. Doster, *Lincoln and Episodes of the Civil War*, pp. 257, 259.
24. Ibid., p. 260.
25. DeWitt, David Miller, *The Judicial Murder of Mary E. Surratt*, Baltimore, John Murpht & Co., 1895, p. 80.
26. Carter III, Samuel, *The Riddle of Dr. Mudd*, New York: G. Putnam's Sons, 1974, p. 167.
27. General Hartranft had a life-long discipline of keeping excellent records including his entire military and political careers. It appears that he may have intended to write his memoirs at some point. Author's note: Also see Letter to Stockham Hartranft from C. A. Hanson, President, Gettysburg College dated October 12, 1965. Shireman Collection. Regrettably, as this book prepares for press, the descendants of Hartranft have requested the return of those documents and the college has refused.
28. Hartranft, *Day Book*, pp. 9-10.
29. Carter, III. *The Riddle of Dr. Mudd*, p. 161.
30. Doster, *Lincoln and Episodes of the Civil War*, p. 282.
31. Hall, James O., *The Surratt Family & John Wilkes Booth*, Clinton, Maryland: The Surratt Society, Circa, 1976, pp. 5, 7-9.
32. Chamlee, *Lincoln's Assassins*, p. 527.
33. Hall, *The Surratt Family & John Wilkes Booth*, p. 10.
34. *Philadelphia Inquirer*, May 13, 1865.
35. Hall, *The Surratt Family & John Wilkes Booth*, pp. 4-5.
36. Poore, Ben Perley, *The Conspiracy Trial for the Murder of the President*, 3 vols., Boston: J. E. Tilton and Company, 1865-1866, Vol. 1, pp. 70, 72, 74-76, 82.
37. Weichmann, Louis J., *A True History of the Assassination of Abraham Lincoln and the Conspiracy of 1865*, New York: Alfred A. Knopf, 1975, p. 188. Hereafter referred to as *A True History of the Assassination*.
38. Most historians accept the fact that Booth broke his leg leaping from the Presidential box at Ford's theater, to the stage. Booth even indicates that in his small diary that was taken from him at Garrett's barn. To demonstrate just how difficult it can be to identify all facts surrounding such an event with assurance, a noted assassination expert, Michael Kauffman, feels that Booth did not break his leg in the leap but rather, it was broken while fleeing. In the process, his

horse stumbled and fell upon him and broke his leg. Mr. Kauffman's research still continues and while it may be tempting to discount such a theory, the author submits that Mr. Kauffman's history of careful research dictate's that his data be considered before being summarily dismissed.

39. Pittman, *The Assassination of President Lincoln and the Trial of the Conspirators*, pp. 85-86.
40. Hall, *The Surratt Family & John Wilkes Booth*, p. 4.
41. Kunhardt, *Twenty Days*, p. 201.
42. Ibid., pp. 187, 193.
43. Ibid., p. 186.
44. Ibid.
45. Clark, *The Assassination*, p. 139.
    Also see Kauffman, "John Wilkes Booth", p. 57. Kunhardt, *Twenty Days*, p. 186.
46. Hartranft, *Day Book*, p. 53.
47. Kauffman, "Fort Lesley McNair", p. 179.
48. Ibid, p. 49.
49. Baker, *History of the United States Secret Service*, p. 509.
50. Hartranft, *Day Book*. pp. 43, 48.
51. Kunhardt, *Twenty Days*, p. 186. Actually, this volume happens to be an excellent basic reference on the subject.
52. Hartranft, *Day Book*, p. 11.
53. *Philadelphia Ledger*, May 12, 1899.
54. Author's note: It should be understood that Hancock always responded positively and promptly to the request made by Hartranft. Space dictates only prevent reproduction of his numerous responses to Hartranft's request'.
55. Hartranft, *Day Book*, p. 68.
56. Ibid., p. 69.
57. Kauffman, "John Wilkes Booth", p. 57.
58. Doster, *Lincoln and Episodes of the Civil War*, p. 276.
    Also see Hartranft, *Day Book*, p. 70.
59. Kauffman, "John Wilkes Booth", p. 57.
60. Hartranft, *Day Book*, p. 4.
61. Letters are part of the Hartranft Collection at Gettysburg College
62. Douglas, Henry Kyd, *I Rode With Stonewall*, Chapel Hill, North Carolina, The University of North Carolina Press, 1940; reprint, St. Simons Island, Georgia, Mockingbird Books, Inc., 1989, p. 323.
63. *Proceedings, Reunion of the Third Division*, p. 57, Shireman Collection.
64. Douglas, *I Rode with Stonewall*, p. 328.
65. Ibid., p. 325.

66. Ibid., p. 330.
67. SSH to JFH, June 28, 1865, Shireman Collection.
68. SSH to JFH, June 22, 1865, Shireman Collection.
69. Unclassified Newspaper clipping, Shireman Collection.
70. Kunhardt, *Twenty Days*, p. 70.
71. Author's note: Actually the Commission had the authority to grant clemency and did not have to approach the President. Some see this as the Commission's way of avoiding the responsibility for Mrs. Surratt's death.
72. Hartranft Collection at Gettysburg College.
73. Ibid.
74. Jordan, David M., *Winfield Scott Hancock - A Soldiers Life*, Indianapolis, Indiana, University Press, 1988, p. 178.
75. Hartranft, *Day Book*, p. 87.
76. *Norristown Times Herald*, Feb. 11, 1957.
77. Hartranft, *Day Book*, p. 87.
78. Katz, D. Mark, "Christian Rath: The Executioner", *Incidents of the War*, Spring 1986, p. 12.
79. Lattimer, John K., *Kennedy and Lincoln, Medical & Ballistic Comparisons of Their Assassinations*, New York: Harcourt Brace Jovanovich, 1980, pp. 116, 118. Hereafter referred to as *Kennedy and Lincoln*. Also, Hartranft Collection, Gettysburg College.
80. Hoehling, A. A., *After the Guns Fell Silent*, New York: Madison Books, 1990, p. 89.
81. Chamlee, *Lincoln's Assassins*, p. 474.
82. Katz, D. Mark, *Witness to an Era, The Life and Photographs of Alexander Gardner*, New York, Viking Press, 1991, p. 178. Hereafter referred to as *Witness to an Era*.
83. Clark, *The Assassination*, p. 159.
84. Hoehling, *After the Guns Fell Silent*, pp. 88-89.
85. *Philadelphia Inquirer*, July 8, 1865.
86. Jordan, *Winfield Scott Hancock - A Soldiers Life*, p. 178.
87. Ibid.
88. Baker, *History of the United States Secret Service*, p. 519.
89. Chamlee, *Lincoln's Assassins*, p. 469.
90. Baker, *History of the United States Secret Service*, p. 512.
91. Chamlee, *Lincoln's Assassins*, p. 470.
92. Weichmann, *A True History of the Assassination*, pp. 318-319.
93. Ibid, p. 316.
94. Chamlee, *Lincoln's Assassins*, p. 471.
95. Lattimer, *Kennedy & Lincoln*, p. 118.
96. Doster, *Lincoln and Episodes of the Civil War*, p. 276.

97. *The Philadelphia Inquirer*, March 22, Circa, 1915. - Shireman Collection.

98. Gray, John, "The Fate of the Lincoln Conspirators", *McClure's Magazine*, [October, 1911]: 636.

99. Times here will vary according to the eyewitness, Author's note.

100. Lattimer, *Kennedy & Lincoln*, p. 118.

101. Katz, *Witness to an Era*, p. 17.

102. Lattimer, *Kennedy & Lincoln*, p. 118.

103. Kauffman, "Fort Lesley McNair", p. 181.

104. Letter of July 17, 1865 to JFH from Secretary of War Edwin Stanton, Shireman Collection

105. Letter from Annie Surratt to JFH dated July 9, 1865, Shireman Collection, It is interesting to note that on August 11, 1897, Louis Weichmann requested a copy of this letter from Hartranft's son Linn for a "historical narrative" he was preparing. Weichmann's original letter is in the Hartranft Collection, Gettysburg College, .

106. Hartranft, *Day Book*, p. 97.

107. Chamlee, *Lincoln's Assassins*, p. 386.

108. Higdon, Hal, *The Union vs Dr. Mudd*, Chicago, Follett Publishing Company, 1964, pp. 131-132.

109. Arnold, *Defence and Prison Experience of a Lincoln Conspirator*, p. 63.

110. Baker, *History of the United States Secret Service*, pp. 548-549.

111. Ibid, p. 546.

112. Ibid.

113. Ibid., p. 548.

114. Ibid., p.555

115. Doster, *Lincoln and Episodes of the Civil War*, pp. 281-282.

116. Weichmann, *A True History of the Assassination*, pp. 293-294.

117. Hanchett, William, *The Lincoln Murder Conspiracies*, Chicago, University of Illinois Press, 1983, p.70.

118. Armor, *Lives of the Governors of Pennsylvania*, p 516.

119. Beath, Robert B., *History of the Grand Army of the Republic*, New York: Bryan Taylor, 1889, p. 163.

# CHAPTER EIGHT

## *WELCOME TO THE WORLD OF POLITICS*

Shortly after the completion of the conspiracy trial, Hartranft returned to Norristown and his family, where on August 2nd, the Montgomery County contingent of the 51st arrived in Norristown to a hailing chorus of cheers and shouts. Leading the parade of those veterans was, of course, General Hartranft. For a couple weeks following, the Norristown area attempted, as many towns did, to show their esteem for their returned soldiers. Bands, parades, and speeches were the standard of the day.

On Monday, August 21st, a group of Norristown citizens made its way up West Main Street along with the local Norristown Band.[1] In the midst of the group was Benjamin F. Hancock, father of the noted Norristown general, and they paused before Hartranft's home and serenaded him and his family. Not being able to resist, the general and Sallie came out to the crowd, and Mr. Hancock delivered a brief but pointed speech on Hartranft's accomplishments and the grateful nature of the local people. During Hancock's speech, he noted to the group that, "you [Hartranft] have been promoted and honored and deservedly so. The government has appreciated your services and bestowed upon you offices of honor and distinction for which we congratulate you. But these military honors and distinctions are not all. Your native State desires to show you, by electing you to the responsible office of Auditor General of this great and loyal Commonwealth, that she appreciates your services."[2]

Hancock was speaking about the fact that Hartranft had already been nominated to the post of Auditor General on August 17th, at Harrisburg.[3] When Hancock finished his remarks, the general then briefly addressed the crowd and told them, "I thank you most sincerely for this compliment tonight. It assures me that you endorse my past public life and that I hold your confidence and support in the public contest soon to be inaugurated. I also thank you, Mr. Hancock, for the kind mention of my military history." Typical of Hartranft's humility, he then added, "Of this [his military life] I will not speak nor detain you but a moment."[4]

At this point, Hartranft then began to pointedly address the issue of making certain that the soldiers of the "conflict," along with their families would not be forgotten. Pensions were the best method in his eyes, and he asked that the veterans should not be forgotten. He also took a brief moment to salute one of his favorite subjects, that of labor.

I need not say that every effort should be made now to protect and encourage labor. You well understand that it is the wealth of a nation. And, while this is so, also from patriotic considerations see that the returned soldier is honorably employed. It is the biggest favor that can be bestowed upon him or his country. He will then soon forget his camp life and become an industrious and prosperous citizen.[5]

With these comments, Hartranft began his long career of public service.

Early on, Hartranft experienced first-hand the world of dirty politics. Immediately following his leave of the military, there was a lot of talk about his running for the governor's office, and that was so positive that it became absolute in his mind.[6] Consequently, when he attended the State's Republican Convention, he was astounded when political differences between the Simon Cameron and Andrew G. Curtin camps led to his nomination as Auditor General instead. This insolent move upset Hartranft, and only after a period of careful thought and reflection did he agree to accept that nomination, which he easily won on the first ballot.[7] His running mate for the office of Surveyor General was Colonel Jacob M. Campbell.[8]

The great Keystone State and its internal politics in 1865 were not exactly morally pristine as one might wish to believe. Smoke filled rooms had become the main innersanctums of political activity and they were attended by such men as 'Bible Banger Browne', a name given to the Rev. Audley Browne of New Castle who was elected as President of the Prohibition Party in 1875;[9] 'Pershing the Pure', Judge Cyrus L Pershing, a Democratic nominee for Governor;[10] 'Pig Iron Kelly', William D. Kelly who was a Congressman from Philadelphia;[11] 'Pauncheous Piollet', Victor E. Piollet, a Democrat who was being sued by his mother-in-law, who claimed he tried to rob her; and later, 'Black Jack', a name given to Governor Hartranft owing to his dark complexion and features.[12]

When Hartranft was nominated for Auditor General, Pennsylvania politics was controlled by Simon Cameron, who had been President Lincoln's first Secretary of War. Cameron was asked to resign that position because of the strong indications that he was stealing and, in an attempt to save face for Cameron, President Lincoln offered him the position as Minister to Russia. Cameron initially refused Lincoln's offer but finally accepted, and later became a Pennsylvania's U. S. Senator.

Many saw the former War Secretary, and now state political boss, as something of a lodestone to the State's ethics but it must be argued that Cameron was a tough fighter, and not one to falter under pressure. One old, but unsubstantiated, story tells that an elderly woman once approached Cameron and asked him, " Why don't you work for the people?" Cameron is reported to have responded in a brisk manner, "Madame, I work for the people that the people work for!" While this statement cannot be verified, it does bring us a bit closer to the Pennsylvania political strongman.

The years following the war and the decade of 1870-1880 in particular proved to be most difficult in the Pennsylvania political arena. Grant had been elected President in 1868, and his own unique style of leadership gave rise to many questions about the integrity of politicians on a national, state, and local level. While politics has always been a tough profession, the tactics at this time, which were not unlike current methods, were frequently to destroy any conceivable value of the opposition. In fact, one might wonder why anyone of good intentions would want to serve in any political office and risk the certain danger of character assassination. But, perhaps these very difficulties and challenges were part of the lure for Hartranft.

The 1865 statewide campaign was particularly vicious, and many charges and countercharges were hurled upon the participants. The Democrats urged voters to support the "white man's" ticket as they steadfastly refused to support voting rights for blacks.[13] Meanwhile, the Republicans pointed toward their war service and the prosperity that the Keystone State enjoyed under the Republican leadership of Governor Curtin.[14]

Hartranft found himself pummeled by the Democrats for the hanging of Mary Surratt, and catcalls of the "Hangman's Party" were leveled at him and the Republicans.[15] Democrats, in a fear ploy, charged the Republicans with courting the Negroes while ignoring the "brave white soldiers and their suffering children."[16]

In the end, when the votes were tallied, the Republican Party had won a plurality of 22,000 votes, while Hartranft edged-out his opponent by only 1,000 votes. Oddly enough, his opponent, who was from Bucks County, beat Hartranft by approximately 1,000 votes in the General's own Montgomery County.

With the election over, Hartranft, his wife Sallie, and their three children, Samuel, Linn and Marion [who had just been born on September 19, 1865][17] were to embark upon nearly twelve tumultuous and trying years. While the constant danger of battle had always worried Sallie, the insulting and demeaning rhetoric of politics was to bring her a new form of fear and pain for her and her husband.

The position of Auditor General is one of financial responsibility and oversees the administration of funds within the state. Because of its highly tempting nature, the state sought out those exceptional individuals of the highest integrity. So it was with Hartranft.

In 1868, Hartranft was again nominated for the Auditor General's office, and this time he won by a majority of 22,600 votes.[18] To prepare for the second campaign, the party prepared a pamphlet that emphasized Hartranft's accomplishments during his first term. One key point was the reduction in the state's debt, and that pamphlet told the public, "This [$5,000,000 reduction in the State's debt] is the record of our candidate for Auditor General, and it only remains for the people to say, by their votes, in the coming election, 'Well done, good and faithful servant'."[19] He also won the support of important newspapers around the State including the *Philadelphia Evening Herald* who told their subscribers, "It gives us exceeding pleasure to recognize sterling merit, especially when it is exhibited in a direction where it was not expected. We have received from General Hartranft, Auditor General of the State of Pennsylvania, his annual report of our canals and railroads for the year 1867, in a durable and handsome volume of five hundred and fifty pages...it will take its place among the most valuable public documents of the day."[20]

The *Harrisburg Daily State Guard* also touted that Hartranft and Campbell, "have reason to be proud of the manly confidence reposed in them by the masses of the Republican party."[21] On March 19, 1868, The *State Guard* again supported Hartranft and Campbell by publishing copies of other newspaper endorsements from around the State. In that same article, that newspaper attempted to further the political fortunes of the State by offering the concept of past Governor Curtin as a Vice Presidential running mate with President Grant. Obviously, this latter attempt failed miserably.[22]

During his terms as Auditor General, Hartranft made every attempt to restore the Commonwealth of Pennsylvania to a position of solvency. One of the many examples of his successful efforts came toward the close of his second term. Hartranft sent a note to Governor John W. Geary on August 8, 1871, informing him that the State had finally received a total of $321,014 from the federal government for military claims that the State had lodged with Washington during the Civil War.[23] No doubt this information was well received in Harrisburg, though few could see that it was soon to lead to a very nasty situation.

While Hartranft's terms as Auditor General were relatively quiet, in 1871 that serenity was broken in a matter that had become known as the "Evans affair." George A. Evans was an obscure state agent who appears to have been utilized as a pawn by far more powerful but unidentified politicians. The result was personal financial gain for those unidentified individuals, while Evans was charged with the collection of war funds due Pennsylvania from the Federal Government.[24] Some in Harrisburg claimed that Washington was remiss or even indifferent towards making these payments and Evans' position was necessary, though it appears that Washington showed no such reluctance.[25] Nonetheless, Evans was appointed by Governor Geary and approved by the legislature as the state's legal agent to collect those funds. As part of his fee, the state "apparently paid him $300,000" for his services.[26]

Out of this affair, it happened that two Philadelphia brokers, who were in prison for another crime, alleged that Auditor General Hartranft had accepted money from Evans as a form of unidentified "pay off". They were also allegedly promised pardons if they retracted their charges against Hartranft. According to one source, "on the eve of the election [Hartranft's Gubernatorial] Governor Geary, under heavy pressure from the organization [unidentified] pardoned the two men; their public retraction followed, and Hartranft was proved innocent."[27] While this comment cast aspersions upon Hartranft, it should be also known that throughout the entire affair, no one was ever found guilty of any charges. Consequently only unsubstantiated insinuations exist.

In fairness to Geary, President Grant applied pressure upon him to get the matter cleared up prior to his own second election. Grant got involved after he held a Philadelphia meeting that included Hartranft, Cameron, and other high party officials.[28] The president feared that the entire mess could damage the party's, and his own chances for reelection.

Nonetheless, in 1873, the Pennsylvania Senate established a judiciary committee to investigate the matter.[29] Hartranft told the committee that he had in fact borrowed $8,000 from Evans and had repaid the money with interest, but he repaid the loan only four days after the "scandal" broke.[30] This led some of his political enemies to point toward it as proof of his involvement. By this time, Hartranft had completed his second term as Auditor General and had also served another partial term because his scheduled successor, David Stanton, died before assuming that office.[31] He was also in the midst of his first gubernatorial term, and all of this made excellent political profit for the Democrats.

The entire affair cast a shadow over many, including Governor Geary whom the *West Chester American Republican* charged, "The unpardonable guilty feather in this whole transaction [Evans affair] rests on the shoulders of the Governor, for without his aid, Mr. Evans could not have secured the money [$300,000 in Commissions]."[32] The newspaper alluded to the fact that Evans was appointed by Geary.

In the notes left by A. K. McClure, author of *Old Time Notes of Pennsylvania*, who was also a member of the Pennsylvania State Legislature at the time,

> It was well known that Evans had not received more than a mere moiety of the percentage paid, as he continued to live obscurely and frugally and died practically without estate. During the campaign of 1872 when I was chairman of the Liberal State Committee[Republican Rump], and employed the best detective force to get into the inner citadel of the State frauds, I obtained positive and indisputable information where $52,000 of the Evans' $300,000 had been received by a prominent man where he invested it and how the securities were held.[33]

Unfortunately for everyone, McClure was no more definitive than this statement, which only leaves room for continuing speculation.

Nonetheless, McClure does write that the work of the Committee came to an abrupt end when the "main individual" suddenly dropped dead. McClure does not identify this person openly but his reference is obviously to Governor Geary himself. Because of that death, "The result was the committee never met again and made no report whatever to the Senate. Most of the Senators understood [McClure does not say what!], and the scandal was dropped by general consent."[34]

Evans stood trial alone, and a civil verdict of $185,663.50 was rendered against him, while he was absolved "from the criminal commitment absolutely."[35] Now the Evans affair was over, if not fully explained. In its wake lay a wounded John F. Hartranft, who had been a focal point of much debate within the party. Because of the accusations leveled against Hartranft, President Grant did not want him to run for the governor's office, fearing he would damage the party and Grant's own election. The President again applied pressure to Cameron to find someone who would better compliment his upcoming second bid.[36] Despite his admiration for the past supreme commander, Hartranft felt that Grant's own name would destroy the Republican party in Pennsylvania during the state's gubernatorial election, which preceded the Presidential election by one month.[37] Obviously, no one was very pleased.

Throughout all of this political infighting, Cameron simply concerned himself with matters that would insure his own return to the U.S. Senate.[38] Cameron was so preoccupied with his own fate that, when the

Democrats charged that Hartranft failed to collect $460,000 in taxes from the Cameron-controlled Northern Central Railroad over the preceding five years, Cameron offered the embattled Hartranft little or no help. This lack of assistance led the Democrats to yell that the public should perceive Cameron's indifference as "proof" that Hartranft was controlled by his office.[39]

While Hartranft had many desirable features stemming from his military career, the Evans affair continued to haunt him. Initially, Cameron chose not to interfere with the general's certain nomination but presidential and party pressure became unbearable even for the old political boss. Consequently, a private meeting was called which included Simon Cameron, Robert W. Mackey, the state's party leader, Hartranft, and other State political leaders. The purpose of the hasty session was to remove Hartranft from the gubernatorial ticket. One individual who was very much in favor of dumping Hartranft was Cameron's son-in-law, Wayne MacVeagh,[40] who felt he might be better suited for the nod. It is reported that Hartranft himself, who was very aware of the controversy, said that he would be willing to step aside if the Republican leaders felt he would be a detriment to the party on either a state or national level.[41]

As the meeting was in progress, Cameron's son Donald, who had not been invited, made his way into the meeting room. Upon entering, the younger Cameron told the group,

> Gentlemen, I know what you are here for. Let me have the floor for three minutes, and leave it without your reply. Your purpose is to take this gentleman [nodding towards Hartranft], Mr. Hartranft, off the ticket and put someone else on. Now I have come here to tell you, by God, that if you take him off and put even this gentleman on [pointing to his father], I will beat him. If you take Hartranft off and put on my brother-in-law, by all the gods, I'll beat him. I swear that, so sure as the day of election comes, if you take off Hartranft and put on any other human being, the Democratic candidate shall be elected. Keep General Hartranft on the ticket, and I will elect him. Gentlemen, good-night I shall take the next train to Harrisburg.[42]

While some feel that the younger Cameron's position was not quite as adamant, McClure had a close tie to one member at that meeting and he accepts this position.[43] Regardless of any arguments on this particular point, Hartranft was not removed from the ticket.

The Democratic party nominated Charles R. Buckalew, a professional politician, while Hartranft was nominated on the first ballot at the Republican convention on April 18, 1872.[44] The race was on and dirty!

Throughout the campaign, Hartranft was frequently vilified over the Evans affair and, despite the endorsement of notables like General Burnside, at times it appeared that he simply was not electable.[45] Even some German newspapers walked away from one of their favorite sons.[46] Yet, when the smoke finally cleared in October, Hartranft had won thirty-five of the state's sixty-six counties[47] and a state-wide plurality of nearly 40,000 votes.[48]

But the ever restless eye of McClure tells us that the Republicans were not lily white in their pursuit of their candidate when he noted,

> Never was a struggle fought more desperately before the people of the state, and the Republicans of Philadelphia, under the registry law, exhausted their power to increase the party majority by frauds in which they had the ripest experience. 'Nick' English, the leader of the "lightning calculation", presided at the meeting of the return judges, when it was known that Hartranft was elected by 35,000 [State wide] majority. He knew also that many bets had been made that Hartranft would carry Philadelphia by 20,000 [votes], and he lacked several thousand of that number, but English solved the problem by simply manipulating the figures, and officially certifying a majority for Hartranft in the city of over 20,000.[49]

As for Grant's concerns about Hartranft being a potential detriment to his own election, the President carried Pennsylvania by a plurality of almost 150,000 votes.[50]

On January 21, 1873, forty-two-year-old John Frederick Hartranft took the oath as Pennsylvania's eighteenth chief executive.[51] Ironically, on that same day, his adversary at Fort Stedman, John Brown Gordon, was elected to the U. S. Senate.[52]

Almost as if by magic, newspapers across the State looked upon Hartranft's Inaugural Address with praise, and most appeared to be impressed with his modest and direct attitude. The *Carlisle Herald* noted that, "He [Hartranft] takes possession of the Chief Magistracy under the most favorable circumstances and with a reputation and experience such as will enable him to make his administration exceptionally brilliant and popular."[53]

The *Bedford Inquirer* reported, "Governor Hartranft's Inaugural address was a subject of much comment and of quite general commendation. His straight forward way of plainly indicating his opposition to certain measures ...is a source of much comfort and confidence to the people at large."[54] While the *Miners Journal* wrote that, "Yesterday General Hartranft was Inaugurated Governor of Pennsylvania...we have full confidence that...he will be able to point to our State debt reduced largely from its present figure...."[55]

In little more than two weeks after his inauguration, the new governor had to issue his first sad proclamation, "With profound regret the announcement is made to the people of the Commonwealth that ex-Governor John W. Geary died suddenly at his home in Harrisburg this morning...."[56] Many felt that with the burial of Governor Geary, the focal point of the Evans affair was also laid to rest.

When Hartranft made his Inaugural Address, which was printed in English and German, he was also presenting the basic framework for his entire six years as governor.[57] John Hartranft was, no matter his human failings, a humanist and a pragmatist. During his entire term, his annual addresses before the legislature included a broad base of concerns that would have long-lasting effects upon the Keystone State. Central to his many concerns as governor were the following areas:

Fiscal responsibility
Education
Welfare for the mentally ill
Peace and harmony between Labor and Management
Respect for the laws
Banking reforms
Insurance
Technical training for the youth
Constitutional reform to curb corruption
Lower Taxes
Effective militia
Elimination of Special Legislation

Education in particular was always high on Hartranft's priority list, and that concern existed before and after his terms as Governor. In his Inaugural Address he pointed out that, "It will be my pleasure, as it is my duty to have a watchful eye over the school system of our State. No part of our governmental policy should command the employment of more wisdom than that which is to promote the instruction of our youth."[58]

Hartranft also made it clear that he was not a proponent of government operated by "Special Legislation", which he thought only furthered "local and private ends to the exclusion of public business."[59] He was already setting the stage that would earn him the new political sobriquet, "Veto Jack."[60] He earned this title because of his promise to veto all bills under the heading of Special Legislation. True to his word, in one incident referred to as the "great veto", Hartranft killed 1622 bills, many of which had been kept alive since 1857.[61] That courageous act won him new admirers and supporters, including the *Reading Gazette and Democrat* which had not been a prior supporter. That newspaper printed that Hartranft, "has pursued since he has been Governor, a manly, honorable and independent course, for which the people of all parties thank him. If he continues through his term the way he has begun, he will be as popular with the masses as a Snyder or a Shunk."[62]

His six years as Pennsylvania's chief magistrate were full of challenges which were frequently rooted in the economic problems of the period. It is not practical in this volume to provide an in-depth review of his total problems and accomplishments as governor; such a study will require its own volume. Consequently, only some of the major areas, including the new state constitution, the Molly Maguires, the great railroad strike, and his bid for the Republican Presidential nomination have been given consideration here. This focus is not intended as a comprehensive review of his gubernatorial term but rather only as an introduction.

During his first term, the issue of a new Constitution for Pennsylvania was the first major challenge he addressed. During his Inaugural Address, Hartranft let the people know that he supported a new Constitution when he told them,

> The subject of constitutional reform is now occupying a large share of public attention. Opinions are various as to its propriety or necessity, as the views of men are conservative or progressive. There is now however, in session in Philadelphia, a convention of respectable and honorable gentlemen, fresh from the people and authorized by them to revise the Constitution. To these gentlemen we confidently refer these questions of constitutional reform, in the belief that out of their combined integrity and wisdom will spring such measures

as will best conduce to our safety, happiness and prosperity.[63]

The initial meeting of the Constitutional Convention met at Harrisburg on November 12, 1872, prior to Hartranft's inauguration. Despite a cutting remark that the convention was comprised of, "one hundred lawyers and thirty-three honest men",[64] the body was composed of a broad base of politicians and businessmen. If there is an objective criticism of that body, it must be directed at the lack of representation for labor and agriculture.[65] Nonetheless, the body was charged to investigate a wide variety of areas including the considerations:

To drop the term free white from the suffrage qualification, which would give blacks access to the ballot box.

To review and correct abuses in management of the State's finances and in the Governor's pardon power.

To modify laws which would prevent fraudulent activities during elections.

To make certain that the sinking fund was limited to the payment of the public debt.

To attempt to curb bribery and corruption of State officials through the administration of oaths and other means.

To modify the terms of office from three to four years for the Governor, plus creation of the position of Lieutenant-Governor and Secretary of Internal Affairs.[66]

In addition to these specific areas, the new constitution would draw many new guidelines to make political corruption far more difficult. When the new constitution was complete it went before the public for its final acceptance. While many felt that the document would incur little or no resistance, they were surprised at the stiff opposition that was offered. Yet, when the vote was taken on December 16, 1873, it was overwhelmingly approved by a vote of 253,774 versus 108,594.[67] When it had been finally accepted by the people, one Philadelphia publication announced that, "No party can 'count' in its candidates at the sweet will of a few leaders. Salaries take the place of fees. The municipality becomes independent ...There is a chance that the practice of politics will become less profitable, and therefore fewer will follow it, and if there be much to regret in the newly accepted Constitution, let us think of all these things and be thankful."[68]

Because of the new constitution, Hartranft would be the last governor to serve a three-year term and the Negro was given the right to vote. In his 1875 address to the State Legislature, after one full year under that new Constitution, Hartranft told that body,

> Being the first Representatives elected under the new Constitution, a grave responsibility rests upon the present Legislature, and the future prosperity of the Commonwealth will depend in large measure upon the wisdom of the counsels that may prevail at the pending session. Additional legislation is needed to give full force and effect to the Constitution, and the importance of framing laws that will be uniform and general in their operation, cannot be urged upon the attention of your honorable bodies with too much earnestness. I feel convinced that you will approach the discharge of this duty with a becoming sense of the magnitude of the trust and an ardent desire to promote the public welfare, and with all efforts in this behalf, I pledge you my heartiest co-operation. My most cordial wishes attend you for an auspicious beginning and a happy close to your labors. Whatever our endeavors may be, let us hope they will redound to the honor and advantage of the State, and to this end we should invoke the maturest judgment and Divine assistance.[69]

This message was delivered in the early part of the year that was to witness Hartranft's second bid for the governor's office. The party faithful gave the governor the nomination, but many in the state felt that the Republicans could not possibly win the election, no matter who the party ran. The economy in Pennsylvania continued to labor under recession, and it represented the single largest concern of the people. Despite this bleak outlook, when the votes were tallied, Hartranft was returned to the governor's office only to face exceedingly difficult problems, not the least of which was the growing menace of a clandestine group known as the Molly Maguires.

1. *The Norristown Herald & Republican*, August 24, 1865.
2. Ibid.
3. 1868 Biographical Sketch of JFH by Republican party, Shire-
      man Collection.
4. *The Norristown Herald & Republican*, August 24, 1865.
5. Ibid.
6. Barrett, "John Frederic Hartranft: Life and Services", p. 351.
7. Ibid.
8. Ibid., p. 352.
9. Evans, Frank B., *Pennsylvania Politics 1872-1877, A Study in Political
      Leadership*, Harrisburg, Pennsylvania: The Pennsylvania Historical
      and Museum Commission, 1966, p. 215. Hereafter referred to as
      *Pennsylvania Politics 1872-1877*.
10. Ibid., p. 195.
11. Ibid., p. 193.
12. Ibid., p. 183.
13. *Register and Watchman*, Norristown, Pennsylvania, October 31, 1865.
14. Barrett, "John Frederic Hartranft: Life and Services", p. 354.
15. *Register and Watchman*, Norristown, Pennsylvania, October 31, 1865.
16. Barrett, "John Frederic Hartranft: Life and Services", p. 353.
17. Brecht, *Genealogical Record*, p. 729.
18. 1868 Republican Campaign Pamphlet, Shireman Collection.
19. Ibid.
20. *Philadelphia Evening Herald*, March 28, 1868.
21. *Harrisburg Daily State Guard*, February 4, 1868.
22. Ibid.
23. JFH from Auditor General's Office, August 8, 1871, Shireman Collec-
      tion.
24. McClure, *Old Time Notes of Pennsylvania*, p. 341.
25. Ibid.
26. Ibid.
27. Evans, *Pennsylvania Politics, 1872-1877*, p. 34.
28. Bradley, Erwin Stanley, *Simon Cameron, Lincoln's Secretary of War*,
      Philadelphia: University of Pennsylvania Press, 1966, p. 339.
29. McClure, *Old Time Notes of Pennsylvania*, p. 341.
30. Evans, *Pennsylvania Politics, 1872-1877*, p. 64 & *Harrisburg Patriot*,
      March 12, 1873.
31. Barrett, "John Frederic Hartranft: Life and Services", p. 356.
32. *West Chester American Republican*, August 29, 1871.

33. McClure, *Old Time Notes of Pennsylvania*, p. 342.
34. Ibid.
35. Barrett, "John Frederic Hartranft: Life and Services", p. 358.
36. Evans, *Pennsylvania Politics, 1872-1877*, p. 34.
37. Ibid.
38. Ibid.
39. Bradley, *Simon Cameron, Lincoln's Secretary of War*, p. 339.
40. *Philadelphia Bulletin*, May 12, 1898.
41. Ibid.
42. Ibid.
43. Bradley, *Simon Cameron, Lincoln's Secretary of War*, p. 338.
44. Barrett, "John Frederic Hartranft: Life and Services", p. 359.
45. *Philadelphia Bulletin*, May 12, 1898.
46. Barrett, "John Frederic Hartranft: Life and Services", p. 360.
47. Evans, *Pennsylvania Politics, 1872-1877*, p. 36.
48. McClure, *Old Time Notes on Pennsylvania*, p. 347.
49. Ibid.
50. Ibid.
51. *Pennsylvania Archives*, Fourth Series, Vol. IX, p. 208.
52. Barrett, "John Frederic Hartranft: Life and Services", p. 362.
53. *Carlisle Herald*, January 23, 1873.
54. *Bedford Inquirer*, January 31, 1873.
55. *Miners Journal*, January 22, 1873.
56. *Philadelphia Free Press*, February 10, 1873.
57. Shireman Collection.
58. Inaugural Address of JFH, January 21, 1873, Shireman Collection.
59. Ibid.
60. Barrett, "John Frederic Hartranft: Life and Services", p. 367.
61. Ibid., p. 364.
62. Ibid., pp. 364-365.
63. Inaugural Address of JFH, January 21, 1873, Shireman Collection.
64. Evans, *Pennsylvania Politics, 1872-1877*, p. 81.
65. Ibid., p. 82.
66. Ibid., pp. 83-83.
67. Evans, *Pennsylvania Politics, 1872-1877*, p. 93.
68. From an article printed in the *Pennsylvania Monthly*, IV - II, 1874. Unfortunately, the title and author have been removed from the remaining pages. Shireman Collection.
69. JFH Message to General Assembly, January 6, 1875, Shireman Collection.

# CHAPTER NINE

## *"A DEAL WITH THE IRISH?"*
## *THE MOLLY MAGUIRES*

During Hartranft's political career, perhaps one of the most difficult challenges to his office was the clandestine group known as the Molly Maguires. Their activities bridged both of Hartranft's gubernatorial terms and his alleged association with them was destined to cast aspersions upon his otherwise spotless character. During his bid for and throughout his tenure as governor, a number of people had the authority while others simply claimed to speak in Hartranft's name. While this practice is not unusual in politics, in 1872, its practice led to some sharp difficulties for the governor.

The entire chapter on the Molly Maguires may never quite be put to rest in terms of total historical accuracy. They certainly appear to arise out of a mixture of violence, local and national pride, and a labor-social struggle that was born of a simple egalitarian attitude characterizing one of the world's warmest people, the Irish. Such a recipe could not help but explode into a carnival of philosophies when many of the participants attempted to prove their own particular point of view or innocence. The Molly Maguire stories run the gamut from the ridiculous to the sublime, right to wrong, and heinous to the charitable. As an indicator of their controversial existence, even today, there are many who refuse to admit that such an organization ever existed. Conversely, and equally absurd, are those who blame them for virtually all the ills and violence that befell the newly reunited nation.

The Civil War was followed by a period of deep financial stress that fell upon the American economy and in the Northeast, in particular. During the war, rapid expansion in almost every type of industry made economic matters a boom period for many as the government's appetite for war materiel made virtually every producer a supplier. Workers were pushed to their maximum for time and productivity, and while labor rates did not necessarily rise in proportion to prices, employment was nonetheless high and steady. Industries including railroads, coal, oil, and other heavy manufacturing began to blossom as a result of the apparent endless demand the nation developed to sustain the war. Enormous and rapid wealth was made by many and in some cases, those fortunes were invested in postwar America. In the populous Northeast in particular, not everyone had been off fighting the Rebels.

The great coal-mining region of Northeastern Pennsylvania matured quickly during the war. Anthracite coal, which was much cleaner burning and more efficient than soft coal, was sought after for a broad-based marketplace. The towns and counties surrounding Scranton became thick with the soot of the "black-gold". Even Confederate blockade runners found that anthracite's clean burning made them less conspicuous on the high seas and they too added to the demands of the region. European immigrants were the main source of the labor who daily rode the rails down into the bellies of those mines for wages that varied between $10.00 and $35.00 per month. Irish, Italians, and Poles flocked to the region in search of a new life and its opportunities. Unfortunately for many, after crossing the Atlantic and making their way to the dusty, dirty coal towns of Pennsylvania, they soon realized that conditions there were not always much better than those in the depressed homelands they had just left.

The working Irish, most of whom were Catholic, arrived with strong ties to the Ancient Order of Hibernians [AOH]. Here in America, that fraternal organization became active around 1836, and one of its main objectives was to assist the Irish immigrants with their adjustments to living in the United States. While new to America, the highly respected AOH had existed in Ireland for over three hundred years and the very name Hibernia is taken from the Latin for Ireland itself.[1] Undeniably, the AOH gave succor to many immigrants who "longed" for the old country while the familiar trappings of the Catholic Church offered a strong sense of pastoral continuity. For a handful of the Irish people who settled in those dank mining regions, the concepts of the AOH, coupled with the teachings of the Catholic Church, would soon be specifically altered to suit their own goals.

From the Irish-Catholic community the American clandestine group known as the Molly Maguires would spring. The Mollies were founded in Ireland around 1845, and while secret in nature, they originally formed to combat the land agents with an eye towards lightening the load of the working people.[2] Tradition has it that the name Molly Maguire comes from a rather ferocious woman in Ireland who personally killed several agents of the landlords, though a variety of tales and traditions exist.[3] From this beginning in Ireland, groups of men came together and called themselves Molly Maguires; even dressing in women's clothing as a disguise as they performed notorious deeds. For unknown reasons, when the organization evolved in America, the men dropped the women's clothing. While the basic concept of the original Mollies was to help and defend the poor and ignorant, their control and strength eventually gave rise to a cruel sense of license.

With the transplanted Mollies here in America, and Pennsylvania in particular, the mine owners and their bosses became the focus of their concern rather than land agents.[4] It was the important mining industry where the Irish felt they were being exploited, since their wages did not increase with soaring prices. In the midst of the Civil War, wages were already a smoldering issue among the miners, and those difficulties, along with poor working conditions, became more intense after the war.

The most plagued time was 1874, which saw the Mollies at their height and that coincided with Hartranft's first term as governor. While the new governor was no stranger to violence, the thought of his fighting with any labor faction troubled Hartranft since labor was always dear to him. However, despite his warm respect for the working people, Hartranft was also keenly aware that over the ten years between 1865-1875, not one Molly had ever been convicted of first degree murder despite the large number of killings that were credited to their organization.[5] With mounting cries and evidence of Molly participation in the growing numbers of murders, the state simply had to do something.

One important focal point of the period was the Philadelphia and Reading Railroad, which was headed by the powerful Franklin Benjamin Gowen, who sought to increase the company's land holdings at almost any cost. Gowen was an aggressive thirty-three-year-old lawyer who was well connected politically and, as matters developed, would later act as a special prosecutor against the Mollies.[6]

One of the major difficulties in understanding the true nature of Mollies lies with the two very strong, divergent views on their existence. Many apologists simply see them as the forerunners of a miners' union -- a band of men who stood united to foster economic gain and working improvements for the miners. It has been argued that poor wages coupled with unethical prices at the company store were designed to hold down the miner to little better than slave status.

Charges of excessive costs for the necessary black powder indispensable in the mines, along with unsafe working conditions essentially forced the miners to contribute substantially to the huge company profits, both real and perceived. When wages fell, these "forced contributions" led to added strife between the miners and management. In support of the miner's position, a typical monthly company statement showed the following gross income and company store deductions:

TYPICAL MONTHLY COMPANY STATEMENT FOR A MINER

| | |
|---|---:|
| Coal Mined, 49 Tons @ 71 1/2 cents | $35.03 |
| Supplies | $ 8.25 |
| Blacksmith | $ .30 |

```
Fixing two drills...............................................................$  .30
Rent...............................................................................$ 6.00
Groceries etc..................................................................$20.18
                                                                              _____
Total..............................................................................$35.03
Net Balance                                                          $00.00[7]
```

Similar monthly statements were very common all over the mining region, leaving many of the miners indebted to the firm for almost a lifetime. Another major complaint was that strong anti-Irish and anti-Catholic sentiments that existed in America at that time, particularly among the owners and bosses of the mines. "Irish need not apply" signs were very common then, and many miners felt that the English Protestants, who generally owned and ran the firms, demonstrated their disdain of the Irish by allowing oppression of the workers. A miner dismissed from one mine found it virtually impossible to find employment anywhere else in the coal fields, owing to the fraternity between the management groups.

Conversely, management viewed the Mollies as representing mob rule. The private lives of a large portion of the mining population were being governed by fear; despite the stated objectives of the AOH, those involved with the organization appeared to be using their positions and AOH membership to further their own personal lot and not the miners in general.

The owners countered that expensive powder forced the miners to utilize that material with great economy and caution, which they would not do if they did not have to pay a handsome price. Management convincingly argued that credit at the company store gave a strong sense of security to a family who always had the basics available to them with no need to worry about cash. Without that credit opportunity, the men in the mines frequently drank away their wages, which could place their families in an utterly hopeless position.

These and endless other arguments make up the contest for the Management-Molly issue, and this small chapter cannot pretend to settle all of those ongoing debates. However, it is clear that arguments aside, both labor and management could have taken steps to avoid the horrible violence that dotted the area and period. With regard to that brand of violence, one New York editor wrote,

> If we are to believe the local journals, a state of disorder
> and brigandage prevails in the mountain districts of that

227

state [Pennsylvania], quite worthy of Mexico, or Calabria, or Greece. The farmers are solemnly warned against sending their boys alone and unarmed to market, as they are thus exposed to robbery and murder at the hands of the gangs of starving and desperate men who infest the roads.[8]

While the total scope and actions of the Mollies cannot be an easy matter to define, several key points are clear and should be noted as follows:

1. Entry into the Mollies required proof of Irish heritage, which sometimes was more a matter of style than precise documentation.
2. To be inducted into the Mollies was also to be inducted into the AOH. However, this induction prerequisite appears to have been more of a tradition rather than a precise requirement.
3. One had to be a Roman Catholic.
4. A secret rite was conducted for new inductees which was a combination of the AOH and Catholic ritual. As matters progressed during this period, a hierarchy of Mollies developed which allegedly detailed men to various functions, including maiming or killing.
5. Maiming or killing was usually directed at mine bosses who were thought obnoxious or odious. Victims were frequently those who fired an Irishman or perhaps offended a Molly member. Those selected for execution were usually sent a "coffin notice" warning them of their impending death. These notices were very cryptic in nature and were frequently festooned with a skull and crossbones cartoon.
6. The organization of Mollies was a male group who kept their women totally ignorant about their activities.
7. The Mollies finally evolved as a labor controlling influence but their effect was also felt in local business and political affairs as well. With that type of growing power, abuse could not be very far behind.
8. As the Mollies developed and matured, they lost favor with the Roman Catholic Church, which ultimately banned their very existence and excommunicated those belonging to the group. The Church simply would not tolerate their reported brutal methods.
9. Men who are concerned only with personal gain do not care much for such ecclesiastical disdain except when it comes to image making. Priests speaking out against the Mollies were as likely as anyone to be the targets of their anger.
10. The men belonging to the Molly organization wrought havoc upon the mine owners but, more importantly and sadly, it was, as usual, the poor miner or worker and his family who would ultimately suffer the most.

Throughout their existence, the Mollies did an excellent job of maintaining their veil of secrecy through fear of physical violence and sworn allegiance from the membership. Their vow of secrecy has been compared to the pledge of "Omerta", or conspiracy of silence utilized by the Mafia. Bent upon a variety of secret salutations, the Mollies even had a number of other names including "Buckshots" and "Sleepers" which were used by the membership to hide their true identity.

Active in a number of Pennsylvania counties including Carbon, Columbia, Dauphin, Lackawanna, Lebanon, Luzerne, Schuylkill, Susquehanna, and Wayne, the Mollies had a substantial population to work upon. The towns of Girardville, Hazelton, Mahanoy City, Mauch Chunk [today, Jim Thorpe], Mount Carmel, Nanticoke, Pottsville, and Shamokin were destined to become famous with their activities.[9]

While it is impossible to pinpoint the exact date that the Mollies emerged in America, their existence was certainly known as early as October 20, 1862. By that date, the draft had been imposed by President Lincoln and almost immediately, resistance began to surface in the coal regions of the Keystone State. In one incident, five hundred civilian men stopped a federal troop train carrying new conscripts, and the mob offered protection to anyone who decided not to enter the army. That band was successful in thwarting the recruiting efforts of the federal government, and it is now generally believed that the ringleaders of that disruption were Mollies.[10] Their success of defying the government won them significant local stature.

Buoyed by that success, the impact of the Mollies began to spread rapidly, and in that same year a colliery, or coal-mine boss, Frank W. Langdon, was beaten and killed for what was believed as a labor reprisal. His death was assumed to have been done by the Mollies but not until 1877, fourteen years later, would the participants in Langdon's death face the gallows.[11] Beginning with Langdon's death, lawlessness in the region grew rapidly and continued during the Civil War, and their activities required federal troops at Reading, Mauch Chunk and other Pennsylvania towns.[12] While there will always be debate about the depth of their involvement, Alexander K. McClure, a Pennsylvania politician and historian wrote that, "victims of the Mollies were entirely innocent of the provocation."[13]

As their network began to spread, the Mollies naturally positioned themselves along mountain regions throughout the coal mining area. Towns and villages had inns or saloons which were owned by "Body Masters", who served as the local Molly leaders, and their buildings frequently served as the local meeting houses. While the organization was growing stronger, the miner's within its ranks were continuing to suffer from the horrible working conditions in the mines. According to James D. Horan, author and historian, in 1871 alone, 112 men were killed in mining accidents while another 332 were permanently injured. During the seven years prior to 1871, a total of 556 men had been killed while another 1,565 had been maimed. Add to this the grisly fact that out of the approximate 22,000 miners in the area, 5,000 were lads of sixteen or younger.[14] All of this provided the Mollies with fertile ground, and those atrocious working conditions soon gave rise to added violence and strikes.

Out of their own network of body masters came a handsome forty-three-year-old Irishman who has been accused of styling himself as sort of the "boss of all bosses" among the Mollies. Jack Kehoe, owner of the Hibernian House in Girardville, reputedly represented the ultimate law within the organization. During the fall of 1873, Kehoe was introduced to an intriguing newcomer in the area, Mr. James McKenna.

Claiming to have been forced to flee Buffalo because of murder, McKenna was really a Pinkerton detective by the name of James McParland, who was a native of County Armagh, Ulster, Ireland.[15] Allan Pinkerton, who had been active with General McClellan during the Civil War, had been hired by Gowen, and Pinkerton is said to have personally selected McParland because of his ability to drink, fight, and keep a cool head. When Pinkerton had to consider the qualifications of the right man for this job, he reportedly envisioned,

> ... no ordinary man that I need in this matter. He must be an Irishman and a Catholic, as only this class of person can find admission to the Molly Maguires. My detective should become, to all intents and purposes, one of the order, and continue so while he remains in the case before us. He should be hardy, tough and capable of laboring, in season and out of season, to accomplish unknown to those about him, a single absorbing subject.[16]

Sometime later, Pinkerton's son Robert noted that, "The man had to feel that he was serving his church, his God, his race and his country."[17]

Posing as a hard-drinking and fighting Irishman, McKenna quickly won the hearts of men in the local saloons with his ability to sing Irish ballads and dance their jigs and his free-spending style when it came to buying drinks. In addition to his alleged murder charge, McKenna claimed to have been wanted by the law for passing the "queer", or counterfeit money. All of this made him a most interesting individual and ultimately, he was introduced to Jack Kehoe, who always viewed him with great suspicion.

In December of 1873, when Hartranft began his first term as governor, McKenna began his secret penetration of the Mollies. Even before being elected Governor, Hartranft was certainly aware of the civil unrest in the coal regions and was well informed about Molly activities. With his bid for the governor's office, there naturally came an entourage of loyal supporters who were eager to make certain that he was elected. That eagerness appears to be the root cause of the many charges and about Hartranft's potential association with the Mollies. Eventually, newspapers all across Pennsylvania, echoed the allegations of his willingness to buy the democratic Molly vote in return for money and gubernatorial favors. Conversely, papers supporting the governor cheered constantly about his adroit handling of a difficult situation and loudly applauded his integrity. This divisive reaction was to serve as the template throughout the entire four year ordeal.

Today, there is still debate whether there ever was a trade of dollars-for-votes relating to Hartranft's second bid for the governor's office. The most generally accepted scenario is that Hartranft's Major General of the National Guard, Joshua K. Sigfried, admittedly struck such a deal with Jack Kehoe and John Slattery and paid them $2,000.[18] This political "arrangement" came to light during the trial of three other Irishmen for the murder of Morgan Powell. When confronted, Sigfried swore that Hartranft never knew about the deal until after his election, but the damage to Hartranft's integrity was still evident.[19]

Despite Sigfried's statements, many felt that Hartranft was never guilty of making any deal with the Mollies. One important individual who felt strongly about Hartranft's innocence was Mr. F. P. Dewees, of Pottsville, a member of the Schuylkill County Bar and a historian as well.[20] Yet, no matter who was pro or con, there is not one thread of evidence that Hartranft ever personally condoned any such treaty.

One damaging, and at the same time, illuminating testimony about Hartranft came from a Molly member and officer of the AOH, John Slattery, who was later charged with murder himself. During his testimony, Slattery reported that,

Last fall we worked hard for Hartranft so that we would have a friend in the Governor's chair who would grant us pardons: money was used to secure the votes for Governor Hartranft; the man who made the agreement said that he would go to Harrisburg to see if he could get the money ... Jack Kehoe and I got $1,000; it was agreed that we were to have each $500.00 more if we carried the county for

Hartranft; I don't think it was so boldly said that pardons would be given to any of our men but that was understood.[21]


Slattery never implicates Hartranft directly and he makes clear that "the man" would have to go to Harrisburg in an attempt to secure the money. The issue of gubernatorial pardons for the Mollies became grossly exaggerated. Few truly understood the new constitutional procedures for pardons which Hartranft had warmly welcomed upon his election. For his judicious use of the pardon, Hartranft actually won the praise of Catholic priests in the area and Father Joseph Koch of Shamokin in particular. Father Koch, who was quite knowledgeable about Molly matters, felt that Hartranft would not be so bold to pardon a convicted criminal and even though he felt that some of the pardons issued were the result of great pressure applied to the governor, he still felt that, "he was acting within the lines of safety for justice."[22]

In terms of pardons, most failed to appreciate that the new state constitution removed the pardoning power by sole discretion of the governor in such matters. The constitution created a pardon board to whom all petitions had to be submitted, in turn, they made their recommendations to the chief magistrate. Hartranft heartily endorsed this procedure when he was first elected, and only on such recommendations were any pardons granted. Still, the governor actually signed the pardons, and whenever one was issued to an Irishman, it was usually assumed to be tied to the Molly deal. This included the September 1874 pardon of John Murphy, who had been convicted of "felonious assault and battery"[23] and the January 1875 pardon of Silas Dougherty, who had been convicted of stealing eight turkeys.[24]

The political problem that developed out of the argument was the potential impediment to Hartranft's ability to govern with all the controversy. Because some newspapers constantly accused him of being involved with the Molly leaders for votes, no matter what sort of decision he might make about them, the opposition simply took a counter stance. Finally, and true to his form, Hartranft ultimately made the required tough decision and issued death warrants instead of the predicted pardons for ten of the Mollies. Given the governor's pragmatic temperament, the anti-Hartranft newspapers could now print whatever they pleased for he was comfortable with his handling of responsibility.

Hartranft was not the only focal point of accusations cast by the Mollies. The entire turbulent time-frame represented a deep frustration for many individuals and organizations including the AOH, which decided to officially discard members of the Mollies. The Roman Catholic Church too, turned away Molly members and local priests predicted that the fires of hell would fall upon the heads of the brotherhood if they continued their godless ways. In a number of parishes in the region, brave priests refused to administer Catholic sacraments to known Molly members or their families. While none of this served to substantially alter the purpose of the silent group, it did raise the level of disdain for the violence among the vast number of innocent Irish people in the area.

During the first half of 1875, miners, or the budding union in the area of Shenandoah and Mahanoy City [the very heart of Molly country] had a number of confrontations with mine management. Equipment and property were destroyed and in June about five hundred miners gathered together to get rid of strike-breakers who were known as "blacklegs". Many with that angry mob were Mollies, and when the sheriff called upon the governor for help, Hartranft immediately sent in troops to restore peace.[25] With a riot narrowly averted by the troops, the Mollies again resumed their clandestine methods of killing and maiming.

Meanwhile, McKenna kept up his penetration into the organization. On October 27, 1873, and for the next two and one half years, this scholarly-looking Irishman, who could have easily passed for a priest, would bring the inner workings of the Mollies to the surface. On April 13, 1874, McKenna was inducted into the AOH by taking the oath on his knees, making the sign of the cross, and paying the treasurer $3.00.[26] McKenna had become a trusted member of the Mollies.

Later that year, when McKenna met Jack Kehoe, the latter's instinctive suspicion drove McKenna to drink harder in an attempt to convince Kehoe of his faithfulness. During the same period, the detective made arrangements to send daily reports of his findings to the Pinkerton office in Philadelphia. All the while his contacts within the organization grew along with his singing, dancing, drinking, and fighting fame.

The reign of terror imposed by the Mollies continued to cause fear and in July of 1875, Bishop James F. Wood of Philadelphia issued a decree that excommunicated anyone involved with the Mollies.[27] This encouraged local priests to become more vocal about their own disdain, but that only served to increase the wrath of local Molly members. Wood's fiat followed the collapse of the "Long Strike" which had begun in December of 1874 and concluded in June of 1875. The net gain of that Molly inspired action was empty for the miners and only served to increase the violence and destruction to both men and equipment.

As the death and destruction increased, so did the anger of some locals which led some of the miners to take up vigilante-type action against the Mollies. On Friday, December 10, 1875, a group of such masked vigilante's broke into the home of a widow, Margaret O'Donnell of Mahanoy City. Seeking revenge against male Molly members, these frustrated and angry men unfortunately beat Mrs. O'Donnell, shot and killed her married daughter, Ellen McAllister, and then wounded her son James, and killed another son, Charles, with "no less than fifteen bullets."[28]

While the O'Donnell boys had been active with the Mollies, Mrs. O'Donnell and her daughter certainly bore no responsibility for the actions of the men. The death of the innocent woman immediately raised the anger of many Mollies including McKenna. At first, the detective threatened to resign his secret assignment over the incident, thinking that it might have been Pinkerton who ordered the action.[29] Many in the area of Mahanoy City prepared for a reign of terror from the Mollies; but instead, the incident seemed to signal the beginning of the end for both the Mollies and McKenna's cover. Kehoe's suspicion of McKenna increased as he noticed too many operations and "hits" were being thwarted, indicating an informer in their ranks; Kehoe rightly suspected McKenna.

In January 1876 two Mollies, Jimmy Kerrigan and Mike Doyle, were completing their defense against murder charges when the jury soon found Doyle guilty; his sentence was death by hanging. That decision prompted Kerrigan to become an informer, and he promptly began to point the finger at his fellow Mollies.[30] Kerrigan's "confession" led to a series of arrests which further threatened McKenna's cover as he began to lose trusted confidantes.

On March 7, 1876, with his cover virtually shattered, McKenna made a hasty exit out of Molly country while a series of Molly trials were already underway. McKenna [McParland] at first was very reluctant to testify at any of the trials though his testimony was thought to be critical. Only after considerable pressure had been applied did McParland [McKenna] agree to take the stand in Pottsville in May 1876. As McParland gave his deadly first-hand testimony, the hunt for other Mollies continued, and on May 6, eleven more Mollies were brought in, including Jack Kehoe, the so-called "King Molly", who had been charged in the 1862 murder of Frank Langdon. The house of Molly was well on its way to ruin.

Predictably, particular attention was paid to the trial of Kehoe because of his high profile. Newspapers from all over Pennsylvania fired off opinions and thoughts on Kehoe's relationship [real and imagined] with Governor Hartranft. They reported the possibility of a quid pro quo arrangement between Hartranft and the "King Molly" for the votes delivered. They further projected that Hartranft would offer asylum to Kehoe for his assistance at the ballot box, and Kehoe is reported to have boldly declared to the warden of the Pottsville jail that, "the old man at Harrisburg [Hartranft] wouldn't go back on us."[31] Despite the fact that

Kehoe's statement was made by the most "notorious" member of the Mollies, many papers found his utterances as absolute proof that he had a connection in Harrisburg.

Emotions throughout the state ran high as newspapers fired daily salvos for and against Hartranft and Kehoe. To this very day some debate lingers over Kehoe's responsibility for the murder of Frank Langdon. Two of Kehoe's "operatives", John Campbell and Neal Dougherty, had already been convicted of second degree murder in the Langdon case, but Kehoe himself was charged with murder in the first degree.[32] Early in 1877, Kehoe was found guilty and sentenced to hang, which led to an immediate appeal.

In January of 1878, one year after Kehoe's conviction, the Pennsylvania Supreme Court reviewed his case and affirmed the lower court's decision.[33] Consequently, he was destined for the gallows unless he received a pardon from Governor Hartranft. However, the decision by the Pennsylvania Supreme Court, refusing Kehoe's request for a new trial, did nothing to settle the Hartranft-Molly dispute and the newspapers continued to question,

 Did Hartranft meet with Jack Kehoe prior to his second election and trade dollars for votes?
 Would the governor, because of Kehoe's alleged voting assistance, pardon the convicted killer and, perhaps, some of his accomplices?[34]
 If there was any connection between Kehoe, the Molly Maguires and the Republican party, was Hartranft aware of what was going on?

Daily, Hartranft was pressed for answers or comments on the Kehoe case, and the entire matter became an ugly political football. Meanwhile, Hartranft was nearing the end of his second and final term, and some charged that he would withhold any decision on pardoning Kehoe to avoid offending partisans of both sides. While it is impossible to determine precisely what went through the governor's mind at the time, we can appreciate that no matter how he might have acted, it would have been used against him by one group or the other. Yet, the newspapers continued to press him, and finally on November 19, 1878, he was quoted as saying,

> I preferred to rest a little longer under the imputation that has been industriously circulated since the trial, rather than use the gallows in a political campaign to reassure those doubters whom sixteen executions could not convince. [Here, Hartranft refers to the sixteen Mollies who had already died on the gallows and some of whom had claimed

235

that they would receive a pardon from him.] Whatever political advantage could be gotten from making the question of pardon or execution a political issue I wished the opposition to enjoy.[35]

Obviously, Hartranft saw the no-win political situation, and for whatever other reasons may be inferred, he simply refused to send Kehoe to the gallows during an impending election where the Democrats could make political fortune from a man's death.

Within days of the Governor's statement, The *Pittsburgh Daily Post*, on Thursday, November 28, 1878, delivered a damaging report against the governor's position. Under the headline, "A Startling Confession ", the *Post* stated,

We print elsewhere the confession of Hartranft's Major General of the National Guard, Sigfried, and since that office was abolished his Boiler Inspector for the anthracite region [a very fat office] testifying to the fact that pending the Gubernatorial election of 1875, he paid two thousand dollars in cash to the Mollie Maguire Chiefs, Kehoe and Slatterly, the conditions being that the Mollie vote was to be transferred to Hartranft. ...The Republican leaders well knew this, and Sigfried, holding high office under Hartranft, was deputed to negotiate the alliance between the Republican Managers and the Mollies. Hoyt at the time was Chairman of the State Committee. Is it a supposable case he did not sanction and authorize the payment? Hartranft was Governor and was to be the chief beneficiary of the infernal alliance. Is it supposable he was not aware of the bribe and the compact? Sigfried is silent about where he got the two thousand dollars, and shirks any mention of Hoyt's name. He says, however, Hartranft was not informed of his indebtedness to the Mollies until some time after his election. This may or may not be true. For our part we don't credit it. Slattery's word is as good as Sigfried's, and Kehoe's as good as either of them, and Jack declared in the Pottsville jail to the warden, as testified in the Mollie trials, that he knew "the old man at Harrisburg [Hartranft] wouldn't go back on us", and that the prosecution "might crack their whips." That showed a close

236

understanding between the Mollies and the Governor, when taken in connection with other circumstances, and especially the payment of the money. Nor do we believe "the old man" will "go back on JACK." The recent issue of the death warrant was the prelude to another move on the Board of Pardons. The warrant will be withdrawn, and the case will go over to Hoyt. It is conceded he will never sign the warrant for execution.[36]

Obviously, the *Pittsburgh Daily Post* with its long history of anti-Hartranft articles, was not a supporter of Hartranft and had, through this article, prejudged Hartranft. The governor was never a person to make snap decisions unless they were required in the heat of battle during his military career. Even then, he always took an extra moment to "think through" his objective and only then did he move forward. Hartranft's patient and reflective attitude in the case of Jack Kehoe was nothing new.

That does not excuse the governor if he was, in fact, knowledgeable about what Sigfried was doing. It is far more likely however that Sigfried operated under the name, but without the prior knowledge and approval of the governor and when Hartranft found out, he simply refused to offer up any supporters as sacrificial lambs for his sake. We will never be able to completely answer the question of what, if anything, Hartranft knew about Sigfried's meeting with Kehoe. We do know that Kehoe's lawyers did apply for a pardon and those very attorneys noted that,

The application for commutation of sentence was argued by Kehoe's counsel, who did openly all the work that was done towards procuring a commutation. No political influence was brought or attempted to be brought to bear upon the Governor or any member of the Board of Pardons. *No old political bargains remain to be fulfilled, for the reason that none were ever made.*

Two of the counsel for Kehoe are now and always have been the political opponents of Governor Hartranft; consequently have no political favors to ask. One of the counsel was, at the time of the trial, and still is, chairman of the Democratic standing committee of Schuylkill county. His efforts, therefore, to secure political favors from Governor Hartranft would be futile and of no avail. Besides, he has not asked and would not ask the same.

We have placed our case before the Board of
Pardons upon its merits, and simply ask that they rise
above the prejudices that have influenced the community
in this case and judge the defendant not as county delegate
of the "Mollie Maguire" organization of Schuylkill county,
as he has heretofore been judged, but as plain John Kehoe,
a citizen of this Commonwealth. We make this statement
in simple justice to Governor Hartranft, who, we believe,
he's [sic] been unjustly assailed, and on behalf of our case,
which may have been prejudged in the minds of the public
through the influence of newspaper articles which have of
late appeared upon the subject.

A. Campbell<br>
S. A. Garret<br>
John W. Ryon<br>
Counsel for John Kehoe[37]

Many of the newspaper attacks upon Hartranft grew more vicious
in nature, while his supporters were equally adamant in their praise. No one
really knew what Hartranft would do about Kehoe in the final analysis.
Some shouted for joy, others decried the Governor's "insensitivity", and
many appeared confused when, on January 18, 1878, Mrs. Kehoe went to
visit her husband to deliver the news that a pardon would not be
forthcoming.[38]

On December 18th, precisely eleven months after his wife's visit
with the bad news, in the midst of the tears and strain, Jack Kehoe remained
stoic as he prepared for death. He took succor from the priest attending him
as he took his last steps walking up to the gibbet, where he said to the
sheriff, "I am not guilty of murdering Langdon, I never saw the crime
committed."[39] Shortly thereafter, the drop fell, and the rope around Kehoe's
neck slipped upon his face more than expected, which prolonged his death.
Despite the driving snow storm, approximately 150 people witnessed
Kehoe's hanging, while another 200 stood outside the prison wall of
Pottsville.[40]

In all, twenty Mollies would be put to the gallows, with the major
hangings at Pottsville and Mauch Chunk. June 21, 1877, would be witness to
twelve hangings alone, and became known as "Black Thursday" among many
Irish-Americans of the area. The last Molly to swing from the gallows was
Martin Bergen, who was put to death at Mauch Chunk on January 16,
1879.[41] While the death of Bergen marked the end of the Molly era, the

debate over Governor Hartranft's alleged relationship with the organization continued.

Through it all, the governor kept his own counsel, which probably fueled his detractors to write their hypothetical points of view. Perhaps the best, final summation of all the charges and countercharges was printed in The *Evening Chronicle* of Philadelphia, on Thursday, November 21, 1878, under the title, THE *TIMES* ON HARTRANFT. This lengthy article tends to vindicate Hartranft's entire scope of activity with the Mollies and their many legal trials. The entire article appears in Appendix B.

The issue of Governor Hartranft's potential relationship with the Mollies or Jack Kehoe in particular, will be long contested. However, when all we know about the governor is considered, the profile offered by The *Evening Chronicle* appears to offer us the best and perhaps most balanced summary of the issue. As for those who might have treated with aides from Hartranft's staff in the belief he would run counter to his own mores, they were wrong; dead wrong!

ENDNOTES FOR CHAPTER NINE
THE MOLLY MAGUIRES

1. Broehl, Wayne G., Jr., *The Molly Maguires*, Cambridge, Massachusetts, Harvard University Press, 1965, p. 3.
2. Horan, James D., *The Pinkertons*, New York, Bonanza Books, 1974, p. 205.
3. Aurand, A. Monroe, Jr., *Historical Account of the Molly Maguires*, Lancaster, Pennsylvania, Aurand Press, [No Date], p. 3.
4. Rhodes, James Ford, *History of the United States from Hayes to McKinley, 1877-1896*, New York, The Macmillan Company, 1919, p. 58.
5. Ibid.
6. Horan, *The Pinkertons*, p. 207.
7. Roberts, Peter, *The Anthracite Coal Industry*, New York, The Macmillan Company, 1901, p. 148.
8. *New York World*, July 7, 1870.
9. Lewis, Arthur, H., *Lament for the Molly Maguires*, New York, Harcourt, Brace & World, 1964, p. 87.
10. Ibid. pp. 29-30.
11. Coleman, Walter J., *The Molly Maguire Riots, Richmond, Garrett and Massie*, 1936, pp. 157-158.
12. Aurand, *Historical Account of the Molly Maguires*, p. 13.
13. McClure, *Old Time Notes of Pennsylvania*, p. 429.
14. Horan, *The Pinkertons*, p. 206.
15. Ibid., p. 209.
16. Ibid., p. 208.
17. Ibid.
18. *Pittsburgh Daily Post*, November 28, 1878.
19. Ibid.
20. Aurand, *Historical Account of the Molly Maguires*, p. 13.
21. Coleman, *The Molly Maguire Riots*, p. 65.
22. Ibid.
23. Documents courtesy of *Pennsylvania Archives*, Harrisburg.
24. Ibid.
25. Lewis, *Lament for the Molly Maguires*, p. 123.
26. Horan, *The Pinkertons*, p. 213.
27. Lewis, *Lament for the Molly Maguires*, p. 245.
28. Horan, *The Pinkertons*, p. 225.
29. Ibid., p. 226.
30. Ibid., p. 228.
31. *Pittsburgh Daily Post*, November 28, 1878.
32. Coleman, *The Molly Maguire Riots*, p. 157.

33. Ibid., p. 158.
34. While these questions are understandable, many within the State, including some newspapers, gave the new governor high marks for his judicious use of pardons. One such report came from *The Press* of Everett, Pennsylvania, on January 21, 1874. That publication stated that, "Forty-five is the number of Governor Hartranft's pardons for the year, which is below the annual average of any of his predecessors, and very far below the average of most of them. This is well; and what is better, most of the pardons seem to have been well bestowed, though there are a few which we think otherwise. The Governor has been exceptionally fortunate in having to sign but one death warrant." - Shireman Collection.
35. *Philadelphia Evening Bulletin*, circa 1878, Shireman Collection.
36. *Pittsburgh Daily Post*, November 28, 1878.
37. *Pottsville Miners Journal*, June 18, 1878.
38. Lewis, *Lament for the Molly Maguires*, p. 304.
39. Ibid., p. 305.
40. Ibid. It should be noted that on January 14, 1971, Pennsylvania Governor, Milton J. Schapp, a Democrat, issued a pardon for Jack Kehoe as a result of 16 years of labor from Kehoe's great-grandson, Joseph Wayne. Mr. Wayne and his family still operate the Hibernian House in Girardville. The author met with Mr. Wayne to discuss Jack Kehoe and encouraged him to provide any/all documents that might prove favorable to his great-grandfather. Despite numerous follow-up calls by the author, and frequent promises from Mr. Wayne, nothing was ever forthcoming.
41. Lewis, *Lament for the Molly Maguires*, p. 308.

# CHAPTER TEN

## *A NON-PRESIDENTIAL BID*

In 1874 the Republican Party suffered from a stinging election defeat as the American people sent 181 Democrats to Congress compared to 107 Republicans and three Independents.[1] Undoubtedly some of that popular discontent resulted from the way President Grant had handled the nation during his tenure in office, and the ire of the public continued right through the year of 1876. While Grant himself did not appear to profit from his two terms as president, many of his appointees certainly did, including Secretary of the Navy George Robeson. When Robeson entered office during Grant's second term, he had a net worth of $20,000. Three years later, with an annual salary of only $8,000, he was able to manage personal bank deposits of approximately $300,000.[2] Many claimed that Robeson had made the term graft synonymous with the U. S. Navy and he is only one example of many who apparently helped themselves to public funds.

While many Americans grumbled about graft in Washington, others were unhappy that the president might be considering an unprecedented third term in the White House. However, President Grant, who was strongly encouraged by his wife Julia to press for a third term, showed distinct signs of really not wanting to weather another four turbulent years as president.[3]

To add to Grant's growing political problems were those Pennsylvania politicians who felt that he was too reluctant to offer Pennsylvania her fair share of patronage. Conversely, the president felt that those begging for more Keystone State appointments had an insatiable appetite and might never be satisfied with any number of appointments.[4] In fairness to Grant, the latter appears to have had some merit. In 1874, Senator Simon Cameron, who had been Lincoln's first Secretary of War, made an unsuccessful bid to have Grant appoint his son, J. Donald Cameron, as Secretary of the Treasury, which was being vacated by resigning Secretary William A. Richardson; Grant refused.[5] A few weeks later, Cameron's ire was again raised when the chief executive turned another deaf ear to his request to appoint his son-in-law, Wayne MacVeagh, as a replacement for the outgoing Postmaster General, John J. Cresswell. That post went instead to Connecticut's Marshall Jewell.[6]

Both of these presidential denials only served to infuriate the Pennsylvania senator and political boss, who was not accustomed to such rough handling. Not one to let such matters pass quietly, Cameron decided to coerce the State Republican convention to flatly reject the thought of a third term for Grant, and to pledge instead, its support for Pennsylvania's "favorite son", Governor John Frederick Hartranft.[7]

Even casual political observers could plainly see the growing erosion between the president and the Pennsylvania political king and they immediately realized that Cameron was spoiling for a fight. Shortly after Grant's 1872 reelection, Cameron had openly supported the idea of a third term for Grant with the hopes of then winning a cabinet seat for his son.[8] Now that he had been spurned, Cameron spoke openly of his displeasure with the man from Galena. With his sudden shift from presidential support, one Philadelphia newspaper wrote, "It seems that the old chieftain [Cameron], having got all out of Grant that he can, but not all that he wants, has resolved to put the knife to the throat of his Excellency."[9] Consequently, Hartranft's Republican nomination was really not rooted in his popularity with Keystone voters or the Republican Party. Instead, it was essentially tied to the vengeance spewed by the state's old political boss against the President of the United States. As the time drew near for the Republican national convention, an article appeared in the *Cincinnati Enquirer* which aptly described Cameron's motives:

> ... But this action [Hartranft's nomination] is not [a] representation of the sentiment of the republican party, as the fact of its isolation shows. It can be very easily explained. Simon Cameron owns the republican party in Pennsylvania, and he owns Hartranft. Simon went down to Washington one day about a year ago accompanied by the mayor of Philadelphia, and Mr. Hartranft and some other noted gentlemen, to ask the President to appoint a certain gentleman post-master of Philadelphia. Grant had a spasmodic and miraculous attack of civil service reform - a disease which never afflicted him before, and which has never manifested any symptoms since - and refused to appoint Simon's candidate. General Cameron wasn't accustomed to such treatment, and it didn't altogether suit him.[10]

The move by Cameron to promote Hartranft was not lost upon Governor Rutherford B. Hayes of Ohio who had assisted Hartranft in his second gubernatorial bid. Understandably, Hayes now looked upon this move to pit the Pennsylvania governor against his own presidential aspirations as "political ingratitude". A comment from the *Harrisburg Patriot* noted that,

> It does seem extremely ungracious now to set up Hartranft as a rival to Hayes for the Presidency, when he ought in gratitude to be a willing ally. But Gov. Hartranft is not in any true sense a candidate for President. His friends neither expect nor desire his nomination. They are only putting him up as a blind until they can determine upon the candidate who is most likely to carry off the prize with their assistance. This is all there is in the talk about Hartranft as a candidate.[11]

In fact, despite the political intrigue, Hartranft was to remain a "willing ally" to Hayes for many years.

So blatant was Cameron's move with the governor that one Democratic journal boldly asked, "What, in the name of Heaven, is the claim of Hartranft to the Presidency...we do think that of all the suggestions for the Presidency, this one...is the most ridiculous."[12] Unfortunately for Governor Hartranft, the rift between Grant and Cameron would take its greatest toll upon himself. He had dealt with the internal machinations of the Pennsylvania system long enough to view matters with a wary eye and he could see his sacrificial lamb status. The only question was under what guise would it develop, and when? Consequently, his personal enthusiasm for the Presidential bid was almost non-existent, and Hartranft did little to promote the idea of his nomination.[13]

Hartranft never had any particular patience for newspaper writers, and he certainly avoided heavy discussion with them as it related to his potential nomination.[14] Despite this disdain, he made one particular exception for the respected Civil War correspondent, George Alfred Townsend who, on May 17, 1876, joined the governor for dinner and an interview.[15]

During their discussion, Townsend reported that, "The Governor had little to say about the Presidency or politics, nor [did he-Townsend] received any hint on that subject but he spoke freely and quietly about the State."[16] When Townsend offered that he felt the governor would receive the Pennsylvania vote in Cincinnati, Hartranft simply said, "I don't see how I could encourage that idea as it would leave the State Government in the hands of the Democrats."[17] [This was a reference to Lieutenant-Governor

James W. Latta who was a Democrat] Beyond that, Hartranft entertained nothing further with the up-coming Republican convention.

It was from this interview where we have Townsend's credible profile of the Governor when he noted that, "He [Hartranft]...had plain manners and an agreeable style ...was easy to get acquainted with, although he is not loquacious. He is a likable man ... large, heavy hipped ..., with predominating German frame and head, yet it is not the blond German of the Prussian type. His hair is black as the raven's wing, his large moustache [sic] is darkish, he has a small forehead, but a good head, a fine soldierly nose and bluish eyes, wide apart. He speaks with an occasionally heavy accent and reminded me somewhat of the late General John A. Rawlins."[18] Rawlins had been General Grant's principal staff officer and confidante. Townsend continued his comments calling Hartranft a, "national subject of curiosity" and he noted that he "liked" the Governor more than he had expected and Hartranft's good memory allowed him to recall matters of years ago with great alacrity.[19] At the time of Townsend's interview, Governor Hartranft was only forty-five years old.

As early as the beginning of 1876, Hartranft received a number of written offers to assist him in his presidential bid, though many of these offers also asked him, at the same time, if he was really sincere about such an effort. These offers were from such diverse sources as Mr. J. B. Russell of the Department of Agriculture; Mr. S. C. Baird, Editor of the *Pittsburg* [sic] *Herald*; Henry M. Needham of New York; Mr. Harrison Allen of Denver, Colorado; to Mr. Hugh Fulton of Nebraska City, Nebraska.[20] These and many other influential friends offered their support to the governor, and they were all eager to campaign for him. Unfortunately, there are no copies of Hartranft's response to these offers, though it would be very much unlike him to let such important matters unanswered.

During the few months prior to the convention, rumors of a deal between President Grant and Simon Cameron became very strong, and threatened to undermine any chance that Hartranft may have had. In late May, Henry Needham advised Hartranft that, "the press all over the country has for a few days past been full of the new deal at Washington and Cameron's arrangement to transfer your delegates to Conkling of this [New York] State."[21] Needham referred to U. S. Senator Roscoe Conkling of New York State who was known to politically "flirt" with Simon Cameron.

From Mr. J. K. Haffey, who was associated with the *Semi-Weekly Era*, in Bradford, Pennsylvania, Hartranft was told that, "Your strength as a candidate for the Presidency, these gentlemen and others of all parties, with whom I have conversed--assert is not realized by those professing to act in your interest."[22]

**Governor John F. Hartranft**

John Hartranft as Governor of Pennsylvania.

*Photographer: H. Winslow Fegley.*
*Source: Library of Congress.*

246

Perhaps the most cryptic note was sent from Washington D. C. and dated May 22nd. Unfortunately the name on the original letter has been obliterated but its concept is similar to, if stronger than, the others as the writer warned the Governor, "You are sold out - you are treated as a mere puppet and one to be used merely to keep Penn. Delegation together for trade.---Don Cameron will be made Sec. of War [which in fact happened]. The affair was final at the White House late on Saturday night at a conference between the President, Conkling and Cameron. Conkling thought about it and the direct consideration is that Cameron is to transfer the Penn. delegation to Conkling."[23]

This letter was highly accurate and the question about the senior Cameron's allegiance was exact.

Still, not all of the information was gloom and doom. One lighter moment occurred when an ex-Congressman and delegate to the convention from North Carolina told a *New York Herald* reporter that he was in favor of Chief Justice Morrison R. Waite for President. Then, moving forward, the ex-Congressman said with a smile, "I don't like Hartranft; it's too much trouble to pronounce his name; and when I stump for a man I want him to have an easy name like my own."[24] Unfortunately, the specific name of the congressman is lost to history.

The dark side of politics, which tends to utilize people and circumstances for personal gain, could be seen by Hartranft and also one of his gubernatorial successors, Samuel W. Pennypacker, who wrote that, "he [Hartranft] ought to have been President of the United States at the time Hayes was elected, and would have been had not the bad Pennsylvania habit of opposing her own prevented [it]."[25] While Pennypacker's thoughts are not shared by everyone, they do represent the thoughts of an important and insightful individual who could definitely understand and relate to Hartranft's political difficulties with the Pennsylvania Republican machine.

While some of the many ills in the nation were due to unethical political dealings, the country was also laboring under the great financial strain and depression that followed the post-war years. Pennsylvania, too, was working its way through that difficult period and Hartranft, as we have already seen, had his hands full with labor problems throughout the state. Now, in the midst of all those difficulties, Simon Cameron was proposing him as a presidential contender, and while the thought must have been flattering, "Black Jack" knew better than anyone that his chances would not be adequate to make him a real presidential contender. Yet, he had something of a debt to pay Cameron, and while he had frequently taken his own counsel in state matters, another affront to the Cameron image would not be politically prudent. Hartranft realized that "bucking the system too far" meant possible Cameron-fueled disruption with legislation that would be designed to embarrass the chief executive. As a result, the governor found himself in a catch-22 situation with very few options to exercise.

The year 1876 was not only active from a political standpoint but also marked the Centennial celebration for the nation, which was to be held in Philadelphia. As governor of the state, Hartranft played an important role in the exposition, but must have found it extremely difficult on opening day when Mrs. Grant became miffed by what she deemed a lack of protocol due her position.[26] It appears that the Emperor of Brazil, Dom Pedro, had come to the United States and handled himself with less than royal countenance. Nonetheless, he was invited to join President Grant at the exposition, to start the Corliss engine which was to put all the exhibition machinery in motion. The Empress of Brazil was also invited to join in this event but, for unknown reasons, the president's wife was not. In her own memoirs, Julia lamented, "I the wife of the President of the United States - I, the wife of General Grant, - was there and was not invited to assist at this little ceremony...."[27] Despite that difficulty with the First Lady, the exposition was well attended, thanks in part to the raging price war among the railroads. One of the special attractions was the uplifted right arm of Lady Liberty who would soon rest, completely assembled, in New York harbor.

Irrespective of the many distractions of 1876, and his lack of enthusiasm for such a political bid, Hartranft had to afford some consideration to his potential Republican nomination. Yet, he knew that he had little popular recognition outside of the Keystone State, though his heroic war record, coupled with his impeccable stint as auditor general and his two elections as governor did offer very desirable traits. While he was seen by some as a potential compromise candidate who might offset the anticipated infighting among a total of six contenders, he clearly understood that his entire potential candidacy was little more than a bargaining chip to benefit the Camerons.[28] Still, he had to make the best of a difficult situation, and his bid as a "non-candidate" therefore really did not enhance his potential.

The selected 1876 Republican Convention site was Cincinnati, Ohio, which was the home of the Buckeye State's favorite son and governor, Rutherford B. Hayes. The actual balloting took place on June 14th, 15th and 16th; and present for that convention were all of the states and territories extant plus Washington D. C. There was a total of 756 voting delegates, and seven ballots would ultimately be taken to reach the required total of 379 votes to produce a winner.[29] Of all the delegates and their alternates from Pennsylvania, none was from Hartranft's home, Norristown.[30]

Late in the afternoon of the 15th, Mr. Lin Bartholomew of Schuylkill County presented Hartranft's name for nomination.[31] During his lackluster speech, Bartholomew said he, "did not claim him [Hartranft] as superior intellectually to all other candidates, but he knows enough to know that he doesn't know everything, and will listen to good, sound, sensible advice."[32] This comment brought a strong applause and the speaker continued and praised Hartranft's "integrity, patriotism, fidelity, purity, modesty and economy."[33] In closing, Bartholomew told the delegates that Hartranft's "nomination here is not of his own seeking, but the spontaneous seeking of the Republican party."[34] Immediately following Bartholomew's speech, the convention adjourned for the evening.

Other contenders for the party's nomination were Roscoe Conkling, Oliver P. Morton, Benjamin H. Bristow, Rutherford B. Hayes, and the anticipated winner, James G. Blaine, a Pennsylvania native who was now a Maine Congressman.[35] Aggressive and savvy, Blaine probably would have won the nomination in a handy manner but for the introduction of the so-called "Mulligan Letters", which alleged that he had accepted cash bribes in return for issuing government contracts. Shocked by the allegations brought by James Mulligan of Boston, Blaine attempted to save his image by theatrics at the convention.[36] However, according to one historian, "Blaine's speech of June 5, is not the speech of an innocent man; but no more adroit and powerful plea from one with an itching palm, who had money illicitly, can be imagined."[37] Blaine, who had attracted some support among Pennsylvanians was sorely hated by Simon Cameron, since the Maine congressman was a leader in the effort to censure Cameron for his conduct as Lincoln's Secretary of War.[38] In the end, Blaine was rejected, though he ran a close second to Hayes.

While there was a modest amount of support for Hartranft from a number of areas outside his home state, the 58 Pennsylvania delegates were led by J. Donald Cameron.[39] It is interesting to note that outside of his home state, where he received the greatest amount of support, all other votes for Hartranft came from southern states, including Florida, Mississippi, Nevada, North Carolina, Texas, Virginia, and West Virginia. He had offers for assistance from Colorado as well, but for unknown reasons, those offers never resulted in any votes.[40] While these southern states offered only very modest support, Hartranft did have indications in early May that he might get a substantial portion of the Texas vote though that support failed to materialize as first thought.[41] Whatever the source of his support, not one delegate from any other northern state came to Hartranft's side.[42]

It appears that the Pennsylvania political intrigue probably kept at least some delegates from consistently voting for Hartranft. Perhaps the only surviving memo from Hartranft's own hand, sent to an aide on May 30th, provides some insight into the anticipated voting ambivalence,

Dear Wills,

There is no intention so far as I can find to transfer the vote of Pennsylvania Delegation to Conkling, neither will my friends who are largely in the majority permit the vote to be transferred to Blaine until it has been clearly demonstrated that I cannot be nominated. All efforts to manufacture public sentiment in favor of any of the prominent candidates with the expectation of riding the winning horse are considered as unfriendly to me and Penna. interest. It will be far better that Penna. goes down with her flag flying than to have her voting for the nominee on last ballot with the charge of bargain and sale clouding the good name of the Delegation.

Yours Sincerely,

J. F. Hartranft.[43]

This memo clearly demonstrates that Hartranft had a good deal of political savvy, but equally indicates his penchant for trusting too many people and being somewhat politically naive.

Despite Hartranft's lack of enthusiasm for the bid, the state of Nevada gave him fairly broad support as witnessed by the comments of the state's two largest newspapers, The *Carson Appeal* and the *Virginia City Sentinel*. According to the *Appeal*, "Hartranft is a representative man of a great powerful Middle State. If the West is to be regarded as having had her share for the present of presidential honors - if the country is not to demand that Grant shall not be renominated at large - let us have John F. Hartranft."[44] The *Virginia City Sentinel* stated, "All the *Appeal* says of Governor Hartranft is true. He is wonderfully loved in Pennsylvania; there is no spot, stain or suspicion on his record; he is a soldier and a statesman, and with him for a leader the Republican party would be sure to win."[45] However, if the Pennsylvania governor was to be nominated, he would need similar support from large urban areas like New York, Philadelphia, and Chicago. The reality was that that type of support simply did not exist for the "likable" man from Norristown.

Some newspapers throughout Pennsylvania offered their support for their favorite son too, though a real strong sense of dedication was lacking. But, one Keystone paper, the *North Wales Record* wrote that, "The Republicans have gained many a hardfought battle at the polls in the last twenty years.... Let them go before the next National Republican Convention with the demand that that body give them one of Pennsylvania's sons to be the standard bearer in the Presidential campaign in 1880 ... that man is Governor John F. Hartranft."[46] Another Pennsylvania paper, The *Times and Dispatch*, noted that, "Should General Hartranft be nominated at Cincinnati there will be in this State the most brilliant and triumphant political campaign on record, and the nation, in its Centennial year, will perform an action altogether worthy of the august occasion by voting to commence the second hundred years of its existence with a President who is one of its ablest, purest and most patriotic citizens."[47] Eighty years after the convention, in Hartranft's hometown newspaper, The *Norristown Times Herald*, a statement appeared that pointedly, if belatedly, exposed the political trickery of the Camerons at that convention when it noted, "The Camerons father and son, controlled the Republican Party of the state. Both had been Secretary of War in Washington and senators from Pennsylvania. It is generally conceded by political historians that the son, J. Donald Cameron, effected the plan to make use of Hartranft in the convention."[48] If their objective was to "make use" of the governor, the Camerons were certainly successful!

Prior to the actual balloting, the Pennsylvania Delegation had agreed to vote for Hartranft on a united front, so long as his total votes, on successive ballots, increased.[49] Despite their stated guidelines, the Pennsylvania delegates began to defect from the Hartranft camp as early as the second ballot even though Hartranft's total votes continued a modest gain right through the fourth ballot. The defection of the Pennsylvania delegates was the result of orchestration led by J. Donald Cameron; and once the erosion began, it essentially continued until the sixth ballot was taken and Hartranft's name was removed completely.[50]

In the end, Hartranft never really was a serious threat to any of the leading potential candidates, as he consistently drew the lowest number of votes cast, and during the seventh and final ballot, he received no votes at all. In the seven ballots, Hartranft's votes numbered 58, 63, 68, 71, 69, 50 and zero, respectively. The votes from his own home state over the seven ballots were 58, 54, 55, 55, 53, 44 and zero. The major part of the contest rested between Blaine and Hayes. However, Blaine, over the first six ballots, had a huge margin over all other contenders, and on the sixth ballot he missed the required total of 378 by only seventy votes. His closest competitor was Hayes, who only had 113 votes in the sixth ballot but, on the seventh ballot, Hayes took the nomination by pulling a total of 384 votes to Blaine's 351. It is interesting to note that throughout the seven ballots, Ohio consistently pledged its 44 votes to her favorite son. Not so with Pennsylvania.[51]

According to the *Norristown Times Herald*, the early voting went as follows:

> Pennsylvania had 58 delegates, and all obeyed instruction by voting for Hartranft on the first ballot, while Blaine received 285 votes. The Blaine supporters wanted to continue the convention at night hoping to connect enough delegates to give their man the necessary majority. But it was found that the gas had been shut off and the convention hall could not be lighted.
>
> So voting could not be continued until the next day. By that time enthusiasms had cooled. Some Pennsylvania delegates forsook Hartranft but he won support in other states. In the fourth ballot he had 71 votes, most he had at any time.[52]

The Republican convention was over, and Hartranft was not sorry to see it pass. He still had two and one-half years to devote to his gubernatorial office, and he had every intention of doing his best. The bid for the presidency was finished, and he was pleased. He never felt quite comfortable in the pursuit of that office, since it did not come with the full support of the people. In other words, John F. Hartranft was not a common politician seeking position for his own benefit. Rather, if called he would serve but, even then, only under the strictures of his own modest attitude.

Following the convention, some questions were raised relating to Hartranft's poor showing in the convention ballots. Some even asked why the delegates voted as they did and why wasn't there more support for Hartranft? This author only knows of one delegate who left any sort of record on these questions. Almost six years after the convention, Colonel Andrew Stewart of Uniontown, Pennsylvania, wrote a letter to Hartranft explaining his position. Attached to that letter was also a clipping taken from the *Pittsburgh Dispatch*, which gave Stewart's rather convoluted response to the charges that he "Defied Instructions in Voting for Blaine."[53] In his response, Stewart told Hartranft that he felt that some of the people in the governor's circle of friends and advisors were really two-faced about their loyalty. Those "friends", Stewart indicated, found it easy to accuse him

[Stewart] of disloyalty when it was they who had the secret agenda.[54] In the news clipping Stewart defended his actions by informing Hartranft that as a county delegate, he first fought against a local resolution that would have bound all those delegates for Blaine, since his locale was definitely for the Maine congressman. Stewart further stated that the reason he fought against the Blaine motion was because he felt it would be improper not to recognize one of Pennsylvania's own at the convention, and he obviously voted for Hartranft at least once.

However, Stewart went on to relate, "So that, *having complimented* [or voted for-emphasis is original] Governor Hartranft, I was justified, if not in duty bound, to vote as I did [for Blaine]."[55] Obviously, Hartranft was a pawn to the Camerons, despite the best intentions of anyone or group within the state's republican party.

There was almost a small bit of irony associated with the outcome of that 1876 Republican convention. In 1880, in the same city where Hartranft had been defeated, General Winfield Scott Hancock was nominated as the Democratic candidate for president. Hancock ran, and lost, against Republican James A. Garfield and Hancock, like Hartranft, was a native of the Norristown area. It would have proved most interesting if Hartranft had won the Presidential election of 1876, Hancock the 1880 convention, which would have pit two Norristown native brothers for the presidential office. Since both men were involved in the Lincoln Conspiracy trial and the hanging of Mrs. Surratt, both were tormented by their political enemies as woman killers.

The final outcome of the 1876 National Convention saw Rutherford B. Hayes nominated as the Republican candidate, and he would have to challenge the Democratic contender, Samuel J. Tilden. The subsequent presidential election almost threw the nation back into armed conflict, and became one of our most interesting national political moments. Tilden had received about 4,300,000 popular votes to Hayes' 4,036,000. Unfortunately for Tilden, he was short by one electoral vote, and accusations of fraud were thrown at both contenders. Through a series of concessions, which became known as the Tilden-Hayes Election Compromise, Hayes was to become the victor and the nineteenth President of the United States. However, even during the swearing-in ceremony, the compromise already began to cast aspersions upon the new president when some of the observers called out, "Rutherfraud Hayes." Through that compromise, Hayes has become known as the president who brought Reconstruction to an end. His wife Lucy, became notable and earned the nickname "Lemonade Lucy", since she refused to serve alcoholic beverages at White House functions.[56] As one might imagine, this was not a very popular concept with politicians.

253

As for Hartranft, he returned to the demanding duties of his gubernatorial office, and left no extensive recorded indication of disappointment that the "bid" for the Presidency failed. We can only view that episode as a trying time for the governor and an incident born of political appeasement and not his personal ambition.

In the wake of the convention, Hartranft was confronted with some personal difficulties when his mother-in-law died, which sorely affected Sallie.[57] Burdened with his wife's grief and the demands of his office, the governor himself was stricken seven days later when he was felled by heatstroke, brought on by his hectic schedule and personal pressures.[58] The year of 1876 was only half over and had already proven itself to be most demanding in nature. All the while, labor and management disputes in Pennsylvania were becoming more and more intense and would soon test the resolve of the governor once again.

ENDNOTES FOR CHAPTER TEN
A NON-PRESIDENTIAL BID

1. McClure, A. K., *Old Time Notes of Pennsylvania*, 2 vols., Philadelphia: Winston, 1905, vol. 2, p. 441.
2. Smith, *Lee and Grant*, pp. 318-319.
3. Anthony, Carl Sferrazza, *First Ladies*, New York: William Morrow, 1990, p. 223.
4. Evans, *Pennsylvania Politics, 1872-1877*, pp. 248-249.
5. Ibid., p. 248
6. Ibid.
7. Bradley, Erwin Stanley, *Simon Cameron, Lincoln's Secretary of War*, Philadelphia: University of Pennsylvania Press, 1966, p. 358.
8. Bradley, *Simon Cameron, Lincoln's Secretary of War*, p. 357
9. Evans, *Pennsylvania Politics, 1872-1877*, p. 248.
10. *Cincinnati Enquirer*, Date Unknown, Shireman Collection.
11. *Harrisburg Patriot*, Date Unknown, Shireman Collection
12. Evans, *Pennsylvania Politics, 1872-1877*, p. 252
13. Barrett, "John Frederic Hartranft: Life and Services", p. 30.
14. *Norristown Herald & Free Press and Republican*, May 23, 1876.
15. Ibid.
16. Ibid.
17. Ibid.
18. Ibid.
19. Townsend, George A., "Hartranft and Cameron", the *New York Daily Graphic*, May 18, 1876.
20. Copies of these letters are contained in the Shireman Collection.
21. Henry M. Needham to JFH, May 25, 1876, Shireman Collection.
22. J. K. Haffey to JFH, June 1, 1876, Shireman Collection.
23. The original letter is contained in the Shireman Collection but the author cannot be identified.
24. *New York Herald*, June 11, 1876.
25. Pennypacker, *The Autobiography of a Pennsylvanian*, p. 87.
26. Anthony, *First Ladies*, p. 204.
27. Grant, Julia Dent, *The Personal Memoirs of Julia Dent Grant*, New York: G. P. Putnam's Sons, 1975; reprint, Carbondale, Illinois: Southern Illinois University Press, 1975, p. 188.
28. Barrett, "John Frederic Hartranft: Life and Services", p. 26. *Also see* Bradley, *Simon Cameron, Lincoln's Secretary of War*, p. 370.
29. Tabulation printed by Bloss & Cogswell, Publishers, Herald Office at Titusville, Penna. No Date, Shireman Collection.

30. Printed listing of Pennsylvania delegates and their alternates, no further identification. Shireman Collection.
31. Evans, *Pennsylvania Politics, 1872-1877*, p. 260.
32. *Norristown Herald and Free Press and Republican*, June 29, 1876.
33. Ibid.
34. Ibid.
35. Barrett, "John Frederic Hartranft: Life and Services", p. 26.
    *Also see* Evans, *Pennsylvania Politics, 1872-1877*, p. 253.
36. Rhodes, James Ford, *History of The United States, 1850-1877*, p. 200.
37. Ibid, p. 205.
38. Evans, *Pennsylvania Politics, 1872-1877*, p. 254.
39. Barrett, "John Frederic Hartranft: Life and Services", p. 26.
40. Harrison Allen to JFH, March 2, 1876, Shireman Collection.
41. J. C. Banden to JFH, May 3, 1876, Shireman Collection.
42. Bloss & Cogswell Tabulation, Shireman Collection.
43. May 30, 1876, JFH to "Dear Wills", Shireman Collection.
44. Press Clippings, Dates and Titles Missing-Shireman Collection.
45. Ibid.
46. North Wales Record, December 7, 1878, Shireman Collection.
47. *Times and Dispatch*, April 25, 1878 - Shireman Collection.
48. *Norristown Times Herald*, June 1, 1956.
49. Evans, *Pennsylvania Politics, 1872-1877*, p. 260.
50. Ibid., p. 261.
51. Bloss & Cogswell Tabulation, Shireman Collection.
52. *Norristown Times Herald*, June 1, 1956.
53. Headline taken from the article appearing in the *Pittsburg Dispatch*, March, 1884, Shireman Collection.
54. Letter from Andrew Stewart to JFH dated March 18, 1884, Shireman Collection.
55. Article appearing in the *Pittsburg Dispatch*, March, 1884, Shireman Collection.
56. Johnson, Donald, *Forging a Nation 1866-1900*, p. 334.
57. *Norristown Herald and Free Press Republican*, July 7, 1876.
58. Ibid., July 11, 1876.

# CHAPTER ELEVEN

## *DEATH RIDES THE RAILS AND*
## *THE BIRTH OF THE "BLOODY BUCKET"*

The year 1877 proved to be another period of deep struggle between labor and management in the United States. Economic strife in the nation followed the Civil War since the government's voracious appetite for goods had fallen off sharply, causing a post-war depression. The East in general and the states of Pennsylvania, Ohio, Maryland, and New York in particular, saw a great number of strikes and other labor difficulties, mainly as a result of wage disputes.

The financial boom that occurred with the Civil War ended abruptly in 1873 and the resulting slump caused havoc for the next five or six years. Depression swept the nation, and in many cases it "caused a veritable paralysis in the industrial regions of Pennsylvania, New York and even extended into the Middle West." Many of these difficulties were triggered by the collapse of Jay Cooke and Company of Philadelphia, which had sold millions of Union bonds during the war, providing Cooke with a fortune for himself. The collapse of Jay Cooke & Company led to a chain reaction of business failures, declining real estate values, strikes, lockouts, and widespread unemployment which would impact upon Hartranft's two terms as Governor.[1]

All sorts of manufacturing facilities became involved in the labor turmoil. Canmakers and boxmakers in Baltimore struck, while Pittsburgh saw strikers at the National Tube Works, The Edgar Thomson Steel Works at Bradocks, and the Bradocks car workers. On the south side of Pittsburgh, the Jones and Laughlin workers went out along with the pipe workers of Evans, Dalzell and Company. In the Buffalo area, planing mills went on strike as did tanneries, car works, hog yards, coal yards, a canal works and a nut and bolt factory. In Zanesville, Ohio, rolling mill workers struck, and their ranks were joined by a pipe works, fire clay works, pot works, and another planing mill.[2]

Strikes of almost every size and description seemed to be the style of 1877, and those labor struggles were exacerbated by the disruptive troubles on the railroad lines. The railroad difficulties had begun as far back as 1873 and during the early days of the depression, railroad revenues began to fall rapidly, which caused a sharp drop in profits. To retaliate, railroad lines became very aggressive competitors and began to undercut each other for freight and passenger fares. Some attempts between the lines were made to stem the fall of profits, but impatient or untrusting rival management groups would not hold the line for any real length of time. Consequently, sales and profits, as well as investments, eroded sharply.

As early as March 1874, employees of the New York and Erie Railroad struck for back pay and began to destroy tracks and other property near the Susquehanna Depot. When the local sheriff appealed to Harrisburg for assistance, Governor Hartranft responded by sending 1500 militiamen.[3] This show of force restored peace to the area, but the use of militia also brought political cries from opponents. Never one to avoid tough issues, Hartranft was quick to silence his detractors by responding,

> As the Chief Executive of the State, I cannot allow creditors [meaning workers who were owed back wages], however meritorious their claims may be, to forcibly seize property of the debtors and hold it without due process of law... Whenever the laws of the Commonwealth shall provide that employees of a railroad may suspend all traffic upon it until their wages are paid I will acquiesce, but I cannot do so while the law refuses to contemplate any such remedy.[4]

From this point until the summer of 1877, friction only increased between the railroad labor and management. All of this plus the price war between the lines developed into disruption to rail service, which in turn impaired material deliveries to many industries throughout the eastern United States. The impact of these disruptions actually affected every industry that they served, and the coal-mining industry in particular; and all of this frequently led to violence.

Faced with falling revenues and profits, Thomas A. Scott, President of the Pennsylvania Railroad, stated that during the first six months of 1877, "not a farthing was made on competitive freight by any line." John Sherman, brother of the general, wrote to an agent in London that, "the railroad companies have competed in a reckless way...[which has] caused a large reduction of net income."[5] This revenue crisis would give rise to the riots that soon followed.

Four of the major railroad lines involved during this troubled period were the New York Central, the Erie, the Pennsylvania, and the Baltimore and Ohio.[6] While the price war meant lower shipping rates for industry, it did benefit the public passengers when lower fares enhanced attendance at the 1876 Centennial Exhibition in Philadelphia.[7]

Despite those lower fares to Philadelphia, the centennial event was also marred by violence. At the height of the celebration, the nation was stunned to learn of the massacre and defeat of Colonel Custer at Little Big Horn. The Ku Klux Klan was developing steam, and even Governor Hartranft noted that the Klan was fostering murder and terror in the country. Sadly, he could also point to Pennsylvania's largest and host city, Philadelphia, where the homicide rate had doubled in recent years.[8] The nation, and Pennsylvania in particular seemed to be seething with unrest and ripe for a violent eruption.

In April 1877, railroad management decided to reduce wages by ten percent in an attempt to offset their ailing sales and profits. This reduction would be the second such cut in about four years, and this very decision, or perhaps its method of implementation, would create the spark to set off harsh riots in Pennsylvania. Between July 19th and 24th, the violence in Pittsburgh would cost somewhere between $4,000,000 and $10,000,000 in destroyed equipment alone.[9] Worse yet, Pittsburgh was also the site of 25 dead and scores of wounded during those six hot summer days of 1877.[10] Other disturbances were reported in New York, New Jersey, West Virginia, Ohio, Illinois, Texas, and Kentucky. All of this was the result of rail problems in one area causing work obstructions in another. Labor in Illinois could not function when no coal was being shipped out of Pennsylvania, and the period became violent and further destructive to the nation's sliding economy which led to even further labor problems.

When the 1877 difficulties ignited in the middle of July, Governor Hartranft was on a train headed for the Pacific coast. While communications were not the convenience of today, the Governor was well informed of developments via the telegraph.[11] By his own admission, he "was constantly advised of the situation" and in frequent contact with key political, military and business advisors.[12] His adjutant-general, James W. Latta, became the focal point for all military matters in the state during his absence.[13]

The initial disturbance began at Martinsburg, West Virginia, on the Baltimore and Ohio line, July 16th, the day the announced wage reduction was to go into effect.[14] Disruption of train service began here and quickly spread to other areas, including West Virginia, Maryland and especially Baltimore. It did not take West Virginia Governor Henry M. Matthews long to realize that he simply did not have adequate manpower within the ranks of his state's own military forces so he asked President Hayes for assistance. Soon, federal troops were on the scene and stability was restored.[15]

While matters settled rather quickly in Martinsburg, conditions were eroding in Cumberland and Baltimore, Maryland. On July 20th, Maryland's Governor, John Lee Carroll, was called upon for troop assistance by the railroad, and he ordered the 5th and 6th militia regiments into action, with the 6th headed toward Cumberland and the 5th to remain in Baltimore. Since matters were deteriorating so quickly in Baltimore, Carroll changed his order when rioters threatened to kill the engineer and fireman assigned to the train that was destined to take the 6th to Cumberland. That train was located at the Camden Station, and when the 250 men of the 5th arrived at the station, they were met by an angry mob. Later in the evening, about 120 men from the 6th were sent to assist the 5th, which had been under constant attack by the mob. En route to the station, the men of the 6th were confronted by a mob of 3,000-4,000 who began to hurl rocks and stones at them.[16] Like bolting race horses, the young men in the ranks began to fire indiscriminately, killing about 12 civilians and wounding another 14. Those shots only served to further fuel the angered mob, causing the troops to seek refuge inside Camden Station. As revenge, the mob set fire to the station, but fortunately it never amounted to much.[17]

As the hours past, Carroll's problems simply got worse and he too sought assistance from President Hayes, who responded with troops under the command of General Winfield Scott Hancock. The presence of the federal troops finally restored order to Baltimore, but not before 59 people were killed in four days of rioting.[18]

On July 19, major troubles began in Pennsylvania and Pittsburgh in particular, when a mob halted all rail freight traffic out of that city.[19] Since the local militia under General Alfred L. Pearson was inadequate to stem the tide of a growing angry mob, General Robert M. Brinton and his First Division were ordered from Philadelphia to Pittsburgh and they took two Gatling guns with them.[20]

The trip between Philadelphia and Pittsburgh took more than two full days of rail travel, and during that time, Brinton's men were treated to less than standard fare. Their meals were very scant, and when they finally arrived in Pittsburgh on the 21st, General Pearson prevented Brinton and his men from firing their weapons, which might have ended the uprising at an early stage.[21] Brinton also found that the rioters had already achieved the upper hand and he asked the mayor to come down to the railroad yard to calm the crowd with his words and a police force. For whatever reason, the mayor failed to show, and mysteriously no police were "available".[22]

Along the Pennsylvania Railroad bed and Liberty Avenue between 25th and 28th streets there were two Round Houses. The "lower" was just off 26th Street while the "upper" was just below 28th street.

When the Philadelphia troops arrived in the Triangle City, they found the local militia fraternizing with the mob. Pressing towards their objective, the Round House at 26th Street, the Philadelphia militia was constantly harassed by the mob and the local troops were ordered to occupy the Round House at 28th Street. General Brinton, wanting to avoid as much bloodshed as possible, had ordered his men not to fire upon the mob unless they themselves were attacked.[23] Much credit must be given to Brinton and his men, who demonstrated great restraint on that day.

En route to their quarters though, Brinton's men were under growing threats from the mob, and he had them form a hollow square with bayonets in place. As his men moved forward, members of the mob became more belligerent, and began to throw rocks and stones. Suddenly, pistol shots rang out from the civilian ranks; and when the militia still failed to react because of Brinton's orders, the mob became overly confident. Rushing toward the advancing troops, the rioters became emboldened and started to reach out for the bayonets of those soldiers in the front line. Understandably, those men of the First became anxious, and some firing began along their line which soon turned into a volley. At least 16 rioters were killed and many others wounded.[24]

Later, when Hartranft addressed the General Assembly, he spoke about that particular firing upon the crowd and he gave his full support to the troops when he stated, "Under the circumstances, they [the soldiers] did right to resist the attempt to disarm or overpower them. A soldier is stationed or commanded to move as a soldier, and had the undoubted right, in the execution of his order, to prevent himself from being forced from his post or disarmed."[25]

The men of the First finally made their way into the Round House at 26th Street and attempted to find protection there. While the firing upon the crowd temporarily dispersed the mob, the men of the First soon found that the Round House at 28th Street was not occupied by the Pittsburgh ranks, as assumed, which allowed the angry mob to regroup and place the 26th Street Round House under siege.

Hartranft soon heard about all of this destruction and anger, and one of the first telegrams to reach him came from General Latta:

HARRISBURG, PA. July 20th, 1877

Gov. J. F. Hartranft:

Mob stopped all freight trains at Pittsburgh. Sheriff called for troops. Ordered [General Alfred L.] Pearson to take charge and put one regiment on duty. Says he may need more.

James W. Latta[26]

Hartranft responded quickly and forcefully to Latta's information and, from Cheyenne, Wyoming Territory, on July 20th, he sent the first of two telegrams to General Latta,

First: ... Order, promptly, all troops necessary to support the Sheriffs in protecting moving trains on the B. and O.R.R. Go to Pittsburg [sic] and keep supervision of all troops ordered out. Will be due at Ogden [Utah] tomorrow, at six o'clock. In the meantime, en route, let me know the situation.

J. F. Hartranft[27]

Then, from Laramie City, Wyoming Territory, Hartranft sent the following, "Spare nothing to protect all persons in their rights, under the Constitution and laws of the State ...Am on train to Ogden.[28]

From this point forward, the telegraph between Hartranft and his aides simply became alive with information, reports and directives. On the 21st, the Governor received the following:

PITTSBURGH, PA. VIA., PHILADIA
JULY 21, 1877
Gov. J. F. Hartranft
Salt Lake [City]

A collision has occurred here [Pittsburgh] between the strikers and the troops. Number of persons have been killed and wounded. Intense excitement prevails in the city and there are indications of further bloodshed and that trouble will be widespread and protracted. I suggest that you return allowing your party to go forward.

M.[atthew] S. Quay[29]

By early evening on the 21st, General Brinton had his First Division located within the Round House at 26th Street, and still assumed that the local Pittsburgh troops would soon occupy the 28th Street Round House. Unfortunately for Brinton and the First, this was not to be the case and throughout the night of the 21st the Philadelphia men were under constant attack from the mob. At one point, some members of the crowd attempted to fire a 12-pounder. In response to the civilian use of a cannon, Brinton's men fired into the mob and brought down 11 men. Unfortunately, instead of dispersing the mob, the gunfire of the First only made matters worse.[30]

The mob then attempted to set the Round house and the outbuildings ablaze by setting fire to railroad cars and sending them into the buildings. While some damage was done to those buildings, most of the fires were extinguished by the militia inside.[31] But, the toll on the men in terms of exhaustion and fear was great, and the damage to the railroad property and equipment was very extensive.

Throughout the night, Brinton and his men had to continuously fight off the mob. During the early morning hours of the 22nd, Brinton had the First form, and he moved them out of the Round house and up Penn Avenue. There, the mob attacked the rear of Brinton's ranks and the troops opened fire again. It did not take the men of the First long to employ their Gatling gun which began to spew its deadly contents upon the crowd. That rapid fire had the desired effect, and the mob began to disperse and never fully recovered from that deadly hail.

During the entire crisis, Scott was in frequent telegraphic contact with the Governor, who was quite disturbed over the amount of casualties and damage done to the railroad's equipment. By mid-morning of the 22nd, Hartranft received the following telegraph from Scott:


PHILADA. July 22, 1877
J. F. Hartranft:

It is not possible to imagine a worse state of anarchy than now exist in Western Pennsylvania. As have twice telegraphed you your presence here is imperatively necessary. All the military forces that have reached Pittsburgh are threatened with destruction by the mob, and since yesterday P. M. great destruction of life and property has occurred every hour. You should not delay by traveling in regular train but should take at once the special which Mr. [Silas H. H.] Clark the General Superintendant of the Union Pacific will place at your disposal the moment you apply to him. In consequence of the widespread trouble our [unintelligible] and the great

263

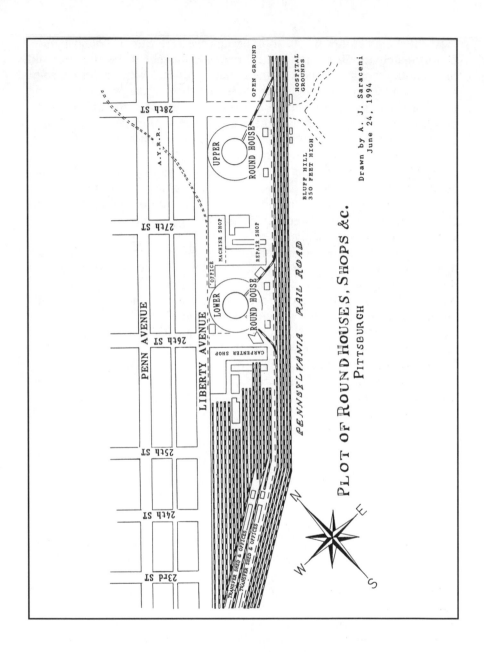

**Pittsburgh Roundhouses During the Riots**

Redrawn by A. J. Saraceni.

danger to persons and property everywhere it is hoped the President of the United States will make a call for additional troops from the various states as authorized by the Constitution. Arrangements have been made for a special [train] for you from Omaha to Pittsburgh.

Thomas A. Scott[32]

All of this frightful information weighed heavily upon Hartranft, and he made arrangements to return promptly to Pennsylvania. Nonetheless, while Scott was preparing his plea to Hartranft, Brinton's First was moving out of Pittsburgh towards Sharpsburg, since the Round House they had occupied was burned by the mob and they were running low on ammunition. In addition, the ranks of the guard had been reduced by four or five killed while civilian fatalities ranged between 15 and 25. Scores more on both sides had been injured, and Adjutant General Latta telegraphed Hartranft to further advise him of the troop movements out of Pittsburgh:[33]

Pittsburgh, Pa. July 22, 1877
Gov. John F. Hartranft
On Special train west of Omaha-Cheyenne

There is from Colonel Scott[*] again a pressing telegram requesting a call upon the President for aid upon which subject there will be a Cabinet session today. The situation does not improve. This city[Pittsburgh] is in the hands of a mob. The First Division after stiff fighting for about fourteen [14] hours have retired to a point near Sharpsburg pursued vigorously by the mob to the bridge at that point under a hot attack. All railways are blocked and no other troops can be gotten here. The Fourteenth [14] & Nineteenth [19] regiments have returned to their homes and the Eighteenth [18] is the only Command on duty here. Roads are blocked at all points & no trains carrying troops are allowed to pass. Colonel Scott also reports that the mob is also collecting at Altoona, Harrisburg & Columbia and will possibly in a few hours extend further east. There

---

[*]Thomas A. Scott served as Assistant Secretary of War in 1861-1862 and was a colonel in the militia.

have been twelve soldiers reported killed in first Reg't. while retreating & some fifteen wounded. The loss among the rioters has been severe said to be about fifty killed, this comprehends the situation as we have it. Please give us specific directions as to whether a call for the United States troops shall be made.[34]

Other telegrams during the day on the 22nd brought the governor a variety of information and requests for decisions. Thomas Scott, again and again, appealed to the governor for action and more troops including federal forces. In one of his messages, Scott pleads with Hartranft: "There is no stopping of it [the mob] without the combined action of National & State Governments and I therefore pray that you will act immediately."[35]

Even before receiving Scott's telegram at 12:30 P.M., Hartranft's own notes tell us that he had already called out all the state forces and had been in communication with the President, requesting federal forces as well.[36] Unfortunately, the governor's request for federal troops encountered some red tape and he was advised by Scott on the 23rd that, "your requisition for troops from the General [Federal] Government is not in the formal shape it should be and as you no doubt intended it should be."[37] Scott then offered the governor some suggestions that he felt might expedite matters. All of this confusion was soon cleared up between the Governor and Washington. President Hayes quickly ordered General Winfield Scott Hancock with "full authority to move any troops within your division as you may think necessary during these disturbances."[38]

Throughout the day on the 22nd, the Pittsburgh mob continued its ravaging of businesses and the railroad in particular. However, innocent people were hurt in the wake of the mob actions too. Fueled by an abundance of liquor, the rioters burned the Union Station, the Railroad Hotel, and a nearby railroad elevator. Looting became rampant and, according to the official history of the militia, "The women engaged in the work of pillage, were most active in carrying the goods away from the cars, used viler epithets and more indecent language than the men and did everything in their power to influence and excite the mob to resistance."[39]

As Hartranft made his way back, he was absolutely determined to put down any rebellion. The governor had always been sympathetic with labor, but his record also clearly showed that he demanded respect for the law as well. Mob rule was not to be tolerated!

By the end of the day on the 22nd, matters were beginning to ease ever so slightly in Pittsburgh, but the cost had been high. In addition to the many dead and wounded, damage to the railroad was extensive, and at least

1600 railroad cars had been destroyed along with some 126 locomotives. Businesses were unable to function and in his history of the 13th Regiment, National Guard of Pennsylvania, Frederick C. Hitchcock estimated that as many as 40,000 men were idled in the Lackawannna Valley because the railroad was unable to transport coal.[40] Other estimates put the number of idle workers as high as 50,000.

Pittsburgh, while the worst hit, was far from the only Pennsylvania city to feel the wrath of the striking railroad members. Philadelphia, Altoona, Harrisburg, Scranton, Wilkes-Barre, Allentown, Reading, Bethlehem and others also felt the sting of violence but to a much lesser degree. By the 24th, General Latta had telegraphed Hartranft from Harrisburg that "Nothing but peace, quiet and good order" existed in the capital city.[41] Yet, in the normally quiet town of Reading, out of an estimated 253 militiamen, 200 were injured when they clashed with a mob after the soldiers killed 11 and wounded almost 60 mob members.[42] In Scranton too, 3 more mob members were killed when they dared to exchange gun fire with the militia.[43]

Destruction was not limited solely to Pennsylvania either. New York City barely avoided serious problems when strikers there were joined by Communists, who made every attempt to fire the people with anger. Fortunately, those efforts never amounted to very much. Chicago was not quite as fortunate; and on July 26th, after making every attempt to avoid bloodshed, the mayor had to agree to use force. At the Sixteenth Street Viaduct, mob members and troops met in a bloody clash that left 10 civilians dead and 45 wounded. Troops continued to pour into the beleaguered city, and final rest came on July 29th when Lieutenant-General Philip Sheridan himself arrived in the city to take command of the troops.[44]

Governor Hartranft returned to Pennsylvania on the 24th. His first stop was in Pittsburgh, where he found things to be quiet. Shortly after his arrival, he was confronted by a group of professional men who urged him to take immediate action to restore basic services for the welfare of the general population.[45] He quickly saw that not only had the city sustained serious damage, but that it was in dire need of staple commodities including food and coal. He promptly determined that the railroad lines must reopen to restore the state to its former routine. The "old soldier" in Hartranft told him that the need for a show of force was still required and before leaving Pittsburgh he issued General Order No. 3. which commanded that, "All other means of quelling riots and restoring order having first been exhausted, the officer commanding the troops shall notify the rioters that they will be fired upon unless they promptly disperse. The order to fire will then be deliberately given, and every soldier will be expected to fire with effect. The firing will continue until the mob disappears."[46] He then hastened to Philadelphia where he would confer with his military commanders.

After his arrival in Philadelphia and following his strategic meetings, the governor personally drew upon his war experience and assumed command of about 4,000 militiamen plus another 600 regulars from Hancock's command.[47] Boarding a heavily guarded train that was led and followed by flatcars loaded with troops and Gatling guns, Hartranft led the men west to Pittsburgh, where they began the work of repairing the damage caused by the riots over the past several days. Through a herculean effort, destroyed railroad cars were removed and damaged rails were replaced. In short order, the railroad soon became operable, which made it possible to supply that beleaguered city with desperately needed goods. According to historian James Ford Rhodes, "On Sunday night, July 29, eight days after the night of riot and terror, the first freight train was sent out on the main line under a military guard, and, although either this one or the one following was wrecked at Spring Hill by a removed switch, the movement was followed up with vigor on the Monday."[48] With this movement, the great railroad riots of 1877 were essentially over for Pennsylvania and its governor.

Some newspapers, and the Pittsburgh Papers in particular, were to have their turn as one after another blamed the damage on the railroad management and its request for troops. *The Globe* cried out that, "The cowardice and imbecility of the railroad sharks, who sought to overawe all this community by imported bummers, met its proper rebuke." Another paper, *The Leader*, blamed everything upon the Philadelphia troops while *The Critic* cried, "arraigned before the board of public opinion, Governor Hartranft, Thomas Scott" and others for the slaughter brought on by the Philadelphia troops. *The Critic* went onto say, "there is tyranny in this country worse than anything known in Russia...Capital has raised itself on the ruins of labor. The laboring class cannot, will not stand this longer. The war cry has been raised...the principle that freed our nation from tyranny will free labor from domestic aggression."[49]

Law and order was restored and the papers were free to print whatever they pleased. During the entire process of re-establishing order, Hartranft kept himself busy by monitoring every detail and making certain that his orders were followed promptly. While the riots proved to be costly in terms of lives and dollars, Hartranft's decisive action with the militia prevented untold added lives and dollars from being lost. Once again, he showed himself to be an excellent administrator and commander. He had always been a proponent of labor, and the economic difficulties that led to the riots only served to heighten those feelings. However, he was also very mindful that law and not mob rule must prevail, and he was prepared to take severe measures and assume full responsibility to return the Commonwealth to normal.

Over the fifteen days of rioting in Pennsylvania, it became clear that a new order of respect and understanding was needed between management and labor. Labor alone could not be expected to subsidize the corporations when economic conditions became difficult. This was particularly true when management itself was the major contributor to a disaster, as was the case with the railroad price wars.

In his 1878 address to the Pennsylvania General Assembly, Hartranft remarked upon the riots. He chastised labor for breaking the law and reminded them that, "No disobedience of regularly constituted authority will be permitted, whether on the part of individuals, corporations, or combinations of men. No sense of wrong, however grievous, will or shall justify violence in seeking indemnity there-for [sic]."[50]

To management, he essentially lectured that, "These great corporations, from the character of the enterprises, are of necessity, in most cases, monopolies. As such, the people have a right to demand that while the profits may accrue to private individuals, their management shall rise above merely selfish aims, and consult also the public utility and welfare."[51]

Then in a philosophical manner, Hartranft told the Assembly that the riots had a "broader and deeper lesson." He told the body that times had changed and that education was the cornerstone of that change. "A little learning is a dangerous thing, it is better than no learning at all," he stated. "While capital held labor in ignorance and bondage, strikes were rare. Their frequent occurrence is a proof that labor is growing, more and more, to an equality in strength and importance to capital."[52]

The riots also clearly demonstrated the failings of the state militia system, which was not prepared for prompt, active service. Hartranft saw the need for a better disciplined militia, and the riots made General Latta's earlier suggestions for change all the more meaningful to him. Latta had seen the need for change in many areas including basics such as a system of rifle practice, more modern weapons and even basic physical and mental examinations for officer competency.[53] Latta made his observations and recommendations known to the governor.

That some of the officers were ill equipped to handle their responsibility during the riots was obvious to both Latta and Hartranft. Some removed their men from advantageous positions while others moved bodies of men through ground "cuts" when the banks were filled with rioters, which gave the mob excellent target practice. Crowds were forced off railroad property and then permitted to return.[54] All of these types of errors were glaring, and emphasized the need for better training and organization.

269

Latta saw that if the militia's organization was left to continue under the current structure, good coordination would not be practical. For one thing, there were entirely too many major-generals. He strongly suggested that there be only one major-general with three or four brigades led by brigadiers. Latta felt that this type of structure would conform to a division in the regular army, and he demonstrated that many of the existing "divisions" had barely enough men to constitute a regiment, and therefore should be led by a colonel and not a general.[55]

Hartranft agreed with Latta's suggestions and confronted the need for militia reform when addressing the General Assembly. He told that body, "the troops, although in receipt of the regular yearly allowance of money, were found provided only with uniforms and arms - all the equipment for active, continuous and independent service, blankets, overcoats, haversacks, canteens, &c, being in part or wholly wanting."[56] He asked the legislature for their cooperation to permit the process of change to begin and to provide the funds required to develop a more effective force. He also focused upon those local troops in Pittsburgh that fraternized with the rioters. With that, he drew a comparison [his only known reference] of his own bad experience with his 4th Pennsylvania regiment at First Bull Run. He told the Assembly, "The behavior of the Pittsburg [sic] troops, in a military sense, is without excuse; but was it any worse than the defection of officers and men in the regular army, who, in 1861, deserted their comrades in arms to join the communities in which they were born and bred?"[57] On the point of the militia, Hartranft concluded by asking for pensions for the families of those militiamen who fell in the service of the state and added that, "The Executive has power by law to reorganize and reduce the National Guard, in accordance with the recommendation of the Adjutant General, but the action of the Legislature will be necessary to re-apportion the annual appropriation among the organizations, and confer authority upon the Adjutant General to issue the allowance in clothing and equipment or in money...."[58]

On June 12, 1878, the Pennsylvania Legislature passed the act that completely reorganized the National Guard of Pennsylvania into its modern structure. The "new" guard would have only one division with five brigades headed by Brigadier-Generals George R. Snowden [1st], Frank Reeder [2nd], Joshua K. Sigfried [3rd], James A. Beaver [4th], and H. S. Huidekoper [5th].[59]

Even five years after the guard was reorganized, many Pennsylvanians did not really understand the need for a new structure. Consequently, on May 18, 1885, the *Gazette & Bulletin* of Williamsport, Pennsylvania, explained the basic reasoning behind the changes; that article is reviewed in Appendix C.

When Governor Hartranft addressed the General Assembly in 1879, he could speak of the progress that had been made in reorganizing the guard when he said,

> When compared with the organization and numbers in 1872, the soldier-like results of the different consolidations and our progress toward a perfect military system are clearly apparent. In 1872, there were twenty-one divisions, with three hundred and twenty-three companies, comprising 1,126 commissioned officers and 13,566 enlisted men. In 1879, the State constitutes one division, divided into five brigades, aggregating one hundred and forty companies of infantry, five cavalry companies, and four batteries of artillery. The muster roll of the Guard now numbers 608 commissioned officers, and 8,200 non-commissioned officers and men.[60]

Less than one year later, Governor Henry M. Hoyt, himself a former Brigadier-General of the Guard, succeeded Governor Hartranft and appointed the former governor "Major General, Division Commander National Guard", a position Hartranft held until his death.[61] This early appointment was to a command first known as the Pennsylvania Division. Later, in October of 1917, the Pennsylvania Division became known formally as the Twenty-Eighth Division, a title it holds to this very day.[62] Because of his tireless efforts with those early troops, Hartranft today is recognized as the "Father" of the modern Pennsylvania National Guard, and rightfully so.

While it must certainly be acknowledged that Latta had the vision to see the need for the new formation, it rested with then Governor Hartranft to make it a reality. In his General Order No. 1 of March 12, 1879, Governor Hoyt honored Latta's foresight by reappointing him Adjutant General.[63]

In August 1879, the keystone was prescribed as the badge for the guard, and it would eventually become known as the "Bloody Bucket".[64] However, before the 28th would earn that sobriquet in World War II, they were first known as the Iron Division during World War I. While the 28th was being observed by General John J. Pershing in France, he was amazed by their tenacity. Turning to an aide, Pershing said, "these are not soldiers, these are men of iron." The name Iron Division stuck with the 28th until it was called into the conflagration of World War II. Known for their ferocity, the men of the 28th became hated by the Nazi troops, who feared them since they were not kindly disposed towards taking prisoners. While the 28th was commonly called the "Keystone Division", the Germans gave them the sanguinary sobriquet, "Bloody Bucket".[65]

Since its initial reorganization in 1878, the 28th Division has seen combat in the Philippines, Puerto Rico, Belgium, Luxembourg, Cuba, France, Germany, and other parts of the world, plus numerous demands from within the confines of Pennsylvania. when her own residents needed the help of the "Bloody Bucket". For Hartranft, his relationship with the Guard was always one of desire and pride. He loved the men of the National Guard and lent all his energy to their well-being until his death. He set the standard for those who came after him, including his fifteenth successor, Major-General Omar N. Bradley, who served the 28th Division during the period of June 1942 to February 1943.[66]

The six years of Hartranft's gubernatorial term were coming to an end and on January 8, 1879, he addressed the General Assembly for the last time and told them, "I think it proper to extend to the people, through their chosen representatives, my thanks for their confidence and support and my earnest desire for the welfare of the State...let us invoke the assistance of the same Power that has guided Pennsylvania to its present high position, to enable us to mould its social relations in accordance with His immutable laws, and hand the noble Commonwealth to our successors with a higher civilization and a yet happier people."[67]

Thirteen days later, Hartranft took his leave of the governor's office. In his last address, Hartranft had touched upon Finances, Savings Banks, Trust Companies, Municipal Government, Education, Labor Arbitration, Penal Reform, the National Guard, State Mental Hospitals, Geological Survey and The Pennsylvania Archives.[68]

Newspapers across the state hailed his final address and many printed the speech in its entirety. In its review, *The Dispatch* from Pittsburgh provides an excellent encapsulation of the Governor and his operation methods when it noted, "In his last message to the legislature of Pennsylvania, Governor Hartranft makes no attempt to leave upon the minds of the people any other impression than he is wholly matter-of-fact, having earnestly at heart the material interest of the State. The message is brief as a whole, considering the number of subjects discussed and each topic is disposed of without waste of words."[69]

For Hartranft personally, now it was a time to return to Norristown and determine exactly how he was going to earn a living to support his family. Despite his lack of employment, he trusted that his own industry, which had never failed him in the past, would continue to sustain him in the future. Hartranft left Harrisburg with a sense of pride and self-confidence.

ENDNOTES FOR CHAPTER ELEVEN
DEATH RIDES THE RAILS AND
THE BIRTH OF THE "BLOODY BUCKET"

1. Dunaway, Wayland Fuller, *A History of Pennsylvania*, New York, Prentice-Hall, Inc., 1935, pp. 532-533.
2. Bruce, Robert V., *1877: Year of Violence*, Chicago, Bobbs-Merrill, 1959, pp. 100-101, 182, 200, and 207.
3. Evans, *Pennsylvania Politics, 1872-1877*, p. 228.
4. Ibid., pp. 228-229.
5. Rhodes, *History of the United States from Hayes to McKinley, 1877-1896*, p. 17.
6. Ibid. p. 12.
7. Ibid, p. 15.
8. Bruce, *1877: Year of Violence*, pp. 9-10.
9. McClure, *Old Time Notes of Pennsylvania*, vol. 2, p. 461.
10. Rhodes, *History of the United States from Hayes to McKinley, 1877-1896*, p. 93.
11. The Shireman Collection contains a large number of telegraphs sent between the Governor and his staff.
12. Message of John F. Hartranft to the General Assembly of Pennsylvania, January 2, 1878. p. 13, Shireman Collection.
13. McClure, *Old Time Notes of Pennsylvania*, p. 454.
14. Rhodes, *History of the United States from Hayes to McKinley, 1877-1896*, p. 19.
15. Ibid., p. 20.
16. Ibid., p. 21.
17. Ibid., p. 22.
18. Ibid.
19. Schlesinger, Arthur M., Jr, *The Almanac of American History*, New York, G. P. Putnam's Sons, 1983, p. 336.
20. Ent, Uzal E., *The First Century, A History of the 28th Infantry Division*, Harrisburg, Pennsylvania, Stackpole Books, 1979, p. 70.
21. Clarke, William P., *Official History of the Militia and National Guard of the State of Pennsylvania*, p. 332.
22. Rhodes, *History of the United States from Hayes to McKinley, 1877-1896*, p. 26.
23. Ibid., p. 29.
24. Ibid.
25. Message of John F. Hartranft to the General Assembly of Pennsylvania, January 2, 1878, p. 11, Shireman Collection.
26. Telegram from James W. Latta to JFH, July 20, 1877, Shireman Collec-

tion.

27. Clarke, *Official History of the Militia and National Guard of the State of Pennsylvania*, p. 307.
28. Ibid.
29. Telegram from Matthew S. Quay to JFH, July 21, 1877, Shireman Collection. N. B., Quay was appointed Secretary of the Commonwealth by Hartranft shortly after he took office.
30. Ent, *The First Century, A History of the 28th Infantry Division*, p. 71.
31. Ibid.
32. Telegram from Thomas A. Scott to JFH, July 22, 1877, Shireman Collection.
33. Ent, *The First Century, A History of the 28th Infantry Division*, pp. 71-72.
34. Telegram from James W. Latta to JFH, July 22, 1877, Shireman Collection.
35. Telegram from Thomas A. Scott to JFH, July 22, 1877, Shireman Collection.
36. Ibid.
37. Telegram from Thomas A. Scott to JFH, July 23, 1877, Shireman Collection.
38. Rhodes, *History of the United States from Hayes to McKinley, 1877-1896*, p. 36.
39. Clarke, *Official History of the Militia and National Guard of the State of Pennsylvania*, p. 276.
40. Ent, *The First Century, A History of the 28th Infantry Division*, p. 70.
41. Telegram From General Latta to JFH, July 24, 1877-Shireman Collection.
42. Rhodes, *History of the United States from Hayes to McKinley, 1877-1896*, pp. 39-40.
43. Ibid, p. 73.
44. Ibid. p. 43.
45. Message of John F. Hartranft to the General Assembly of Pennsylvania, January 2, 1878, p. 13, Shireman Collection.
46. Clarke, *Official History of the Militia and National Guard of the State of Pennsylvania*, p. 271.
47. Rhodes, *History of the United States from Hayes to McKinley, 1877-1896*, p. 37.
48. Ibid., p. 38.
49. Bruce, *1877: Year of Violence*, p. 164.
50. Message of John F. Hartranft to the General Assembly of Pennsylvania, January 2, 1878, p. 16, Shireman Collection.
51. Ibid.
52. Ibid., p. 17.

53. Clarke, *Official History of the Militia and National Guard of the State of Pennsylvania*, p. 270.

54. Ibid., p. 271.

55. Ent, *The First Century, A History of the 28th Infantry Division*, p. 75. N.B. Mr. Charles B. Oellig, Curator for the Pennsylvania National Guard Museum, feels that Mr. Ent is in error on this point and notes that, "There were no divisions in the regular army at this time. That is why the 28th or Penna. division receives credit for being the oldest division in the U. S. Army."

56. Message of John F. Hartranft to the General Assembly of Pennsylvania, January 2, 1878, p. 25, Shireman Collection.

57. Ibid.

58. Ibid., pp. 25-26.

59. Ent, *The First Century, A History of the 28th Infantry Division*, pp. 76-77.

60. Message of John F. Hartranft to the General Assembly of Pennsylvania, January 8, 1879, p. 19, Shireman Collection.

61. Ent, *The First Century, A History of the 28th Infantry Division*, p. 77.

62. Clement, Charles M., et al., eds., *The 28th Division*, 2 vols, Pittsburgh: States Publications Society, 1921, vol 1, pp. 136-137. Here again, Mr. Oellig of the National Guard Museum points out that while the Guard's change in status was referred to as the Pennsylvania Division, it "was also officially the National Guard of Pennsylvania." Mr. Oellig continues that, "In 1916 when it went to the Mexican border the U. S. Army called it the 7th Division. When federalized in 1917 it then became the 28th Division."

63. Ibid, p. 79.

64. Ibid, p. 77.

65. This bit of history supplied by Lt. Colonel William O. Hickok, past historian for the 28th Infantry Division. Mr. Oellig adds that the red Keystone also reminded the Germans of a "bucket of blood" which assisted in the development of the sobriquet,"Bloody Bucket".

66. Ent., *The First Century, A History of the 28th Infantry Division*, p. 251.

67. Message of John F. Hartranft to the General Assembly of Pennsylvania, January 8, 1879, p. 25, Shireman Collection.

68. Ibid., pp. 23-24.

69. The *Pittsburg* [sic] *Dispatch*, January 9, 1879.

# CHAPTER TWELVE

## *"THE LAST TRUMPET"*

When Hartranft left Harrisburg, he was only 48 years old, and he and Sallie still had four children that were dependent upon them. Never a wealthy man, the ex-governor was now faced with the challenge of finding suitable employment to support his family. This concern of employment would be the first time in fifteen years he had been confronted with such a problem.

While he and Sallie had accumulated a number of properties in Norristown, a review of his deeds show them to be mostly land holdings that would not yield much in the way of income.[1] In addition to land, he continued his horse trading which was more a labor of love than a means of support. As a result, when President Hayes offered him the position of Postmaster of Philadelphia in 1879, he promptly accepted though some of his friends thought that job beneath him.[2] This was the beginning of a hectic decade of positions, appointments, and civic duties that he was to accept and execute with his customary zeal.

While in the military, his life seemed charmed, as he missed severe wounds on a number of occasions though at least two horses were shot out from under him. It appears that his worst experience came from a bout with dysentery which beset him while serving in the western theater. Aside from that, his only other problem was his susceptibility to colds. Hartranft did have an annoying minor kidney problem from time to time but nothing that ever created any major difficulties. However, in terms of health, his good fortune was not to last forever.

While he was still serving as Governor, Hartranft was also an active member of the General Samuel K. Zook Post No. 11 of the Grand Army of the Republic, and in June of 1875, he was made Chief Marshall of that national organization.[3] It was only natural then that he soon became an active member of the Military Order of the Loyal Legion of the United States, where he would serve as Junior Vice-Commander.[4]

There was almost a decade between his leaving the Governor's office and his death, and Hartranft wasted no time during that period. The day after he left the state house, he was appointed Major-General Commanding the Pennsylvania National Guard by Governor Henry M. Hoyt. About the same time, he was also being considered for the position of Secretary of Legation at Berlin, and one compelling reason for his consideration was his fluency with the German language. Regrettably, that appointment never materialized though it was one that he would have thoroughly enjoyed.[5] In 1880, President Hayes appointed him Collector of the Port of Philadelphia, a post he held until 1885.[6] He also served as Chairman of the Board of Trustees for the State Hospital for the Insane at Norristown, and just before his death, he issued a cost analysis for that institution which demonstrated that cost/patient had increased in one year from $3.47/week in 1888 to $3.67/week in 1889.[7] While this increase might appear modest by today's standards, the increase of six per cent in the late nineteenth century was not good news.

In July 1888, Hartranft was appointed by the U. S. Congress as Manager of the National Home for Disabled Volunteer Soldiers.[8] Later that same year, he was honored by the Pennsylvania National Guard when, three days before Christmas, it held a banquet to honor his reappointment to the command of the division. At that celebration, General George R. Snowden addressed the soldiers and told them, "whatever the National Guard is to us and whatever its fame abroad is due to the sagacity and work of General Hartranft."[9]

In 1889, President Benjamin Harrison appointed him a member of the Cherokee Indian Commission, and for that post he headed west in the month of July and wrote home to Sallie that he meant "to civilize the Indians."[10] In that same letter, he told his wife, "if the government insists on the present programs [for the Indians], it will certainly take sometime, entirely long for me."[11] It is unclear if his statement relates to his desire to return home or his own internal knowledge that he did not have long to live. Yet typically, the very next day Hartranft wrote to Sallie and told her of his excitement about meeting the Chief of the Cherokee Nation, and further stated that he thought that he was now physically better than when he left home. He even told his wife that he would not object to staying in the West for another year. This was in sharp contrast to his somber statement the day before. Still, he told Sallie that he was anxious to return home and thought it might be physically good for him to travel to Europe.[12] In May 1889, Governor James A. Beaver fortuitously appointed him Commissioner to represent Pennsylvania at the Universal Exposition in Paris, and that appointment did indeed send him and Sallie to Europe.[13]

At the time that Hartranft was preparing to leave for Europe, he was already showing some obvious signs of failing health. One newspaper reported that, "General John F. Hartranft, whose health has been poor for some time past, being made worse by his performance of his duties as commissioner to negotiate a treaty with the Cherokees, has sailed for Europe in the hope of improvement. He will carry with him the hearty wishes of the people of Pennsylvania for his early recovery."[14] Unfortunately, little is recorded about this trip, and his health would not be restored.

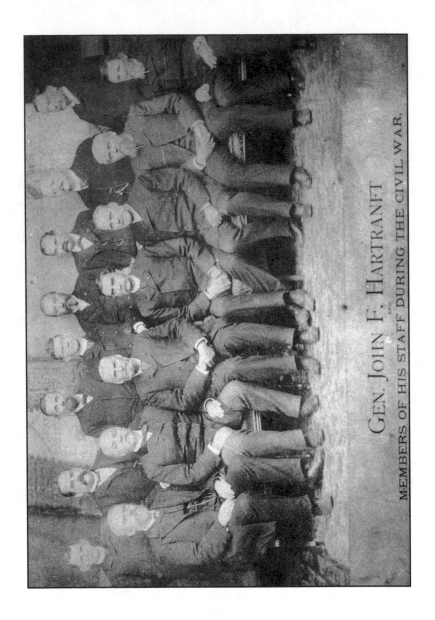

GEN. JOHN F. HARTRANFT
MEMBERS OF HIS STAFF DURING THE CIVIL WAR.

**Reunion of Hartranft's Civil War Staff**

Hartranft with his military staff after the war. There were a number of reunions for the Fifty-first and while Hartranft is seated in the center of the first row, the other men are not identified.

*Photographer: Copy by Frank D'Amico.*
*Source: Shireman Collection.*

278

**Hartranft at Inaugaration of President Benjamin Harrison**

This is the only known photo of General Hartranft upon a horse. It is believed that this photo was taken on March 4, 1889 when the Pennsylvania National Guard participated in the innaugaration of President Benjamin Harrison.

*Photographer: Copy by Frank D'Amico.*
*Source: Shireman Collection.*

279

In addition to his various political and military appointments, upon his return from Europe, Hartranft also found time to serve as a trustee of the Pennsylvania Military Academy at Chester, Pennsylvania, and became President of the Lynchburg Manufacturing and Mining Company and President of the Quinnimont Coal and Iron Company.[15] The Lynchburg position in particular cost him much in the way of financial and mental strain after it sank into bankruptcy. For the balance of his life, he took it upon himself to endeavor to return as much money as possible to his friends who invested based upon his suggestion.[16] He also became President of The Commercial Mutual Accident Insurance Company, which he helped form in 1888, a position he held until his death.[17] In the same year, he was appointed President of the Pennsylvania Boiler Insurance Company as well, and he also served as a member of the Norristown Board of Trade.[18] Unfortunately, none of these positions had any history of paying Hartranft any appreciable money, much less making him wealthy. The reality is that Hartranft would die as he was born, a man of very simple means.

In between all of his demanding activities, Hartranft also gave a lot of his time to Veterans Organizations throughout the state and nation. During March 1889, he was asked to assist in the creation of homes for disabled and destitute Confederate veterans and his prompt response to Oliver Downing, Esq., of New York City was,

> The movement to establish homes in the South for destitute and disabled Confederate veterans meet[s] my hearty approval. After every battlefield in the war, the gallant and generous foeman, vied with each other in relieving the suffering and the wounded. There are no longer foes but fellow countrymen. I do not see that the lapse of 25 years makes any difference in the principles or the obligation. I shall rejoice to do all in my power to aide the southern people in binding up their wounds and moving from the land every cause for a single bitter recollection of the contest which, will not have left us "a more perfect union."

> J. F. Hartranft[19]

One issue that was always close to Hartranft's heart was education, and he was pleased to become President of the Board of Trustees for the University of Pennsylvania. In the Spring of 1889, at the dedication of a new veterinary hospital, Hartranft told the crowd that the state's policy of offering free veterinary education to twelve deserving young men at a time was, "in keeping with the generosity of the great State which gave this institution its corporate existence, and is to-day, and it is hoped always, will be proud of her offspring, the University of Pennsylvania."[20]

Perhaps sometime during the late summer or early fall of 1889, Hartranft began to feel some of the sharp effects of a worsening kidney disorder. While there is ample evidence that he had been suffering from some sort of kidney malady since at least 1873, circumstances now began to take their full effect.[21] The pain became more acute, and his ability to expunge body fluids became ever more difficult. As his condition grew worse, Hartranft sought and received the best possible treatment of the day, but medical science of the time paled when compared to the standards of today.

Despite his growing ailments, he made every attempt at remaining active and was even being considered for the position of Commissioner of Pensions by President Harrison. While there was a lot of support for him, even he finally had to acknowledge his failing health, and on October 1, 1899, Hartranft reluctantly sent the following brief note to Washington,

Dear Sir:

I am very much pleased and gratified at your kind offer of support in case I am a candidate for the position of Commissioner of Pensions. I thank you as fully as if I were a candidate and successful; but my present state of health and business affairs will not permit me to consider myself as such.

Yours very truly,
J. F. Hartranft[22]

As the weeks passed, Hartranft's condition did not improve. Based upon modern medical knowledge, he was undoubtedly suffering from a compound condition brought on by his advanced uremia, which could include anorexia, nausea, and malnutrition. Owing to what must have been an advanced condition, he probably also suffered from what is commonly called "uremic frost." This condition discolors the skin when the urea excreted in the sweat crystallizes and irritates the skin's surface. If Hartranft were alive today and suffering similar conditions, he would at least be subject to dialysis or a kidney transplant.[23]

On Friday evening of October 11th, Hartranft fell gravely ill with severe chills and became extremely weak physically.[24] The family immediately summoned his physician, Dr. L. W. Read, who found the general in serious condition at his West Main Street home in Norristown. Now, in addition to his kidney problems, Dr. Read determined that he was also suffering from pneumonia and malaria.[25] Dr. Read did all that he could to make his patient as comfortable as possible and while his condition worsened over the weekend, Hartranft did show slight signs of improvement in the early part of the following week. Although deeply drained and weak, the general was able to rest comfortably and he even engaged in some light conversation with family members.

But then, on Thursday morning, Hartranft took a turn for the worse. His pain became more serious and he was unable to pass his urine. Dr. Read was again summoned, and he called upon Dr. James Tyson, Dean of The University of Pennsylvania, to render his opinion.[26] Upon completing his analysis, Dr. Tyson told Dr. Read that he could not make any further suggestion beyond that which Read had already prescribed for Hartranft. That statement was the equivalent of a medical death warrant as far as Read was concerned, though it came as no surprise. It now fell to Read to confirm for the family their worse fears, the general was indeed dying.

Throughout the night, a vigil was kept by Sallie and the general's aged mother, Lydia. For Sallie, matters were compounded since she desperately made every effort to comfort her dying husband while contending with his mother, who was not exactly in command of all of her faculties. Through it all, Hartranft's labored breathing filled the room through the long, dark, and unforgiving night.

Then, about 2:00 A.M. on Friday morning the 17th, Sallie noticed that his breathing was becoming even more erratic and she again summoned Dr. Read, who came immediately. When Read entered the room, he addressed the general and asked him, "How do you feel, General?", but Hartranft simply did not understand, did not have the strength to respond, and turned his head away and closed his eyes.[27]

As morning broke upon Norristown, many friends of the family came to call and check on the general's progress. By eight that morning, shortly after Dr. Read had again looked in upon his patient, callers were told that the general was dying and the word began to spread quickly.

Meanwhile, Sallie was joined at Hartranft's bedside by their two daughters, Anna and Marion, and their sons, Samuel and Linn. All the while, Lydia continued to remain in the room, though she did not exactly understand what was happening.

As the morning wore on, Hartranft fell deeper and deeper into oblivion, and just around noon, 58 year-old John Frederick Hartranft answered the call of the last trumpet.[28] Characteristically, Hartranft died quietly, without fanfare, and oblivious to pain. The final cause of death was listed as Bright's disease, a kidney ailment named for its key researcher, Dr. Richard Bright, and also commonly called uremia, which was compounded by his pneumonia.[29] The telegraph spread word of his death quickly throughout the immediate area, the state and the nation.

Almost immediately, the family began to receive many expressions of sorrow and condolence. The court house bell in Norristown began a melancholy toll, while its flag was draped in black and lowered to half staff to let the residents know that one of their favorite sons had died.[30] The whole region seemed to be thrown into sorrow as businesses, clubs, and the Grand Army headquarters adopted expressions of mourning.[31] Other organizations like the Republican Invincibles, to which Hartranft had belonged, also joined in the chorus of sadness.[32]

It did not take long before details for the funeral began to unfold. As with many notable people, his burial was to be a compromise between the personal wishes of the family and the desire of the public to have one last glimpse of one of their heroes. Through all of this, Sallie and her distraught family were most cooperative, as representatives from various groups, military, political, and business, came to offer their condolences and to request some participation in the final recognition of the general.

The Pennsylvania National Guard would play a very conspicuous part in the program, along with the remnants of his beloved 51st. Sallie agreed that he should have a military funeral befitting his rank of Major-General. Pall-bearers would include President and Major-General Rutherford B. Hayes, Hartranft's Ninth Corps Commander Major General John G. Parke, past Pennsylvania Governors Curtin, Pollock, Hoyt and Pattison, along with Brigadier-General James W. Latta and Major General William J. Bolton, who had replaced Hartranft as commander of the 51st Pennsylvania.[33]

His final resting place was selected at the Montgomery Cemetery, which is located on the soft banks of the Schuylkill River in West Norriton Township, immediately over the line from Norristown. The plot would be on the immediate north end of the river bank, where one could sit and muse with the never-ending flow of that gentle waterway. In that cemetery already lie some of the Hartranft's closest friends and commrades-in-arms. General Winfield Scott Hancock had been laid to rest there on February 13, 1886.[34] General Samuel K. Zook had also been buried there after being killed at

Gettysburg in July of 1863.[35] Lieutenant-Colonel Edwin Schall, who was killed at Cold Harbor while leading Hartranft's own 51st Pennsylvania, had also been interred there.[36] General Adam Jacoby Slemmer, who lived through the war only to die of heart disease at Fort Laramie almost one year prior to Hartranft's death, was also laid to rest here.[37] In addition to these distinguished officers, Montgomery Cemetery had already become a final resting place for many other officers and men of the area who had given so much to the cause of the Union.

On Monday morning at 9:00 A.M., standing outside the general's home on West Main Street near Haws Avenue, the honor guard of the First Brigade, National Guard of Pennsylvania, paused for a moment to permit the family another few precious moments of privacy. When the honor guard finally entered the Hartranft living room they moved softly, quietly but resolutely, and took their own last look upon the remains of the general. Taking the nearby coffin cover, which bore the simple inscription "JOHN FREDERICK HARTRANFT 1830-1889", they affixed it and placed the coffin upon the awaiting caisson outside. Then a long, precise military line moved eastward towards the Montgomery County Court House, where the general's remains would lie in state for three hours.

Upon reaching that beautiful marble edifice on Swede Street between Main and Airy Streets, the coffin was carried inside and preparations quickly made for a public review, which would last from 11:00 A.M. to 2:00 P.M. Resting the coffin inside one of the upper court rooms, the cover was again removed so the public might briefly look upon the remains of their governor, general, friend and neighbor for the last time.

When the doors swung open to the public, people promptly began to file past the bier. Most were somber, a few were curious, but at least one failed to understand the total gravity of the moment. One unidentified woman, while waiting in line, continued to talk and laugh and joke until she was sternly approached by a Colonel Robert P. Dechert with the question, "Do you think you are going to a circus?" The Colonel's reproach so embarrassed the woman that she simply glided past the bier without taking any particular note of its content.[38] All the while, the chime atop the court house pealed its sad toll while the bell atop Independence Hall in Philadelphia also rang out for the deceased general.

Perhaps the most poignant moment of all was when his aged mother entered the room to gaze upon her only child for the last time. Assisted to the bier, Lydia Hartranft approached the casket when a newspaper reporter caught the sorrowful moment,

### Hartranft's Home in Norristown

The Hartranft Home on West Main Street in Norristown, where he died. Today, it has been converted into apartments.

*Photographer: Frank D'Amico*

**Headquarters of Pennsylvania National Guard**

During Hartranft's funeral proceedings in October of 1889, the Divisional Headquarters of the Pennsylvania National Guard, located at City Hall in Philadelphia, was draped in his honor.

*Photographer: Copy by Frank D'Amico.*
*Source: Shireman Collection.*

It soon became apparent that she did not fully realize that before her lay all that was mortal of her most distinguished son, and soon his loved features would be forever hidden in the darkness of the grave. As she looked at the quiet features of her son she smiled, and, extending her left hand, laid it on his brow, lovingly smoothing back the hair, as if she only comprehended that he was sleeping and refrained from making any further demonstration through fear of awakening him.[39]

Almost 20,000 people passed the bier of "Old Johnny". The great and not so great came to pay their last farewell to a man who had unselfishly devoted his entire life to the public. As such, he was respected as a patriot, soldier, adversary, commander, politician, and a defender of justice. He was a gentleman and a gentle man, with a constitution of steel and a keen mind that possessed unusual mental acumen. Despite these qualities he had a tendency to trust too many people, which brought its fair share of havoc upon him at various times in his life. This failing was never more evident than in some moments of his political and business careers. Whatever the case, and equally important, John Hartranft was a model husband, father and neighbor, who won the respect of all that knew him.

At two o'clock, Rev. Dr. Henry C. McCook, from the Tabernacle Presbyterian Church in Philadelphia, delivered an eloquent eulogy. In his closing statement, Dr. McCook appeared to find the proper words to capture Hartranft's profile. This was not such an easy matter since at the time of death, people want the consolation of religion and the traditional assurances that a benevolent God will render suitable justice and care.

McCook had some appreciation for Hartranft's atypical religious values, and knew that he was not one to seek solace through ceremony only. Hartranft respected everyone's right to pursue his God as he deemed fit, but for himself, he led his religious life, almost unwittingly, just as his Schwenkfelder forbears prescribed. God to Hartranft was not affiliated with any particular building or creed, but rather recognized by one's respect for all that rest under His dominion, no matter how or where it might be found. With this in mind, Dr. McCook focused rather upon Hartranft's genuine ethical values and said that he was,

Great in warfare, he excelled also in civil life. Twice the ordained magistrate of a great Commonwealth, he so bore himself in the ordinary details of government and in the extraordinary responsibilities of the Centennial year, that neither the office nor the man suffered discredit. He was not rich, but no temptations of opportunity or necessity could swerve him from his high integrity, and his hands were not besmirched with illicit gain. After a life spent in enriching this Nation and State, he lies there as he died, a poor man.[40]

Following Dr. McCook's comments, Hartranft's remains were again covered and placed upon the caisson. With the traditional riderless horse with boots reversed in the stirrups following, the sad procession wound its way west onto Main Street and headed toward the cemetery. When the line arrived in front of the general's home, the party stopped for a moment and permitted the family to join the procession.[41]

Upon reaching the cemetery, about 5,000 people crowded around the gravesite and listened to a number of brief eulogies. As the brilliant October sun began to fall in the western sky, Rev. T. W. Davidson, D. D., of the Episcopal Church offered a final prayer and Sallie and her children approached the edge of the grave along with Governor Beaver and others. Rev. Davidson then recited the Lord's Prayer, slipped into a brief benediction, and stepped aside.[42]

Then, the military took over and offered its final salutes. Following their great thundering reverberations, there was a brief moment of total silence which was rudely broken by the woeful wail of the bugler's taps. As those sorrowful notes fell upon the soft countryside and the ears of the gathered mourners, few were the eyes that could hold back the strain of tears. With the last drawn out closing note, the crowd slowly began to move toward home. For the better part of forty years, the name of John Frederick Hartranft had come to mean so much to so many of those on the field that day. Many knew that the passing of the "General" would leave a permanent void in their lives, while others felt certain that he would continue to live through the memory of his greatness.

Unfortunately, like so many fallen heroes, Hartranft too fell under the prophetic words spoken about 700 years before the birth of Christ. Laboring under his own anguish of the moment, Job was shaken by Bildad the Shuhite when he told the Oriental Chieftain the fate which awaits an impious man. Little did Bildad realize that he was also speaking to the memory of many good men as well, when he told Job,

288

Below, his roots dry up,
and above, his branches wither.
His memory perishes from the land
and he has no name on the earth.

Job 18:16 & 17

# ENDNOTES FOR CHAPTER TWELVE
## "THE LAST TRUMPET"

1. Courtesy, Montgomery County Recorder of Deeds Office.
2. Presidential appointment, February 17, 1879, Shireman Collection.
3. *Norristown Register*, October 22, 1889, Shireman Collection.
4. *Memoriam of the Military Order of the Loyal Legion of the United States*, Issued January 20, 1890, Shireman Collection.
5. Williamsport *Daily Gazette & Bulletin*, January 16, 1879.
6. Barrett, "John Frederic Hartranft, Life and Services", p. 35.
7. JFH memo to Honorable Thomas McCamant, October 7, 1889, Shireman Collection.
8. U. S. Department of State Appointment, August 3,1888, Shireman Collection.
9. *Philadelphia Weekly Times*, December 23, 1888.
10. *Philadelphia Free Press*, October 18, 1889.
11. JFH to SSH, July 28, 1889, Shireman Collection.
12. JFH to SSH, July 29, 1889, Shireman Collection.
13. Document, Courtesy of Pennsylvania State Archives.
14. Unclassified newspaper clipping, Shireman Collection.
15. Barrett, "John Frederic Hartranft, Life and Service", p. 35.
16. McClure, *Old Time Notes of Pennsylvania*, vol. 2, p. 428.
17. *Philadelphia Free Press*, October 22, 1889.
18. Barrett, "John Frederic Hartranft, Life and Services", p. 35. Also see, *Norristown Weekly Herald*, October 21, 1889.
19. Unidentified [Norristown] Newspaper clippings, Shireman Collection.
20. Pennypacker, Samuel W., *Pennsylvania in American History*, Philadelphia: W. J. Campbell, 1910, pp. 453-454.
21. Letter from Joseph F. Tobias to JFH, October 18, 1873, Shireman Collection.
22. *Philadelphia Weekly Times*, October 3, 1889.
23. Opinion of Dr. Ian Lawson, M. D., Danbury, Connecticut.
24. *Philadelphia Free Press*, October 18, 1889.
25. Ibid
26. Ibid
27. *Philadelphia Public Ledger*, October 18, 1889.
28. Ibid.
29. Clendening, Logan, *Source Book of Medical History*, N. C., P. B. Hoeber, Inc., 1942, p. 530.
30. *Philadelphia Public Ledger*, October 18, 1889.
31. Ibid.

32. Memorial offered by the Republican Invincibles-Shireman Collection.
33. *Norristown Weekly Herald*, October 21, 1889.
34. Tucker, Glen, *Hancock The Superb*, Indianapolis, Indiana: Bobbs-Merrill, 1960, p. 311.
35. Warner, *Generals in Blue*, p. 577.
36. Taylor, Vivian F, *Memorials in Stone*. Norristown, Pennsylvania: The Historical Society of Montgomery County Pennsylvania, 1985, p. 63.
37. Warner, *Generals in Blue*, p. 452.
38. *Norristown Weekly Herald*, October 22, 1889.
39. *Norristown Register*, October 22, 1889.
40. *Philadelphia Public Ledger*, January 22, 1889.
41. *Philadelphia Press*, October 22, 1889.
42. *Norristown Weekly Herald*, October 22, 1889.

# HARTRANFT EPILOGUE

The first monument to bring honor upon General Hartranft and the 51st Pennsylvania was dedicated at Antietam Bridge on October 8, 1884. That monument stands on the north side of the creek near the mouth of the bridge and fortunately Hartranft himself was present for this dedication and he presented a review of his actions that fateful day in September of 1887.[1]

After Hartranft's death, there were several other tributes that also warrant particular notice here. On October 19, 1889, the city of Allentown, Pennsylvania, unveiled its massive Civil War monument. According to one newspaper report, "the slides are ornated with medallion bust pictures of Generals Meade, McClellan, Hancock and Hartranft who represented Pennsylvania among the generals of the Union Army."[2]

In that same year, C. E. Bair & Sons of Harrisburg offered to the public a substantially less enduring tribute when they introduced the "General Hartranft" cigar. While little is known of the success or quality of this item, there is no evidence to support the thought that the general himself ever indulged in any sort of tobacco.

In 1900, the Smith Memorial was unveiled in Fairmount Park in Philadelphia. According to the *Philadelphia Ledger*, the monument included a "colossal...bust of General Hartranft, by Sterling Calder." The Hartranft bust would join similar tributes to Generals George Gordon Meade and James A. Beaver and Admiral David Porter.[3]

On May 19, 1909, President William H. Taft was joined by Virginia Governor Claude A. Swanson and Pennsylvania Governor Edwin S. Stuart for the unveiling of the 60-foot-tall obelisk near Fort Mahone at Petersburg. This monument also honors Hartranft, but primarily, the fighting men of the Third Division. This monument was designed by F. W. Ruckstuhl, who earlier also designed Hartranft's bronze statue in Harrisburg.[4]

But, even while the general's funeral ceremonies were under way, plans were already being discussed for some sort of gravesite monument to be erected by the Pennsylvania National Guard. Those plans rapidly materialized into a fund raiser within the Guard, and each member was asked to contribute one dollar. It did not take long before the funds began to mount and a suitable monument was selected at a cost of $5,000.[5] Made of granite, the monument consisted of five separate parts, with the top being an obelisk rising to a height of thirty-six feet.[6] At the base is a relief of the General plus a listing of his major military accomplishments.

On June 7, 1891, with a throng approaching 10,000 or more spectators and participants, the people turned out to see the Hartranft monument unveiled at his gravesite on the banks of the Schuylkill River.[7]

The dignitaries included Governor Robert E. Pattison, ex-Governor/General James A. Beaver and Generals George R. Snowden, who succeeded Hartranft as Commander of the Pennsylvania Division, and James W. Latta who would deliver a keynote address.[8] A large parade began about 2:15 P.M. and wandered its way westerly from the center of Norristown at Main and Swede Streets, and included 20 remaining members of the 51st Pennsylvania Regiment who were led by Colonel George Schall.

Bands provided stirring martial music, while thousands more lined the streets on that hot but cloudy June day. When the parade finally made its way into Montgomery Cemetery and arrived at Hartranft's gravesite, Governor Pattison addressed the crowd, and said that Hartranft, "was as modest as he was brave, as wise in counsel as he was bold in the field. He was a good citizen and a faithful friend."[9]

General Snowden then addressed the crowd, and stated that, "This monument selected from a number of handsome designs which reflect credit upon the competing artists was in a measure chosen to set forth the character of the hero in whose memory it was raised. It is as plain and simple as his manner, without ostentation or display, of fine and elegant proportions like the manly personage who rests under its shadow."[10] With Snowden's closing comments, ten-year old Margaret Y. North pulled the cord which held a great American flag around the 36-foot-high obelisk. With the main flag released, hundreds of smaller American flags were also released, and they floated down upon the heads of the thousands of spectators. Then fifteen cannon opened their salute, causing the ground to shake so vigorously that it appeared to start the summer rain that began to fall.[11] That rain led General Latta to cut his comments short and prompted the Reverend Henry C. McCook, D.D., to expedite the benediction.

Today, Hartranft's gravesite receives only modest care from a few private individuals though it used to be regularly maintained by the National Guard of Pennsylvania. Other Union generals laid to rest in that totally unmaintained cemetery are Generals Hancock, McClennan, Slemmer and Zook. Today, there is no organization or individual with direct maintainance responsibilities owing to some legal disputes over ownership of the burial grounds. Consequently, those interred there lie within the rubble of broken stones, weeds, and unkept grounds. Unfortunately, all of this speaks to our local, state, and national indifference toward men to whom we are so greatly indebted for our current, unified existence.

Perhaps the most important tribute to Hartranft was unveiled in Harrisburg on May 12, 1899, in front of the new State Capitol Building which replaced the one that had burned two years earlier. There, a bronze statue of General Hartranft was unveiled with much pomp. The State of Pennsylvania ordered the monument at a cost of $18,000; and Mr. F. W.

Ruckstuhl of New York, Secretary of the National Sculpture's Association, was selected to execute the piece, which he did in Paris.[12] The statue is approximately 1 1/2 time life size and represents a mounted Hartranft receiving the plaudits of his hometown people with humility and strength. Ruckstuhl's portrayal faithfully represents Hartranft's exceptional equestrian ability, wherein man and beast act as one.

Requiring more then a year to complete, the monument was placed directly in front of the new Capitol Building in November of 1898 but the official unveiling was delayed until May of 1899 due to the war with Cuba. Present for the ceremony were Mrs. Sallie Hartranft, widow of the General/Governor, his sons Samuel and Linn plus his two daughters Marion and Anna. Many dignitaries were also there including Governor and Mrs. William A. Stone, Postmaster General Charles E. Smith and the U. S. Army Adjutant General Henry C. Corbin, along with over 3,000 veterans who would be in the line of march.

The actual unveiling was done by Miss Lenora Embick, daughter of M. A. Embick, who had served in Hartranft's Division. The keynote speech was offered by Major Isaac B. Brown, who also served under the general and he stated that, "In the fortunes of war, it fell to General Hartranft to meet, check and repulse the last grand offensive movement of Lee's army in Northern Virginia."[13] Brown was referring to Hartranft's heroic attack and recapture of Fort Stedman.

One of the more interesting speeches made during that celebration weekend came from one of Hartranft's foes at Fort Stedman, General Henry Kyd Douglas. At the time of that fight, Douglas was commander of the First Brigade of Gordon's Division, and he negotiated the truce with Hartranft so the dead and wounded could be gathered.[14] When he began his comments, Douglas told those Yankees, "my fellow Union Soldiers, for we are all that now, I do not feel it out of place on this occasion for me to be here with you to honor the name of General Hartranft. I feel that I have a peculiar right to be here. I am here as a Confederate soldier to pay my little tribute to the man whose name would blaze in any country."[15]

With a feeling of genuine warmth and respect, Douglas saluted Hartranft's personal character along with his traits as a superior soldier and statesman.  He went on to evoke much laughter from the crowd when he stated that he did not wish to offer an apology for breaking Hartranft's center that fateful day [Fort Stedman], but was also quick to add that he had no suitable explanation for the sudden reversal of his organization's good luck, once Hartranft began his counterattack.[16]

The ex-Confederate officer then praised Hartranft's humane treatment of Mrs. Surratt during the conspiracy trial. Citing his own detention at the  Penitentiary as a suspect in the death of Lincoln, Douglas told the crowd of veterans that when he was given a choice of where he should be incarcerated, he chose that facility because he knew that Hartranft was in charge and he would receive humane treatment from the general. Douglas continued that during his brief stay at the Penitentiary, he bore witness to Hartranft's kind treatment of Mary Surratt.[17] For his statement, General Douglas was rewarded with applause and a warm reception from Hartranft's comrades.

Douglas continued with his healing comments as he told the crowd that he again met Hartranft when, "he was Auditor General of Pennsylvania. He went with me as a representative of the Confederate Society of Maryland before the Military Committees of the House and Senate of Pennsylvania, and personally stood by my side and requested the Legislature of Pennsylvania to appropriate the sum of $5,000 to remove and bury the Confederate dead who fell on the field of Gettysburg." This comment brought a burst of applause, and Douglas then mentioned that Pennsylvania did appropriate the funds because of Hartranft's efforts.[18]

Douglas also praised Hartranft's work with the State's National Guard. "He organized them as a soldier; he headed them as a soldier; he disciplined them as a soldier; he commanded them as a soldier and on every occasion he conducted himself like a soldier. He was not there for military fame or for political prestige; he was not trying to capture the eyes of the ladies - he was afraid of his wife at home [laughter]."[19]

Then, Douglas concluded his remarks on a very sober plane when he said that Hartranft,

> ...was a man of sound judgment and of the most uncompromising honesty; modest, retiring, diffident, and reticent. He knew his own counsel and kept it. He was true to his friends and to his word of honor. He was never known to desert a friend for any purpose on earth, in adversity or in trouble. He was silent, heroic and manly. At a time when it would have been easy for him as for others to enrich himself from the public treasury, his hands remained pure and clean [applause]. Even in political excitement no one ever questioned his honesty and integrity. If misfortune was brought upon him by too great generosity, by too great trustfulness, by believing that all men were as honest as he was, in these times of mammoth fortunes, it is well to remember that amidst all temptations, in all circumstances, and with every opportunity, General Hartranft died a poor man [Applause].[20]

With all the speeches and parties completed, the statue had been placed on a prominent landing directly in front of the Capitol facing West, towards the majestic Sesquehanna River. Anyone approaching the State House could not possibly avoid the impressive casting which upon its base carries the simple inscription "John Frederic Hartranft".[21] When the festivities were complete, many participants made their way home including those from Norristown. Unfortunately, the Norristown-bound train ran into the rear of another train at Exerter Station, six miles from Reading, and the tragic result was 29 killed, 16 of whom were from Norristown directly.[22] In addition, 40 others were seriously injured. Consequently, the entire festive occasion was promptly turned into a horrible nightmare. The general's family members were sorely troubled by this disaster, and they would make many visits to the hospitals and homes of the dead and injured around the state to help bolster their morale.

With the passing of time and the fading memories of the great war and its heroes, some believe that the arena of partisan politics took its toll upon the once famous Pennsylvania General/Governor, which resulted in his statue being moved in September of 1927.[23] The monument was removed from its place of prominence in front of the State House and moved toward the southerly portion of the esplanade, where it overlooks a small park. Whatever the cause, today Ruckstuhl's exceptional bronze likeness of Hartranft sits quietly as it overlooks the pleasant foliage and walkways on that common.

Today, few visitors to the State Capitol venture to that southern end of the esplanade, and most residents of Harrisburg know nothing about the proud man set upon that bronze horse. With a sense of fallen history, Hartranft has slid into relative obscurity in Norristown, Harrisburg, and Pennsylvania in general. Only a small handful of Civil War students, along with some specialized historians, maintain any contact with and appreciation for his accomplishments.

Perhaps the last major monument to Hartranft, and other Pennsylvania soldiers, was unveiled on March 24, 1906, on the battlefield of Vicksburg, Mississippi. Amidst a highly decorated Vicksburg, dignitaries from Pennsylvania that included Governor Samuel W. Pennypacker and former Governor James A. Beaver, gathered to honor five of the Keystone State's sons which included Colonel John I. Curtin, Lieutenant-Colonel Thomas S. Brenholts, Colonel John F. Hartranft, Colonel Daniel Leasure, and Captain George W. Durrell.[24]

Just below the top of the tall granite monument there is a large marble tablet with the following inscription: "Here brothers fought for their principles; here, heroes died for their country and a united people will forever cherish the precious legacy of their noble manhood." Immediately below this tablet are the five bronze medallions, before identified.[25]

It appears that with the dedication of the Vicksburg-Pennsylvania monument, Hartranft's valorous deeds as a Union soldier and his strong leadership as a statesman began their fall into dusty archives waiting to be searched and rediscovered by modern students. To all of this, we can only relate and paraphrase the famous words of one of Hartranft's true friends and admirers, General William T. Sherman, who said, "war is all hell...and war is being killed on some obscure battlefield and having your name misspelled in the newspapers." Unfortunately, that sad legacy befell Hartranft along with hundreds of thousands of brave Americans who dared to fight for what they believed to be right.

Woodbury, Conn.

**Hartranft Obelisk, Shortly After Its Dedication in June of 1891**

Hartranft's monument as given by the Pennsylvania National Guard, shortly after its dedication.

*Source: Shireman Collection.*

**Hartranft's Grave Site, Today**

Sallie and other family members are buried here as well.

*Photographer: Frank D'Amico.*
*Source: Montgomery Cemetery.*

## Bronze Equestrian Statue of John F. Hartranft

A modern photo of the Hartranft monument in front of the Capitol Building in Harrisburg. It is this pose and position that leads local people to refer to the statue as "The General in the Park".

*Photographer: Jim Schmick.*

300

**Hartranft Equestrian Monument**

The Hartranft Monument in the front of the Pennsylvania Capitol Building.

*Source: Shireman Collection.*

**Hartranft's Equestrian Statue**

The Presidential party moving toward the stands on May 12, 1899, at the unveiling of the Hartranft statue in Harrisburg. President William McKinley was ill and unable to attend. Representing the President was Secretary of War, Russell Alger, who leads the group.

*Photographer: Copy by Frank D'Amico.*
*Source: Shireman Collection.*

**Hartranft's Equestrian Monument in Front of the Capitol Building**

Hartranft's Equestrian Monument in its original position.

*Photographer: Copy by Frank D'Amico.*
*Source: Shireman Collection.*

**Hartranft and Sheridan at Gettysburg Encampment**

Generals John F. Hartranft and Philip Sheridan on the far right. Taken in August of 1884 when the Pennsylvania National Guard camped at Gettysburg. During that encampment, Lieutenant-General Sheridan reviewed the troops. Immediately behind General Sheridan is his brother Michael.

*Photographer: Copy by Frank D'Amico.*
*Source: Shireman Collection.*

**A Rare Photograph of Sallie Hartranft, Wife of the General**

This photograph appeared in the Philadelphia Press on May 12, 1899 when the paper ran a feature article on the dedication of Hartranft's Equestrian Statue in Harrisburg.

*Photographer: Copy by Frank D'Amico.*
*Source: Shireman Collection.*

**Sallie Hartranft, the General's Wife**

One of the rare existing photos of Sallie Hartranft as she participated in the Norristown Centennial Celebration. Mrs. Hartranft is located in the rear seat, to the far left. The theme of this particular parade was "Military Day" and the photo appears to have been taken in front of the Montgomery County Court House in Norristown.
**[*Information courtesy of HSMC*]**

*Photographer: Copy by Frank D'Amico.*
*Source: Shireman Collection.*

**Pennsylvania Monument at Vicksburg National Military Park**

The Pennsylvania Monument at Vicksburg, Mississippi, that honors five of her sons. Hartranft is in the center.

*Source: Vicksburg National Military Park.*

**Pennsylvania Monument at Vicksburg National Military Park**

Close-up of the Pennsylvania Monument at Vicksburg, Mississippi, that honors five of her sons. Hartranft is in the center.

*Source: Vicksburg National Military Park.*

# ENDNOTES FOR EPILOGUE

1. Hartranft, John F., *Oration. Report of the Sixth Annual Meeting of the Association of the 51st Regiment P.V., Dedication of Monument at Antietam Bridge*, October 8th, 1887. Shireman collection.
2. *Allentown Chronicle News*, October 19, 1899.
3. *Philadelphia Ledger*, July 26, 1900.
4. Ibid., May 19, 1909.
5. *Philadelphia Weekly Press*, June 7, 1891.
6. Ibid.
7. Ibid.
8. Norristown *Register*, June 8, 1891.
9. Ibid.
10. Ibid.
11. Ibid.
12. *The Philadelphia North American*, May 12, 1899.
13. Ibid.
14. *Philadelphia Public Ledger*, May 13, 1899.
15. *The Uniontown Standard*, May 18, 1899.
16. *Philadelphia Weekly Press*, May 13, 1899.
17. Philadelphia *North American*, May 12, 1899.
18. Ibid.
19. Ibid.
20. Ibid.
21. Kolatch, Alfred J., *The Name Dictionary, Modern English and Hebrew Names*, New York: Jonathan David, 1967, p. 51. According to this volume, Frederick and its various forms are from the German meaning "peaceful ruler". The name may be spelled Frederic, Frederick, Fredric or Fredick.
22. New York *Independent*, May 18, 1899.
23. Pennsylvania State Archives, File Number #662.
24. Winschel, Terrence J., "The Day They Raised a Monument in Dixie", *Pennsylvania Heritage*, [May 1992], pp. 33-37.
25. Ibid.

# APPENDIX - A

The following is the list of men of the 51st Pennsylvania that were either killed or wounded during the charge over Rorbach's Bridge at the Battle of Antietam, September 17, 1862.

\* \* \* \* \* \* \* \* \* \*

## HEADQUARTERS

*Killed*        Lieutenant-Colonel Thomas S. Bell.

*Wounded*    Quartermaster Sergeant John J. Freedley.
Sergeant Major Curtin B. Stonerod.
Adjutant George W. Shorkley.

## COMPANY - A

*Killed*        Corporal James Coulston.
Private William Somerlot.

*Wounded*    Captain William J. Bolton.
Corporal Levi Bolton.
Private James M. Bolton.
Private George S. Buzzard.
Private Charles Keyser.
Private Andrew Widger.
Private Harry C. Wood.

## COMPANY - B

*Killed*        Sergeant Richard J. Williams.
Corporal George W. Bird.
Private David S. Hutman.
Private Henry C. Moore.

| *Wounded* | Sergeant George Bobler. |
|---|---|
| | Corporal Valentine Stocker. |
| | Private Aaron Thatcher. |
| | Private Lewis Young. |

## COMPANY - C

| *Killed* | Lieutenant Davis Hunsicker. |
|---|---|
| | Corporal David Kane. |

| *Wounded* | Lieutenant Thomas J. Lynch. |
|---|---|
| | Sergeant Benjamin F. Miller. |
| | Corporal Samuel Egolf. |
| | Corporal Simon P. Emery. |
| | Corporal James Sullivan. |
| | Private Thomas Allen. |
| | Private Levi Baum. |
| | Private Henry Davis. |
| | Private Ruben De Haven. |
| | Private Charles R. Fox |
| | Private William H. R. Fox. |
| | Private William Gunn. |
| | Private Marcus A. Gross. |
| | Private John Hollowell. |
| | Private Henry Jago. |
| | Private Benjamin Johnson. |
| | Private George Kevin. |
| | Private William Lath. |
| | Private Henry Lightcap. |
| | Private George Mercer. |
| | Private Patrick Rogan. |
| | Private Levi W. Shingle. |
| | Private David R. Spare. |
| | Private John M. Springer. |
| | Private James Sullivan. |
| | Private John Umstead. |
| | Private Abraham Walt. |

## COMPANY - D

*Killed*        Private Michael Mooney.

*Wounded*       Sergeant Edward Bennett.
                Sergeant John W. Gilligan.
                Corporal John Gilligan.
                Corporal William Jenkins.
                Corporal Isaac Tolan.
                Private John Earls.
                Private William Essick.
                Private William Faulkner.
                Private Hector Gillian.
                Private William Hamburger.
                Private George Haybeery.
                Private Samuel McDade.
                Private William McManamy.
                Private William Mogee.
                Private Isaac Sloan.

## COMPANY - E

*Wounded*       Sergeant James P. Cornelius.
                Sergeant George C. Gutilius.
                Corporal George W. Foote.
                Private Abraham Benfer.
                Private Lewis Klines.
                Private Jackson McFadden.
                Private James Marson.
                Private Martin G. Reed.
                Private C. W. Woodward.

## COMPANY - F

*Killed*        Private William Conner.
                Private Hertz Lentz.
                Private Henry Shultz.

| Wounded | Captain Lane S. Hart. |
|---|---|
| | Sergeant Howard Bruce. |
| | Sergeant Allen H. Fillman. |
| | Corporal William Montgomery. |
| | Private James Dolan. |
| | Private D. Freas[e]. |
| | Private R. McGee. |

## COMPANY - G

| Killed | Corporal James Dowling. |
|---|---|
| | Private Miles Dillon. |
| | Private William Wenrick. |
| | Private Wallace Wiggins. |

| Wounded | Corporal Geogre Armstrong. |
|---|---|
| | Private Jacob Casher. |
| | Private George Dutott. |
| | Private Houston Heichel. |
| | Private Robert Hinton. |
| | Private Jesse Lucas. |
| | Private William Maurer. |
| | Private William Wilson. |
| | Private William Young. |

## COMPANY - H

| Killed | Lieutenant Jacob G. Beaver. |
|---|---|
| | Sergeant Levi Marks. |
| | Sergeant Matthew Vandine. |
| | Private Edward Bear. |
| | Private Isaac Beck. |
| | Private Isaac Witters. |

| Wounded | Lieutenant William F. Campbell. |
|---|---|
| | Sergeant Hugh McCluc. |
| | Sergeant Jacob H. Santo. |

Sergeant Daniel M. Wetzell.
Corporal H. C. McCormick.
Corporal James Schooley.
Private John W. Erdley.
Private John Rain.
Private Daniel M. Wetzell.
Private Anthony Wiesenback.


## COMPANY - I

*Killed*        Sergeant J. Clark Davis.
               Corporal Thomas P. Davis.

*Wounded*     Sergeant Thomas H. Parker.
               Sergeant George W. S. Pennell.
               Private Charles Buley.
               Private Jacob Emrich.
               Private John Murphy.
               Private Jacob H. Myers.


## COMPANY - K

*Killed*        Private William Scott.

*Wounded*     Sergeant Daniel W. Eichman.
               Corporal Thomas Foster.
               Private Jacob Fortner.
               Private Paul McBride.
               Private Irwin Richards.
               Private Samuel Royer.
               Private Joseph Sarba.
               Private Albert Snyder.
               Private Joseph Snyder.
               Private William Yates.

* * * * * * * * * *

Total
    *Killed:* 2 officers and 23 enlisted men.
    *Wounded:* 5 officers and 102 enlisted men.


Source: Parker, *History of the 51st*. At the time of the attack at Antietam, Parker was a Sergeant in the 51st with Company I and was wounded. He would later win promotion to the rank of Captain.

    *Also see* the *O. R.* I, vol. XIX, part I, pp. 420-421., and the *Bolton Diary*. The above values represent a combination of the three sources since none agree with every detail.

# APPENDIX - B

The following article about Governor Hartranft and his alleged relationship with the Mollies appeared in the *Philadelphia Evening Chronicle* on November 11, 1878.

Yesterday's *Philadelphia Times* indulges in two full columns of rather badly jumbled rhetoric on the Kehoe case. It is a matter of some difficulty to discover what it is all about, beyond the personal malignity towards Governor Hartranft and Attorney General [George P.] Lear which pervades every sentence. The course of the *Times* in this matter has been conspicuously unfair towards Governor Hartranft from the beginning. It will be remembered that away back in June the *Times* raised a hue and cry around the Governor's ears because he had thus far neglected to sign Kehoe's death warrant; and a number of other newspapers in Pennsylvania, which hadn't any more definitive idea of what they were talking about than the *Times*, took up and prolonged the howl. It remains for the *Chronicle* to give the fact of the case in a letter from Lieutenant Governor [James] Latta, published on the 20th of June, which stated that the board of pardons had not yet passed on Kehoe's application.

It seems to us that the *Times* logic and its facts don't jingle together very harmoniously. If Kehoe's neck was to be on the condition that the vote of Luzerene and Lackawanna counties should be given for Hoyt, we can't exactly comprehend why the governor was in such haste to issue Kehoe's death warrant as soon as the majority for Hoyt in those counties was announced. So far as the vote for Schuylkill County is concerned there is no indication of any such bargain.

It is but justice to General to say that the case made out for Kehoe at the second hearing before the board was a much stronger one than that presented at the first hearing. That second hearing was brought about by the persistency by Kehoe's counsel, who produced the affidavits of Neal Dougherty and John Campbell, the two men who were convicted of murder in the second degree for the same crime, and who testified that Kehoe had nothing to do with the Langdon murder; and also the affidavit of M. M. L'Velle, Esq., who testified that Yellow Jack Donohue stated to him in his cell at Mauch Chunk, on the day before his execution for the murder of Morgan Powell, that Jack Kehoe was not guilty of the murder of Langdon.

The *Times* reviews the disgraceful chapter in our political history in which the Mollie Maguire vote of Schuylkill County was purchased for Hartranft in 1875, and intimates that the pardon of certain criminals was a part of that bargain. This was doubtless true, but Jack Kehoe was not at that time under suspicion of any of these grave crimes, and it is unfair to insinuate that his pardon for offenses with which he had not then been charged, was part of the consideration agreed upon.

The *Chronicle* is neither the apologist nor the defender of Hartranft and his administration. In the fight for the suppression of Mollie Maguireism it was always in the forefront of the battle. It was the first journal which exposed the bargain and sale of 1875. The *Times* so frequently asserted that the forfeit of Jack Kehoe's neck was to be made an element of the recent political canvas that we took pains to get all the information we could on the subject. We repeat that we have seen no indication of such a bargain in this county - and if there was such an understanding in other counties and the Mollie Maguire cutthroats performed their part of the contract, we are at a loss to know why Hartranft went back on his part.

We venture the assertion that not one of the dozen gentlemen who are now just writing so vigorously about the Kehoe case never read the evidence, or have the least idea of the testimony on which Kehoe was convicted. The *Times* and other journals fall back on the decision of the Supreme Court affirming the judgment of the court below; but if the affirmance is final and governs the action of the board of pardons and the governor, then the pardoning power may as well be stricken from the executive prerogative. It is evident that the governor and half the members of the board, after a careful review of the testimony, were inclined to think that a verdict of guilty was not warranted by the evidence. The board refusing to recommend a pardon, the governor's duty was merely ministerial. Nothing was left for him to do but to affix his signature to the death warrant. This he has done in compliance with the law.

# APPENDIX - C

The following article appeared in the *Williamsport Gazette & Bulletin* on May 18, 1885. The purpose of the article was to explain to the public the need for restructuring the National Guard of Pennsylvania.

Prior to the [railroad] riots of 1877, there was in effect, no organized militia in the state of Pennsylvania. The call for troops in 1861, and their subsequent service in the field, had depleted the state of its serviceable soldiers, and the general apathy following the war rendered the formation of an efficient militia almost an impossibility. But the martial spirit gradually revived and attempts were made from time to time to reawaken the latent energies of our citizen soldiery. Nothing definite was accomplished until 1874. There then existed in the state twenty-one divisions, each commanded by a major general. They were furnished nothing by the state, but were compelled to equip themselves and pay their own expenses in keeping up their organization. Some of the major generals commanded less than 100 men, while a colonel might call himself fortunate, could he muster a corporal's guard. In that year however, a long advance was made. By act of the general assembly the number of divisions was reduced to ten, an appropriation of one and two hundred dollars yearly, for armory rent, was passed, the legislature of the previous year having allowed the sum of four hundred dollars per annum to each company for ordinary expenses. But the Commonwealth was still chary of its favors. There was no attempt at equipment. Each organization purchased its own uniforms and most of them were armed with the old muzzle loading rifles, and a filled cartridge or bullet was a genuine curiosity. There was no uniformity in dress, but each organization selected its own, and thus the guard was made up of the tinsel and show, bear skin hats and gaudy uniforms, which generally make up the dress of the modern militiaman.

Thus matters until the sudden call to arms in 1877 to suppress the formidable riots existing at Pittsburgh and other parts of the state. ... in 1878 the legislature passed a law providing for the complete reorganization of the guard, its thorough equipment and in effect, putting it upon what might be termed a "war footing." This result was largely due to the untiring efforts of Governor Hartranft and Adjutant General Latta...

Thus stands the National Guard of to-day; a body of men that has taken the palm at two successive inaugurations at Washington under the critical eyes of army officers, and which General [William T.] Sherman declared was the finest body of men ever seen by him.

# HARTRANFT BIBLIOGRAPHY

## MANUSCRIPTS

Bolton Diary or "War Journal." This is the diary of Captain William J.
Bolton an officer, under Hartranft, in the 51st Pennsylvania Volunteers. Hartranft and Bolton were very close and Bolton's diary, which actually begins with his birth, is an invaluable vehicle for the study of Hartranft and the war years. After the war, Bolton became a Major General of the National Guard of Pennsylvania. This manuscript was provided by historian, Dr. Richard Sauers, with orignal owned by the Civil War Library and Museum, Philadelphia.

"General Ambrose E. Burnside's 1862 North Carolina Campaign." This is a thesis written by Dr. Richard Sauers in 1987 toward his Ph.D. at Pennsylvania State University Graduate School, Department of History. This work is slated to appear soon in book form.

Hartranft Gubernatorial Correspondence. This information came from two sources including The Historical Society of Montgomery County at Norristown, and the Shireman Collection. Each source has approximately eight volumes of correspondence copies reproduced by some wet process that was popular at the time. The data in both sources is different and covers a wide variety of subject matter.

Hartranft Journal or "Day Book." Hartranft kept these records while he was Special Provost Marshal General during the Lincoln Conspiracy Trial. This daily information is frequently redundant about the status of the prisoners but does offer keen insight into how they were treated and his own efforts to improve their care. Perhaps the most astonishing point made in these volumes is the fact that Hartranft never made any statement that indicated he felt Mrs. Surratt innocent. This position had been held by many historians and it simply is not true. Hartranft's grandson, Hartranft Stockham, lent these document to the Musselman Library at Gettysburg College, before his own death, and they still reside there.

Hudson, John William, Letter. Hudson was a lieutenant with the 35th Massachusetts and in October of 1862 he sent his sweetheart "Spohy" a letter regarding the fight for Burnside's bridge at Antietam. This letter was supplied by author John M. Priest and the original resides in the Western Maryland Room, Washington County Free Library. It should be noted that the author believes that many of Hudson's thoughts on the taking of the bridge are very flawed.

Shireman Collection. This is a very large collection of primary material which was assembled by Hartranft and ultimately passed down to family members. The collection contains thousands of documents including personal letters, plus official military and political data as well. In addition, the collection contains hundreds of newspaper clipping that pertain to Hartranft's military and, more heavily, his political career. It is obvious that as governor, he utilized a "clipping" service plus the eyes of his own staff. The collection can boast numerous original letters from many of the notable Civil War officers including, William T. Sherman. References to any of these papers is always noted as "Shireman Collection."

Townsend, George Alfred. Townsend was a well known newspaper reporter during the war and he kept extensive records. In addition, he also interviewed Hartranft as Governor and left behind a clear written description of the Keystone State's Chief Executive. Particular mention of his interview with Hartranft appears in his Scrapbook #133, and this data was provided by Michael Kauffman, Chesapeake Beach, Maryland.

U. S. Army Military History Institute, Carlisle Barracks, Pennsylvania. The Institute has a wealth of information on the Civil War and many of its participants. For Hartranft, they offered a letter from Private David Benfer, of the 51st Pennsylvania, and Colonel Zenas R. Bliss, a regimental commander in the Ninth Corps. Both of these letters offer keen insight into the military life and personality of John F. Hartranft.


NEWSPAPERS


*Agitator*, Wellsboro, Pennsylvania.
*Allentown Chronicle*, Allentown, Pennsylvania.
*American Republic*, West Chester, Pennsylvania.
*Bedford Inquirer*, Bedford, Pennsylvania.
*Bloomfield Times*, New Bloomsfield, Pennsylvania.
*Bradford Daily Breeze*, Bradford, Pennsylvania.
*Carlisle Herald*, Carlisle, Pennsylvania.
*Carson City Appeal*, Carson City, Nevada.
*Chronicle-Herald*, Philadelphia, Pennsylvania.
*Cincinnati Enquirer*, Cincinnati, Ohio.

*Commercial Gazette*, Pittsburgh, Pennsylvania.
*Daily Evening Telegraph*, Philadelphia, Pennsylvania.
*Daily Gazette & Bulletin*, Williamsport, Pennsylvania.
*Leader*, Pittsburgh, Pennsylvania.
*Daily Graphic*, New York, New York.
*Daily Miners Journal*, Pottsville, Pennsylvania.
*Daily Post, Pittsburgh*, Pennsylvania.
*Daily Record Times*, Wilkes-Barre, Pennsylvania.
*Daily State Guard*, Harrisburg, Pennsylvania.
*Daily Telegraph*, Harrisburg, Pennsylvania.
*Dispatch*, Pittsburgh, Pennsylvania.
*Evening Bulletin*, Philadelphia, Pennsylvania.
*Evening Chronicle*, Philadelphia, Pennsylvania.
*Evening Herald*, Philadelphia, Pennsylvania.
*Free Press*, Easton, Pennsylvania.
*Free Press*, Philadelphia, Pennsylvania.
*Franklin Herald*, Philadelphia, Pennsylvania.
*Globe*, Pittsburgh, Pennsylvania.
*Grand Army Scout and Soldier's Mail*, Philadelphia, Pennsylvania.
*Herald*, New York, New York.
*Herald & Free Press*, Norristown, Pennsylvania.
*Herald & Free Press & Republican*, Norristown, Pennsylvania.
*Independent*, New York, New York.
*Industrial Advocate*, Scranton, Pennsylvania.
*Inquirer*, Philadelphia, Pennsylvania.
*Morning Herald*, Titusville, Pennsylvania.
*National Defender*, Norristown Pennsylvania.
*North American*, Philadelphia, Pennsylvania.
*North Wales Record*, North Wales, Pennsylvania.
*Patriot*, Harrisburg, Pennsylvania.
*Philadelphia Ledger*, Philadelphia, Pennsylvania.
*Philadelphia North American*, Philadelphia, Pennsylvania.
*Philadelphia Weekly Press*, Philadelphia, Pennsylvania.
*Picayune*, New Orleans, Louisiana.
*Press, The*, Everett, Pennsylvania.
*Public Ledger*, Philadelphia, Pennsylvania.
*Register*, Norristown, Pennsylvania.
*Register & Watchman*, Norristown, Pennsylvania.
*Sentinel & Republican*, Mifflintown, Pennsylvania.
*Standard*, Uniontown, Pennsylvania.
*Times*, New York, New York.
*Times Herald*, Norristown, Pennsylvania.

*Tribune*, New York, New York.
*Virginia City Sentinel*, Virginia City, Nevada.
*Uniontown Standard*, Uniontown, Pennsylvania
*Weekly Herald*, Norristown, Pennsylvania.
*Weekly Times*, Philadelphia, Pennsylvania.
*World*, New York, New York.

Alexander, Edward P. *Military Memoirs of a Confederate*. New York: Charles Scribner's Sons, 1907; reprint, Dayton, Ohio: Morningside Bookshop, 1977.

Armor, William C. *Lives of the Governors of Pennsylvania from 1609-1872*. Philadelphia: J. K. Simon, 1873.

Arnold, Samuel Bland. *Defence and Prison Experience of a Lincoln Conspirator*. Hattiesburg, Mississippi: The Book Farm, 1943.

Atlas, to accompany the *Official Records*, U. S. Government Printing Office, Washington D.C., 1891-1896.

Aurand, A. Monroe, Jr. *Historical Account of the Mollie Maguires*, Lancaster, Pennsylvania: Aurand Press, no date.

Aurand, Harold and William Gudelunas. *The Mythical Qualities of Molly Maguire*. Hazelton, Pennsylvania: Pennsylvania State University Press, 1982.

Bailey, Ronald H., et al., eds. *The Bloodiest Day, The Battle of Antietam*. Alexandria, Virginia: Time-Life Books, 1984.

Baker, Lafayette C. *History of the United States Secret Service*. Philadelphia: By the author, 1867.

Barrett, Eugene A., "John Frederic Hartranft; Life and Services", *Bulletin of The Historical Society of Montgomery County, Pennsylvania*, Norristown, Vols. VII & VIII [April & October, 1951].

Bates, Samuel P. *History of Pennsylvania Volunteers, 1861-5*, 5 vols. Harrisburg: B. Singerly, State Printer, 1869-1871.

_____, *Martial Deeds of Pennsylvania*. Philadelphia: T. H. Davis & Co., 1875.

Bean, Theodore W., ed. *History of Montgomery County Pennsylvania*. Philadelphia: Everts & Peck, 1884.

Bearss, Edwin Cole. *The Campaign for Vicksburg*, 3 vols. Dayton, Ohio: Morningside House, Inc. 1986.

Beath, Robert B. *History of the Grand Army of the Republic*. New York: Bryan Taylor, 1889.

Blaine, James G. *Twenty Years of Congress: from Lincoln to Garfield*. vol. 1, Norwich, Connecticut: Henry Bill, 1884.

Board of Publication of the General Conference of the Schwenkfelder Church. *A Brief Statement on the Schwenkfelder Church*, Pennsburg, Pennsylvania, 1985.

_____, *Who Are the Schwenkfelders?*, Pennsburg, Pennsylvania: 1923.

Bosbyshell, Oliver C. *Pennsylvania at Antietam*. Harrisburg, Pennsylvania: Harrisburg Publishing Company, 1906.

Bradley, Erwin Stanley. *Simon Cameron, Lincoln's Secretary of War*. Philadelphia: University of Pennsylvania Press, 1966.

Brecht, Samuel Kriebel, ed. *The Genealogical Record of the Schwenkfelder
Families*. New York: Rand McNally & Company, 1923.

Brock, R. A. ed. *Southern Historical Society Papers*, vol. 31, Richmond,
Virginia: By The Society, 1903.

Broehl, Wayne G., Jr. *The Molly Maguires*. Cambridge, Massachusetts:
Harvard University Press, 1965.

Brooks, Thomas R. *Toil and Trouble, A History of American Labor*. With a
Foreword by A. H. Raskin. New York: Delacorte Press, 1964.

Brown, Isaac B., "Address at the Unveiling of the Hartranft Statue", *Philadelphia Press*, May 13, 1899, Shireman Collection.

Bruce, Robert V. *1877: Year of Violence*. Chicago: Bobbs-Merrill, 1959.

Carter, Samuel III. *The Final Fortress: The Campaign for Vicksburg 1862-
1863*. New York: St. Martin's Press, 1980.

_____, *The Riddle of Dr. Mudd*. New York: G. P. Putnam's Sons, 1974.

Catton, Bruce. *Grant Takes Command*. Boston: Little, Brown and Company,
Inc., 1968.

Cavanaugh, Michael A. and William Marvel. *The Petersburg Campaign-
The Battle of the Crater*. Lynchburg, Virginia: H. E. Howard, Inc.,
1989.

Chambers, Lenoir. *Stonewall Jackson*, 2 vols., New York: William Morrow
& Co., 1959.

Chamlee, Roy Z. Jr. *Lincoln's Assassins*. Jefferson, North Carolina: McFarland & Company, Inc., 1990.

Clark, Champ, et al., eds. *The Assassination, Death of The President*. Alexandria, Virginia: Time-Life Books, 1987.

Clark, Dennis. *The Irish in Pennsylvania*, Pennsylvania Historical Association, Camp Hill, 1991. Harrisburg Publishing Company, eds.,
Proceedings–Reunion of the Third Division, Ninth Corps, Army of
the Potomac, Held at York, Pa., March 25, 1891, Harrisburg, 1892.

Clarke, William P., "Official History of the Militia and the National Guard
of the State of Pennsylvania", Harrisburg, 1912.

Coleman, J. Walter. *The Molly Maguire Riots*. Richmond: Garrett and
Massie, 1936.

Congdon, Don, ed. *COMBAT: The Civil War*. Secaucus, New Jersey: The
Blue and Grey Press, 1985.

Davis, Burke. *Gray Fox*. New York: Reinehart, 1956.

Davis, Jefferson. *The Rise & Fall of the Confederate Government*, 2 vols. New
York: Appleton, 1881; reprint, New York: DaCapo Press, 1990.

Davis, William C., et al., eds. *Death in the Trenches, Grant at Petersburg*.
Alexandria, Virginia: Time-Life Books, 1986.

Davis, William C. *Battle at Bull Run*. Garden City, New York: Doubleday
    & Company, Inc., 1977.
De Witt, David Miller. *The Judicial Murder of Mary Surratt*. Baltimore:
    John Murphy & Co., 1895.
Doster, William E. *Lincoln and Episodes of the Civil War*. New York: G. P.
    Putnam's Sons, 1915.
Douglas, Henry Kyd. *I Rode With Stonewall*. Chapel Hill, North Carolina:
    The University of North Carolina Press, 1940; reprint, St. Simons
    Island, Georgia: Mockingbird Books, Inc., 1989.
Dowdey, Clifford and Louis R. Manarin, eds. *The Wartime Papers of R. E.
    Lee*. New York: Bramhall House, 1961.
Dunaway, Wayland Fuller. *A History of Pennsylvania*. New York: Prentice-
    Hall, Inc., 1935.
Eckert, Ralph Lowell. *John Brown Gordon*. Baton Rouge: Louisiana State
    University Press, 1989.
Editors, Civil War Times Illustrated, *Great Battles of the Civil War*. New
    York: Gallery Books, 1989.
Eisenschiml, Otto. *Why was Lincoln Murdered?*. Boston: Little, Brown and
    Company, 1937.
Embick, Milton A., ed. *Military History of the Third Division, Ninth Corps,
    Army of the Potomac*. Harrisburg, Pennsylvania: O. E. Aughinbaugh,
    1913.
Ent, Uzal W. *The First Century 1879-1979*. Harrisburg, Pennsylvania: Stack-
    pole Books, 1979.
Erb, Peter C. *Schwenckfeld in His Reformation Setting*. Pennsburg, Pennsyl-
    vania: Schwenkfelder Library, 1978.
Evans, Eli N. *Judah P. Benjamin, The Jewish Confederate*. New York: The
    Free Press, 1988.
Evans, Frank B. *Pennsylvania Politics, 1872-1877: A Study in Political Leader-
    ship*. Harrisburg, Pennsylvania: The Pennsylvania Historical and
    Museum Commission, 1966.
Forney, John W. *Life and Military Career of Winfield Scott Hancock*. Phila-
    delphia: Hubbard Bros, 1880.
Fowler, Robert H. *Album of the Lincoln Murder*. Harrisburg, Pennsylvania:
    Stackpole Books, 1965.
Fox, William F. *Regimental Losses In The American Civil War*. Albany, New
    York: Albany Publishing Company, 1889.
Frassanito, William A. *Antietam - The Photographic Legacy of
    America's Bloodiest Day*. New York: Charles Scribner's Sons, 1978.
Freeman, Douglas Southall. *Lee's Lieutenants*, 3 vols. New York: Charles
    Scribner's Sons, 1942-44.
_____, *R. E. Lee*, 4 vols. New York: Charles Scribner's Sons, 1934-35.

Gallagher, Gary W. *Antietam, Essays on the 1862 Maryland Campaign*. Kent, Ohio: Kent State University Press, 1989.

Gavin, William Gilfillan. *The 100th Regiment Volunteers, The Round-head Regiment*. Dayton, Ohio: Morningside House, Inc., 1989.

Godcharles, Frederick A. *Pennsylvania - Political, Governmental, Military and Civil History*, 2 vols. New York: American Historical Society, 1933.

Goodrich, Frederick E. *The Life and Public Service of Winfield Scott Hancock*. New York: Lee and Shepard, 1880.

Gordon, John B. *Reminiscences of the Civil War*. New York: Charles Scribner's Sons, 1903; reprint, Alexandria, Virginia: Time-Life Books, Inc., 1981.

Grant, Julia Dent. *The Personal Memoirs of Julia Dent Grant*. New York: G. P. Putnam's Sons, 1975; reprint, Carbondale, Illinois: Southern Illinois University Press, 1975.

Grant, Ulysses S. *Personal Memoirs of U. S. Grant*, 2 vols. New York: Charles L. Webster & Company, 1886.

Gray, John, "The Fate of the Lincoln Conspirators", *McClure's Magazine*, [October, 1911].

Hall. James O. *The Surratt Family & John Wilkes Booth*, Clinton, Maryland: The Surratt Society, no date.

Hanchett, William. *The Lincoln Murder Conspiracies*. Chicago: University of Illinois Press, 1983.

Hancock, Almira. *Reminiscences of W. S. Hancock*. New York: Charles L. Webster & Co., 1887.

Hartranft, John F. *Inaugural Address, Delivered at Harrisburg on Tuesday, January 21, 1873*, Shireman Collection.

_____, *Message[s] of John F. Hartranft to the General Assembly of Pennsylvania, for the years, 1874, 1875, 1876, 1877, 1878 and 1879*. Shireman Collection.

_____, *The Recapture of Fort Stedman*, Philadelphia Press, March 17, 1886.

_____, "The Schwenkfelders", *The Schwenkfeldian*, [October, 1914]. N.B. This paper was originally prepared by Hartranft in 1886. In the introduction of the 1914 printing, the Magazine stated that, "We deem it very appropriate that we should print in this issue cut of the late Governor John F. Hartranft, who just thirty years ago in connection with Ex-Judge Christopher Heydrick, of Franklin and others started the movement that led to the publication of the Corpus Schwenckfeldianorum." It should also be noted that there is reason to believe that Hartranft knew little or nothing about his Schwenkfelder heritage until later in his life.

_____, *Speech at the Sixth Annual Meeting of the 51st Regiment P.V., Dedication of Monument at Antietam Bridge*, October 8th, 1887.

Hauze, Gary C. *A History of America's Oldest German Reformed Church, The Falkner Swamp Reformed Church*, Gilbertsville, Pa., 1975.

Henderson, G.F.R. *Stonewall Jackson*. New York: David McKay Company, Inc., 1968.

Hendler, Charles J. *Official History of the Militia and the National Guard of the State of Pennsylvania*. 2 vols. Harrisburg, Pennsylvania: Charles J. Hendler, Third Infantry N.G.P., 1912.

Higdon, Hal. *The Union vs. Dr. Mudd*. Chicago: Follett Publishing Company, 1964.

Higginbotham, Sanford, W., William A. Hunter, and Donald H. Kent. *Pennsylvania and the Civil War - A Handbook*, The Pennsylvania Historical and Museum Commission, Harrisburg, 1961.

Hodgkins, William H. *The Battle of Fort Stedman*. Boston: Privately Printed, 1889.

Hoehling, A. A. *After the Guns Fell Silent*. New York: Madison Books, 1990.

_____ and Mary Hoehling. *The Day Richmond Died*. New York: Madison Books, 1981.

Horan, James D. *The Pinkertons*. New York: Bonanza Books, 1974.

Howe, Thomas J. *The Petersburg Campaign-Wasted Valor June 15-18, 1864*. Lynchburg, Virginia: H. E. Howard, Inc., 1988.

Johnson, Curt and Mark McLaughlin. *Civil War Battles*. New York: Crown Publishers, Inc., 1977.

Johnson, Robert U. and Clarence C. Buel, eds. *Battles and Leaders of the Civil War*, 4 vols. New York: Century Company, 1887; reprint, Secaucus, New Jersey: Castle, 1989.

Jordan, David M. *Winfield Scott Hancock - A Soldiers Life*. Indianapolis, Indiana: University Press, 1988.

Katz, Mark D., "Booth's First Attempt & Christian Rath: The Executioner", *Incidents of the War*, [Spring 1986].

_____, *Witness to an Era, The Life and Photographs of Alexander Gardner*. New York: Viking Press, 1991.

Kauffman, Michael W., "Fort Lesley McNair and the Lincoln Conspirators", *Lincoln Herald*, [Winter 1978].

_____, "The Lincoln Assassination", *Blue & Gray Magazine*, [April, 1990].

Kennedey, Francis H. *The Civil War Battlefield Guide*. Boston: Houghton Mifflin, 1990.

Kolatch, Alfred J. *The Name Dictionary, Modern English and Hebrew Names*. New York: Jonathan David, 1967.

Korn, Jerry, et al., eds. *The Fight for Chattanooga, Chickamauga to Missionary*

*Ridge*. Alexandria, Virginia: Time-Life Books, 1985.

_____, *Pursuit to Appomattox, the Last Battles*. Alexandria, Virginia: Time-Life Books, 1987.

Kunhardt, Dorothy and Philip. *Twenty Days*. New York: Harper & Row, 1965; reprint, North Hollywood, California: Newcastle Publishing Co., Inc., 1985.

Lang, Jack H. ed. *The Wit and Wisdom of Abraham Lincoln*. Cleveland, Ohio: World Publishing Company, 1941.

Lattimer, John K. *Kennedy & Lincoln, Medical & Ballistic Comparisons of Their Assassinations*. New York: Harcourt Brace Jovanovich, 1980.

Lens, Sidney. *The Labor Wars, From the Molly Maguires to the Sitdowns*. New York: Doubleday & Company, Inc., 1973.

Lewis, Arthur, H. *Lament for the Molly Maguires*. New York: Harcourt, Brace & World, 1964.

Lindsey, Almont. *The Pullman Strike*. Chicago: University of Chicago Press, 1942.

Livermore, Thomas L. *Numbers & Losses in the Civil War*. Bloomington, Illinois: Houghton, Mifflin and Company, 1901.

Longstreet, James. *From Manassas to Appomattox - Memoirs of the Civil War in America*. Philadelphia: J. Lippincott Company, 1895.

Lowry, Don. *No Turning Back*. New York: Hippocrene Books, 1992.

Luvaas, Jay and Harold W. Nelson, eds. *The U.S. Army War College Guide to the Battle of Antietam*. New York: HarperCollins Publishers, 1987.

Luvaas, Jay and Harold W. Nelson, eds., *The U. S. Army War College Guide to the Battles of Chancellorsville & Fredericksburg*, Carlisle, Pennsylvania: South Mountain Press, Inc., 1988; reprint, New York: Harper & Row, Inc, 1989.

Macdonald, John. *Great Battles of the Civil War*. New York: Macmillan Publishing Company, 1988.

Matter, William D. *If It Takes All Summer: The Battle of Spotsylvania*. Chapel Hill, North Carolina: University of North Carolina Press, 1988.

Martin, David. *The Vicksburg Campaign*. New York: Gallery Books, 1990.

Marvel, William. *Burnside*. Chapel Hill, North Carolina: University of North Carolina Press, 1991.

McCabe, James D. *The Centennial History of the United States*. Philadelphia: National Publishing Company, 1876.

McClure, A. K. *Old Time Notes of Pennsylvania*. 2 vols. Philadelphia: Winston, 1905.

McFeely, William S. *Grant, A Biography*. New York: W. W. Norton & Company, Inc., 1981.

Medal of Honor Recipients, 1863 - 1978, In the name of the Congress of the

United States, U. S. Government Printing Office, Washington D.C.,
  1979.

Miller, William J. *The Training of an Army - Camp Curtin and the North's
  Civil War*. Shippensburg, Pennsylvania: White Mane Publishing
  Company, Inc., 1990.

Mitchell, Joseph B. *Decisive Battles of the Civil War*. New York: G. P.
  Putnam's Sons, 1955.

Mogelever, Jacob. *Death To Traitors*. Garden City, New York: Doubleday &
  Company, Inc., 1960.

Moore, Guy W. *The Case of Mrs. Surratt*. Oklahoma City: University of
  Oklahoma Press, 1954.

Murfin, James V. *Battlefields of the Civil War*. East Granby, Connecticut:
  CLB Publishing, Inc., 1990.

Nicolay, John G., and John Hay. *Abraham Lincoln - A History*. 9 vols. New
  York: The Century Co., 1890.

Oldroyd, Osborn H. *The Assassination of Abraham Lincoln*. With a Foreword
  by T. M. Harris, Washington D. C.: O. H. Oldroyd, 1901.

Parker, Thomas H. *History of the 51st. Regiment of P.V. and V. V.* Philadelphia: King & Baird, Printers, 1869.

*Pennsylvania in the World War: An Illustrated History of the 28th Division*, 2
  vols. Pittsburgh: States Publication Society, 1921.

Pennypacker, Samuel W. *The Autobiography of a Pennsylvanian*. Philadelphia: J. C. Winston Company, 1918.

_____, *Pennsylvania in American History*. Philadelphia: W. J. Campbell,
  1910.

Pinkerton, Allan. *The Mollie Maguires and the Detectives*. New York: G. W.
  Carleton, 1877.

Pitman, Benn. *The Assassination of President Lincoln and the Trial of the
  Conspirators*, New York: Wilstach & Baldwin, 1865; reprint, Bir-
  mingham, Alabama: The Legal Classics Library, Gryphon Editions,
  Ltd., 1982.

Poore, Benjamin Perley. *The Conspiracy Trial for the Murder of the President,
  and the Attempt to Overthrow the Government by the Assassination of its
  Principal Officers*. 3 vols. Boston: J. E. Tilton and Company, 1865-
  1866.

Porter, Horace. *Campaigning With Grant*. New York: The Century Co.,
  1897; reprint, Alexandria, Virginia: Time-Life Books Inc., 1981.

Powell, William H. *The Fifth Army Corps* - [**Army of the Potomac**]. New
  York: G. P. Putnam's Sons, 1896.

Priest, John M. *Antietam: The Soldiers' Battle*. Shippensburg, Pennsylvania:
  White Mane Publishing Company, Inc., 1989.

_____, *From New Bern to Fredericksburg: Captain James Wren's Diary*.

Shippensburg, Pennsylvania: White Mane Publishing Company, Inc., 1990.

*Public Service of Brevet Major General John F. Hartranft and Colonel Jacob M. Campbell.* Norristown, Pennsylvania: Wills, Iredel and Jenkins, 1865.

Putnam, Sallie B. *Richmond During the War.* New York: G. W. Carleton & Company, 1867.

*Republican Candidate for the Governorship of Pennsylvania in 1875*, Hartranft Campaign pamphlet, Shireman Collection.

Rhodes, James Ford. *History of the United States 1872-1877.* New York: The Macmillan Company, 1906.

_____, *History of the United States From Hayes to McKinley, 1877-1896.* New York: The Macmillan Company, 1919.

_____, *Historical Essays.* New York: The Macmillan Company, 1909.

Richards, James K., "Trial by Combat, Ambrose Burnside's Civil War", *Timeline Magazine*, [December 1990/January 1991].

Roach, Harry, "Defender of the Union - John F. Hartranft", *Military Images*, [January/February, 1982].

Roberts, Peter. *The Anthracite Coal Industry.* New York: The Macmillan Company, 1901.

Roland, Charles P. *Albert Sidney Johnston, Soldier of Three Republics.* Austin, Texas: University of Texas Press, 1964.

Sandburg Carl. *Abraham Lincoln - The War Years.* 4 vols. New York: Harcourt, Brace & Company, 1939.

Schildt, John W. *The Ninth Corps at Antietam.* Chewsville, Maryland: By the author, 1988.

Schlesinger, Arthur M. Jr. *The Almanac of American History.* New York: G. P. Putnam's Sons, 1983.

Schmucker, Samuel M. *The History of The Civil War in The United States*, Philadelphia: Jones Brothers & Co., 1865.

Schultz, Gerhard Selina. *Caspar Schwenckfeld von Ossig* (1489-1561). Pennsburg, Pennsylvania: The Schwenkfelder Church, 1977.

_____, *Caspar Schwenckfeld von Ossig - A Course of Study.* Pennsburg, Pennsylvania: The Schwenkfelder Church, 1964.

Scott, James G. and Edward A. Wyatt IV. *Petersburg's Story.* Richmond: Titmus Optical Company, 1960.

Sears, Stephen W. *George B. McClellan: The Young Napoleon.* New York: Ticknor & Fields, 1988.

_____, *Landscape Turned Red - The Battle of Antietam.* New York: Ticknor & Fields, 1983.

Sideman, Belle Becker and Lillian Friedman, eds., *Europe Looks at the Civil War*, New York: The Orion Press, 1960.

Sifakis, Stewart. *Who Was Who in the Civil War*. New York: Facts on File
      Publications, 1988.

Slotkin, Richard. *The Crater* [A Novel]. New York: Antheneum, 1980.

Smith, Benjamin B. and Robert Tomes. *The War with the South - A History of
      the Late Rebellion*. New York: Virtue & Yorston, 1867.

Smith, Gene. *Lee and Grant*. New York: McGraw-Hill Book Company,
      1984.

Snow, William P. *Lee and His Generals*. New York: Fairfax Press, 1982.

Sommers, Richard J. *Richmond Redeemed*. New York: Doubleday &
      Company, Inc., 1981.

Steiner, Bernard C. *Life of Reverdy Johnson*. Baltimore: The Norman,
      Remington Company, 1914.

_____, *Life of Roger Brooke Taney*. Baltimore: Williams & Wilkins, 1922.

Stevens, George T. *Three Years in the Sixth Corps*. Albany, New York: S. R.
      Gray, 1866.

Surratt Society eds., *In Pursuit of ... Continuing Research in the Field of the
      Lincoln Assassination*, [This is a compilation of articles taken from
      the newsletters of the Surratt Society], The Surratt Society, 1990.

Symonds, Craig L. *A Battlefield Atlas of the Civil War*. Annapolis, Maryland:
      The Nautical and Aviation Publishing Company of America, 1983.

Taft, Philip. *Organized Labor in American History*. New York: Harper &
      Row Publishers, 1964.

*The Congressional Medal of Honor, The Names, The Deeds*. Forest
      Ranch, California: Sharp and Dunnigan, 1984.

Thomas, Benjamin P. and Harold M. Hyman. *Stanton - The Life and Times of
      Lincoln's Secretary of War*. New York: Alfred A. Knopf, 1962.

Trudeau, Noah Andre. *The Last Citadel*. Boston: Little Brown and
      Company, 1991.

_____, *Bloody Roads South*. Boston: Little, Brown and Company, 1989.

Tucker, Glenn. *Chickamauga*. Indianapolis, Indiana: Bobbs-Merrill, 1961,
      reprint; Dayton, Ohio: Morningside Bookshop, 1976.

_____, *Hancock The Superb*. Indianapolis: Bobbs-Merrill, 1960.

Turner, Thomas Reed. *Beware The People Weeping*. Baton Rouge: Louisiana
      State University Press, 1982.

United States War Department. *War of the Rebellion: A compilation of the
      Official Records of the Union and Confederate Armies*, 70 volumes in
      128 parts. Government Printing Office, Washington, D. C., 1880-
      1901.

Wallace, Willard M. *The Soul of the Lion*. New York: Thomas Nelson &
      Sons, 1960.

Walker, Francis A. *History of the Second Army Corps*. New York: Charles

Scribner's Sons, 1887; reprint, Gaithersburg, Maryland, Olde Soldiers Books, Inc., 1990.

Walker, Peter F. *Vicksburg - A People at War*. Wilmington, North Carolina: University of North Carolina Press, 1960; reprint, Wilmington, North Carolina: Broadfoot Publishing Company, 1987.

Warner, Ezra J. *Generals In Blue*. Baton Rouge: Louisiana State University Press, 1964.

_____, *Generals In Gray*. Baton Rouge: Louisiana State University Press, 1959.

Weichmann, Louis J. *A True History of the Assassination of Abraham Lincoln and of the Conspiracy of 1865*. New York: Alfred A. Knopf, 1975.

Wheeler, Richard. *Sword Over Richmond*. New York: Harper & Row, 1986.

Wilkinson, Warren. *Mother, May You Never See the Sights I Have Seen*. New York: Harper & Row, 1990.

Wilshin, Francis F., *"Manassas" [Bull Run]*, National Park Service, Washington D.C., 1955.

Winschel, Terrence J., "The Day They Raised a Monument in Dixie", *Pennsylvania Heritage*, [May, 1992].

Winslow, Richard Elliot III. *General John Sedgwick*. Novato, California: Presidio, 1982.

Woodbury, Augustus. *Major General Ambrose E. Burnside and the Ninth Army Corps*. Providence, Rhode Island: Sidney S. Rider & Brother, 1867.

Zbick, Jim, "Coalfield Terror", *America's Civil War*, [March, 1992].

# HARTRANFT INDEX

*A*

Auditor General,  210, 211, 213, 214
Avery House,  131, 136
Ayres, Romeyn B.,  109, 113


### B


Babcock, Orville E.,  82
Bachman, Michael,  5
Bair, C. E. & Sons,  292
Baird, S. C.,  245
Baker, Lafayette C.,  159, 160, 191
Baker, Luther B.,  159
Baltimore, Maryland,  10, 188, 257, 259, 260
Baltimore & Ohio Railroad,  258, 259
Banks, Enoch A.,  52
Barlow, Francis C.,  62
Barney, Benjamin,  105
Bartholomew, Lin,  248
Bartlett, William F.,  105, 108, 111
Bates, Edward,  171
Baxter Road, Fort Stedman,  127
Beauregard, Pierre Gustav Toutant,  18-20, 23, 100
Beaver, James A.,  270, 277, 288, 292, 293, 296
Bedford County, Pennsylvania,  201
*Bedford Inquirer*,  218
Belgium,  272
Bell, Thomas S.,
   Battle of New Bern,  48-50
   Battle of Roanoke Island,  45
   death of,  67
   elected Lt. Colonel,  37
Benfer, David,  85
Benjamin, Judah P.,  42, 47
Benning, Henry L.,  63
Bergen, Martin,  238
Berks County, Pennsylvania,  3
Bertolette, John D.,  140, 147
Bethlehem, Pennsylvania,  267
Bible, Daniel P.,  38
Bildad the Shuhite,  288

Bingham, John A.,  171, 172
"Black John",  204
Black Soldiers,  94, 103
"Blacklegs",  233
Blaine, James G.,  249, 251-253
Blair County, Pennsylvania,  52
Bliss, Zenas R.,  81, 82
"Bloody Bucket",  271, 272
"Bloody Lane",  60
Blue Bell, Pennsylvania,  13
"Body Masters",  229
Bolton, Joseph K.,  54, 113
Bolton, Levi,  40
Bolton, William J.,  32, 59, 99, 113
  at the funeral of JFH,  283
  Battle of Bull Run,  28
  Battle of the Crater,  108, 109
  comments on McDowell,  28
  diary of,  24, 25, 30
  enlist in the 4th Pennsylvania,  18
  takes command of the 51st Pennsylvania,  99
  Wilson's Station,  152, 154
Booth, John Wilkes,  1, 201
  at Garrett's barn,  160
  burial of,  162
  death of,  160
  reward for,  159
  testimony of John Lloyd,  180
  testimony of Louis J. Weichmann,  176, 178
Boston, Massachusetts,  201, 249
Boyd, James,  6
Boyer, Michael C.,  6
Boyertown Inn,  5
Boyertown Militia,  5
Boyertown, Pennsylvania,  5
Brackett, L. Curtiss,  139
Bradford, Pennsylvania,  245
Bradley, Omar N.,  272
Bradocks, Pennsylvania,  257
Bradocks Car Works,  257
Bragg, Braxton,  18
Brenholts, Thomas S.,  297

335

Bright, Richard, Dr.,  283
Bright's Disease,  283
Brinton, Robert M.,  260-263, 265
Bristow, Benjamin H.,  249
Brooks' Stable,  178
Brophy, John P.,  188, 199
Brown, Isaac B.,  294
Brown, John,  41
Browne, Audley "Bible Banger",  211
Buchanan, James,  8
Buckalew, Charles R.,  217
Bucks County, Pennsylvania,  3, 212
"Buckshots",  229
Buffalo, New York,  230
Bull Run, First battle of,   13, 20, 26-28, 32, 33, 37, 193, 270
  4th Pennsylvania leaving the field of,   25, 38
  comments from General McDowell,  31
  creek of,  20
  letter from General Heintzelman on,  68
  Stanton's comments of,  27
Bull Run, Second battle of,  53, 55, 57, 70
Burnett House,  82
Burnett, Henry L.,  172, 173
Burnside, Ambrose E.,  38, 53, 78, 94-96, 100, 130, 217
  Battle of Antietam,  62, 63, 68
  Battle of the Crater,  103, 104, 107-109, 111
  Battle of Fredericksburg,  68, 70
  Battle of New Bern,  49, 51
  Battle of Roanoke Island,  42, 47
  commands the Department of North Carolina,  39, 40
  Knoxville Campaign,  82-86
  "Mud March",  72
Burnside Bridge,  60
Burrage, Henry,  86
Butler, Benjamin F.,  11, 12
Butler, John G.,  188

C

Calabria,  227

Camden, North Carolina, 52, 70
Camden Station, Maryland, 260
Cameron, J. Donald, 216, 242, 244, 247, 249, 251, 253
Cameron, Simon, 11, 13, 22, 23, 28, 53, 211, 212, 244
  "Evans affair", 213-218
  JFH 1876 Presidential bid, 242, 243, 245, 247, 249, 251, 253
Camp Curtin, 9, 10, 37, 94
Camp Hale, 13, 25
Camp Hartranft, 51
Camp Nelson, Kentucky, 93
Camp Union, 38
Campbell, A., 238
Campbell, Jacob M., 211, 213
Campbell, John, A., 119, 235, 316
Campbell's Station, 83, 88, 99
Canada, 173
Cape Hatteras, 48
Carbon County, Pennsylvania, 229
*Carisle Herald*, 217
Carroll, Annex, 161
Carroll, John Lee, 259
*Carson Appeal*, 250
Carter, Joseph T., 151
Catholic, Roman
  miners, 176
  Molly Maguires, 225, 227, 228, 230, 232, 233
Cemetery Hill [at Crater], 105, 110
Centential Celebration-Exhibition, 258
Centre County, Pennsylvania, 37
Centreville, Virginia, 23, 25, 26, 33, 54
*Century Magazine*, 151
Chain, Benjamin E., 93
Chambersburg, Pennsylvania, 102
Chancellorsville, Virginia, 96
Chantilly, 55-57
Chapultepec, Mexico, 22
Cherokee Indian Commission, 277
Chesapeake Bay, 39
Chester, Pennsylvania, 280
*Chevaux-de-frise*, 125, 128, 131-133
Cheyenne, Wyoming Territory, 262
Chicago, Illinois, 250, 267

Curtin, Andrew Gregg, 9, 38, 92, 211-213, 283
Curtin, John I., 296
Custer, George A., 18, 259
Cutter, Calvin, 88


## D


Dabney, V., 122
*Daily Citizen Newspaper*, 79
Dalien, Prosper, 140
Dare, Charles P., 10, 140
Dauphin County, Pennsylvania, 37
Davidson, T. W. Reverend, 288
Davis, Ann [Sebring], 8, 254
Davis, Jefferson, 42, 47, 120, 121, 144
Dechert, Robert P., 284
Delack, J.P., 133
Delaware, 10
*Delaware, U.S.S.*, 44
Democratic Party, 211, 212, 216, 217, 237, 242, 244, 245, 253
Denver, Colorado, 245
Department of Agriculture, 245
Dewees, F. P., 231
Dimmock line, 138
Diven, Charles W., 130
Dodd, Levi A., 182, 189
Donohue, Jack, 316
Doster, William, E., 172, 173, 175, 180, 184, 192, 200, 202
Dougherty, Edward, 159
Dougherty, Neal, 235, 316
Dougherty, Silas, 232
Douglas, Henry Kyd, 144, 151, 185, 294, 295
Douty, Jacob, 104
Downing, Oliver, 280
Doyle, Michael, 234
Dry Tortugas, 200
Dunkers, 60
Dunker Church, 60
Dunn House Battery, 138
Durrell's Battery, 56, 58

Durrell, George W.,   54, 297
Duryea, J. Eugene,   63


**E**


Earle, William P.,   18
Early, Jubal,   26, 101, 102
Easton, Pennsylvania,   6, 8
Eckert, Thomas T.,   184, 188
Edgar Thomson Steel Works,   257
Elliot's Salient,   103
Embick, Lenora,   294
Embick, M. A.,   294
Emperor of Brazil, Dom Pedro,   248
Empress of Brazil,   248
England,   39, 5, 160, 172
Engle, Mary Elizabeth,   3
English,   2, 227
English, "Nick",   217
Eisenhower Senior High School,   i
Erie Railroad,   258
Europe,   172, 176, 225, 277, 280
"Evans Affair",   213-218
Evans, Dalzell & Company,   257
Evans, George, A.,   213-215
Evans, John F. Dr.,   5
*Evening Chronicle*,   239
Ewell's, [Richard S.] Corps,   97
Ewing, Thomas, Jr.,   173
Exerter Station, Pennsylvania,   296


**F**


Fagleysville, Pennsylvania,   5
Fairfax, Virginia,   29, 57
Fairfax Court House,   22, 55
Falkner Swamp Reformed Church,   3, 5
Ferrero, Edward,   68, 79, 103

Graham, William M., 54
Grand Army of the Republic, 276, 283
Grand Review, 154
Grant, Julia Dent, 248
Grant, Ulysses, S., 18, 84, 86, 94, 95, 97, 99, 100, 111, 114, 144
  as President, 212-215, 217, 242-245, 247, 248, 250
  Battle of Fort Stedman, 119-122, 136, 137
  Petersburg, 101-104
  Vicksburg Campaign, 78-83
Greece, 227
Greenleaf Point, 175
Griffin, Simon, G., 81, 82, 108, 110, 111
Grimes, Bryan, 124


*H*


Habeas Corpus, 12
Haffey, J. K., 245
Hains, Peter C., 30
Hall, John, P. H., 201
Halleck, Henry Wager, 53, 83, 97
Hampton Roads, 119, 120
Hancock, Benjamin F., 210
Hancock School, i
Hancock, Winfield Scott, 18, 97, 100, 104, 109, 161, 181, 182, 184, 204, 253,
  283, 292, 293
  Lincoln Conspiracy Trial, 174, 187-189, 191, 192, 198
  Railroad Strikes, 260, 266
Haner, George, 131
Harden, Henry, 114
Hare, Otway O., 128
Hare's Hill, 128
Harper's Ferry, 20, 41, 57
Harrisburg, Pennsylvania, 9, 10, 37, 94, 186, 203, 204, 214, 216, 220, 231,
  232, 234, 235, 258, 261, 265, 267, 272, 276, 292, 293, 296
*Harrisburg Daily State Guard*, 213
*Harrisburg Patriot*, 244
Harrison, Benjamin, 277, 281
Harrison, *Mr.*, 186, 187
Harrold, Daniel C., 159

345

Colonel Hartranft Quick Step, 53
comments on troops' actions, 261
confronts 1874 railroad strike, 258
congratulates troops, 147
controversy over 4th Pennsylvania Volunteers, 27, 28, 38
controversy over battle, 150-152
"Daybooks" of, 174, 182
death of children, 52
death, 283
declines appointment as colonel, 204
describes attack of Yellow Tavern, 113-114
drills troops, 12, 13, 20, 44, 79
early career, 6
education, 5, 6
estimates Confederate casualties, 144
evaluation of, 287, 288, 293, 295, 296
"Evans affair", 213-218
first combat experience, 13
"Fred" nickname, 6
funeral, 284, 287
Hayes appoints JFH Collector of the Port of Philadelphia, 277
Hayes appoints JFH Postmaster of Philadelphia, 276
health deteriorates, 281, 282
implores troops to stay for the Battle of First Bull Run, 23
inaugural address, 218-220
Jack Kehoe controversy, 237-239, 316, 317
JFH realizes debt to Cameron, 247
known as "Veto Jack", 219
life before the outbreak of the war, 6
marriage to Sallie Douglas Sebring [SSH], 6, 8
Mary Surratt controversy, 2, 181
memorials to, 292-297
Molly Maguires, 224-239, 316, 317
named Chief Marshall of the Grand Army of the Republic, 277
national support for JFH, 249-251
new Pennsylvania Constitution, 219-221
newspaper accounts of JFH and Kehoe, see Appendix B, 239
newspapers comment on inaugural address, 219
nominated for Auditor General of Pennsylvania, 210
"Old Johnny", 96, 105, 287
ordered to join Burnside's North Carolina expedition, 40
ordered to Knoxville, 82

Hartranft, Sallie [Wife],  9, 12, 13, 88, 94, 103, 154, 186, 204, 210, 212, 254, 276, 277, 294
children,  8
death of children,  52, 53
funeral of JFH,  288
illness and death of JFH,  282, 283
JFH writes to,  21, 37, 39-41, 51, 55, 68, 70, 78, 94, 100, 102, 112, 113
marries JFH,  8
Hartranft, Samuel Engle [Father],  3, 5, 6, 22, 29, 37, 53, 92
Hartranft, Samuel S. [Son],  8, 212, 276, 282, 288, 294
Hartranft School,  i
Hartranft Avenue,  ii
Hartranft, Wilson [Son],  8, 52
Hartrauth [sic], General,  162
Hartsuff, George L.,  145
Hawkins, Rush C.,  45
Hayes, Lucy,  253
Hayes, Rutherford, B.,  276, 277
1876 Presidential election,  243, 244, 247-249, 251, 253
attends funeral for Hartranft,  283
Railroad strikes,  259, 260, 265, 266
"Rutherfraud" nickname,  253
Hazelton, Pennsylvania,  229
Heintzelman, M. T.,  152
Heintzelman, Samuel P.,  25, 26, 67, 68
Herold, David E.,  1, 2, 159, 173, 179, 180, 187, 188, 202
arrested,  162
executed,  191, 192
Herterranft, Abraham,  3
Herterranft, Anna,  2
Herterranft, Barbara,  2, 3
Herterranft, George,  2, 3
Herterranft, Maria,  2
Herterranft, Melchior,  2
Herterranft, Rosina,  2
Herterranft, Tobias,  2, 3
Heth's Brigades,  127
Hibernian House,  230
Hicks, Thomas H., Governor,  11
Hill, Ambrose Powell,  56
Hill, Daniel Harvey,  41
Hitchcock, Frederick C.,  267

Hobbs, *Colonel*, 152
Hobbs, *Mrs.*, 154
Hodgkins, William, 144
Holmes, Joseph G., 152
Holmes, William R., 62, 67
Holohan, John T., 198
Holt, Joseph, as Judge Advocate in Lincoln Conspiracy Trial, 171, 174, 176, 182, 184, 187, 199, 203
Hood, John Bell, 60, 84
Hooker, Joseph, 18, 60, 72
Horan, James D., 229
Hosack, John P., 37
Hough's Ferry, Tennessee, 83
Howard's Stable, 178
Hoyt, Henry M., 271, 276, 283
  Jack Kehoe case, 236, 316
Hudson, John Williams, 67
Huidekoper, H. S., 270
Humphrey's Brigade, 97
Humphreys, William, 84
Hunsicker, Charles, 10
Hunsicker, Davis, 64
Hunter, David, 25
Hunter, R. W., 122
Hunter, Robert, M. T., 119, 120


*I*


Illinois, 259
Independence Hall, 284
Iredell, C. Jones, 23, 25
Ireland, 225
Irish, 224, 225, 228, 233
"Iron Division", 271
Italians, 225

# J

# K

McKenna, James,  230, 231, 233, 234
McLaughlen, Napoleon Bonaparte,  137, 145
McLaws, Lafayette,  58, 83, 84
McParland, James,  230, 234
McPhail, Marshall,  188


### M


Mac Veagh, Wayne,  216, 242
Mackey, Robert, W.,  216
Mafia,  229
Mallory, Daniel G.,  38, 80
Mahanoy City, Pennsylvania,  229, 233, 234
Mahone, William,  107, 113
Maine,  249
Maine troops
  4th Infantry Regiment,  128
Manassas Junction,  20-22, 29, 54
Markoe, Frank, Jr.,  122
Marlboro, Maryland,  180
Marlborough Township, Pennsylvania,  3
Marshall College,  6, 144, 185
Marshall, Elisha G.,  104, 105
Martinsburg, West Virginia,  259
Marye's Heights,  68-70
Maryland,  10-12, 38, 60, 172, 176, 257, 259
Maryland troops
  2nd Infantry Regiment,  62, 63, 83
  5th Militia Regiment,  260
  6th Militia Regiment,  260
Masonic Lodge,  8
Massachusetts troops
  5th Infantry Regiment,  25, 26
  6th Infantry Regiment,  10
  11th Infantry Regiment,  25, 26
  12th Infantry Regiment,  60
  21st Infantry Regiment,  55-57, 83
  24th Infantry Regiment,  42, 45, 49
  25th Infantry Regiment,  45
  27th Infantry Regiment,  45, 49

Nazi, 272
Nebraska City, Nebraska, 245
Needham, Henry M., 245
Negroes, 212, 220
Nevada, 249, 250
New Bern, North Carolina, 41, 48, 51, 52, 70
New Hampshire troops
  6th Infantry Regiment, 62
  11th Infantry Regiment, 80, 84
New Hanover Township, Pennsylvania, 3, 5
New Jersey, 259
New Jersey troops
  9th Infantry Regiment, 45, 49, 59
New Orleans, 40
New York and Erie Railroad, 258
New York Central Railroad, 258
New York City, 227, 245, 248, 250, 267, 280
New York troops
  14th Artillery Regiment, 104, 105, 124, 126, 133
  16th Cavalry Regiment, 159
  9th Infantry Regiment [Zouvaves], 45
  51st Infantry Regiment, 45, 50, 59, 62-64, 67, 80
  61st Infantry Regiment, 62
  64th Infantry Regiment, 62
  79th Infantry [Highlanders] Regiment, 84
  109th Infantry Regiment, 25, 28
  8th Militia Regiment, 95
*New York Herald*, 247
New York State, 80, 245, 257, 259
*New York Tribune*, 21, 203
New York Union League, 94
Newport News, Virginia, 53, 78
Nicholasville, Kentucky, 78, 82
Noble, James D., 38
Norfolk, Virginia, 42
Norris Rifles, 8
Norristown Board of Trade, 280
Norristown, Pennsylvania, 3, 5, 6, 8-10, 13, 21, 22, 52, 53, 57, 94, 103, 109,
  130, 154, 204, 210, 248, 250, 253, 272, 276, 277, 282, 293
  Borough Council, 8
  JFH death and funeral, 283
  JFH monument, 296

newspapers,   78, 93, 94, 251, 252
soldiers associated with,   19, 22, 32, 37, 78, 92
*Norristown Times Herald,*   251, 252
North Carolina,   8, 40, 68, 119, 120, 247, 249
North Carolina troops
  8th Infantry Regiment,   44
  35th Infantry Regiment,   100
  37th Infantry Regiment,
Northampton County, Pennsylvania,   37
Northern Central Railroad,   216
North, Margaret Y.,   293
*North Wales Record,*   250
Northington, O. F., Jr.,   137, 138
Nothey, John,   178
Nye, E. B.,   133

## *O*

O'Donnell, Charles,   234
O'Donnell, James,   234
O'Donnell, Margaret,   233, 234
O'Neill, Thomas,   53
Oakland Female Institute,   53
Ocracoke Inlet,   48
Ohio,   243, 251, 257, 259
Ohio troops
  11th Infantry Regiment,   62
O'Laughlin, Michael,   162, 173, 200
Old Capitol Prison,   161
"Old Penelope",   161
*Old Time Notes of Pennsylvania,*   215
Olustee, Florida,   128
Omaha, Nebraska,   265
"Omerta",   229
O'Sullivan, Timothy,   189
Ox Hill,   55

State Supreme Court, 235
Surveyor General, 52
Pennsylvania troops
2nd Provisional Heavy Artillery, 105
1st Infantry Regiment, 128
4th Infantry Regiment, 10-13, 19-23, 25, 27-33, 37, 38, 51, 193, 270
23rd Infantry Regiment, 10
48th Infantry Regiment, 83, 103
50th Infantry Regiment, 97
51st Infantry Regiment, 37-39, 44, 45, 48-50, 52, 54, 55, 58-60, 62-64, 67,
    70, 72, 78-82, 84, 85, 92-98, 101, 108, 109, 114, 152, 154, 283, 284, 292,
    293
100th Infantry Regiment, 150-152, 210
200th Infantry Regiment, 130, 131, 139-141, 144, 145, 151
205th Infantry Regiment, 130, 140, 141, 152
207th Infantry Regiment, 135, 140, 141, 152
208th Infantry Regiment, 130, 140, 141, 152
209th Infantry Regiment, 130, 131, 137, 139, 140, 143
211th Infantry Regiment, 135, 141
Pennsylvania Boiler Insurance Company, 280
Pennsylvania Division, 271, 293
Pennyslvania Farmer Inn, 5
Pennypacker, Samuel W., 247, 296
Perryville, Maryland, 10, 11
Pershing, Cyrus, L. "Pershing the Pure", 211
Pershing, John J., 271
Petersburg, Virginia, 100, 103, 113, 124, 127, 292
    siege of, 119-121
Petersburg National Military Park, 138
Philadelphia, 2, 3, 5, 79, 201, 211, 214, 217, 219, 220, 233, 284, 287, 292
    1872 gubernatorial election, 217
    1876 Presidential election, 243, 250
    1876 Centennial Celebration, 248, 258, 259
    Fairmount Park, 292
    JFH ancestors settle in, 2
    Railroad strikes, 257, 260, 262, 263, 267, 268
Philadelphia and Reading Railroad, 226
*Philadelphia Evening Chronicle*, 316, 317
*Philadelphia Evening Herald*, 213
*Philadelphia Ledger*, 292
*Philadelphia Times*, 239, 316, 317
Philipine Islands, 272

## R

Ragenfrid,  3
Railroad Hotel, Pittsburgh,  266
Ramph,  3
Randall, George M.,  124, 133
Ranf,  3
Ranfd,                                    Ranfd,  3
Ranft,  3
Ranph,  3
Rapidan River,  95, 101
Rappahannock River,  68, 70
Rath, Christian,  188, 189, 192
Rauft,  3
Rawlins, John A.,  245
Read, L. W., Dr.,  282
*Reading Gazette and Democrat*,  219
Reading, Pennsylvania,  200, 229, 267, 296
Reconstruction,  253
Red Hill, Pennsylvania,  3
Ree's, Henry,  104
Reeder, Frank,  270
Reed, Joseph C.,  23, 25
Reno, Jesse Lee,  40, 45, 47-49, 54-58
  on JFH,  50
  mortally wounded,  59
Republican Invincibles,  283
Republican Party,  53, 211, 219, 221, 236, 242, 243, 247
  1865 gubernatorial election,  212
  1872 election,  215-217
  1876 National Convention,  245, 248-253
  "Evans affair",  213-218
Reynolds, John F.,  ii
Rhode Island troops
  4th Infantry Regiment,  45
  27th Infantry Regiment,  81
Rhodes, James Ford,  268
Rhumer, Llewelyn,  13
Richardson, Israel B.,  62

Richardson, William A., 242
Richmond, Virginia, 21, 22, 41, 47, 72, 79, 99, 120, 137, 144
Ricketts, James B., 26
Ricketts Battery, 26
Rittenhouse Jr. High School, i
*River Queen*, 130
Roanoke Island, 41, 42, 48, 52, 70
  activities of JFH at, 45, 47
  arrival of Burnside, 42
  battle of, 44, 47
  landing of the 51st Pennsylvania, 42
  strength of General Wise at, 42
Robeson, George, 242
Rogers, James A., 152
Rohrbach's bridge, 60, 62
Roundheads, *see 100th Pennsylvania Infantry Regiment*
Roundhouse, Lower, Upper, Pittsburgh, 260-263
Ruckstuhl, F. W., 292, 294
Runyon, General, 24
Russell, J. B., 245
Russell, William Howard, 32, 33
Russia, 211, 268
Ryon, John W., 238


S


Saint Paul Lutheran Church, 3
*Saint Andrew*, 2
Saint Clairsville, Ohio, 200
Salford Township, Pennsylvania, 3
Salt Lake City, Utah, 262
Sarget, *Colonel*, 107
Saylor, James C., 18
Schall, Edward, 10, 13, 25, 78
Schall, Edwin, 10-12, 37, 54, 82, 154, 284
  killed at Cold Harbor, 99, 100
Schall, George, 293
Schenectady, New York, 6
Schriver, Edward, 109
Schubert, Susanna, 3

Smith, John, 188
Smith Memorial, 292
Smith, Charles E., 294
Smyser Daniel M., 32, 33
Snowden, George R., 270, 277, 293
Snyder County, Pennsylvania, 37
Snyder's Bluff, 78
South Mountain, 57-59, 70
Spangler, Edward, 162, 184, 200, 202
Speed, James, 171, 189
Spotsylvania, 97, 99, 103, 109
Spring Hill, Pennsylvania, 268
Spring Hill, Virginia, 124
Stanford, Kentucky, 78
Stanley, Wesley, 105, 109
Stanton, David, 214
Stanton, Edwin, 27, 53, 95, 98, 204
    Lincoln Conspiracy Trial, 159, 160, 162, 163, 175, 181, 182, 200, 201
    praises JFH, 193
Starke, William E., 56
State Hospital for the Insane at Norristown, 277
Statue of Liberty, 248
Stedman, Griffen A., Jr., 124
Stedman, John, Captain, 2
Stephens, Alexander H., 119
Stevens, Issac Ingalls, 55-57
Stevenson, John H., 151
Stewart, Andrew, 252, 253
Stockham, Hartranft, 174
Stockham, Hartranft [Grandson], 174
Stone, Frederick, 173, 184
Stone, William A., 294
Stone, William A., Mrs., 294
Stonewall Brigade, 122, 185
Stony Creek Railroad Company, 8
Stryker, A. P., Rev., 188
Stuart, Edwin S., 292
Stuart, James Ewell Brown, 18, 41
Sturgis, Samuel D., 59, 62
Sudley Ford, 26, 27
Suffolk and Petersburg Railroad, 101
Sumner, Edwin Vose, 68

Toombs, Robert,  62, 67
Townsend, George Alfred,  244, 245
Treemount Seminary,  5, 6
Trent River,  51
Triangle City,  260
Trimble, James, H.,  130
Turner, John W.,  111
Twenty-Eight Division, [N.G.P.],  271, 272
Tyson, James, Dr.,  282


## U


Union College,  6, 104
Union County, Pennsylvania,  37
Union House,  5
Union Pacific Railroad,  263
Union Station, Pittsburgh,  266
Union Telegraph Company,  186
Uniontown, Pennsylvania,  252
United Confederate Veterans,  131
United States of America,  11, 172, 225, 243, 247, 257
   1876 Presidential election,  242, 253
   1877 Railroad strike,  266
   Centennial Celebration,  248, 258
   Constitution,  95, 161
United States Catholic Historical Society,  191
U. S. Cavalry
   3rd, 2nd Division,  25
United States Government,  2, 180
United States Naval Academy,  12
*U.S.S. Cossack*,  40, 42, 48
*U.S.S. Delaware*,  44
*U.S.S. Montauk*,  161
*U.S.S. Saugus*,  161
*U.S.S. Scout*,  40
United States Senate,  128, 215
United States Supreme Court,  119
University of Georgia,  120
University of Pennsylvania,  280-282

### V

Valley Forge, Pennsylvania, 5
Van Bibber, Henry, 5
Vicksburg, Mississippi, 72, 82, 296, 297
   Grant's siege of, 78-80, 104
Virginia, 8, 19, 57, 122, 131, 249, 292, 294
Virginia troops
   13th Infantry Regiment, 132
   49th Infantry Regiment, 132
   59th Infantry Regiment, 44
*Virginia City Sentinel*, 250


### W

Waite, Morrison R., 247
Walker, James A., 122, 131, 132, 136, 143
Walter, Father J. Ambrose, 188, 191, 199
Walter, William, F., 130
Wannerskerch, W. M., 181
War of 1812, 18, 22
War Department Secret Police, 159
Warrenton Junction, 94
Warrenton Road, 27
Washington Arsenal, 1, 187
*Washington Chronicle*, 204
Washington, D.C., 10-13, 19, 20, 55, 57, 97, 101, 102, 154, 161, 176, 185,
   202, 203, 214, 242, 246, 251, 281
   Battle of First Bull Run, 27
   Lincoln Conspiracy Trial, 171, 172, 188, 201
   manhunts for suspects after Lincoln assassination, 259
   Railroad strikes, 266
Washington Elementary School, i
Washington Schwenkfelder Cemetery, 3
*Washington Star*, 162
Water Gap Railroad, 6
Watt, Richard, 189
Wayne County, Pennsylvania, 229
Wayne, General "Mad" Anthony, 5

Weichmann, Louis,  176, 179, 202
Weldon Railroad,  112-114
Weldon Station,  112
*West Chester American Republican*,  214
West Norriton Township, Pennsylvania,  283
West Point,  19, 20, 62, 130
West Virginia,  249, 259
Wheeler, Rose,  188
White House,  1, 8, 188, 191, 198, 242, 247
Whiting, William H. C.,  42
Wigget, Father Bernardin F.,  188
Wilcox, Cadmus M.,  127
Wilderness,  95, 103
Wilkes Barre, Pennsylvania,  267
Wilkes Barre Railroad,  6
Williamsport, Pennsylvania,  270
*Williamsport Gazette & Bulletin*,  318
Wills, John A.,  18
Wills, *Mr.*,  179
Wilmer, S.,  122
Wilmington, Delaware,  10
Wilson, Henry,  88
Wilson Station,  152
Wirz, Henry,  193
Wisconsin troops
  38th Infantry Regiment,  98
Wise, Henry,  41, 42, 47
Wise, Jennings,  47
Wise, John,  47
Wise, O. Jennings,  44, 47
Wood, James F., Bishop,  233
Wood, *Mr.* [Alias used by Lewis Paine],  179
World War I,  128, 271
World War II,  271
Wright, Angeline,  201
Wright, Caroline,  201
Wylie, Andrew,  189, 191

## Y

Yale, 172
Yellow Tavern, 112, 113

## Z

Zainsville, Ohio, 257
Zook, Samuel K., 18, 276, 283, 293